Prime Ministers and Premiers

Political Leadership and Public Policy in Canada

edited by
Leslie Pal and David Taras
The University of Calgary

Prentice-Hall Canada Inc., Scarborough, Ontario

Canadian Cataloguing in Publication Data

Main entry under title·

Prime ministers and premiers

Bibliography: p.
Includes index.
ISBN 0-13-704959-5

1. Political leadership – Canada. 2. Political planning
– Canada. 3. Prime ministers – Canada.
I. Pal, Leslie Alexander, 1954-   . II. Taras,
David, 1950-   .

JL99.P74 1987   354.7103' 13   C87-094795-8

73612

Prentice-Hall Inc., Englewood Cliffs, New Jersey
Prentice-Hall International, Inc., London
Prentice-Hall of Australia, Pty., Ltd., Sydney
Prentice-Hall of India Pvt., Ltd., New Delhi
Prentice-Hall of Japan, Inc., Tokyo
Prentice-Hall of Southeast Asia (Pte.) Ltd., Singapore
Editora Prentice-Hall do Brasil Ltda., Rio de Janeiro
Prentice-Hall Hispanoamericana. S.A., Mexico

Copy Editor: Magda Kryt
Production Editor: Kateri Lanthier
Typesetter: Cundari Group Ltd.
Printed and bound in Canada by The Alger Press Limited

ISBN 0-13-704959-5

1 2 3 4 5 AP 92 91 90 89 88

Chapter Credits

The following page constitutes an extension of the
copyright page. Every reasonable effort has been made to
find copyright holders. The publishers would be pleased
to have any errors or omissions brought to their attention.

Chapter 3
This chapter first appeared in *Entering the Eighties:
Political Leadership in Crisis,* edited by R.K. Carty and
W.P. Ward, Oxford University Press Canada, 1980.
Reprinted by permission of Robert Craig Brown.

Chapter 5
The original version of this chapter, entitled
"Organizational Change in the Management of Canadian
Government: From Rational Management to Brokerage
Politics" first appeared in *The Canadian Journal of
Political Science,* XIX, I, March, 1986. Reprinted by
permission of the CJPS and Peter Aucoin.

Credits

Christopher Armstrong, "Ceremonial Parties: Federal-Provincial Meetings Before the Second World War" in *National Politics and Community in Canada,* edited by R. Kenneth Carty and W. Peter Ward, Vancouver: University of British Columbia, 1986, pp. 142-3.

Peter Aucoin and Richard D. French, *Knowledge, Power and Public Policy,* Ottawa: Science Council of Canada, 1974, p. 12.

James David Barber, *The Presidential Character: Predicting Performance in the White House,* Englewood Cliffs, N.J.: Prentice-Hall, 1972, pp. 5-6.

Bélanger, A.-J., *L'apolitisme des idéologies québécoises,* Québec: Les Presses de l'Université Laval, 1974, p. 287.

Colin Campbell, *Governments Under Stress: Political Executives and Key Bureaucrats in Washington, London and Ottawa,* Toronto: University of Toronto Press, 1983, pp. 351-52.

Clive Cocking, *Following the Leaders: A Media Watcher's Diary of Campaign '79,* Toronto: Doubleday Canada, 1980, pp. 31, 33, 53, 139.

Thomas E. Cronin, *The State of the Presidency,* Second Edition, Boston: Little, Brown, 1980, p. 81.

Andrew Dunsire, *The Execution Process,* Volume 2, *Control in a Bureaucracy,* London: Martin Robertson, 1978, pp. 207-8.

Stefan J. Dupré, "Reflections on the Workability of Executive Federalism," in *Intergovernmental Relations,* edited by Richard Simeon, Toronto: University of Toronto Press, 1985, p. 26.

J. Eichmanis and G. White, "Government by Other Means: Agencies, Boards and Commissions" in *The Government and Politics of Ontario,* Third Edition, edited by Donald C. MacDonald, Toronto: Nelson, 1985. Used with permission of Nelson Canada, A Division of International Thomson Limited.

Edward Jay Epstein, *News from Nowhere: Television and the News,* New York: Vintage Books, 1973, p. 215.

Frederick J. Fletcher, "The Contest for Media Attention: The 1979 and 1980 Federal Election Campaigns" in *Politics and the Media,* Toronto: Reader's Digest Foundation of Canada and Erindale College, University of Toronto, 1981, p. 134.

Michel Foucault, *Power/Knowledge: Selected Interviews and Other Writings, 1972-1977,* edited by Colin Gordon, New York: Pantheon Books, 1980, p. 187.

Roger Gibbins, *Conflict and Unity: An Introduction to Canadian Political Life,* Toronto: Methuen, 1985, p. 253.

Ron Graham, *One-Eyed Kings: Promise and Illusion in Canadian Politics,* Toronto: Collins, 1986, pp. 58 and 397. With permission from Collins Publishers.

Richard Gwyn, *The Northern Magus: Pierre Trudeau and the Canadians,* Toronto: McClelland and Stewart, 1980, p. 272. Used by permission of the Canadian Publishers, McClelland and Stewart, Toronto.

Sidney Hook, *The Hero in History: A Study in Limitation and Possibility,* Boston: Beacon Press, 1943, p. 7.

Donald Johnston, *Up the Hill,* Montreal and Toronto: Optimum Publishing International, 1986, p. 135.

Harold Lasswell, *Psychopathology and Politics,* Chicago: University of Chicago Press, 1930, pp. 53, 78, 127.

Peter C. Newman, *The Distemper of Our Times: Canadian Politics in Transition: 1963-1968,* Toronto: McClelland and Stewart, 1968, p. 69. Used by permission of the Canadian Publishers, McClelland and Stewart, Toronto.

Peter C. Newman, *Renegade in Power: The Diefenbaker Years,* Toronto, McClelland and Stewart, pp. 79-91. Used by permission of the Canadian Publishers, McClelland and Stewart, Toronto.

R.M. Punnett, *The Prime Minister in Canadian Government and Politics,* Toronto: Macmillan, 1977, p. 28.

Clinton Rossiter, *The American Presidency,* p. 102, copyright © 1956 by Clinton Rossiter; renewed 1984 by Mary Crane Rossiter, Caleb S. Rossiter, David G. Rossiter. Reprinted by permission of Harcourt Brace Jovanovich, Inc.

Richard Simeon, *Federal-Provincial Diplomacy: The Making of Recent Policy in Canada,* Toronto: University of Toronto Press, 1982, pp. 144, 191-2, 229-33, 235, 239, 311.

Donald V. Smiley, *Canada in Question: Federalism in the Eighties,* Third Edition, Toronto: McGraw-Hill Ryerson, 1980, pp. 99-100.

Geoffrey Stevens, "Prospects and Proposals" in *Politics and the Media,* Toronto: Reader's Digest Foundation of Canada and Erindale College, University of Toronto, 1981, p. 102.

Garth Stevenson, "Federalism and Intergovernmental Relations," in *Canadian Politics in the 1980's,* edited by Michael Whittington and Glen Williams, Toronto: Methuen, 1984, p. 386.

Pierre Elliott Trudeau, *Federalism and the French-Canadians,* Toronto: Macmillan of Canada, 1968, pp. xxiii, 203.

Richard Van Loon, "The Policy and Expenditure Management System in the Federal Government: The First Three Years" in *Canadian Public Administration,* 26, 2 (1983), p. 285.

Richard Van Loon, "Planning in the Eighties" in *How Ottawa Decides: Planning and Industrial Policy Making 1968-1984,* edited by Richard French, Toronto: James Lorimer, 1984, p. 177.

Max Weber, "Politics as a Vocation" in *From Max Weber: Essays in Sociology,* edited by H.H. Gerth and C. Wright Mills, New York: Oxford University Press, 1973, p. 128.

Aaron Wildavsky, *The Nursing Father: Moses as a Political Leader,* Tuscaloosa, Ala.: University of Alabama Press, 1984, pp. 187, 190.

CONTENTS

SECTION III: LEADERSHIP IN THE CANADIAN PROVINCES

PREFACE

The purpose of this book is to reassert the importance of leadership in the study of public policy. Prime ministers and premiers, while the focus of enormous popular attention and speculation, have been largely neglected in scholarly analysis. Concerned principally with the constraints on action, scholars have often ignored the importance of individual initiatives, the possibilities for "strategic intervention" by leaders capable of altering the balance of forces and decision within governments, and the impact of ideals, egos, and idiosyncrasies on the shaping of events. This book does not put a gloss on our highest office holders. Their roles are not glamourized. Rather, our view is that prime ministers and premiers operate in increasingly complex milieux, face tremendous obstacles, and live under a harsh and unceasing media spotlight. The heights of power are densely crowded with demands, deadlines, tensions, and public performances. Yet opportunities for strong action remain. Character has its impact on policy and history.

This book is aimed primarily at a university audience, although the general reader will also find much that is of interest. It is one of the few books that deals with prime ministerial power and it is the first attempt to describe the office of premier in each of the major regions of the country. It is also the first book that directly examines leadership and public policy in Canada. Robert Craig Brown's article and portions of Peter Aucoin's have been previously published. All others were commissioned specifically for this volume. The essays are linked by the hypothesis, articulated in the Introduction, that as government has grown in size and complexity, the skills required for successful leadership in Ottawa and in the provinces have become more varied and demanding. Those at the pinnacle of power must learn to wear many masks.

Prime Ministers and Premiers is divided into three sections: Perspectives on Leadership, The Exercise of Power: Prime Ministerial Arenas, and Leadership in the Canadian Provinces. The first provides an overview of the scholarly literature and suggests some approaches that might be taken in deciphering the roles and styles of leaders in Canadian political systems. It also contains an assessment by Robert Craig Brown of some of the common patterns shared by prime ministers throughout Canadian history. The second section examines six arenas of prime ministerial power, each having its own characteristics, routines, symbols, and pressures. The last section is on the office of premier in Atlantic Canada, Quebec, Ontario, in the Prairie West, and in British Columbia, respectively.

As always, there are debts of thanks that must be acknowledged. Keith Archer, Alan Cairns, Sylvie d'Augerot-Arend, Lorry Felske, Thomas Flanagan, Roger Gibbins, Guy Laforest, Ronald Landes, Howard and Tamara Palmer, and Elly Silverman each refereed at least one of the chapters. Dianne Fox, Keith McKenzie, Judi Powell, and Michael Pretes helped with preparation of the manuscript and went to efforts beyond the call of duty. We are very appreciative. We also thank Ian Stewart of Acadia University, and other anonymous reviewers, who reviewed the manuscript for Prentice-Hall Canada. Pat Ferrier, David Jolliffe, and Kateri Lanthier of Prentice-Hall Canada were gracious and helpful in shepherding the manuscript to completion. Magda Kryt's copyediting was a virtuoso performance of literary discipline applied to a sometimes recalcitrant text.

We owe the greatest debt to our wives, Mary Pal and Daphne Gottlieb Taras, for their loving encouragement and critical eye. Matthew Pal and Matthew Taras, both toddlers, kept their fathers busy and alert on matters having nothing to do at all with this book.

CONTRIBUTORS

Peter Aucoin is Professor of Public Administration and Political Science at Dalhousie University. He is the author and/or editor of *The Structures of Policy-Making in Canada* (with G. Bruce Doern); *Knowledge, Power and Public Policy* (with Richard French); *Public Accountability in the Governing of Professions; Public Policy in Canada* (with G. Bruce Doern); and *Party Government and Regional Representation in Canada,* among other works. Professor Aucoin served as a research co-ordinator for the Royal Commission on the Economic Union and Development Prospects for Canada (Macdonald Commission).

Robert Craig Brown is Professor of History at the University of Toronto. His books include *The Canadians, 1867-1967; Canada's National Policy, 1883-1900;* and a biography of Robert Laird Borden.

Robert Malcolm Campbell is Associate Professor and Chairman, Department of Political Studies, Trent University. Among his recent publications is *Grand Illusions: The Politics of the Keynesian Experience in Canada 1945-1975.*

Daniel Latouche is Professor at the Institut National de la Recherche Scientifique, Université du Québec. He served as an advisor to Premier René Lévesque and appears frequently as a writer and commentator in the Quebec media. He is the author of *Le Système politique québécois* (with Edouard Cloutier); *Premier Mandat;* and *Canada and Quebec, Past and Future: An Essay.*

Kim Richard Nossal is an Associate Professor of Political Science at McMaster University. He is the author of *The Politics of Canadian Foreign Policy* and a number of articles on Canadian foreign policy which have appeared in leading journals.

Leslie A. Pal is Associate Professor of Political Science at the University of Calgary. He is the author of *Public Policy Analysis: An Introduction* and *State, Class, and Bureaucracy: Canadian Unemployment Insurance and Public Policy.*

Jennifer Smith is Assistant Professor of Political Science at Dalhousie University. She is a former Parliamentary Intern and a member of the Board of Directors of the Canadian Political Science Association. She has written a number of articles on federalism and constitutional issues.

Neil A. Swainson is Professor Emeritus of Political Science at the University of Victoria. He is the author of *Conflict over the Columbia* and editor of *Managing the Water Environment.*

David Taras is Assistant Professor of General Studies and Director of the Canadian Studies Programme at the University of Calgary. He is editor of *Parliament and Canadian Foreign Policy* and *A Passion For Identity: Introduction to Canadian Studies* (with Eli Mandel).

Donald C. Wallace is Research Officer for the Faculty of Arts and lecturer in the Department of Political Science at York University. He is the author of *Canadian Politics Through Press Reports* (with Frederick J. Fletcher) and has contributed the chapter on "Ottawa and the Provinces" to the *Canadian Annual Review of Politics and Public Affairs* for a number of years.

Robert G. Weyant was trained as a research psychologist and has been Dean of Arts and Science and Dean of General Studies at the University of Calgary. He is now Professor of General Studies and has published in psychology, the history and philosophy of science, women's studies and post-secondary education.

Graham White is Assistant Professor of Political Science at Erindale College, University of Toronto. He worked for several years at the Ontario Legislature and has served as Director of the Ontario Legislative Internship Programme. He is editor of *Politics: Canada,* sixth edition (with Paul Fox) and has contributed articles and chapters to a number of journals and collections.

Nelson Wiseman is Associate Professor of Political Science at the University of Toronto. He is the author of *Social Democracy in Manitoba* and editor of *Government and Enterprise in Canada* (with K. J. Rea).

INTRODUCTION

The Changing Faces of Political Power in Canada

David Taras and Leslie A. Pal

It would appear, at first glance, that in Canadian politics all roads lead to the prime minister and the provincial premiers. The individuals who occupy these offices attract an extraordinary amount of media and public attention. To judge from press reports, those at the apex of political power in the Canadian system are, or should be, responsible for almost every important decision emanating from government. During elections, this focus on leaders intensifies, almost to the exclusion of other political participants and even of political issues. Prime ministers and premiers are so much a part of the public consciousness that terms such as "the Diefenbaker period" or "the Duplessis years" are commonplace.

This popular attention to leaders and to leadership issues is sometimes denigrated as mere voyeurism, a sort of *People* magazine approach to politics. Certainly the academic study of leadership in Canada has not been extensive. In the social sciences, with the exception of psychology, there has been more emphasis on the role of large political and economic forces than on the effect of individuals or personalities. In our view, this focus has neglected important aspects of the political process. While political leaders may not have all the impact or effect that is ascribed to them in the popular press, neither are they completely overshadowed by larger forces. This book helps to adjust the perspective, at least in

the study of Canadian politics, by refocussing attention on leaders, leadership, and their relationship to public policy.

Leadership is so pervasive a phenomenon that it almost defies definition. In the political sphere alone, the varieties of leadership are staggering. Intellectuals may lead the political process in championing new and arresting ideas; interest groups may lead in defining policy problems; the media may lead by drawing public attention to some neglected social issue; the opposition may lead by challenging government to deal with particular problems. Not only will the type of leadership itself vary according to the nature of the group within which it is practised, but the personalities will differ, each adding special and unique ingredients to the alchemy of power.

Leadership is thus exercised throughout the political system at virtually every level. This book cannot hope to capture all its expressions, certainly not at a time when the serious study of political leadership in Canada is barely in its infancy. Accordingly, we have decided to train our attention on the apex of the political process: the offices of prime minister and premier. As mentioned earlier, there are several good reasons for beginning here. First, in formal terms, these offices are defined by our traditions of government as being the most pivotal in the policy process. The individuals who occupy them are "first among equals." Second, the informal networks of power which bind these offices to other components of the political system are so extensive and so sensitive that to study these leaders is also to comprehend a great deal about the broader phenomenon of leadership itself.

Since this volume is exploratory, and since, as David Taras and Robert Weyant show in Chapter 1, there is no consensus on the best approach to leadership, we did not impose a rigid theoretical framework on our contributors. Instead, we asked them to address several themes. First, we asked them to explore the relationship between political leaders and social context. Our interest was in the specific sphere of autonomy that leaders exercise, and moreover, in the way that leaders express and channel social forces. Second, we asked for some consideration of the impact of personality on politics. How do different individuals handle similar problems and opportunities? Third, we asked for some reflection on the nature of the policy process, since it would seem to be one of the critical targets of leadership activities. Our suggestion was to consider the policy process as a series of loosely connected arenas, each with different actors and dynamics. This is similar, of course, to the old interest in the different "roles" which leaders play, but differs in that we assume that these arenas now represent what can almost be considered subgovernments in their own right. The challenge of co-ordinating these diverse arenas is commensurably greater.

The result has been a rich array of essays drawing on different approaches and providing a kaleidoscope of insights on the place of prime ministers and premiers in the Canadian political system. The first section of the volume sets the stage for these essays by reviewing the leadership literature, addressing the connection between policy and leadership, and describing the types of men who have held highest office throughout Canadian history. The remaining essays all probe, in various ways, the balance between character and circumstance, the strategies of intervention, and the broad role of leaders in our political system. There are two strong implications in this volume about the capacity of individuals to exercise leadership. The first is that institutional arrangements place certain constraints (while also providing opportunities) on what leaders can do.[1] Canadian leaders, especially prime ministers, are, as it were, stranded between a cabinet and presidential style of government, between their old pre-eminence under the traditional Westminster system, and the new fragmentation which has apparently all but eliminated any clear centre of power. The second implication is that leadership is not a single phenomenon but many; it is exercised in different ways requiring different skills. Prime ministers, and to a lesser extent, premiers, must play several roles, master several vocabularies, and dominate and transcend several different universes. They must wear many masks.

"THE STRANDED LEADER"

Canada inherits from Great Britain a cabinet system of government. The Cabinet symbolizes collective authority and fuses party, politics, and government. It is supreme, and traditionally the epicentre of the rumblings of power. Prime ministers in cabinet-style systems are expected to serve long apprenticeships in their political parties and in Parliament. For instance, British prime ministers serve an average of over a quarter of a century in Parliament before assuming the highest office.[2] In the classic formulation, the prime minister is "first among equals" at the cabinet table. In more contemporary parlance, he or she is expected to be foremost a "team captain" or "coach." The Cabinet, not the prime minister, is the mainspring of government.

A vigorous debate has flourished in Britain over whether cabinet government has given way to prime ministerial government. A former cabinet minister, Richard Crossman, argued in 1965 that "'the hyphen which joins, the buckle which fastens' the legislative part of the state to the executive has become one man."[3] Others contend that the Cabinet remains the linchpin, and that, as former Prime Minister Harold Wilson once put it, "it is the Cabinet, not the prime minister, who decides."[4]

The traditional cabinet model certainly dominated in Canada until after the Second World War. Prime ministers from John A. Macdonald up to at least Diefenbaker were "party men," and the Cabinet brought together powerful regional spokesmen and political barons. Quite small by present standards, it was a key instrument for "elite accommodation" and governance.

The contrasts between the cabinet system and the American presidential system are glaring. In the American political system, power is diffused and fragmented. Presidential power is checked by congressional veto and Supreme Court judgements. In the postwar period, political parties have declined in importance and single-issue interest groups have grown in the force of their demands and political effectiveness. Richard Neustadt has argued in his well-known book *Presidential Power* that because the president does not control many of the instruments of decision directly, in order to be successful he must be a persuader.[5] This is the meaning behind Teddy Roosevelt's description of the office as a "bully pulpit." Richard Rose has described the president as "more like a golfer who has just won the National Open by playing against and defeating everyone around him" than as a team player.[6] The image is that of the lonely individual at the top, surrounded by government on all sides — in effect, "stranded." Significantly, presidents like Carter and Reagan could remain "outsiders" and vehement critics of government even while they served as president.

Since 1945, the Canadian political system, like other cabinet systems of government, has developed some of the features of the American political process. It has become increasingly pluralistic and disjointed. In the 1960s and 1970s, provincial governments assumed impressive powers in many areas of Canadian life. Although they can rarely exercise a veto over Ottawa's decisions, their co-operation is essential to the successful implementation of many policies. The Meech Lake Accord of 1987 may disperse even more power to the provinces. As in the United States, political parties have declined in importance. Indeed, Pierre Trudeau did not have to serve any significant apprenticeship at all within the Liberal party before being propelled to the top. Interest groups have grown in number and influence and often vie for power within the government itself. The Cabinet, grown increasingly large and cumbersome, has, in the view of many, lost ground to central agencies such as the Privy Council Office and the Prime Minister's Office. That Joe Clark and Brian Mulroney could both become prime minister without previous cabinet experience is perhaps the best testimony to the waning influence and power of that institution. The prime minister has had to become much more of a broker of societal interests. Unlike his predecessors, the modern prime minister is now much more than a team captain or coach. Yet he lacks the prestige of the American leader. He is deprived of the pageantry and mystique that surrounds the presidency and enables the president to be an effective persuader. The prime minister falls between the two systems, between two chairs, and has not yet found the right footing.

THE MASKS OF POWER

A second problem is that as a consequence of this diffusion of power and the tremendous growth of government, the prime minister no longer presides over a monolithic system but over a number of what can best be described as subgovernments. Several subgovernments co-exist within the Ottawa political universe. While some problems are pervasive enough to have an impact in many areas of government, other problems affect one area only. The machinery of government, federal-provincial relations, international diplomacy, the economy, and the political realm of party and media relations constitute some of the principal subsystems. Each involves different players, calls for different instincts and knowledge, has different rules, and requires a different vocabulary. Mastery of each demands expertise and the development of special personas or masks. Unfortunately, few leaders command such a diverse range of skills or manage to perform in so many arenas simultaneously. As R.M. Punnett has written,

> the skills that the Prime Minister is required to possess are so numerous and so varied that it is almost inevitable that he will be found to be deficient in at least one of them.... Indeed there may be something of an "iron law" of unavoidable prime ministerial failure: every Prime Minister will have an Achilles' heel on which critics can focus, so that no matter how successful he may be in most aspects of his job, his reputation is liable to be undermined by his lack of even one of the necessary talents.[7]

These subsystems also operate according to their own rhythms. The diplomatic calendar is arranged around annual summit meetings between the prime minister and the American president, the annual meeting of the heads of government of the Group of Seven industrial nations, and the meeting of Commonwealth leaders. Foreign guests and visits abroad are also part of the diplomatic cycle. The economic cycle, in turn, has its own relentless schedule. The budget address, the speech from the throne, the seasonal problem of unemployment, and the Bank of Canada's responses to monetary fluctuations often fall into predictable patterns. Intergovernmental relations is yet another area that has its own rhythms and seasons. First ministers' conferences, economic summits, and bargaining over Established Programmes Financing all have been regularized to some degree.

Faced with demands from so many sectors, prime ministers have tended to confine themselves to specialized areas of interest. Lester B. Pearson was a leading diplomat before his entry into politics. As prime minister, he retained a strong interest in international affairs and sought to translate these diplomatic skills to the field of federal-provincial negotiation. Media management, party affairs, and economic matters were largely left to others. Prime Minister Trudeau gave priority to constitutional struggles and intermittently to foreign policy offensives. He also gave considerable time and thought to the organization of his government. Party affairs, his media image, and economic issues did not seem to compel his interest. Brian Mulroney seems to be foremost a party politician who is skilled at keeping the party machine well-oiled and the partisans happy. He seems to be less comfortable dealing with economic or foreign policy issues or with administrative matters.

It is tempting to argue that because provincial premiers preside over smaller governmental systems, they dominate all significant realms of government. Certainly one expects that the premiers of Newfoundland or Saskatchewan should put their personal stamp on all major initiatives. It is open to question, however, whether the premiers of the larger provinces do not face a multifaceted political system in which they must exercise diverse skills and instincts in order to function effectively.

This book explores the varied terrain of political leadership in Canada. The chapters in the second section on the exercise of power describe how prime ministers have dealt with and influenced major issue areas. David Taras argues that strategies of media management and the advent of a television prime ministership have altered many of the old political rules. Taras contends that the ability of prime ministers to get a positive message through to the public may now be the single most important ingredient determining political survival. The appropriate metaphor is that of a battleground in which the prime minister uses defences, devises strategies, and keeps an arsenal of weapons at the ready. The relationship between prime ministers and the media seems to operate with its own rituals and codes.

The machinery of government as it evolved under Pierre Trudeau and Brian Mulroney is described by Peter Aucoin. Trudeau's "rational management" is compared to Mulroney's "brokerage politics." As these organizational styles are the extensions outward into the governmental system of a prime minister's character and world view, they indicate a great deal about how much influence prime ministers really do have in shaping bureaucratic instruments. But as Hugh Heclo has written, "Between the politician's intentions and the government's final action passes the shadow of the bureaucrat."[8] Aucoin has described the workings of the "administrative minds" of Trudeau and Mulroney. The third chapter in this section, by Donald Wallace, discusses the influence that prime ministers have had in the intergovernmental arena. Wallace describes the rules of the game, and the hobbles on prime ministerial initiatives, as prime ministers meet premiers at the bargaining table. Those at the pinnacle of the federal system struggle for power against each other, each using different resources and tactics. As is the case with other subgovernments, there is a particular set of skills needed in this area. In the next chapter, Leslie Pal discusses prime ministers and their political parties. The forging of "enduring coalitions" is the key to leadership within the party, and the gateway to the prime ministership. Unless alliances are maintained, the grass roots cultivated, and cash kept flowing into party coffers, the leader is vulnerable to rebellion and disaffection. In a sphere of ambitious men and women, loyalty can never be taken for granted. Pal stresses the differences between government leadership and party leadership. These roles, or, more broadly speaking, systems, are often contradictory.

Yet another set of skills is needed in the management of the economy. Robert Campbell describes the impact that prime ministers have had on economic policy. Prime ministers must deal with a company of actors entirely different from that in the media or in intergovernmental relations. Business associations, the banking community, large corporations, and regional interest groups expect to have access at least to the minister of finance, and ultimately hold the prime minister responsible for the direction of the economy. Campbell reminds us that economic policy in the 1980s is adrift among the reefs of apparently intractable problems of trade, unemployment, and inflation. Leaders are drawn either to impose solutions based on arid economic principles, or to design compromises that ultimately involve the "dismal science" less than they do politics. Foreign policy, the subject of the last essay in this section examining the exercise of power, represents yet another world. Kim Richard Nossal describes how both Trudeau and Mulroney, when they first assumed office, thought they could with relative ease redirect Canadian foreign policy. This was before they learned the ropes. International realities, together with Canada's relative powerlessness in world affairs, imposed severe constraints on their capacities to manoeuvre. Both Trudeau's and Mulroney's early hopes for new departures in Canadian foreign policy were dashed by powerful domestic and external forces.

In the book's final section, the office of premier is analyzed from a number of perspectives. The political culture of each province or region, rather than the notion of subgovernments, seems to be the key to understanding the world of Canadian premiers. The central idea in Jennifer Smith's "Political Leadership in Atlantic Canada" is that the small size of the Atlantic provinces and their poor economic conditions determine political behaviour. Because they preside over relatively small governmental systems, premiers are involved directly in almost all aspects of policy and administration. The relative poverty of Atlantic Canada dictates that economic issues are inevitably at the top of a premier's agenda. Daniel Latouche has described vividly the problems of power at intoxicating heights, developing an extensive physiology of the office of Quebec premier. Indeed, Latouche argues that the office has been transformed along with transformations in Quebec society. Keying his description to the evolution of political regimes, Latouche shows that the Quebec premiership has itself evolved to a new level of complexity and responsibility. Moreover, the practice of leadership in Quebec is complicated by the problem of having to be simultaneously a political leader and a societal leader. The Quebec premier has emerged as the voice of Quebec society and this has brought unique and intense pressures.

In the third chapter in this section Graham White compares the structures used in governing Ontario under Conservative William Davis and Liberal David Peterson. The two premiers developed different mechanisms for directing a large and complex government. White shows that even within a highly developed and conservative governmental system, structures can be shaped to fit the needs, styles, and outlooks of the individuals who become premier. It can be argued that premiers change the office even as the office changes them.

In a sweeping review of prairie leadership, Nelson Wiseman describes how premiers reflect and symbolize the values of the societies that elect them. The careers of John Bracken, T.C. Douglas, and William Aberhart are used to illustrate the ideological patterns that dominated politics at formative stages in the development of distinct political cultures in Manitoba, Saskatchewan, and Alberta, respectively. Neil Swainson's chapter on the premiers of British Columbia is of necessity quite different, as he portrays premiers who have governed amid fierce ideological strife. Swainson analyzes how premiers from W.A.C. Bennett to William Vander Zalm have carried out the major tasks associated with British Columbia's

highest office. Taken together, the chapters in this section suggest that premiers are still able to affect almost all of the important areas that are under their direction. Perhaps these separate political cultures each have their own historic priorities that subsume other interests or tasks.

Prime ministers and premiers can easily become victims of a political system that leaves them "stranded" and demands that they play a variety of sometimes mechanical roles. The vague but vast distrust of modern leaders may be rooted in these realities: as the policy process becomes more fragmented and arenas multiply, the masks become even more elaborate and contrived. Who can trust the faceless? While job descriptions have changed and tasks have become herculean and more numerous, public expectations have not diminished. The desire for a saviour who will nobly sweep away the problems that confront society seems to be as pressing and pervasive as ever. The media have done little to alter these expectations. What is needed, perhaps, is a greater understanding of the poisons, delights, and passions of politics, and most importantly, of its complexities. We hope that this book will shed some needed light on our highest political offices.

Notes

1. See for instance Campbell, *Governments Under Stress.*

2. Rose, "Government against Sub-governments," p. 313.

3. Quoted in Weller, *First Among Equals,* p. 5.

4. Quoted in Weller, p. 6.

5. Neustadt, *Presidential Power.*

6. Rose, "Government against Sub-governments," p. 315.

7. Punnett, *The Prime Minister,* p. 28.

8. Heclo, *A Government of Strangers,* p. 6.

Perspectives on Leadership

This section seeks to introduce the concept of leadership, and to illustrate the wide variety of approaches to the subject. David Taras and Robert Weyant review writings on leadership, and particularly the treatment of leaders in the social science literature. They find that there is little consensus; on the contrary, the number of theories and approaches is staggering. In the latter part of their essay, they focus on the question of political leadership and political leaders.

Leslie A. Pal reviews the treatment of leadership in the public policy literature and the treatment of public policy in the leadership literature. He discovers a curious disjunction: those who study policy see a need for leadership but assume that it is difficult, if not impossible; those who study leadership seem to conclude that its impact on policy is minimal. Pal argues for a different conceptualization of power to resolve the tension. The ideas of strategic intervention and arenas of power are developed.

Historian Robert Craig Brown describes the "curious creatures" who have in their time served as prime ministers of Canada. According to Brown, they have been primarily conciliators, skilled at fashioning compromises and walking the safe middle ground. The historical record reveals, however, a variety of personalities, perspectives, and approaches.

CHAPTER 1

Dreamers of the Day: A Guide to Roles, Character and Performance on the Political Stage

David Taras and Robert Weyant

> *All men dream; but not equally. Those who dream by night in the dusty recesses of their minds wake in the day to find that it was vanity; but the dreamers of the day are dangerous men, for they may act their dream with open eyes, to make it possible.*
>
> T.E. Lawrence

The study of leadership has generated a vast body of literature. While the main work has been conducted in psychology, psychiatry, political science, history, sociology, international relations, and management, interesting insights have also arisen from less obvious disciplines such as biology, chemistry, medicine and feminist scholarship.[1] However, without diminishing the impressive biographical work done by Canadian historians, it must be said that Canadian scholars have tended to avoid the subject. Several factors may explain this apparent disinterest among students of Canadian politics. Insofar as analysis from the political economy perspective has been influential in Canadian scholarship, it has portrayed economic forces as paramount in shaping behaviour. While a John A. Macdonald or a Pierre Trudeau may act out important dramas, they are not seen as setting the stage or even inventing the major

themes in the plot. Another impediment to the analysis of Canadian leadership has been the official secrecy of cabinet deliberations and documents, which impedes serious study of recent or current leaders. While American presidents leave entire libraries to mark their years in office, and ex-cabinet-level officials in the United States receive lucrative book contracts to recount their battles and describe the foibles of others, Canadian cabinet ministers are restrained by the requirement and tradition of secrecy. Memoirs by Jean Chrétien, Keith Davey, Donald Johnston and others dwell on personal impressions and colourful anecdotes, and not on the substance of policy-making.[2]

Another possible reason why the subject has been avoided is that Canadian leaders have rarely been graced by the aura of greatness that is conferred on leaders in other countries. Clinton Rossiter, for instance, has described the myth of presidential greatness accepted by many Americans, especially up until Watergate.

> Lincoln is the supreme myth, the richest symbol in the American experience. He is, as someone has remarked neither irreverently nor sacrilegiously, the martyred Christ of democracy's passion play. And who, then, can measure the strength that is given to the President because he holds Lincoln's office, lives in Lincoln's house, and walks in Lincoln's way? The final greatness of the Presidency lies in the truth that it is not just an office of incredible power but a breeding ground of indestructible myth.[3]

Indeed, it can be argued that Canada's internal divisions, its complex federal system and the constant need for compromise have militated against the emergence of "great men." Canadians have tended to be highly critical of their leaders. Indeed, Gaile McGregor has argued that Canadians not only expect but have even come to admire evasion, scheming, and "magical" tricks from their leaders.[4] The cultural landscape with its brooding moral restraint and sharp satire has not been conducive to creating heroes. It is fitting, perhaps, that most of the paintings of Canada's best-known artists, the Group of Seven, are landscapes devoid of human figures.

This chapter will survey some of the important developments that have taken place in the study of leaders. Out of necessity we have been highly selective, plucking a number of major strands out of a rich and varied tapestry. In the first section, several general approaches are described. A second section focusses on political frameworks which are relevant to the study of Canadian leaders.

For the purposes of this chapter, leadership will be defined as "the process of influence between leaders and followers."[5] We do not view leadership as an attribute that one possesses at birth, but rather as an active, ongoing, developing relationship with others in society. While leadership can be exercised in a variety of settings, we are concerned with political leadership in a governmental context. Our central concern is with the effects which leadership may have on public policy.

STUDYING LEADERSHIP

Eponymous history emphasizes the role of outstanding individuals (typically males, hence the sexist "great man" approach) in the formation and development of policies, institutions and actions. The idea of the great person as an agent of social and political change has a long history. The Iliad is very much a tale of heroes, and names such as Hammurabi, Lycurgus, Solon, Alexander, and Caesar have come down to us from antiquity as denoting social and political leaders of almost godlike stature. Biblical leaders, such as Moses and David, and the figures of Mohammed and Joan of Arc have been portrayed as instruments for divine intervention in human affairs. On the other hand, the practical idea that rulers can, and indeed must, be trained, that a deity should not always be depended on for guidance, also developed. Philosophers from Plato to Machiavelli have discussed the attributes of leadership and have given advice about everything from the type of education that leaders should receive to the strategies that they should employ in war. An oft-quoted example of such advice is Machiavelli's dictum in *The Prince:*

> A prince must imitate the fox and the lion, for the lion cannot protect himself from traps, and the fox cannot defend himself from wolves. One must therefore be a fox to recognize traps, and a lion to frighten wolves. Those that wish to be only lions do not understand this. Therefore, a prudent ruler ought not to keep faith when by so doing it would be against his interest, and when the reasons which made him bind himself no longer exist. If men were all good, this precept would not be a good one; but as they are bad and would not observe their faith with you, so you are not bound to keep faith with them.

Daniel Bell found that the main theme in early discussions of leadership is the "image of the mindless masses...and the strong-willed leader."[6]

While heroic figures have been recognized throughout recorded history, a vigorous debate on the merits of the "great man" approach did not arise until the nineteenth century. This was due largely to a growing interest in individual achievement in response to a number of factors, including the emphasis on the individual that arose during the Renaissance, growing speculation on the psychological equality of human beings, and an increasing interest in history and historical method. An important contribution to the debate was made by Thomas Carlyle. In his *On Heroes and Hero Worship,* the great person was depicted as a prophet whose role was to bring a supreme spiritual meaning into the sterile and meaningless material world. According to Carlyle,

> Universal History, the history of what man has accomplished in this world, is at bottom the History of the Great Men who have worked here. They were the leaders of men, these great ones; the modellers, patterns, and in a wide sense creators, of whatsoever the general mass of men contrive to do or to attain; all things that we see standing accomplished in the world are properly the outer material result, the practical realisation and embodiment, of Thoughts that dwelt in the Great Men sent into the world: the soul of the whole world's history, it may justly be considered, were the history of these.

For Carlyle, the appearance of the hero was a mystical event, separate from and above mundane social forces. William James, an American philosopher and psychologist influenced by the writings of Charles Darwin, argued that the critical issue is not how great persons are produced but, rather, how they are selected by particular societies at particular times.[7] The essential question is why persons with certain attributes were chosen as leaders or heroes, while others were ignored. Leaders are closely linked to, and reflect and symbolize the social evolution of their societies.

Two basic positions that emerged in the "hero in history" debate have been summarized by Sidney Hook as follows:

> Either the main line of historical action and social development is literally inescapable or it is not. If it is, any existing leadership is a completely subsidiary element in determining the main historical pattern of today and tomorrow. If it is not inescapable, the question almost asks itself: to what extent is the character of a given leadership causally and, since men are involved, morally responsible for our historical position and future?[8]

If history is the product of great persons, then, as Barbara Kellerman has written, "without Moses the Jews would have stayed in Egypt; without Lenin there would have been no Russian Revolution; without Churchill the Nazis would have conquered Great Britain."[9] If, on the other hand, leaders are products of particular forces and events and cannot shape outcomes, then "greatness" cannot in fact be thrust on individuals. According to this view, Lenin would not have emerged as the leader of the Bolshevik Revolution without the massive upheavals caused by large economic and social forces. It was economic and technological developments, not Abraham Lincoln, that freed the slaves. Both of these arguments are, of course, extreme positions, but they are not straw men. For instance, in the theory of historical materialism proposed by Karl Marx, the laws of social and economic change are portrayed as inevitable and immutable. At most, a leader can hasten or retard slightly the pace of history's implacable march to an already determined end. Class conflict and the engines of history devour individual actions. Daniel Latouche, in his contribution to this volume, discusses Marx's depiction of Louis Napoleon as a prisoner of a providential role, having virtually "no freedom of action." Although Marxist scholars have now developed more sophisticated approaches, the role played by leaders remains a thorny and perplexing question that is yet to be fully resolved. Ironically, the "cult of leadership" has been especially evident in Marxism. Marx himself, Lenin, Stalin, Mao, Castro, Che, and others have been the subjects of idolatry on a scale rarely parallelled in history.

Sociologists Robert Michels and Max Weber made significant contributions by linking leadership to economic and social developments, and particularly to the growth of bureaucracies. Michels argued that even within the most democratic organizations there is an "iron law of oligarchy" which ensures that power is held by a small group of individuals. Since full political participation of large numbers is impractical, an elite inevitably assumes control. Leaders, having attained power, immediately have a vested interest in maintaining the privileges of rank and keeping control of the resources necessary to perpetuate themselves in office. Elitism, bureaucratic rigidity, and corruption triumph eventually. Michels argued that even if the leaders are overthrown, the replacements will soon undergo a "transformation which renders them in every respect similar to the dethroned tyrants.... The revolutionaries of today become the reactionaries of tomorrow."[10]

Max Weber's main thesis regarding leadership was that the stability of societies depended on the relationship of leaders to followers.[11] The focus was on the needs and expectations of the led as much as on the qualities exhibited by those who lead. Weber argued that legitimate authority was based on three types of leadership. "Charismatic authority" is assumed by those who are seen as possessing extraordinary gifts. Obedience comes from a sense of awe inspired by those who seem to have special grace or even magical powers. The prophet, the warrior, and the hero lead through personal magnetism and outstanding accomplishment. A second type of leadership is "traditional authority." Traditional leaders inherit their position as a birthright. They symbolize to their followers a historic chain of authority and allegiance. Monarchy is the clearest form of traditional leadership. The third type described by Weber is "legal authority." Legal authority is based on bureaucratic or technical expertise

and on rational impersonal processes. The bond of obedience comes from a respect for law and the obligations of citizenship. According to Weber, charismatic leaders introduce new values and create new institutions, traditional leaders uphold the status quo, and those vested with legal authority can, if they want, bring incremental change.

Psychoanalysis has also been brought to bear on the study of leadership. The actual value of the psychoanalytic contribution is open to question, both because of the problematic nature of psychoanalytic theory and because of its use in a number of controversial studies. Among the most controversial was the study by Sigmund Freud and William C. Bullitt of United States President Woodrow Wilson.[12] Their book was personal and vindictive rather than scholarly. Less controversial is Harold Lasswell's *Psychopathology and Politics,* now regarded as something of a modern classic.[13] Basing his study on extensive interviews with public personalities, Lasswell concluded that leaders externalize inner conflicts, acting out their internal dramas and crises on the political stage. He arrived at a formula to describe how psychological drives impel political behaviour: "$P > D > R = P$, where P equals private motives; D equals displacement onto a public object; R equals rationalization in terms of public interest; P equals the political man; $>$ equals transformed into."[14] He found three types of leaders, with each type linked to a psychological predisposition: the agitator, the administrator, and the theorist. According to Lasswell,

the essential mark of the agitator is the high value which he places on the emotional response of the public.... The agitator has come by his name honestly, for he is enough agitated about public policy to communicate his excitement to those about him.

[The administrator is tied] to the members of his own environment, whose relations he seeks to co-ordinate. The administrator is a co-ordinator of effort in continuing activity.

Marx, [a theorist], wanted to impress himself

upon mankind, certainly.... But more: Marx wanted unreserved admiration for the products of his mind. He toiled through years of isolation and poverty to make his assertions impregnable...[15]

Erik Erikson, T.W. Adorno, Bruce Mazlish and Victor Wolfenstein, among others, also discovered relationships between the inner play of needs and conflicts, and the values espoused by public figures.[16] Erikson found that Luther, Gandhi, Woodrow Wilson, and Eleanor Roosevelt all suffered from low self-esteem in adolescence, and that the need to overcome these feelings fuelled their political actions and beliefs.[17] Lucille Iremonger concluded from a study of twenty-four British prime ministers that "the driving force in their lives emerged from their being deprived in childhood of the love of their parents."[18]

Psychoanalytic interpretations have also been applied to the behaviour of followers. In his classic work *Escape From Freedom,* Erich Fromm has argued that the rise of capitalism and the advance of industrialization created severe alienation in entire populations.[19] Explosive urbanization and the subsequent decline of rural life, the growth of large and anonymous bureaucracies, the decline of religious observance and the breakdown of traditional ways of life and institutions all occurred over a relatively brief period in history. According to Fromm, the resulting feelings of insecurity brought a craving for authority and the desire to submit blindly to powerful leaders, father figures, men who would be sturdy anchors in a sea of change. This submission, in that it meant relinquishing both personal responsibility and the necessity of thinking for oneself, was in fact an escape from freedom.

The varied nature of the work that has been done in this area raises a number of questions. What is it that we need in order to proceed with reasonable expectation of producing an accurate understanding and assessment of a leader's character? At the very least we need three things — reliable data on leaders, a verifiable theory of personality development, and criteria for what constitutes good and bad leadership performance in specific situations. This task is made difficult by the secrecy that surrounds politics and political figures. Theirs is a world of smoke and mirrors, difficult to penetrate. Too often we are dealing with evidence that is impressionistic, second-hand, speculative, and biased by political and other considerations.

Eponymous history often attempts to account for the greatness of the particular individual in terms of family, education, personal experiences, general character, and a host of other variables. Most historians no longer find the eponymous approach to be adequate. Nevertheless, no one can seriously doubt the important role played, on occasion, by individual human beings. Consequently, biography remains an important part of both historical and political writing. Many biographies, in addition to furnishing the historical and political facts, seek to explain the behaviour of the individual in terms of his or her psychological character. Some of this literature qualifies as "psychohistory" in that it takes figures of historical significance and attempts to reconstruct their psychological traits, as well as the sources of those traits in unconscious motivations, from evidence that varies in quantity, quality and reliability. Noteworthy examples are Doris Kearns's work on Lyndon Johnson, Fawn Brodie's portrait of Thomas Jefferson, Erikson's analysis of Martin Luther, and a study of Woodrow Wilson by Alexander and Juliette George.[20]

In addition to the variation in quality evident in these biographical works, the reason for which they appear to have been written has also varied widely, ranging from analysis of a political power structure (Dale Thomson, *Jean Lesage and The Quiet Revolution*) to popular quasi-history (George Radwanski's or Richard Gwyn's biographies of Trudeau) to ideological argumentation (Donald Creighton's two-volume biography of John A. Macdonald) to political analysis (H. Blair Neatby's study of Mackenzie King) to wartime evaluation of an enemy leader (Walter C. Langer, *The Mind of Adolf Hitler: The Secret Wartime Report*).[21] There are, of course, examples of both cloying adulation and near-libel written by hacks for purely political purposes. The genre has become broad and diverse in both quality and approach. Unlike mainstream psychohistory, many of the more recent reconstructions of the personalities of historically prominent leaders do not necessarily depend upon some variation of psychoanalytic theory, though psychoanalytic concepts and ideas may occasionally be used either explicitly or implicitly. However, the "hero in history" perspective tends to live on in many of these works.

One of the more interesting psychological approaches to leadership has been that of David C. McClelland and his associates.[22] Although McClelland's major focus has not been leadership characteristics as such, his work on power and the motivation for achievement is relevant. McClelland has emphasized factors involved in leadership behaviour, such as the need for power, the need for achievement, and the need for affiliation. One might add to McClelland's list an additional need for recognition or notoriety. McClelland has suggested a fourfold system of classification that relates the source of the power motivation to the object of the power behaviour. Early in life, other persons (parents, teachers, etc.) are the sources that strengthen the individual and satisfy the need for power. Later, in the second stage, a person can satisfy his or her own power needs. Acquiring objects that provide prestige is associated with this stage. Having become a source of power on his or her own, the individual then moves on to use power to influence or manipulate others. Finally, at what McClelland saw as the most mature state, the source of power again moves outside the individual in the form of ethics, laws, religion, political values, etc., and power is directed at influencing or serving other people for some external, higher purpose. The resulting matrix provides what McClelland has called four "stages" of power

Figure 1.1 — McClelland's Four Stages

	SOURCE OF POWER	
	OTHERS (influence)	SELF (feel stronger)
SELF	*Stage I* "They" strengthen me.	*Stage II* I strengthen myself.
OBJECT OF POWER		
OTHERS	*Stage IV* "It" (ethics, laws, etc.) moves me to influence or serve others.	*Stage III* I influence others.

orientation.

The result is a developmental hierarchy of behaviour. The idea is not that an individual moves forever out of one stage and into another, but rather that the mature person is capable of applying any of the appropriate behaviours, from any stage, in the appropriate situation. One of the most interesting aspects of McClelland's work is that he saw power as satisfying personal needs and, consequently, discussed actual ways in which the need for power, achievements, and affiliation might be satisfied. McClelland also applied his schema to political situations, such as periods of peace and war in English history. Canadian leaders and their decisions have yet to be analyzed from this perspective.

An interesting alternative approach has been suggested by a social psychologist, Dean Keith Simonton. Simonton has done considerable work on the characteristics that seem peculiar to historical figures of genius. He defined genius in terms of fame or eminence (recognizing, nius in terms of fame or eminence (recognizing, in the process, the difficulties inherent in such a definition). This led him to argue that there is no fundamental distinction between creativity and leadership: "Creativity, by this definition, can be considered a special form of leadership: creators are cultural leaders."[23] Using a set of statistical techniques which he termed "historiometry," Simonton attempted to determine if there are any general hypotheses about the characteristics of the creators or leaders which could be found. These hypotheses could then be applied to individual leaders to determine if the particular leader conforms to a general norm.

Simonton found that leaders appear, as a group, to possess above-average intelligence. It was not the case, however, that continued increases in intelligence correlated with increased fame as a leader. It would appear that one can be too bright, perhaps too esoteric in one's plans, to obtain and hold popular support. On the other hand, leadership does seem to be related to versatility — the range of areas in which one excels. That is, all other things being equal, generalists become more prominent than specialists. While historiometric research gives the strong impression of objectivity and scientific credibility — for example, it is replete with coefficients of correlation, measures of variability, and the like — there are problems with historiometric research, just as there are with psychoanalytic biographies. Assessment of traits such as intelligence and mental pathology is based on biographical data that is of varying quality, and comparisons are made across centuries of changing social conditions. Also, because of gender discrimination and inequality of access, the subject pool is almost totally male. A number of additional factors lead one to hesitate about making any strong claims based on Simonton's methods. Nonetheless, this approach would seem to be useful in tracing trends within one culture during a particular time period. Simonton's approach might be espe-cially illuminating in the Canadian context, as the characteristics of federal and provincial party leaders could be tabulated and hypotheses formulated.

In the period since World War Two, attention has been directed less at grand theories about leaders and societies than to an analysis of how particular situations condition or elicit behaviour. According to one of the leading "situationists," Ralph Stodgill, the "qualities, characteristics and skills required in a leader are determined to a large extent by the demands of the situation in which he is to function as a leader."[24] The focus has been on the interaction of leaders, followers, situations, and tasks. The situational requirements imposed on gang leaders, union bosses, business executives, or legislators make them different creatures.

Management and business studies have been the areas perhaps most influenced by the situationist perspective. Certainly it has been the basis of a large number of tests devised to screen potential employees and even chief executives. Katherine Briggs and Isabel Briggs Myers developed one such test using personality traits first identified by Carl Jung in 1921. The Myers-Briggs Type Indicator, or MBTI, poses questions which ask respondents to react to different situations. It has become the personality test most widely used by North American companies.[25]

Another situationist approach which gained wide acceptance for some time within management and business studies is the "theory X" and "theory Y" assumptions developed by Douglas McGregor in 1960.[26] McGregor argued that managers worked according to one of two basic assumptions about human nature. Theory X managers assume that their employees need constant monitoring and goading because workers will, if left to their own devices, show little initiative. Theory Y managers believe that their charges are fundamentally hard-working and responsible and need only supportive conditions and encouragement from the top to do their work well. One management type wants tight control, the other is comfortable with looser supervision. McGregor's description of diametrically opposite management types spurred considerable research and myriad studies on the leadership requirements of corporate culture.

In the situationist perspective, the needs of the group, the tasks to be accomplished, and the structure of organizations are seen in each case as being the most powerful determinants of leadership. One that has emerged from this research is that, as groups have so many diverse needs, it is possible for numerous group members to play leadership roles of some kind. Leadership can be exercised in some way by almost every group member. Aaron Wildavsky has been critical of this perspective on leadership:

> Thus begins the blurring; as leaders merge into followers, social life becomes a seamless web. With increasing sophistication, scholars succeed only in making leadership indistinguishable from other phenomena.[27]

The chief thrust, however, is that leaders emerge as a result of their behaviour in particular circumstances. Leadership is different from headship, where the mantle of formal authority is bestowed by an established organization, for a definite time period during which real leadership may or may not be exercised. Leadership is diverse and pluralistic and can be seen in many facets of daily life. It is not synonymous with political power, although politics remains the main medium in which we observe leadership.

POLITICAL LEADERSHIP

Wildavsky has argued that "the most remarkable feature of the literature on leadership is the near-total neglect of large-scale politics."[28] While studies of individual leaders and specific historical events have proliferated, little work has been done on the various types of leaders produced by different political systems, on methods for classifying leaders, or on criteria for evaluating the performance of officeholders. The literature is particularly sparse on the role of leadership in Canadian politics. Few Canadian scholars have engaged in psychohistorical research on Canadian personalities, many of the tools developed to analyze decision-making have not been applied to Canadian events or policies, and there has been no thorough attempt to classify Canadian leaders using typologies from other political systems or situations. In this section, several approaches to studying political leadership will be described. While hardly exhaustive, these approaches provide frameworks for organizing thoughts and evidence and are in themselves interesting and provocative.

Stanley Hoffman has argued that essentially there are only two kinds of leader: the heroic and the routine.[29] Different terms have been used in different contexts to describe approximately the same phenomena. For example, psychologist Abraham Zaleznik described leaders as having either a charismatic or consensus style, while John Stoessinger has labelled the makers of American foreign policy as being either crusaders or pragmatists.[30] In his 1938 book on power, Bertrand Russell contrasted what he called "soldiers of fortune" with those he described as "believers in a cause." The former were driven by ambition and opportunism, while the latter were often individuals of profound religious faith who regarded themselves as instruments of extra-human purpose.[31] Hoffman's characterization is perhaps the most applicable to the purposes of this volume, since his focus is on heads of government.

Hoffman used as his model of heroic leadership the dynastic leaders of modern France; Maréchal Pétain, Pierre Mendès France and Charles de Gaulle. The heroic leader arrives from outside normal organizational or political life to rescue the nation in crisis or pluck a political regime from the brink of collapse. He remains an "outsider." Above the ordinary politics, he "reasserts individual exploits after and

and "the drug of drama" are part of the heroic leader's operating style.[33] Each of the leaders that Hoffman described appears to have had unshakable confidence in his own beliefs and greatness, and a personal vision of France's destiny. The heroic figure is shrouded in mystery and conveys a distant magnetic power.

Routine leaders differ from heroic leaders in almost every way. They have risen to positions of power because of their mastery of party and bureaucracy and are the products of organizational life. Hoffman tells us that "smoothness, unobtrusiveness, procedural self-effacing skill, flexibility, what the French call *astuce* — a somewhat subdued brand of cleverness — these are the functional requirements of 'routine authority'."[34] These are leaders found in normal times and situations. They are the leaders of everyday life.

One can argue that setting up polar opposites is a kind of strait-jacket. The danger is that these black-and-white archetypes do not capture the numerous shades of grey that lie in between. Yet, if we were to apply Hoffman's descriptions to Canadian political life, an obvious conclusion would be that prime ministers have been, for the most part, leaders of routine. Men such as Macdonald, Borden, Laurier, King, St. Laurent and Pearson were consummate "insiders." They were the products of organizations and each, in his own way, was a master of *astuce*. In a country divided by language and regional differences and governed by a complex federal system, this type of leader has predominated. As Robert Craig Brown has observed about Canada's prime ministers, particularly before the Second World War,

> the prescription for success was a restrained approach to partisanship and a wary attitude towards innovation. Sir John A., Creighton observed, "was not a crusader with a mission; he thumped no tubs and he banged no pulpits." Similarly, Laurier, as Skelton put it, "was never a man to raise questions before they were ripe." And King, the master of the "half measure," saw no need for political action when political har-

mony did not seem threatened.[35]

Lester B. Pearson has written: "No strong man in the emotionally satisfying sense has ever ruled this country — none will if it is to survive. Attempting to reconcile what appears to be the irreconcilable will continue to be the task of the Prime Ministers and in this task Prime Ministers tend to look uninspiring."[36] Yet there have been Canadian leaders who seem closer to the heroic, "outsider" type than to routine politics: John Diefenbaker, René Lévesque, Joey Smallwood and Pierre Trudeau. They were powerful speakers, thrived on drama, cherished visions of Canada's or their province's destiny, and possessed unshakable confidence in the correctness of their ideas. One can argue that they came to power as a result of some measure of dissatisfaction with old ways or old regimes and that each had to face "emergencies" of some kind, even if in some instances these emergencies were fabricated or self-imposed. Although the fit with Hoffman's heroic leader may not be exact, these men cannot be described as administrators of routine.

One is tempted to argue that success in the Canadian political system is most readily achieved by conciliators, and that heroes have not done particularly well in terms of concrete achievements, whatever glamour and panache they might bring to the process. As Margaret Atwood has written about heroic figures in a different context: "'Prophets' here don't get very far against the civil service."[37] There is no evidence, however, that their performance is consistently better or worse than that of "routine" leaders. One might suspect that there still is in Canada a discernible longing for the "hero in history." It may come from the traditional view of Western culture that leaders should be competitive and aggressive and ultimately conquerors. To characterize Joe Clark as a "wimp," regardless of how competent he may be, is to label him unfit for the prime ministership. Mackenzie King and Lester Pearson, among others, were also ridiculed because of their innate caution and conciliatory style. In a presidential address to the American Psychological Association, Kenneth B. Clark has argued that it is childish to use "macho" concepts of leadership as the standard to which leaders must measure up.[38] These qualities can do serious harm to tenuous economic and political arrangements and are immensely dangerous in the nuclear age. It would be interesting to study whether Canadians see the attributes of leadership differently from other nations, and also whether distinct expectations can be identified among different linguistic and ethnic groups and in different regions.

Several studies have examined leadership in the context of national political cultures. In his examination of American politics, Samuel Huntington has argued that there is a distinct "creed" that makes up American national identity.[39] Successful politicians operate according to codes, and use language and symbols that emanate directly from this creed. For instance, Huntington noted that the verbal symbols used in presidential inaugural addresses have changed little over time. Again, no systematic attempt has been made to study the language and symbols used by Canadian leaders or their operating codes and styles to see whether there is a distinct political creed that is innately a part of Canadian politics.

One of the most interesting systems for evaluating leaders was developed by James David Barber.[40] Barber created a schema for classifying American presidents based on three factors: self-image, world view, and style. His method of classification may be a useful device for studying and comparing leaders and, according to Barber, it is also a means of predicting the behaviour of present and future office-holders. "Self-image" describes the president's self-esteem and confidence. Childhood experiences, relations with parents, siblings, and peers, and early successes and failures are crucial factors in creating self-esteem. This is the measure a leader has of his own abilities and importance in the larger scheme of things.

"World view" is the leader's image of the political landscape, how the leader views historical events, his or her country's place in the world, and social and class relations. These images, which are shaped by parents, schooling, the media, or by personal experiences, tend to "harden," persisting in the leader's mind long after the events that gave rise to these images have faded from the headlines. The last element in Barber's so-called pattern of character is "style." Style is how leaders perform the roles expected of them in the positions that they hold. Barber breaks style into three component parts: speaking to the public, whether to audiences directly or through the media; face-to-face dealing and bargaining; and the handling of administrative chores. Style encompasses how decisions are made, strategies employed in communicating to the public and negotiating with others, and the extent to which leaders immerse themselves in detail or delegate tasks and authority to others.

In Barber's schema there are four types of presidents; active-positive, active-negative, passive-positive, and passive-negative. Barber first analyzed political character (self-image, world view, and style) using the terms "active-passive." The simple question is whether presidents are essentially active or passive in pursuing their goals. Do they initiate policies and pursue their implementation vigorously, or do they wait for events to dictate how and when they will respond? Do they strive for change, or attempt to preserve the status quo? Barber also attempted to assess whether presidents had a positive or negative orientation to their jobs. Presidents with a positive orientation enjoyed holding office, thriving in the limelight and under pressure. Those with negative feelings found some aspects of the job distasteful and tended to view the holding of office as a task performed out of a sense of obligation. They did not delight in political encounters or struggles, enjoy the spotlight, or feel enlivened by the sensations of power.

According to Barber, active-positive presi-

Figure 1.2 — Barber's Schema of Presidential Types

POSITIVE

	ACTIVE		PASSIVE	
	active-positive	passive-positive	
	active-negative	passive-negative	

NEGATIVE

dents are the most successful. They are open to new ideas, can deal with stress, and know how to draw on the sources of power available to them. Leaders who are not active-positive types are likely to fail in some way. Passive-negative types are dangerous for the systems that they govern. Their thinking is closed, they tend to rely on methods and strategies that have worked in the past, regardless of their relevance to the present, they do not initiate actions or policies, and are incapable of using resources and the instruments of power imaginatively. They retreat from power.

In an article published over a decade ago, John Courtney used Barber's schema to analyze the political character of Mackenzie King.[41] Courtney argued that King could best be described as an active-positive leader. In a reply published together with Courtney's article, Joy Esberey contended that Courtney had glossed over some of the more disturbing and unsavoury aspects of King's behaviour and that it was more accurate to describe him as having an active-negative political character.[42] The gauntlet has not been retrieved by other scholars. While Barber's schema is not a very refined analytical instrument, it can be effective in organizing information. A history of prime ministers or provincial leaders using Barber's typology might prove to be exceptionally useful.

Valuable insights have also been derived from relatively recent developments in the study of foreign policy and international rela-

tions. Robert Jervis has perhaps gone the furthest in analyzing how the cognitive processes of key decision-makers have determined their images of international reality and, hence, the decisions that they have made.[43] Jervis's work is based on cognitive approaches pioneered by Ole Holsti and Michael Brecher, among others.[44] The images held by decision-makers are based on early experiences with others, the values that predominate when leaders are just becoming aware of politics, strategies and tactics that they have used successfully in the past, the organizational memory of the institutions involved in decisions, and the personal idiosyncrasies of those at the top. These perceptions can mask reality and distort the way in which new information is interpreted. In one frequently cited study of American foreign policy failures, Irving Janus has attempted to show that in each instance "groupthink" was at fault.[45] Groupthink occurs in situations where leaders choose subordinates in their own image and thus find themselves surrounded by lieutenants who will not challenge their views. Those within the inner circle are isolated from opinions other than those which prevail in the group. Group dynamics create the illusion of unanimity and a false confidence sets in. In these circumstances, leaders are artificially shielded from reality and inevitably stumble.

While Richard Simeon has drawn a parallel between international diplomacy and federal-provincial relations in Canada, there have been few attempts to follow through on this comparison by applying decision-making theories used in the study of international relations to federal-provincial diplomacy.[46] A study that examined the cognitive masks of prime ministers and premiers is likely to yield valuable insights. There has also been no shortage of fiascos in Canadian domestic politics, caused by the false confidence of leaders who have insulated themselves from opposing views and, ultimately, from reality.

The prime minister's and the premier's job descriptions have also not been dealt with in any great detail in Canadian political science literature. These job requirements can be seen quite apart from the skills needed in understanding and transcending the different systems and subgovernments that are described in this volume. There is, however, a large body of scholarly work on almost every aspect of the U.S. president's responsibilities. One of the most interesting descriptions appears in *The State of the Presidency* by Thomas Cronin,[47] in which standards have been identified that could apply just as readily to Canadian prime ministers and premiers. The seven activity areas described by Cronin are:

1. Crisis Management
2. Symbolic or Morale-Building Leadership
3. Priority Setting and Program Design
4. Recruitment Leadership
5. Legislative and Political Coalition Building
6. Program Implementation and Evaluation
7. Oversight of Government Routines and Establishment of an Early-Warning System for Future Problem Areas

While one could argue that Canadian prime ministers and premiers do not have to face crises such as those faced by an American president, on the scale of a Cuban missile crisis or a Vietnam War, Canada has had its share of wars and no shortage of internal crises. How leaders like Robert Borden or Mackenzie King coped with the stresses of war, or how Trudeau and Bourassa behaved during the October Crisis have not been studied in detail. Canadian office-holders should be judged on whether they have inspired, given purpose and boosted morale. Leaders should also symbolize societal values and stand for principles that are cherished in the political system. One can argue that most leaders are "screened" with this in mind, so that holding these values is in fact a prerequisite for leadership.

Priority-setting involves determining which initiatives will be undertaken and how limited resources are to be allocated. The job, as Cronin put it, is "to clarify many of the major issues of the day, define what is possible, and harness the governmental structure so that new initiatives are possible."[48] A fourth measure is the ability to attract the most able people available to government. A large number of appointments are made at the discretion of first ministers. There are not only cabinet and judicial positions but appointments to a number of agencies, boards and commissions. In an oft-cited example, Lester Pearson was able to save the deteriorating political situation by recruiting the so-called three wise men, Gérard Pelletier, Jean Marchand, and Pierre Trudeau, into the Liberal party in 1965. This move not only shored up Liberal fortunes in Quebec in the short term, but altered the political balance in that province in the long run. John Diefenbaker and Joe Clark both failed to build bridges into Quebec by neglecting to recruit able people. The Conservative party paid dearly for this failure during the 1960s and 1970s.

The fifth criterion is the building of a broad governing coalition. In a minority government, prime ministers and premiers must strike deals with the opposition and find votes wherever they can in order to maintain power. Broadly based support in the regions, among powerful interests and in both linguistic communities, is necessary if a prime minister is to move decisively on important national questions. The forging of consensus is especially critical in the Canadian situation, where feelings of alienation from Ottawa can have dangerous consequences. Another important criterion of leadership is the energy to ensure that policies are implemented correctly and that the effects of policy changes are evaluated accurately. Office-holders often encounter bureaucratic resistance to their programs for change. Non-compliance, stalling, and poor communication of directives occur frequently. First ministers must persuade senior officials of the rightness of their chosen courses of action and be vigilant in seeing that their wishes are followed.

The last task outlined by Cronin is the monitoring of the government's basic structures and toring of the government's basic structures and routines and scanning the horizon for new developments, prospects, and threats to the operations of the government. One might enlarge on Cronin's idea by arguing that prime ministers and premiers should anticipate change, not only in the government, but in society as a whole. Not unlike biblical prophets, modern leaders must warn of the dangers and opportunities that they foresee for the future. Cronin's description stresses that leaders must ensure that the engine of government, and each part of the overall machine, functions smoothly. Each task described by Cronin can be applied in each of the systems or subgovernments that are described in this volume.

CONCLUSION

We have attempted to map some difficult terrain. Far from being explicit about what leadership is or should be, or how research should be conducted, we have described a number of possibilities, a number of paths that might be taken. We have also expressed skepticism about the possibility of finding easy or convenient solutions. The entire subject is mired in complexity, secrecy and even mystery.

The question which still persists, despite the large corpus of research, is whether leaders do affect the outcome of events — whether leaders make a difference. To some, the evidence that leaders are decisive to any political equation is overwhelming. Evidence has been presented by Valerie Bunce, for instance, that political leadership has made a difference in the types of policies that have been enacted in both Western and Eastern European countries.[49] Their influence is felt especially during so-called honeymoon periods just after an election, when they are given a fresh mandate to establish policies and priorities. James David Barber has written about the important role played by American presidents.

> Who the President is at a given time can make a profound difference in the whole thrust and

direction of national politics.... even the most superficial speculation confirms the common-sense view that the man himself weighs heavily among other historical factors.... Only someone mesmerized by the lures of historical inevitability can suppose that it would have made little difference or no difference to government policy had Alf Landon replaced FDR in 1936, had Dewey beaten Truman in 1948, or Adlai Stevenson reigned through the 1950s. Not only would these alternative Presidents have advocated different policies — they would have approached the office from very different psychological angles.[50]

Others remain cautious. Fred Greenstein has argued that leaders can only affect the course of policy within limited parameters. According to Greenstein, the impact that can be made by any individual depends on "(1) the degree to which actions take place in an environment which admits of restructuring, (2) the location of the actor in the environment, and (3) the actor's peculiar strengths or weaknesses."[51] Even the most skilled leader cannot necessarily alter policies or events, in Greenstein's view. There must be the right combination of circumstances — and unscientific variables such as chance and luck play a major role.

We believe that there are strong reasons for vigorously pursuing leadership studies in Canada. A number of the approaches that we have described have been used effectively in examining historical figures, foreign leaders, and the processes that have shaped how decisions have been made in a variety of situations. These tools can be used to tell us more about the nature of Canadian political cultures. Every country must ultimately come to terms with its own "dreamers of the day." Greater illumination can also help to dispel the pervasive myth, particularly in the public mind, that able leadership is, of itself, a magic solution to problems. Most important in a democracy, leaders must be watched, their motives understood, their values questioned. Power can be a dangerous instrument. As Francis Bacon observed several centuries ago, "nothing doth more harm in a state than that cunning men pass for wise."

Notes

1. Some of the more interesting works that have appeared include Karlen, *Napoleon's Glands;* Renshon, "Assessing Political Leaders"; Millan, *Monstrous Regiment;* Hartsock, *Money, Sex and Power.* See also Willhoite, "Primates and Political Authority."

2. Chrétien, *Straight From The Heart;* Davey, *The Rainmaker;* Johnston, *Up The Hill.*

3. Cronin, *The State of the Presidency,* p. 81.

4. McGregor, *The Wacousta Syndrome,* Chapter 9.

5. The definition is taken from Hollander's work *Leadership Dynamics,* quoted in Kellerman, *The Political Presidency,* p. 18.

6. Quoted in Wildavsky, *The Nursing Father,* p. 183.

7. See James, *The Will to Believe.*

8. Hook, *The Hero in History,* p. 7.

9. Kellerman, "Leadership As A Political Act."

10. Michels, *Political Parties,* p. 195.

11. Weber, "Politics as a Vocation."

12. Freud and Bullitt, *Thomas Woodrow Wilson.*

13. Lasswell, *Psychopathology and Politics.*

14. Ibid., p. 75.

15. Ibid., pp. 78, 127, 53.

16. Erikson, *Gandhi's Truth;* Adorno et al., *The Authoritarian Personality;* Mazlish, *In Search of Nixon* and *The Revolutionary Ascetic;* and Wolfenstein, *The Revolutionary Personality.*

17. Fox, "Psychology, Politics and Hegetology."

18. Ibid., p. 688.

19. Fromm, *Escape From Freedom.*

20. Kearns, *Lyndon Johnson and the American Dream;* Brodie, *Thomas Jefferson;* Erikson, *Young Man Luther;* George and George, *Woodrow Wilson and Colonel House.*

21. Thomson, *Jean Lesage and The Quiet Revolution;* Radwanski, *Trudeau;* Gwyn, *The Northern Magus;* Creighton, *John A. Macdonald: The Young Politician* and *The Old Chieftain;* Neatby, *William Lyon Mackenzie King;* Langer, *The Mind of Adolf Hitler.*

22. McClelland, *The Achieving Society,* and *Power.*

23. Simonton, *Genius, Creativity and Leadership,* p. 2.

24. Quoted in Wildavsky, *The Nursing Father,* pp. 183-84.

25. Moore, "Personality Tests Are Back."

26. McGregor, *The Human Side of Enterprise.*

27. Wildavsky, *The Nursing Father,* p. 185.

28. Ibid., p. 190.

29. Hoffmann, "Heroic Leadership."

30. Zaleznik, "Charismatic and Consensus Leaders"; Stoessinger, *Crusaders and Pragmatists.*

31. Russell, *Power.*

32. Hoffmann, "Heroic Leadership," p. 123.

33. Ibid., p. 136.

34. Ibid., p. 120.

35. Brown's article appears in this volume.

36. Matheson, *The Prime Minister and the Cabinet,* p. 29.

37. Atwood, *Survival,* p. 172.

38. Clark, "The pathos of power."

39. Huntington, *American Politics.*

40. Barber, *The Presidential Character.*

41. Courtney, "Prime Ministerial Character."

42. Esberey, "Prime ministerial character."

43. Jervis, *Perception and Misperception in International Politics.*

44. Holsti, "Foreign Policy Formulation Viewed Cognitively"; Holsti, "The 'Operational Code' Approach to the Study of Political Leaders"; Brecher, *The Foreign Policy System of Israel.*

45. Janus, *Groupthink.*

46. Simeon, *Federal-Provincial Diplomacy.*

47. Cronin, *The State of the Presidency.*

48. Ibid., p. 163.

49. Bunce, *Do New Leaders Make a Difference?*

50. Barber, *The Presidential Character,* pp. 5-6.

51. Greenstein, "The Impact of Personality on Politics."

CHAPTER 2

Hands at the Helm?
Leadership and Public Policy

Leslie A. Pal

> They don't know that for the true pilot it is necessary to pay careful attention
> to year, seasons, heaven, stars, winds, and everything that's proper to the art,
> if he is really going to be skilled at ruling a ship.
>
> Plato, *The Republic*

Political theorists have often portrayed the state as a ship navigating a sea of circumstance. In an earlier age, the metaphor was particularly apt in its depiction of class structure (lower and upper decks), division of labour (crew and passengers), and the role of chance (changeable winds). It still affects the way in which we conceive of our political leaders: they are pilots or helmsmen, navigating by some secret astronomy and inner will, steering a clear course from storm to calm. The metaphor casts the leader as hero, possessed of inner strength, hands firmly on the helm, directing what in today's parlance is known as the policy process. The discourse of modern politics echoes this characterization: we call for leaders who are strong, wise, bold, brave, determined, popular, and persuasive. The comedy of their errors and the tragedy of their falls are the chief preoccupation of the media.

In sharp contrast to ancient metaphor and modern discourse, the study of public policy has taken almost no serious account of leadership. It has had something to say about specific leaders and administrative processes at the executive level, but with only a few exceptions has preferred to explain the policy process in macro-political terms such as class, bureaucracy, federalism, or ideology. When it focusses on individual behaviour, it tends to analyze the pure logic of decision-making, separate from the influence of personality. Yet leadership is inseparable from character, however much character may be challenged by circumstance. It is people, after all, who make policy, people with different personalities and talents. Leaders are not merely amusing themselves with empty rituals; they are trying to shape events. While the results vary, their efforts must invariably have some effect. What, then, is the relationship of leadership to public policy?

POLICY STUDIES AND LEADERSHIP

The Traditional Approaches

The modern study of public policy has a markedly paradoxical character. Much of it contains suggestions for reform and policy improvement, yet simultaneously assumes that public policy is determined by large aggregate forces beyond government control. The *prescriptive* side of the literature assumes that effective leadership is possible; the *descriptive* side contends that it is not. To understand why this is so, we need to review briefly the development of the so-called policy sciences in Canada and the United States.

The policy sciences are grounded in the social sciences. The various disciplines which today constitute the social sciences have only gradually, over the last century, established themselves as repositories of policy expertise.[1] The turning point came with World War II, when governments discovered the usefulness of the social sciences for the war effort and for the planning of postwar reconstruction. The new optimism generated by these efforts led some pioneers, like Harold Lasswell, to proclaim the era of a unified, practical, problem-solving approach to public policy — the policy sciences.[2] In Lasswell's original formulation, the policy sciences were to be multi-disciplinary, problem-oriented, and normative. Some proponents even went so far as to proclaim a new supra-science of societal management.[3]

This philosophical orientation to public policy was clearly prescriptive, for it openly encouraged the view that social processes were amenable to organized human intervention. Government, equipped with the proper tools, could become a cogent force in the battle against poverty, unemployment, inadequate housing and other social ills. The "evaluation movement" which swept American government in the 1960s, and Canada slightly afterwards, was an offshoot of this new hubris. The movement was multifaceted. It included, for example, a panoply of management techniques and approaches to organizational design such as PPBS (Planning-Programming-Budgeting System), MBO (Management by Objectives), ZBB (Zero-Based Budgeting), and more recently in Canada the "envelope" system of expenditure management.[4] These systems assumed that since organizations made policy, better policy would come from more rational organization.

Another aspect of the evaluation movement focussed on efficiency and effectiveness. It rested on a simple yet profound insight: if public policy is normally about solving problems at reasonable cost, then the scrutiny of impact and real benefit must result in better policies. The measurement of impact varies with different policies, but always boils down to the question of whether a policy intervention makes a difference of the desired magnitude and in the desired direction. Experimental and quasi-experimental techniques were developed in the 1960s to measure impact in these terms. Their justification was also simple: if policies were not having the desired impact, they clearly needed to be changed. The key measure of efficiency, as opposed to effectiveness or impact, was cost-benefit analysis. Presumably almost any collective problem can be resolved if society is prepared to spend unlimited resources on it. But because resources are scarce, allocations have to be made which maximize the yield of benefits. The partisans of cost-benefit analysis argued that their techniques could help decision-makers determine rational allocation of resources to programs.

Yet another dimension of the evaluation movement was the more regular provision of expert advice to government. Policy analysts sprang up like mushrooms after rain in almost every fissure of government. Advisory bodies multiplied, councils appeared, analytical units materialized. When Pierre Trudeau became prime minister in 1968 he encouraged and accelerated these developments at the federal level.[6] Ottawa's decision-making machinery was thereby dipped into a rich protein bath of policy advice and technical information.

Organizational design, evaluative technique and complex information were the main themes in practical and applied policy analysis in North America. The original optimism of the evaluation movement became tinged with pessimism by the early 1970s, however, and the current "evaluation of evaluation" is quite a gloomy process indeed. In the United States, racial tensions and the Vietnam War severely discredited the government, as did the growing evidence that grand, well-intentioned policy interventions in areas ranging from education to housing have had negligible or even undesirable effects.[7] The Canadian evaluation movement was discredited in similar if less dramatic ways. Prime Minister Trudeau's penchant for priority exercises abated in the face of economic and political issues such as inflation and Quebec separatism. Policy and planning units, it came to be realized, paid little attention to either policy or planning, and when they did, they were without influence.[8] By the late 1970s, numerous studies had appeared which showed that policy analysis had virtually no direct impact on the policy process.[9] Instead, bureaucratic self-interest and intrigue, along with the machinations of interest groups and politicians, seemed to be the critical forces.

The world, it appeared, was not ruled by reason. As trite as this observation may seem, it has contributed to the current absence of theoretical interest in leadership in the policy sciences. The fantasy of a world ruled by reason assumes reasonable people; moreover, it assumes rational processes of decision-making within which conscious human action outweighs caprice and the forces of circumstance. A world of "irrational" policy is messy, without direction or plan. Outcomes are impelled by chance, rarely determined by reason. Policies pop up unpredictably, like rugby balls from furious scrums. The leader as helmsman or pilot cannot exist, because there is no helm, no rudder, no stars by which to navigate: all is Sturm und Drang.

The academic, explanatory orientation in the policy sciences has arrived at much the same impasse, albeit by a different route. In political science the debate has somewhat perversely revolved around the issue of "whether politics matters." Political science has traditionally approached the study of public policy through an analysis of process, probing into its determinants. As one would expect, the tradi-

tional answer to the question of "whether politics matters" within the discipline stressed political forces. In the early twentieth century, ideology and institutions topped the list; after World War II, party competition and interest groups were favoured.[10] By the early 1960s, however, several studies had appeared which purported to show that political variables had little or no statistical effect on levels of government expenditure, when compared to broader socio-economic variables. Given a certain level of socio-economic development, governments would tend to spend about the same amount on roughly similar programs, whatever their ideological stripe or political position.[11]

A debate was thereby launched concerning the role of intermediate political forces such as party competition, legislative structure, ideology and the presence of unions and a social democratic movement. While none of these was synonymous with leadership, they did assume a relatively large role for human agency in the policy process. The opposite view, that socio-economic variables were fundamental, reduced human agency, indeed the entire political process, to epiphenomenal froth on the tidal wave of social development. The inevitable reaction was a vigorous counter-offensive, which succeeded in undermining the socio-economic approach.[12] One simple objection was that the "politics doesn't matter" literature measured policy almost entirely in terms of expenditures. Yet two governments might spend identical amounts on education and still organize service delivery entirely differently. Another problem was that many of the socio-economic variables which supposedly explained policy (e.g., level of GNP) were themselves the *result* of previous policy interventions.

The result of these debates has been to acknowledge that politics does matter. However politics and leadership are not the same thing. Indeed, they would appear to be entirely different. Two main schools of thought, for example, consider politics either as competition between left- and right-wing parties, or as governmental efforts to promote re-election. The first argues that large trade union movements spawn social democratic parties, which if they win election, will tend over time to pursue class-oriented policies (i.e., a larger welfare state.[13] The second school is represented in several interpretations of election cycles, with the common theme that governments will tend to make policies which maximize chances of re-election.[14] Thus the strongest tendency in social scientific explanations of public policy is to emphasize broad-gauged, aggregate forces rather than the strategic intervention of political leaders.

An Emerging Focus

Policy studies of both the applied and academic variety have little to say about political leadership. Human agency seems less important in the policy process than broad structures and long-term forces. There are several reasons, however, why this perception is unsatisfactory. At the simplest level, the literature cannot ignore so vital an issue of practical contemporary politics. Any student of public policy who is inarticulate on the question of leadership lacks an element of the grammar of politics. At a more complex, epistemological level, it seems highly implausible that the entire policy process can be explained without recourse to human agency. Indeed, it is fallacious to view factors such as "degree of unionization" as purely structural: unions have to be created and maintained, and at least part of that involves human agency and leadership. The influence of leadership is therefore an ineluctable element in the policy process.

There is evidence that the policy literature is beginning to rediscover the traditional elements of leadership in the policy process, but that it lacks an integrating conceptual framework to carry the burden of observation. For example, there is a recent emphasis, by both Marxist and non-Marxist students of public policy, on the autonomy of the state.[15] Though

individual authors put the point differently, even suggesting that state autonomy rests on structural forces, the state autonomy thesis reopens the question of a specific political realm, separate from larger socio-economic determinants. Indeed, the idea of autonomy compels the ultimate consideration of factors such as creativity, subjective interests, conjunctural interventions, and conflict.

Another recent development has been the idea of the policy process as a succession of distinct phases, each with its own dynamics.[16] While names for the stages may vary, they usually include: problem definition, agenda-setting, policy formulation, policy adoption, implementation, and evaluation. It is increasingly clear that while each phase has its own dynamics, the critical stages of the cycle are the early ones. Problem definition is crucial because it outlines the object of policy interventions.[17] Those who excel in this early phase, even if they absent themselves from the rest of the policy process, have scored a significant triumph. Agenda-setting involves the selection of policy problems for public action. Since the scope of problems is virtually infinite, while political resources are finite, competition is intense. Once more this orientation compels the consideration of leadership. While arguably some problems and their place on the policy agenda are due to broad structural forces, leadership must be a critical variable. Defining problems is a creative act, as is the manoeuvring of one's preferred definition onto a crowded agenda.

Finally, the applied tradition of policy analysis has recently reconsidered the problem of influence in the policy process in ways which encourage consideration of leadership. As noted earlier, the "evaluation of evaluation" has revealed that policymakers rarely rely on their experts. Policy analysts are heeded when their advice suits political and bureaucratic interests; otherwise their specific recommendations rarely get reflected in public policy. It is now widely accepted that the absence of this direct impact may mask fairly substantial indirect influence. Expert policy advice is only one source of information among many.[18] Its value may be less in its "factual content" than in the way it frames problems, provides alternative perspectives, verifies facts, and challenges operating assumptions. The policy analyst as advocate rather than expert implies many of the intellectual qualities usually associated with leadership, e.g., creative insight and a strong sense of political feasibility.

The study of public policy thus appears, in a halting and uncoordinated fashion, to be groping its way toward the concept of leadership. The rediscovery of leadership at the heart of the state, the policy process, and policy analysis leads naturally to the question of the balance between structural forces and political intervention. Unfortunately, while the policy literature seems to show an emerging focus on leadership, it has no indigenous conceptual framework upon which to draw. There is, on the other hand, a separate and highly developed literature on leadership itself, with its psychological, social, and political foundations, which also addresses the role of leaders in politics and the policy process. Here again we confront a paradox. The policy literature has little to say about leadership, even though it appears in great need of the concept. The leadership literature collectively concludes that leaders have little impact on policy, though what else can political leadership be about if not about policy? Leadership is acclaimed as the central variable in all social processes, but leadership literature collectively concludes that leaders have only modest impact on public policy.

LEADERSHIP: THE POLICY PARADOX

Thomas Carlyle is frequently perceived as an extreme proponent of the view that all history is "the biography of great men," although in one less-frequently quoted passage, he laid the foundation for leadership studies in quite reasonable terms:

> Show our critics a great man, a Luther for example, they begin to what they call "account" for him; not to worship him, but take the dimensions of him, — and bring him out to be a little kind of man! He was the "creature of the Time," they say, the Time called him forth, and Time did everything, he nothing — but what we the little critic could have done too! This seems to be but melancholy work. The Time call forth? Alas, we know Times *call* loudly enough for their great man; but not find him when they called! He was not there; Providence had not sent him; the Time, calling its loudest, had to go down to confusion and wreck because he would not come when called.[19]

The modern study of leadership depends, in large part, on the argument that structural forces ("the Time") are an insufficient explanation of social processes. At the very least, leaders may be eventful in that they appear at history's "forking points," and so act as conduits for historical forces.[20] At best they generate events, taking history in directions it might not otherwise have gone.

The leadership literature is vast, including sociological and psychological, as well as political, approaches. It is argued that almost "any task related to organized activity involves leadership,"[21] and that leadership is the essence of politics.[22] James MacGregor Burns has provided one of the most widely cited definitions of leadership:

> Leadership over human beings is exercised when persons with certain motives and purposes mobilize, in competition or conflict with others, institutional, political, psychological, and other resources so as to arouse, engage, and satisfy the motives of followers. This is done in order to realize goals mutually held by both leaders and followers.[23]

The above statements notwithstanding, the leadership literature as a whole tends to conclude that leaders exercise relatively little influence in the policy process. Public policy is apparently made within so many constraints that leaders have relatively little scope within which to act. Burns, for example, acknowledges that policymakers "transact more than they administer, compromise more than they commend, institutionalize more than they initiate."[24] Somewhat paradoxically in light of his emphasis on leadership in the modern world, when discussing the relationship between leadership and public policy, Burns seems to stress the constraints and impediments that confront leaders in the policy process. "Executive leaders in a power struggle may appeal to public opinion, but lack the machinery to activate it, shape it, channel it, and bring it to bear on the decision-making process."[25] He suggests that the idea of event-altering "decisions" is too pat; leaders make decisions which may have long-term effects insofar as they allow the "institutional embodiment of purpose."

Other prominent students of political leadership echo this ambivalence towards influence in the policy process. Edinger pointed out years ago that the event-making leader was "emphatically rejected by most contemporary American social and political scientists."[26] Stanley Hoffman called the study of political leadership the "orphan" of political science.[27] Richard Neustadt's classic study of the American presidency concludes that the balance of power between the president and other actors in the policy process may "balance to the point of immobility."[28] Surveying the role of the British prime minister, Richard Rose finds that she "can influence policies only indirectly, through responsible ministers."[29] Rose examines the prime minister's influence in foreign affairs, concluding "Not much."[30] The most recent detailed overview of the role of the Canadian prime minister also emphasizes the constraints he faces in the policy arena,[31] though there is evidence that the Canadian P.M. wields more power than his British counterpart.[32] A recent review of leadership at the provincial level has produced mixed results: leadership seems critical and potent in Newfoundland, P.E.I., Nova Scotia, Quebec, Saskatchewan, and Alberta; in the remaining provinces, it has been of medium to low importance.[33]

Students of leadership assume its importance, and yet the evidence seems to suggest a relatively modest role for leaders in the policy process. We seem to have returned to the dreary conclusions of the public policy literature: leadership is necessary and important, but impossible. Leaders cannot, in most circumstances, make events; they lack the necessary power and face far too many constraints. It may be, however, that the problem lies not with how we conceive of leadership, but in the assumptions that we make about the nature of power. After all, the metaphor of the helmsman or pilot assumes a single helm respondent to a single will. The ship of state is steered through the shoals of public policy by one will flowing through one instrument. This concept of power may be as outmoded as Jason's Argo.

POWER, POLICY, AND LEADERSHIP

It is commonplace to speak of power as a possession, something lost and gained, stolen or eroded. The more power one "has," the greater one's ability to effect one's will. If power is a commodity to be possessed and accumulated, then the more equal the distribution of power the less powerful any single actor can be. In the metaphor of the helmsman or pilot, there is only one helm, hence only one avenue for the exercise of power, only one leader. The crew is powerless not only because it lacks knowledge (as Plato argued) but because it cannot collectively grasp the helm. It is fated to follow.

Both the policy studies and leadership literature argue that modern political systems are fragmented, and that in actuality power is shared among many subgovernments which face modern leaders as feudal barons might have faced a weak king. Among the authors cited above, Neustadt observes that the modern president faces new "chiefs" in the people in charge of client groups created in the Great Society programs.[34] Rose ascribes the British P.M.'s impotence in part to "opposition from sovereign forces outside the control of Whitehall."[35] In an essay on the American presidency, Rose explicitly refers to the problem in modern states of the plurality of quasi-autonomous units and the lack of one single institution to declare the will of the government as a whole.[36] The American system encourages a high degree of fragmentation, so that the sum of the parts is greater than the whole, but even cabinet government along British lines faces (though somewhat more successfully) the problem of integrating these subgovernments into a single will. In discussing executive leaders, Burns points out that they must deal with extra-organizational influences as well as conflicts within government. "In fact the executive leader deals with executive subleaders with needs of their own and power resources and skills of their own."[37] He refers to their real influence in the policy process as a function of the "harnessing" of pre-existing resources and powers among other groups and interests. However, Burns leaves the insight undeveloped.

The traditional understanding of power, in the circumstances of fragmentation just described, indicates the conclusion that leaders cannot lead. A revised philosophy of power, on the other hand, might open new possibilities in the conceptualization of leadership. It is beyond the scope of this essay to develop such a philosophy, but it is worth noting signs of its emergence in disparate places. The work of radical social critic Michel Foucault and of Andrew Dunsire, a student of public administration, will serve as examples.

Foucault's central statement about power is that it is not localized in the state apparatus, it is "never in anybody's hands, never appropriated as a commodity or piece of wealth. Power is employed and exercised through a net-like organization."[38] For Foucault, the exercise of political domination involves linking or harnessing pre-existing systems of power. It requires an

assembly of forces and institutions. The *result* of such an assembly can be dramatic and overpowering, although the "power" required to form the original chain may be slight.

> Between every point of a social body, between a man and a woman, between the members of a family, between a master and a pupil, between every one who knows and every one who does not, there exist relations of power which are not purely and simply a projection of the sovereign's great power over the individual; they are rather the concrete, changing soil in which the sovereign's power is grounded, the conditions which make it possible for it to function.[39]

Andrew Dunsire, though far removed from Foucault ideologically, examines much the same problem and arrives at much the same conclusion. His purpose is to analyze the control mechanism in bureaucracies, but his portrait of opposing forces within bureaux perfectly replicates the policy world faced by modern leaders. Dunsire begins with a simple model of "opposed maximizers."

> There is a type of desk-lamp which is supported by two strong springs pulling in opposite directions, so that when (with a fingertip) you move it to the angle and position you desire, you are effectively inhibiting the action of one of the springs and allowing the other to "win", temporarily.[40]

Brute strength is unnecessary; a simple touch will alter the balance of pre-existing forces and move the lamp through various angles and arcs. "The activity of 'controlling' a bureaucracy, or governing, or ruling, or commanding it, is an activity of adjusting an equilibrium of forces that are already there."[41] While Dunsire and Foucault certainly differ on details and context of argument, their work suggests an alternative view of power, and hence of the effects of leadership in the policy process.

The "special-interest state,"[42] "bureaucratic politics"[43] and subgovernments are persistent themes in the modern literature on politics, public policy, and leadership. They denote fragmentation, countervailing powers, and immobility. What do leaders do in these circumstances? Apparently not very much, if we think of power in traditional terms. But leadership may be more a matter of strategic interventions in ongoing processes, linkages between disparate chains of power, deflection and redirection. These all require effort, but not centralized, monopolized, or overweening power. In the modern state, the art of leadership consists of finding the nodal points in existing networks of power and conflict, and applying sufficient pressure to alter flows in desired directions. This is admittedly abstract, but it helps make more rigorous sense of some of the prevailing platitudes about leadership.

This conceptualization of power helps us remember that political leaders never face an undifferentiated mass of "followers," or indeed, an undifferentiated political process. Subgovernments or multiple authorities may be organized into "arenas," and the secret of effective leadership is a reasonable mastery of the dynamics of separate arenas, as well as an ability to harness those dynamics towards a single purpose. For Canadian prime ministers and premiers, all of the following can be considered arenas: the party, the Cabinet, the Legislature, the media, intergovernmental relations, elections, and interest groups. These overlap in practical politics, of course, but remain distinct contexts for the exercise of leadership. The personal qualities of leaders are tested differently in each arena. Prime Minister Diefenbaker, for example, was a master of parliamentary cut and thrust and electoral politics, but failed dismally in his relations with the media and in control of the Cabinet. Joe Clark was in control of his Cabinet, but could never bridle the rest of his party. Pierre Trudeau performed well in all arenas most of the time, and that is why, in retrospect, he appears as a "successful" leader, whatever we may think of his policies. The Liberal party never revolted and while the Cabinet may have lost bright lights over time, it remained cohesive. Trudeau was an uneven performer in the House, but,

when moved, could speak forcefully. He dominated the media by disdaining them. He won elections and patriated the Constitution. The point here is not to celebrate Trudeau, but to illustrate that the true measure of leadership is a simultaneous mastery of key arenas.

This mastery can express itself in different ways, few of which involve the exercise of brute power. The trick is to understand the dynamics and forces in each arena, and to channel them in the desired direction. The party, for example, operates by the fact that many people work voluntarily for their party and their leader, without conscious intent to benefit thereby, but with some need for reward, symbolic or otherwise. The systematic use of patronage, symbolic gestures of approval, and a demonstration of willingness to consult the rank and file are standard strategies in a leader's repertoire. The principle of balanced control among arenas is essential; for example, a leader who cannot defend and justify his party activities in the electoral arena is in trouble.

Some arenas lend themselves to more direct control by leaders than others. Political leaders can, for instance, change some of the rules, and hence, the dynamics of the Cabinet, as Joe Clark did when he established an Inner Cabinet and the envelope system of expenditure management. They are somewhat more constrained in the party arena, but even here may exercise influence on the rules of the game. The media, on the other hand, cannot be restricted this way, and so leaders must accept the dynamics of the media arena, satisfying themselves with influencing pre-existing forces. In television news, for example, they must simply accept the primacy of iconography over content: the picture *is* the word, and so leaders must convey their intentions, their attitudes, their personalities visually. Television in many ways is unsuited for the coverage of democratic politics, since so much of that politics is talk. Talk is usually unexciting, and so television images, however trivial in themselves, tend to carry a disproportionately heavy symbolic burden.

The famous "bum-patting" incident during the 1984 federal election branded John Turner as sexist, and Turner's failure to immediately enact the rituals of apology and contrition only made matters worse.

If the essence of leadership is the ability to master the dynamics of disparate arenas, how is this done, and how is it done with an economy of effort? What are the real counterparts in the policy process of the "fingertip" in Dunsire's analogy of the lamp? The answer cannot lie, as we argued above, with instruments of domination; to conceive of leadership as the exercise of "more power" is to miss its real character. In fact, in a paradoxical way, leadership would seem to consist of the exercise of "less power" in that the individual leaders must try to deflect or channel large social forces. Two alternative yet complementary modes of mastering arenas that fit this conceptualization of power are leadership as problem definition and as symbolic politics.

The policy process in liberal-democratic states is locutionary — it is about talk. The political process cannot be simply reduced to pure interest or pure power; it involves debate over ideas, alternative formulas of right and wrong, conflicting goals and remedies. If the policy process is conceived in this way, then one of its most crucial phases is problem definition. Recent work on public policy has on the whole agreed that this is a fruitful way of conceptualizing the policy process.[44]

Problem definition involves various aspects. Problems, at least the bulk of those addressed in the policy process, do not exist "out there" in some objective sphere. To define a problem in policy terms means first, to claim its existence, second, to argue that it falls into the public domain and hence may be treated as an item of *public* policy, and third, to elaborate its character. Political leaders at every level are those who excel or at least prevail in the definition of problems. Tucker refers to this as their "diagnostic function."[45] Modern government is too complex for political leaders to

have any realistic role in formulating and implementing policy solutions, but leaders can play a critical role in problem definition. The arenas described earlier are, with respect to the policy process, institutional expressions of different ways of defining public problems. One comprehensive strategy of political leaders such as prime ministers and premiers is to coin new definitions which can be employed across arenas. The leadership literature in the past noted most leaders must have a vision and set agendas. Leaders today can, with skill and empathy, set the terms by which actors in different arenas will orient themselves in the policy process. Even his most uncompromising critics will admit that Pierre Trudeau, whatever his failings as prime minister, set the public agenda on key policies: the Just Society, wage and price controls, Quebec separatism, and the Constitution were public policy issues fought out largely within a conceptual terrain charted by one man. The point is not that Trudeau won every fight or overwhelmed opponents (leadership as power), but that he influenced debate and thus directed the course of forces larger than himself (leadership as problem definition).

Political leaders rely on another overarching strategy for dealing with various arenas. Problem definition depends in large part on rational persuasion, but leaders have tremendous symbolic resources (whatever their personal qualities) that automatically make them a focus or compass point in the policy process. At times this can be a handicap, but, if carefully nurtured, the leader's symbolic power may be a prime asset. As Edelman suggested:

> Governmental leaders have tremendous potential capacity for evoking strong emotional response in large populations. When an individual is recognized as a legitimate leading official of the state, he becomes a symbol of some or all the aspects of state.[46]

The policy process is uncertain, liable to ignorance and happenstance, and incumbents thus perform an important function in appearing to act decisively and with conviction. Indeed, they can refrain from acting, adopting instead a relatively passive posture of symbolic proclamations on unspecified ills or non-controversial policies.[47] Prime ministers and premiers, whether they wish it or not, occupy centre stage in the drama of politics. The public, as audience, invests them with symbolic potency which may then be used to master and unify competing arenas. Mackenzie King, during World War II, used this symbolic power to bring economic groups and the provinces into line. Peter Lougheed capitalized on his symbolic importance as spokesman for the province against Ottawa to manage the policy process in Alberta. Every leader is aware of the symbolic energy latent in the formal political office. The exploitation of this energy to elicit particular responses is a large part of the leader's art.

CONCLUSION

The metaphor of the pilot or helmsman is rooted in the idea that the state is a single vessel steered by a single will. The modern state, however, resembles a ragged flotilla more than it does a single ship. The vessels are of different shapes and under separate commands, each responding to wind and wave in peculiar and singular fashion. In these conditions, the imposition of a single will is considerably more complex than Plato's parable of the pilot might imply. The power expressed in leadership consists, of necessity, of signals, or perhaps of a broad strategy on direction and speed. Signals and strategy, it is true, have none of the immediate, visible, and uncompromising force of a single hand at the helm, but if they succeed in shepherding fleets of interest across oceans of politics, their ultimate effect may be vastly more dramatic.

Notes

1. See, for example, Owram, *The Government Generation.*
2. Lerner and Lasswell, eds., *The Policy Sciences.*
3. Dror, *Design for Policy Sciences.*
4. French, *How Ottawa Decides.*
5. Described in Pal, *Public Policy Analysis,* Chap. 3.
6. Doern, "The Policy-Making Philosophy of Prime Minister Trudeau and his Advisers."
7. Pressman and Wildavsky, *Implemenation,* and Murray, *Losing Ground.*
8. Prince and Chenier, "The Rise and Fall of Policy Planning and Research Units."
9. Patton, *Utilization-Focused Evaluation.*
10. See, for example, Key, *American State Politics: An Introduction.*
11. The best example is Dye, *Politics, Economics, and the Public.*
12. See, for example, Cameron, "The Expansion of the Public Economy," and Castles, "How Does Politics Matter?"
13. Schmidt, "The Welfare State and the Economy in Periods of Economic Crisis."
14. Tufte, *The Political Control of the Economy.*
15. See Pal, *Public Policy Analysis,* Chap. 10 for a discussion. Also see, Evans, Rueschemeyer, and Skocpol, eds., *Bringing the State Back In.*
16. May and Wildavsky, eds., *The Policy Cycle.*
17. Dery, *Problem Definition in Policy Analysis.*
18. Lindblom and Cohen, *Usable Knowledge.*
19. Carlyle, *On Heroes, Hero-Worship, and the Heroic in History,* pp. 16-17.
20. Hook, *The Hero in History,* and Paige, *The Scientific Study of Political Leadership.*
21. Hollander, *Leadership Dynamics,* p. 3.
22. Tucker, *Politics as Leadership.*
23. Burns, *Leadership,* p. 18; original emphases removed.
24. Ibid., p. 405.
25. Ibid., p. 372.
26. Edinger, "Editor's Introduction," *Political Leadership,* p. 14.
27. Hoffman, "Heroic Leadership," p. 108.
28. Neustadt, *Presidential Power,* p. 180.
29. Rose, "British Government," p. 33.
30. Ibid., p. 33.

31. Hockin, "The Prime Minister and Political Leadership".

32. Weller, *First Among Equals.*

33. Dyck, *Provincial Politics in Canada,* passim.

34. Neustadt, *Presidential Power,* pp. 177-80.

35. Rose, "British Government," p. 40.

36. Rose, "Government Against Sub-governments."

37. Burns, *Leadership,* p. 377.

38. Foucault, *Power/Knowledge,* p. 98.

39. Ibid., p. 187.

40. Dunsire, *Controls in a Bureaucracy: The Execution Process,* Vol. 2, pp. 207-208.

41. Ibid., p. 226.

42. See Pross, *Group Politics and Public Policy,* especially Chaps. 10 and 11.

43. See the review of this concept in Pal, *State, Class, and Bureaucracy,* Chap. 5.

44. Dery, *Problem Definition in Policy Analysis.*

45. Tucker, *Politics as Leadership,* pp. 18-19.

46. Edelman, *The Symbolic Uses of Politics,* p. 73.

47. Ibid., p. 81.

CHAPTER 3

Fishwives, Plutocrats, Sirens and Other Curious Creatures: Some Questions About Political Leadership in Canada

Robert Craig Brown

Perceptions of political leadership are like images in a hall of mirrors. They are partial, shifting, transitory. They often reveal more of the eye and mind of the beholder than of the image reflected. Consider, for example, a recent cartoon which characterized the leaders of our three national parties as fish-bodied creatures with cone-shaped mouths from which emanated pulsing waves of sound. Behind the rock on which they sit, the Canadian voter, in a rowboat, utters a tiny "Help."[1] The whole, captioned "The Sirens," is intended to remind us of Circe's warning to Odysseus. The Sirens, she admonished, "bewitch all men," they "enchant... with their clear song... and all about them is a great heap of bones of men, corrupt in death."

Our history is rich with characterizations of our political leaders from the cartoonist's pen, all drawn to accent a momentary image of the leaders' characters or circumstances or both. In 1934 Arch Dale of the *Winnipeg Free Press* placed R.B. Bennett, a portly plutocrat, at the edge of an enormous pile of surplus wheat, the result of R.B.'s high-tariff policy. What, the citizen asked, are we going to do with it? "Eat it!" Bennett replied.[2] In 1917 Sir Robert Bor-den, whose government had just passed the Wartime Elections Act, was portrayed as a U-boat captain, on the deck of his submarine, forcing "Justice," a delicate, scantily clad, and blindfolded beauty, to walk the plank.[3] In 1888 the great cartoonist J.W. Bengough drew Sir John A. as an ugly fishwife haggling over a basket of mackerel with Grover Cleveland.[4] At other times Macdonald became a wee lad in tartan short pants, "Little Johnnie," led by the hand to some dreadful destination or other by John Bull, or a Canadian businessman wearing a vest decorated with dollar signs.

Word portraits by pundits and poets have had the same effect. Recall Dafoe's apt assessment of Laurier as "a man who had affinities with Machiavelli as well as with Sir Galahad,"[5] or A.R.M. Lower on Meighen, "the lean and hungry Cassius," and Bennett, "the lord of the iron heel." When he came to King, Professor Lower found that a pungent phrase would not do. Appropriately, more words were needed to capture the essence of this "typical," this "essential" Canadian: "He spoke as the plain man did — with all the repetitions, the painful elaboration of the obvious, the turgidity of the ordinary man — only more so!"[6] "We had no

27

shape," Frank Scott wrote of King,

> Because he never took sides,
> And no sides
> Because he never allowed them to take shape.[7]

These images have a lasting appeal. They pinpoint, in their simplicity and directness, contemporary views of leadership, and shape the historical judgement of our political leaders. Even leaders who get scarcely a mention in our texts cannot escape the mirrors of characterization. Because their images are blurred, they neatly fit into the eager student's most frequent class of inquiry: "Sir J.J.C. Who? Sir Mackenzie Who?"

There is an elemental truth about these images which we would be foolish to ignore. But, as our friends in political science warn us, we must not stop here. As if to indicate the seriousness of the matter, they have disputed at length the origins and nature of political leadership and constructed a variety of categories in which to put and from which to compare political leaders as diverse as Louis XIV, Gandhi, Charles de Gaulle, and Alexander Mackenzie. Their scholarship goes a long way towards explaining what is and what is not indigenous to political leadership in Canada.

In the typology of leadership political leaders are said to have received their "legitimization" from any of three sources: God, their own charismatic qualities, or the laws and institutions of the states over which they rule. Numerous musings in Mr. King's diary notwithstanding, we can, I think, agree that none of our political leaders received his authority by divine right. (Their pretensions to infallibility are another matter!) On the other hand, journalists and hypesters for the Liberal Party a decade ago tried very hard to convince us that P.E.T. was the very personification of charismatic leadership come to Ottawa. At last we had our own Luther, our own Gandhi, our own Nkrumah, complete with a red Mercedes, with quips for every occasion, and with an adoring cast of thousands of children of all ages. Behind all the flapdoodle, however, was Mr. Trudeau the leader we were told that we had been waiting for for so long?

Charismatic leaders are "transitional figures between old and new forms of authority" — in Charles Taylor's words; "charisma is like lightning: it is very powerful in short bursts but it does not last very long." Anyone who listened to Mr. Trudeau realized instantly that ushering in a New Order was not his "thing"; no comment on his longevity seems necessary here. Moreover, charismatic leaders, as an American political scientist puts it, "believe that they have access to a specific variety of truth" and "that they have a call to overcome the ignorance and perhaps the evil of those who have not accepted their doctrine."[8] Again, apart from some opposition politicians, few of us would agree that Mr. Trudeau as party leader and prime minister, whatever else you may think about him, has measured up to this rigid but necessary qualification for charismatic leadership. No, all that happened was that journalists and Liberal propagandists confused a colourful personality with charisma. And, given the rarity of colourful personalities among our political leaders, they may be forgiven their confusion, if not the shallowness of their analysis of Mr. Trudeau's character. Roger Graham, in a brilliant essay written shortly after Mr. Trudeau came to power, punctured the balloon of charismatic leadership in Canada with a witty question: "Sir Wilfrid Laurier, let us say, sliding down a banister? Sir Robert Borden in goggles and flippers? Arthur Meighen in a Mercedes? Mackenzie King at judo? R.B. Bennett on skis?"[9]

We are left as we should be, with our leaders deriving their authority from laws, institutions, and customs that are the fabric of our "liberal-conservative democratic tradition." They are selected by political parties operating with formal rules and accepted procedures. They carry out their functions in long-established institutions, like the Cabinet and Parliament. A closer look at this process will reveal some of the boundaries and some of the opportunities of Canadian political leadership.

William Lyon Mackenzie King in 1919, and Richard Bedford Bennett almost a decade later, were the first national party leaders elected by party leadership conventions. Earlier leaders had been selected by the party hierarchy or by the party caucus. Borden's selection in 1901 illustrated the latter case; he was elected from among contenders in the caucus with the open support of the retiring leader, Sir Charles Tupper. Arthur Meighen was the last party leader to be chosen by caucus and the mode of his selection was probably unique. The Unionist caucus cast preferential ballots for their new leader. But the caucus also specified that the ballots were advisory and explicitly delegated to Borden the unwelcome task of selecting his own successor and persuading his colleagues to support Meighen.[10]

Even in these extraordinary circumstances, a primary criterion for selection as leader was a broad measure of demonstrated support in the ranks of the caucus, or, after 1919, in the party's convention. Borden and King, and probably Laurier and Macdonald, among others, were elected because, to borrow Frank Underhill's phrase, they were leaders "who divided us least." They were leaders who had been loyal party men, men who recognized that they were creatures of their parties. "I am their leader, I must follow them," quotes Léon Dion: "the leader's role as innovator will be accepted only after he has given proof of his absolute loyalty to the group."[11]

No one demonstrated this axiom of interdependence between the leader and his party more deliberately or more expertly than Mr. King. He might outrage functionaries in the national Liberal Federation[12] and he might cow his colleagues into submission to his will with a pointed reminder of *his* role as leader, as he did during the 1944 conscription crisis when he told the Cabinet that "as the leader of the Party... I had to consider what was owing to the Party."[13] Nevertheless, as Blair Neatby observes,

the caucus was King's "sounding board" and "his test for any measure was its effect on party unity or national unity." Because King believed the Liberal Party was the "political embodiment" of the diverse interests and regions of the nation, party unity and national unity were usually synonymous.[14]

Interdependence required that prime ministers should have, as Lord Dufferin said of Macdonald, a "great faculty for managing other people." Macdonald's problems with "loose fish" never ceased. "It has kept me constantly at work to the exclusion of everything else," he wrote in 1881, "to strengthen the weakhearted in both Houses."[15] "Loose fish" were less a problem for Macdonald's successors as party discipline stiffened and the institution of the caucus became formalized. Even so, the papers of every prime minister are filled with comments echoing Sir John A.'s. Every party, every caucus, and every Cabinet has had its quota of "weak-hearted" and the not-always-gentle art of persuasion remains an essential attribute of a party leader.

The nature of the national parties, with some exception granted for the Co-operative Commonwealth Federation and the New Democratic Party, also discourages dramatic policy initiatives by party leaders. The problem was twofold: not to alienate the support the leader enjoyed and to acquire new adherents to the party. The aim of a party's spokesman, Borden argued, was to "seek to reach and influence men of moderate opinion who vote now with one and now with the other party."[16] The prescription for success was a restrained approach to partisanship and a wary attitude towards innovation. Sir John A., Creighton observed, "was not a crusader with a mission"; "he thumped no tubs and banged no pulpits."[17] Similarly, Laurier, as Skelton put it, "was never a man to raise questions before they were ripe."[18] And King, the master of the "half measure," "saw no need for political action when political harmony did not seem threatened."[19]

At first sight we have a paradox here. The

party leader as manager, as persuader, as "Old Tomorrow," as the artisan of half-measures, projects an image of pandering to debilitating but necessary compromise. But Charles Taylor reminds us, albeit disapprovingly, that national parties that aim at this kind of broad support must, of necessity, emphasize their capacity for leadership. Eschewing specific program promises, they offer electors "a leadership which claims the competence to extract and act on the consensus at any given time, rather than a specific view of what should be done."[20]

"Reforms are for Oppositions," Laurier once remarked. "It is the business of governments to stay in office."[21] Put another way, the business of government is power, and the power of the prime minister to do something — and to do nothing — is most evident in the Cabinet. Here too a complex relationship between the government leader, his party, his caucus, and his cabinet colleagues is constantly at work, creating opportunities and imposing limitations on his leadership.

Macdonald, who described himself as a "cabinetmaker," told a friend that "a good carpenter... can work with indifferent tools."[22] He was referring, confidently, to his ability to get the best out of indifferent cabinet colleagues. But there was a limit. Both he and Laurier began their administrations with Cabinets composed of able and powerful men. Both had to rely on men of lesser talents as time went on, and their own power and prestige slipped accordingly. Borden began with a relatively weak Cabinet; the infusion of new blood in 1917 freed him to implement a creative initiative in external affairs and gave his Union government the power and prestige that were not evident in his first administration. Clearly, a powerful and talented colleague like C.D. Howe,[23] given the freedom to pursue innovative policies, contributed to the impression of strong leadership by Mackenzie King. Indeed, Samuel Tilley's National Policy and Clifford Sifton's immigration policy, to cite two examples, became hallmarks of the Macdonald and Laurier governments.

Each prime minister, of course, had his own style of cabinet leadership. Laurier often conveyed an impression of aloofness from the business of government and liked to say, "I'm a lazy dog."[24] But his ears were always up. "A masterful man set on having his own way," Sifton remarked; "and equally resolute that his colleagues shall not have their way unless this is quite agreeable to him."[25] Borden generally presided over his Cabinet as a genial committee chairman. King, Mr. Pearson observed, "was the headmaster!" — adding that "my philosophy was to let a Cabinet Minister, as far as possible, run his own show and that it was not my job to be interfering in details."[26] Most prime ministers worked hard to avoid divisions in their Cabinets, but when difficult and divisive decisions had to be made, as Mr. Diefenbaker said, "the final responsibility rests on the Prime Minister. No one else."[27] The prime minister, if he wished, could also assume initial responsibility for some policy and ignore his cabinet colleagues. but the historical record suggests that this has been a game full of risks. Laurier's schools policy for the new provinces, Bennett's "New Deal," Pearson's compromise with Quebec on the pension plan, and, in some respects, Borden's conscription policy, remind us of leaders in trouble rather than in control.

The price for such daring and sometimes desperate gambles is usually paid in the House of Commons. Political scientists differ sharply on the role the House of Commons plays in an evaluation of political leadership. Thomas Hockin reminds us that the rules and procedures of the House are designed to favour the opposition and that the prime minister, who can speak as the leader of the nation outside the House, is forced to play the part of partisan chieftain in that "theatre for political upheavals."[28] But, Denis Smith replies, "in its less spectacular day-to-day performances, the House of Commons normally, if grudgingly, does the work the Government directs it to do."[29]

The first article in every prime minister's profession of faith must be, as Pearson put it, "a deep and genuine feeling for Parliamentary institutions." That does not mean that they all liked their work there. "I never had any great love of Parliamentary battles and rows," Pearson said. "I used to get impatient because you couldn't get things done quickly enough because of those struggles in Parliament that other people may have loved."[30] St. Laurent, King, and Borden would have agreed. And recalling that Diefenbaker, Drew, Meighen, and Laurier sat across the aisle, the sentiment is understandable. Other prime ministers obviously enjoyed the place: Diefenbaker for its theatrical potential; Laurier as an arena for his eloquence; Macdonald as a partisan battleground and as the most congenial club in Canada.

This suggests a necessary change of focus in our examination of political leadership. So far I have concentrated upon the role that the political institutions of our society play in restraining or encouraging displays of leadership. I have been using, and no doubt abusing, what political scientists call a "situational" mode of evaluation and it does yield essential insight into the nature of leadership in a democratic society. There is, however, a whiff of stasis and determinism in all this. It is already apparent in the examples I have cited that institutional limits and opportunities are only one factor in our inquiry.

As Donald Creighton observed, every historical study is an "encounter between character and circumstances."[31] Both beg far more questions than can be answered, or even acknowledged here. But a few examples of the influence of circumstances and character on the decisions of our political leaders are in order.

Circumstances, political deadlock in the Canadas, indecisive tinkering with the idea of union in the Maritimes, civil war in the United States, and growing problems in Anglo-American relations, among many factors, provided the opportunity and shaped the nature of Confederation, Macdonald's — and George Brown's — greatest political achievement. And circumstances, the unforeseen growth of provincial powers and responsibilities, dramatically altered the nature of Confederation before Macdonald's death. Circumstances, a decade of prosperity, low interest rates, expanding export markets for Canadian natural products, cheap shipping fares, industrial innovation and expansion in Canada, and a shrewd sense of timing, made the Laurier government's immigration policy a success. That, in turn, made the creation of the new provinces necessary and politically opportune. Moreover, circumstances, the legacies of earlier school crises and the dwindling influence of the francophone minority in the Territories, influenced the nature of Laurier's original schools clauses in the Autonomy Bills *and* the opposition to them in his own ranks and in the opposition party. Circumstances played a major role in Borden's decision to abandon his pledge that there would be no conscription in World War I. Conscription, another circumstance, helped King to win the Liberal Party leadership and a long series of elections. It also deeply influenced his tenacious resistance to conscription in World War II and his eventual half-abandonment of voluntary enlistment.

But remember that at every moment in a political leader's career there is an interplay, an "encounter", between circumstances and character. His own perception of the restraints and the opportunities of institutions and of circumstances is also shaped by his own personality. In the end, I think, this is the most important determinant in what he does, in what he refuses to do, in the quality and the success or failure of his leadership.

Leaving aside the pretensions Mr. King confided to his diary, none of our political leaders had been born to rule. But wanting to rule and having extraordinary confidence in their capacity and fitness to rule are characteristics that set our memorable political leaders apart from other men. Compare, for example, the responses of Mr. Diefenbaker and Sir Mackenzie Bowell to the cabinet revolts each endured. "The Chief" faced his down; Bowell succumbed. Poor Sir Mackenzie, unlike Diefenbaker, seems not to have wanted to fight for his leadership. As Laurier said of Alexander Mackenzie, "he has no zest to carry a party on." Mackenzie admitted as much. "From the first," he said while prime minister, "I was more willing to serve than reign."[32] And yet another prime minister, Sir John Joseph Caldwell Abbott, began his term of office with what amounted to an apology: "I am here very much because I am not particularly obnoxious to anybody."[33] A redeeming quality, no doubt, and one that was true of many other Canadian political leaders. But Abbott was not "here" long — five months and eight days. The lack of "zest" for leadership, then, is a sure first step to oblivion.

But listen to Laurier's reaction to his first election to the Quebec legislature: "I have scored a triumph, a real triumph." His goal, he said, was "making my ideas triumph," surely the most ambitious of all political goals.[34] His confidence occasionally wavered but never died. Towards the end of his long career, early in the 1917 conscription crisis, Laurier told a friend that "if at the present time anybody can restrain and face the extremists, I think I am the man."[35]

King shared Laurier's confidence and his will to triumph, but not his "zest". Here is King on his last electoral victory:

It was almost as if I had had a bath after a dusty and dirty journey, with the storm of lies, misrepresentations, insinuations and what in which I have had to pass during the past few weeks — I might even say over most of the years of the war. One could go back and say almost over one's public life. I felt a real vindication in the verdict of the people and a sense of triumph therefrom.[36]

That speaks volumes about King's perception of his leadership and reminds us of the striking differences that accompanied the similarities in the personalities of two of our most successful political leaders.[37]

Courage, determination, patience, tolerance, all in varying measure, are also characteristics of nearly all our political leaders. Each of us can supply his own examples. I think of Macdonald, who had all these qualities. Macdonald, however, seemed to find his way through encounters with circumstances with an especial flair. A less demanding and inquiring, or prying, age, of course, allowed more assistance from the grape and the grain and Macdonald took full advantage of that. But Macdonald bore his defeats and dreadful tragedy in his private life with uncommon cheer and wit and a healthy pinch of fatalism. "Take things pleasantly," he told a friend, "and when fortune empties her chamber pot on your head — smile and say, 'we are going to have a summer shower.'"[38]

One final example of how personality encounters and moulds circumstances. Compare, for a moment, the approaches of Borden and King to conscription in 1917 and 1944. There are, in fact, remarkable similarities in the circumstances leading to each crisis, but the motivations of the two men were as different as day and night. Borden's decision was rooted in his complete commitment to the soldiers, a commitment steeled by his hours of visits with wounded men during his trips to England and France in 1915 and 1917. Borden had made a covenant with "his boys." "No man wanting inspiration, determination or courage as to his duty in this war ... could go to any better place than the hospitals in which our Canadian boys are to be found," he said on the day he announced his decision for conscription. "I should feel myself unworthy... if I did not fulfill my pledge."[39]

Mr. King was no less concerned about the welfare of the Canadian troops in World War II, but his concern was more abstract; the emotional fervour that drove Borden was absent. And King was torn, far more than Borden, between the demands of the military and his fear of national disunity and internal strife. In the end King rationalized his turnabout with two imagined conspiracies by opponents of his social reforms and by plotters in the army. "King," Professor Granatstein remarks, "had to create these dark shadows before he could bring himself to take drastic and difficult action."[40]

Our perception of political leadership are shaped by a host of images. We probably judge yesterday's fishwives more justly than we do today's Sirens, if only because time add evidence, balance, and perspective. Our political institutions, our history and contemporary circumstances, create restraints upon and offer opportunities for initiative and innovation by our political leaders. But institutions, history, and circumstances are their chamber pots of fortune. How did they, with their complex and unique personalities, respond when the chamber pots tipped? That is the most important question in our inquiry. Did they smile — or curse the gods?

Notes

1. *Globe and Mail,* 2 January 1980, p.2.
2. Careless and Brown, eds., *The Canadians, 1867-1961,* p.245.
3. *Regina Morning Leader,* 13 September 1917, p.1.
4. Brown, *Canada's National Policy, 1883-1900,* p.87.
5. Dafoe, *Laurier,* p.15.
6. Cited in Beck and Dooley, "Party Images in Canada," in Thorburn, *Party Politics in Canada,* pp.33, 37.
7. "W.L.M.K." in Scott and Smith, *The Blasted Pine,* p.27.
8. Taylor, "Political Leadership," in Hockin, *Apex of Power,* p.112; Robins, "Paranoia and Charisma" (unpublished paper).
9. Graham, "Charisma and Canadian Politics," in Moir, ed., *Character and Circumstance,* p.26.
10. Brown, *Robert Laird Borden,* Vol. 1, Chap. 3, Vol. 2, Chap. 14.
11. Dion, "The Concept of Political Leadership," p. 4.
12. Whitaker, "The Government Party".
13. Cited in Granatstein, *Canada's War,* p.347.
14. Neatby, *William Lyon Mackenzie King,* Vol. 3, pp.4-14.
15. Creighton, *John A. Macdonald: The Old Chieftain,* pp.251, 309.
16. Borden, ed., *Letters to Limbo,* pp.68-69.
17. Creighton, *John A. Macdonald: The Young Politician,* p.180.
18. Skelton, *The Life and Letters of Sir William Laurier,* Vol. 1, p.362.
19. Neatby, *William Lyon Mackenzie King,* Vol. 3, pp.11-13.
20. Taylor, "Political Leadership", p.110.
21. Cited in Stevens, "Wilfrid Laurier: Politician," in Hamelin, ed., *Les Idées politiques,* p.54.
22. Cited in Waite, "The Political Ideas," in Hamelin, *Les Idées politiques,* p.54.
23. Bothwell and Kilbourn, *C.D. Howe.*
24. Skelton, *Laurier,* Vol. 2, p.163.
25. Cited in Stevens, "Laurier," p.73.
26. "Interview with the Right Honourable Lester B. Pearson," in Hockin, *Apex of Power,* p.197.
27. "Interview with the Right Honourable John G. Diefenbaker," Hockin, p.185.
28. Hockin, "The Prime Minister and Political Leadership", *Apex of Power,* pp.7-10.
29. Smith, "President and Parliament", Hockin, p.234.
30. "Interview with Pearson," Hockin, p.194.
31. Creighton, *Towards the Discovery of Canada,* p.19.
32. Skelton, *Laurier,* Vol. 1, pp.187, 181.
33. Ibid., p.430.
34. Ibid., pp.110-111.
35. Brown, *Borden,* Vol. 2.
36. Cited in Granatstein, *Canada's War,* p.410.
37. Laurier saved his darker reflections for electoral defeats. "It is becoming more and more manifest to me," he wrote in October 1911, "that it was not reciprocity that was turned down, but a Catholic premier."
38. Cited in Waite, "The Political Ideas," p.66.
39. Canada, Parliament, House of Commons, *Debates,* 18 May 1917, pp.1539, 1542.
40. Granatstein, *Canada's War,* p.423.

SECTION II

The Exercise of Power:
Prime Ministerial Arenas

This section focusses on the office of prime minister and the exercise of power throughout a variety of key arenas. The authors review the dynamics of prime ministerial leadership in the media, the Cabinet, intergovernmental relations, political parties, and in economic and foreign policy.

While the approach differs essay by essay, the inevitable theme which binds them together is that prime ministers must cope with very different demands and dynamics in different arenas. As David Taras shows, the "media battle" requires certain skills and qualities which may be quite irrelevant to success elsewhere. While Taras focusses on strategies in this arena, Peter Aucoin concentrates on the way in which cabinet structure, and hence the pinnacles of the policy process, reflect prime ministerial priorities and preferences. Donald Wallace reveals the limitations and constraints leaders face in the intergovernmental arena, and traces some of the patterns of power as they have evolved there. Leslie A. Pal's essay on political parties explores some of the tensions and demands which prime ministers face as leaders of partisan organizations.

Robert Campbell and Kim Richard Nossal tackle the policy connection head-on by exploring leadership in terms of economic and foreign policy. Not surprisingly, they conclude that leadership is difficult to exercise in either arena, though they do explore the influence that some leaders have had at specific conjunctures.

CHAPTER 4

Prime Ministers and the Media

David Taras

In order to be successful, a prime minister must be first and foremost "a public persuader."[1] The media are the instruments for transmitting the prime minister's message to his or her party, the government, and the public. Yet the media have their own priorities and interests and vigorously pursue their own agendas. The prime minister must have an understanding of media routines and be skilled in packaging, choreographing, and manipulating in order to have his or her intentions and ideals conveyed in a positive light. The relationship is one in which both sides are seeking definition and recognition and are constantly struggling against each other. Various analogies have been used to describe the relationship: Larry Zolf called it a dance; others have described it as a game.[2] The experiences of Joe Clark and John Turner suggest a harsher reality. Prime ministers must survive in the "battleground" of media relations. They have at their disposal a well-stocked arsenal of weapons with which to wage the media battle.

This chapter will describe the interests of the two sides, the resources and tactics employed by prime ministers, and the media-management styles of each of the modern prime ministers. A second section will examine the consequences of the prime minister's relationship with the media for the political system as a whole. Particular attention will be on the influence that television has had on the nature of leadership in Canada.

CLASH OF INTERESTS

Prime ministers and the media have different interests, agendas, and codes of conduct. To remain in office, prime ministers must satisfy large and disparate blocs of voters and many divergent interests. Their desire to avoid offending significant constituencies predisposes them to general statements of principle more than narrow appeals. Canadian politics, because of linguistic and regional differences, tends to produce prime ministers skilled in the art of compromise and conciliation. Divisive language is rarely used when the prime minister speaks to the country as a whole. The prime minister is also constrained by his position as chief diplomat responsible for Canada's international relations and as the principal manager of the Canadian economy. The prime minister's many roles dictate a language, a vocabulary, and a personal style that project a sense of national responsibility, general principles, and conciliation.

For the media, the stakes in covering Ottawa are high. The Prime Minister's office (PMO) has a monopoly on information about many aspects of government and of course most tantalizingly, about the prime minister's daily schedule, thoughts, opinions, experiences, and aspects of his personal life. Almost any item about the prime minister is newsworthy. For Ottawa reporters, among whom there is a significant turnover, covering the prime minister is an opportunity to make a name and establish a professional reputation. Of the press gallery's approximately 350 members only a few will emerge as "stars."

The premium for the news industry is on

stories that are eye-catching, dramatic, and have so-called spin. Selling the size, and in some cases, the characteristics, of audiences and readerships to advertisers is what sustains television networks and newspapers. This requires stories that have news appeal; that is, stories that stress conflict, can be easily condensed and labelled, and involve some degree of sensationalism and excitement. High-impact visuals are critical for television, and controversy is what is required for newspaper headlines. These are the essentials of newsworthy features according to most journalists. A CBC news editor has admitted: "We look for confrontation often to the exclusion of a story. It's overwhelmingly prevalent. It's the nature of journalism to be a storyteller. It needs drama." A senior editor at the *Globe and Mail* put it even more succinctly: "Conflict is news. That's basic." According to Anthony Westell, "most editors believe...the harder the statement, the better the news story."[3]

While these differences in priorities and purposes between prime ministers and the media are critical, there are other sources of conflict. Those interviewed for this study believed that the media had an obligation to criticize and to play an opposition role. This ethic is deeply embedded in the Canadian journalistic psyche. One senior *Globe and Mail* editor made the distinction between being a critic of the government and being an opponent. His view was that while some newspapers crossed that line frequently, television was almost inherently an opponent of the government because of its constant requirement for exciting stories. According to him, in both media "the best stories are always government-in-trouble stories." A CBC producer argued that criticizing the government was "one of the rituals of civilization" and that interviews on television had to be aggressive and challenging, with the interviewer "taking the opposite position."

One can argue that Canadian journalists have been influenced by the post-Watergate machismo that became prominent in American journalism during the 1970s. This trend emerged as much out of the Vietnam War as out of Watergate itself. The prevailing view was that politicians were to be looked upon with suspicion; approval of government policies or statements was a sign of weakness, and careers could be made by exposing incompetence and corruption at the top. According to Edward Jay Epstein,

> the working hypothesis almost universally shared among correspondents is that politicians are suspect; their public images probably false, their public statements disingenuous, their moral pronouncements hypocritical, their motives self-serving, and their promises ephemeral. Correspondents thus see their jobs to be to expose politicians by unmasking their disguises, debunking their claims and piercing their rhetoric. In short, until proven otherwise, political figures of any party or persuasion are presumed to be deceptive opponents.[4]

Whatever the validity of Epstein's description of the prevailing attitude among American journalists, few would dispute that similar currents can be found in the Canadian media community. Strong skepticism and a "culture of disparagement"[5] seem firmly embedded. A former parliamentary correspondent for the CBC has complained that "everybody wants to write like Allan Fotheringham. Journalists have been reduced to a bunch of smart-alecks. Can't a P.M. ever be right? Can't a policy ever be good?" Pierre Trudeau used the term "Watergate envy" to characterize the media's cynicism.[6] In Canada, investigative journalism almost always means exposing government flaws and ineptitude.

A dominant feature of much news reporting is what has been called "horse-race" journalism. The media give overwhelming attention to politics, specifically the race for power, rather than to policies. How party leaders are perceived, their daily performance in Question Period, any moves against them from the ranks of their own parties, and their future prospects have become the bread and butter of reporting.

Policy developments are often too complex to follow or explain, given the time and space pressures that journalists are under. The horse race is a convenient metaphor for addressing (or perhaps for failing to address) almost any policy issue, and it makes news items seem exciting.

Politicians have come to fear not only the media's criticisms, but their need for drama and conflict. Many have difficulty understanding why so large a proportion of what they say and of what they find important goes unreported. Minor scandals, peripheral topics, and gaffes are often seized on as news, while larger issues and broader indicators of performance are sometimes neglected. They are afraid that their messages will not get through. Prime Minister Pearson complained in his day that

> newspaper editors are always bleating about the refusal of politicians to produce mature and responsible discussion of the issues. The fact is, when we do discuss policies seriously, we are not reported at all, or reported very inadequately. Reporters do not appear even to listen, until we say something controversial or personal, charged with what they regard as news value.[7]

Virtually every modern prime minister has voiced a similar complaint. Brian Mulroney has charged: "There's a cottage industry in this country that deals with facile and mostly pejorative references to what any prime minister is doing at a given time... I'm not saying it with bitterness. I'm saying it calmly, as a matter of fact. The message has been distorted in going out."[8]

A second fear is that labels and images will be applied too readily by the media and that these cannot easily be removed. Images can take on a life of their own and remain long after the events that inspired them have faded from public consciousness. One might argue that Pierre Trudeau, based on the media's very first descriptions of him as bold, charismatic, and exciting, acquired political capital that would last him for years. Robert Stanfield, Joe Clark, and John Turner, on the other hand, had difficulty with the negative images affixed to them from the beginning of their tenure as party leaders, and these images coloured all subsequent reporting.

PRIME MINISTERS' WEAPONS

Prime ministers are not without formidable resources of their own in dealing with the media. They can have coverage monitored constantly, they can dispense information and grant access at times, and to journalists, of their choosing, they can engage in numerous image-building exercises, and they can manipulate events, issues, and situations so that the media has little choice of what to report. The prime minister has a director of communications and press secretary with a sizeable staff to help devise an overall media strategy and handle the daily requirements of dealing with the press. Every cabinet document now contains a communications strategy which spells out in considerable detail how policies should be sold. The art of media management has been well developed. Strategies, however, are difficult to implement. With the media naturally suspicious of the machinations of political leaders, attempts at overt manipulation can easily backfire. Politicians who are too clever and too slick will arouse distrust. Subtlety is the key to successful application of media-management techniques.

A most formidable weapon in the prime minister's arsenal is the ability to grant or deny access. Under Trudeau and Mulroney, in particular, access has been limited and often held out as a reward to favoured reporters. The basic understanding is that journalists who are allowed an exclusive interview or story will in return report favourably on the prime minister. Being singled out by the prime minister gives journalists a tangible advantage over their rivals and enhanced credibility with their news organizations. Moreover, reporters and columnists who are treated as important by the prime minister are likely to be treated as important by others. Press officials do not expect these favoured reporters to be uncritical in every instance. But the prime minister's staff minimizes risk by selecting reporters with care, knowing as much as possible about reporters' views and predicting how they will use the information provided by the prime minister.

Leaking a story to a favoured reporter has a number of advantages. A leak about an impending policy announcement, for instance, gives the government at least two opportunities, instead of only one, to get its message through to the public. The first is when the leak is reported, the second is the coverage given to the announcement. Most important is that the reporter's positive tone creates a first impression about the intended policy, and first impressions tend to have the greatest impact on public opinion.

Correspondents who are seen as unfriendly are frozen out by the prime minister, as well as by ministers and key government officials. As one former press secretary said: "We never had lists but I privately knew that I was not going to put the prime minister in an interview with X or Y. Put it this way, they were not going to be at the top of my list for interviews." According to one reporter, Prime Minister Mulroney is especially "knowledgeable about where his precious words and time will go" and tends to punish reporters for stories he does not like. The reporter observed that "nothing hurts a journalist more than being denied access, because we lose favour with our bosses." A former Ottawa columnist believed that his fellow journalists were constantly afraid of this kind of retaliation. "They watch for it to a degree you wouldn't believe," he said. Being frozen out has consequences for daily reporting. Reporters often need facts confirmed before they file their stories. If officials do not cooperate, the reporters' jobs become more difficult. In some instances reporters will be frozen out for short periods, as a warning.

Direct access to the prime minister is not as important as it may have been at one time. With power increasingly diffused, many journalists rely heavily on contacts in the bureaucracy; a never-ending source of insights about struggles for position and control.

Another common technique is to create circumstances that narrow the available options for journalists. The strategy is to make the stories that the prime minister wants reported readily available, while hindering reporters' efforts to pursue stories that could be damaging. A favourite tactic is the release of information late on Friday afternoons. The story will make the Saturday papers, which in most cases have a larger circulation than weekday news. Since civil servants and opposition M.P.s will have left for the weekend, they are largely not available for needed background or critical comments. Correspondents facing deadlines have little choice but to file the stories they have. The government has "at least a twenty-four-hour free ride before the critics get their turn." A former field producer for the CBC told of being always anxious as Friday afternoons approached. He commented that after a long week almost everyone in the press gallery was "tired and didn't want to scramble." Not surprisingly, Friday has often been the day for prime ministerial press conferences.

A variant of this tactic was used with some measure of success by Trudeau and Clark, during the 1974 and 1979 elections, respectively. Policies and promises would be announced just before many of the correspondents had to file their stories. Without much time to digest or evaluate the substance of the announcements, reporters had little choice but to give a verbatim account of Trudeau's or Clark's statements. Their messages got through relatively free of commentary or criticism. This tactic eventually proved counterproductive, for Trudeau in particular. Flagrant manipulation of the media during the 1974 election contributed to bitter relations later on. In subsequent years journalists were tougher on Trudeau because of the election experience, and news organizations were better prepared to deal with such tactics.

Another device is the effective use of news releases. Releases with the important remarks underlined or highlighted are served up as a steady diet to correspondents. The idea is to supply journalists with enough information, carefully explained and made to appear newsworthy, that they will have little inclination to look elsewhere or chase other stories. Politicians can depend on a certain degree of journalistic inertia, as some reporters will be content with this ration of packaged stories. As reporters have to produce news stories almost every day, whether or not there is real news, some reporters will take the path of least resistance and report the "news" they have been given.

Yet another tactic is to avoid the suspicious and unfriendly Ottawa press gallery by making announcements to less critical journalists somewhere else. Statements about oil or farm policy, for instance, are likely to be received more favourably in Calgary or Regina than in Ottawa. When the prime minister is on tour there is often a high degree of enthusiasm and receptivity on the part of the local media. As a reporter for the *Ottawa Citizen* explained, "Moving out of Ottawa you get more uncritical coverage. Local reporters are not as informed on some of the issues and as familiar with the nuances."

News conferences also are an opportunity for manipulation. A prime minister, who can set the tone and agenda, always has the advantage. Announcements about policies or appointments can be made that will dictate the content and flow of the news conference, and there are few questions for which answers have not been prepared in advance. Key phrases are repeated often so that correspondents will not fail to include them in television and radio clips or as quotes in articles. One CBC news editor believed that Trudeau eventually banned scrums simply because he could not control them to the same degree as formal news conferences. Mary Comber and Robert Mayne quote a former Trudeau aide as saying that Trudeau would

have in reserve a number of dramatic and controversial declarations which he freely used...to deflect questions away from...sensitive areas. When particularly critical questions were expected, the Prime Minister would embellish his answer to a relatively innocuous question. This lively quote would then be picked up and become the theme for subsequent questions.[9]

For a strong thinker and debater, the news conference is always an opportunity; for a less able politician it can degenerate into a nightmare.

One tactic often used by governments is to plant stories in the media as a means of testing public opinion. Correspondents are leaked information about proposed policy initiatives or appointments. If response to reports that appear in the media are unfavourable, the government can retreat without suffering a loss of prestige. Such "trial balloons" have kept more than a few political leaders from possibly squandering much-needed public goodwill. The PMO usually orchestrates the release of such information through members of the Cabinet or party, as the dangers of a trial balloon backfiring prevent the prime minister from using this strategy himself.

A senior editor with the *Globe and Mail* complained that prime ministers can create a sense of crisis to make themselves appear to be saviours of a particular situation. Correspondents would be given gloomy reports or told that solutions were unlikely. For instance, the *Globe and Mail* journalist recounted how during the 1981 struggle for a revised Constitution, government spokespersons stressed repeatedly the impasses that were likely to make an agreement impossible. When a settlement was finally reached, the media, having anticipated failure, were quick to pronounce it a major historic achievement, notwithstanding the fact that Quebec had not given its approval, because the prime minister appeared to have triumphed against seemingly insurmountable obstacles.

Above all, prime ministers attempt to control the rules and setting. One former press secretary related how, by demanding that a television interview be done "to time", whereby it was a predetermined length and not subject to editing, the show's producers were forced "to go with what had been said" rather than their repackaged and highly selective version of the interview. Patrick Gossage, a press secretary to Pierre Trudeau, described "the old PMO trick" of stipulating publication of the text of a newspaper interview in its entirety as a condition of granting an interview. This ensured that "the PM's views get out clean."[10]

It is evident that prime ministers have enough knowledge of the media's rules that they can package their comments and images in a way that can be irresistible. Staged events, flashy comments or put-downs, press releases that do the work for the journalist, and the promise of exclusive stories in exchange for favourable coverage have become part of the prime ministers' arsenal. Prime ministers have learned to use the media's needs and routines to their own advantage.

THE ARENA OF CONFLICT

While a similar arsenal of weapons has been available to all modern prime ministers, each has had a different style in dealing with the media. Despite the availability and variety of media-management techniques, no prime minister, regardless of his approach, has avoided some measure of bitter and hostile relations with the press. A magic formula for dealing with the media has eluded even the most skilled and adroit prime ministers.

Veteran reporters can remember a relationship that was more direct and personal than the one that exists today. This was due largely to the small size of the Ottawa press gallery. When election travel was by train, journalists and political leaders spent long periods in close proximity to each other. Diefenbaker and Pearson, for instance, each knew virtually all the

major reporters personally and spent long hours in cozy conversation with their favoured reporters, exchanging anecdotes and even soliciting advice. Yet this relatively small and personal system of relationships did not always produce positive coverage. Diefenbaker reacted bitterly to press criticism, and as Charles Lynch has observed, "it wound up a total adversary situation — Diefenbaker versus the press."[11] He was convinced to the end that "the press gallery contributed to his losing office."[12] Despite his more affable disposition and greater tactfulness, in hindsight Pearson also believed that "the press had done him in."[13]

Diefenbaker was the first prime minister to employ a press secretary. Jim Nelson, then the Ottawa bureau chief for the British United Press, had been recruited in 1957. Nelson found the position frustrating and demeaning. Diefenbaker was not open to advice and frequently made impromptu statements and announcements. He remained convinced that his abilities and charm needed no further orchestration. In 1958, while Opposition Leader, Lester Pearson hired Dick O'Hagan of MacLaren Advertising to be his press secretary. O'Hagan remained until 1966, and, unlike Jim Nelson, was to assume important responsibilities. He spoke for Pearson on some occasions and helped shape Pearson's public persona. O'Hagan was the first to institute the regular prime ministerial press conference. He also encouraged informal exchanges between Pearson and groups of reporters, feeling that Pearson was far more effective in personal encounters than in public performances. Pearson, more conscious of image than Diefenbaker, once had a poll taken to gauge the reaction of Canadians to his wearing a bow tie.

Trudeau's relations with journalists were cool and distant. Seeing himself in part as a philosopher and educator, he developed a strong dislike for the media's tendency to simplify and sensationalize. He also resented their intrusions into his private life. His contempt became palpable. A CBC journalist recalls that

Trudeau viewed journalists as "ink-stained wretches" and that he "despised" them. Although he had a few favourites such as Jack Webster, George Radwanski, and Jim Munson, Trudeau developed an intense antipathy toward journalists as a group while he was prime minister, though, ironically, during his formative years of political experience in Quebec, before he became prime minister, some of his closest associates — Jacques Hébert, Blair Fraser, and Gérard Pelletier — had been journalists. These feelings of animosity were reciprocated. Clive Cocking found in an informal survey of the Ottawa press gallery taken in 1978 that there was "not one reporter who likes Trudeau" and that "the gallery vultures seem distinctly bloody-minded."[14] There is little doubt, however, that Trudeau was respected, and even feared. His intelligence, independence, and charismatic appeal won grudging admiration from the journalists covering him. One journalist described him as "an appealing if unnerving figure."

Unlike Diefenbaker and Pearson, or Clark and Mulroney, Trudeau made few efforts to cultivate good media relations. Only from necessity, as part of struggles for political survival, did he swallow his natural feelings of enmity. Access to Trudeau was always difficult. One former Ottawa columnist for the *Globe and Mail* was never granted an interview despite repeated requests. He complained that his paper went without access to Trudeau for close to ten years. According to Patrick Gossage, the "'Interview Request File' was definitely the office's most swollen and lethargic paper-collector. It was virtually a one-way dossier — 'in' only!"[15] A former columnist for a financial newspaper noted as well that "access to Trudeau's ministers was often difficult largely because of the boss's view that we were dangerous idiots." Trudeau believed that he could be most effective if he could reach the public directly, bypassing the Ottawa press gallery. He made use as much as he could of airtime to speak to Canadians directly, and had federal-

provincial first ministers' conferences televised. Most significant was that Trudeau had proceedings of the House of Commons televised beginning in 1977.

During his long period in office, Trudeau was served by a succession of press secretaries. Roméo Leblanc, Peter Roberts, Pierre O'Neill, Courtney Tower, Jean Charpentier, Dick O'Hagan, Arnie Patterson, Patrick Gossage, Nicole Sénécal, and Ralph Coleman each seemed to have encountered numerous frustrations. Some enjoyed a place in Trudeau's inner circle while others had little power at all. When Dick O'Hagan was called in to be press secretary in 1975 he again, as he had with Pearson, instituted regular press conferences. He reportedly told a resistant Trudeau, "Okay, so these aren't journalists of the caliber of those who work for *Le Monde* or the *London Times*. This is the press you have to deal with and it's necessary to respond to their needs at their level."[16] O'Hagan attempted to get Trudeau to acknowledge key journalists when they rose to ask questions, but he often forgot their names.

Trudeau's news conferences have been described as having a "chess-match" quality. Trudeau's answers were nimble but his tone often aggressive. Occasionally he would challenge the intelligence and appropriateness of questions. According to a former CBC correspondent, "it was Trudeau versus the press. His intellect against theirs. There was fear that he would make a fool of you in front of your colleagues." As one former columnist described Trudeau's performance:

> He would answer parts of questions, walk right through them, or turn it around on you. You had to ask questions just right, shutting off avenues of escape anticipating his getaway and shutting it down. It became a game.

He noted, however, that if questions were challenging intellectually, Trudeau was more likely to respond, even if it was not politically advantageous for him to do so.

Much of the antagonism between Trudeau and journalists was a result of the Liberals' successful manipulation of the media during the 1974 election campaign. During that campaign, as stated previously, policy statements would be presented close to deadlines and Trudeau would remain inaccessible. He would appear only in contrived or controlled circumstances. Thus, while the media were given a regular flow of reportable news, grievances were developing. The adversarial relationship that characterized the 1974-to-1979 period was a direct result of this campaign. Liberal policies were intensively scrutinized and Trudeau was often vilified by the media. As Charles Lynch described the situation that then prevailed,

> it's been total war 'tween Trudeau and the press for a long, long time.... And the press gallery is just full of people who would love to get that sonofabitch, and who savour the fact that now he's on the skids they want to be there for it.[17]

There was little repair work that could be done in the 1980-to-1984 period. Both sides retained their earlier impressions and beliefs. Trudeau's public performances did become more effective as a result of advice, from Patrick Gossage in particular. After 1980, Trudeau used a podium more often and practiced a more relaxed delivery for television. There was a sophisticated transcription service in place, and a "Visiting Editors" program was instituted. Gossage also supplied the media with photographs of private events.[18] On the whole, Trudeau's distaste for the media fostered his reliance on a repertoire of formal media-management tactics, with little attempt to build interpersonal skills or relationships.

In contrast to Trudeau, perhaps no modern prime minister has been as accessible to the media as Joe Clark. Clark scrummed outside the House almost daily while Parliament was in session, held a weekly press conference, and granted frequent interviews. One senior journalist recalls being able to see Clark with only a day's notice. Another remembers reaching him directly by phone to have a news story confirmed. Yet despite — or perhaps even because of — his availability, Clark received harsh treat-

ment from the media.

Clark's trials began when he invited journalists to accompany him on his world tour in 1978. The tour was designed to acquaint Clark with international problems and trouble spots. No statements of policy, outlook or philosophy were delivered; it was intended as a learning experience. With little hard news to report, journalists were left to focus on Clark's personality and whatever "human interest" stories the tour could provide. The tour soon became a public-relations disaster. Luggage was lost, Clark nearly walked into a soldier's bayonet while reviewing Canadian troops in the Golan Heights, and his questions and demeanour were awkward and showed inexperience. The image of his lost luggage was to remain with the media for many years.

To compound his troubles, Clark did not come across well on television. His weak chin, stilted laugh, and gawky movements were magnified on television. Clark arrived at the prime ministership with an image of ineptitude that proved difficult to shake. Desmond Morton argued that

> whoever it was who decided that Joe Clark was a wimp established a framework of interpretation in which every action, in victory or defeat, could be located. The image, at least in my view, preceded the evidence and distorted it.[19]

Indeed, there is strong suspicion that some producers and editors began soliciting stories about Clark's alleged bungling from their correspondents because they thought that these stories would be popular with audiences. Hubert Gendron, who covered Clark during the 1979 election campaign, admitted that the psychology was indeed such that "during the tours of Maritime steel mills and shipyards everyone was looking for him to fall into a steel vat or something."[20] Expectations of this kind undoubtedly conditioned the type of coverage that Clark received during what reporters had begun to call the "wimp-watch."

That the Conservatives were able to win the election in 1979 despite the negative stereotyping of Clark suggests that the media may not be as powerful a force in Canadian elections as many believe. It may also be that the electorate was determined to defeat Trudeau whatever the consequences. The 1979 election campaign had been tightly orchestrated with Clark placed by his advisors in what Cocking refers to as "eight weeks in a cocoon."[21] He was suddenly inaccessible to journalists and his appearances were as contrived and his words as guarded as had been Trudeau's in 1974. Everything was done to avoid mistakes.

Upon assuming power, Clark returned to the open style. What did not change was the negative reporting from the media. One former Clark advisor complained, "The more he was open, the more they attacked. The bastards trashed us." The view of Stephen Handelman, who reported for the *Toronto Star,* was that

> the seeds of ridicule and disbelief planted in the public mind long before he became Prime Minister grew until they choked off the life of his government when it had barely got started.... Long before the press had come to accept and respect Clark's ability as Prime Minister the public was still looking at him with a jaundiced eye. Clark's jerky awkwardness became a metaphor for his government.[22]

It might be argued that had the Conservatives won a majority, the media might have been more circumspect in its approach, and given the government time to find its legs. But as the Conservatives seemed to be having difficulty from the beginning, appearing indecisive and inexperienced, many journalists apparently took the view that they "wouldn't be there for long and could be attacked right away." As the Conservatives made few firm policy decisions, and took over four months to call Parliament into session, reporters were left with little to report except the government's apparent infighting and indecision.

John Turner, while prime minister for only a brief period in 1984, also received a great deal of negative coverage. Indeed, in a survey of how party leaders were covered by the CBC and the *Globe and Mail* during the 1984 election, Comber and Mayne found that in stories that gave assessments, Turner received negative treatment 90 percent and 84 percent of the time respectively.[23] Turner was not helped by his intense and starchy appearance on television. With a burning stare, staccato speaking style, and stiff movements, he was unable to make himself seem comfortable to viewers. His long absence from the political wars had left him strangely inexperienced, and there was no shortage of wrong moves and inappropriate gestures, not the least of which was the damaging "bum-patting" incident. Turner was clearly denied a honeymoon period in which to regain his political legs. The media seemed to delight in revealing the weaknesses of the once-powerful Bay Street baron.

Prime Minister Brian Mulroney did not have Clark's or Turner's endemic problems with the media. To begin with, he is highly effective on television. He has strong features, a resonant voice, and no apparent nervous mannerisms. His speaking style is conversational, and he can be persuasive. He clearly defeated Liberal leader John Turner in their televised debates during the 1984 election. More than one observer has commented that his performance in French is stronger than in English, as his use of rhetoric and general political style are rooted in Quebec politics. Moreover, Mulroney is highly conscious of, some would even say obsessed with, the media. He is a voracious consumer of media reporting, and has made extraordinary efforts to cultivate contacts with journalists.

During the years that he was out of politics, following his 1976 loss of the Conservative leadership race, Mulroney sought to rebuild his political fortunes by strenuously lobbying important journalists. He met frequently with those he saw as influential, was a source of information about the Conservative party, and according to a *Globe and Mail* reporter would often "flatter them excessively." In a book on the 1983 Conservative leadership race, Allan Gregg, George Perlin, and Patrick Martin wrote:

Quick to contact journalists with whose work he agrees and equally quick to call those who disappoint, Mulroney cajoled and bullied, leaked and stonewalled his way into the professional lives of many journalists, until he became able to do a little "trafficking" of his own.[24]

By the time he became prime minister, a large number of journalists could be counted among his friends and were clearly in the Mulroney camp, although others had already developed a deep skepticism about his character and intentions.

Yet relations with the media were to sour quickly once Mulroney became prime minister. Access to Mulroney was highly restricted during the 1984 election campaign and his first months in office were characterized by an obsession with secrecy. Most significant was that Mulroney tended to become irritable and exasperated when coverage was not to his liking. According to Charlotte Gray, "he will phone a publisher, editor or reporter to complain. He attributes a poor showing in the polls directly to negative publicity."[25] Bill Fox, his first press secretary, sometimes got into heated battles with reporters over the tone of their stories. One measure of the deteriorating relationship was that press conferences, which Mulroney promised would be held twice every month when he came to power, had become almost non-existent by the middle of his term.

Journalists interviewed for this study pointed out that Mulroney lost a great deal of credibility because of a penchant for exaggeration and bluster. Too much slickness and "blarney" apparently aroused the suspicion and cynicism of the media. Having made patronage and the Liberals' style of governing the main issues in the 1984 election, Mulroney had set a moral standard that he was unable to live up to. As one reporter commented: "He accused us of being trivial but the trivial was what his campaign was based on." While less open to the media than Clark, Mulroney is more accessible than Trudeau. Relations are at once highly personal and informal, as Mulroney continues

to mine his friendships and contacts, yet also presidential and formal, for he has consciously adopted some aspects of the Reagan style. His press secretaries, Bill Fox, and later Michel Gratton and Marc Lortie, were given an official spokesperson's role similar to that of White House press secretaries, and attempts were made to centralize the flow of government information through the press office. Mulroney usually speaks in carefully controlled settings where a dignified prime ministerial image can be preserved. His instinct for partisan statements, embellished rhetoric, and jabs at the opposition, however, often upset the best planning. Mulroney believes that he can find the magic formula to deal with the media, and seeking that formula continues to consume much time and energy.

What is evident is that no prime minister since Diefenbaker has been able to win the media battle. Living with intense criticism and little praise is simply one of the conditions of office.

THE TELEVISION PRIME MINISTER

While the prime minister was once a distant figure to the majority of Canadians, television's intimacy has made him familiar: familiar not only in the sense that we recognize him because he is seen frequently, but familiar in that his presence is part of our lives. Much has been written about the power of television to make audiences feel that they have a relationship to those that they see on the screen. As Robert Lichter and his colleagues have pointed out, "the stars of television, from anchormen, to rock performers, to politicians, have become pseudo-intimate acquaintances."[26] Today's political leaders are nakedly exposed to public view in a way that their predecessors were not.

Newspapers, although they have maintained a strong position in Canadian society, are no longer the primary source for news. Generally they are looked to by those who wish to gain

more in-depth coverage and by a better edu-
cated and more prosperous audience than that
which relies on television for news coverage.

There are two contending views about the
impact of television on the way that political
leaders are perceived. One school of thought
argues that how leaders appear on television
carries little political weight. Robert Stanfield's
gaunt cheeks, Joe Clark's weak chin, and John
Turner's burning stare, all of which were exacerbated on television, had little to do with their
electoral defeats. Telegenic politicians such as
Pierre Trudeau and Brian Mulroney are not
guaranteed success merely because of their
seemingly made-for-television charms. These
factors are window dressing, irrelevant to a
public that ultimately will judge its leaders on
policies carried out, performance as organizers
and administrators, and the ability to express or
symbolize the national mood. A CBC producer
interviewed for this study pointed out that
under Mulroney, Erik Nielsen became deputy
prime minister and arguably the second most
powerful person in Ottawa, yet possessed none
of the attributes normally associated with television image-making. One might say the same
of Nielsen's successor Donald Mazankowski.
The dynastic rule by Jean Drapeau over Montreal was carried out by a politician who largely
avoided media coverage for almost a decade,
often refusing to appear on television at all.
According to this view, even the wily and
neurotic Mackenzie King, given the potency of
his other skills, could have survived the intrusion of the cameras.

The opposing view is that success on television can be translated directly into political
success or that it can mask or deflect attention
from failures on other fronts. Scholars have
noted that after the fiasco of the Bay of Pigs
invasion in 1961, John F. Kennedy's popularity
increased dramatically. A foreign policy failure
was transformed into domestic political success through a brilliant television performance
by Kennedy. A senior editor at the CBC observed that although in transcripts of news

conferences President Reagan's statements appeared "idiotic," on television they had soun-
ded good. Some would argue that it is because
of his televison magic that Reagan was able to
maintain his popularity for so long, despite
dubious foreign policy adventures, a mixed record on arms control, and increased economic
and social disparities in American society.

An Oxford scholar, Max Atkinson, contends
that some styles and techniques are more successful than others on television. He argues that
the most effective communicators are those
who adopt a cool, low-key, relaxed manner and
a conversational speaking style. Slow gestures
and a relaxed casualness are the prerequisites
for a convincing performance. According to
Atkinson, Ronald Reagan and Francois Mit-
terand have fit the television mould because
they have used a conversational approach and
made no sudden or expansive gestures. Stump
speakers, emotional oratory, and exaggerated
body movement tend to be too "hot" for television. Many of the great orators of history, with
their fiery rhetoric and dramatic gestures, probably would have appeared foolish on television:

> Practices which are visible, audible and impres-
> sive to those sitting in the back row of an
> auditorium are likely to seem greatly exagger-
> ated, unnatural and even oppressive when
> viewed on a small screen from a distance of a
> few feet.[27]

Moreover, television by its nature coarsens
and distorts. Imperfect chins look more imperfect, a hand seems to shake more than it actually does, bald pates can become elongated and
pear-shaped. As John Meisel described John
Turner's performance during the 1984 election
debates:

> The debates stripped the emperor of his clothes
> and destroyed the image he had acquired over
> the years of being the natural, uniquely qualified
> and inevitable leader. The camera exaggerated
> his mannerisms, hand movements, lip noises
> and a certain stiffness.[28]

Another concern is that political leaders are
unlikely to look as good on television as the

journalists that are reporting on them. Tele-journalists have several advantages. They are often chosen for their jobs because they appear attractive and comfortable on-camera and sound authoritative. Their reports are often practised and edited until their words, glances, and delivery are perfect. Most important, they are able to put the politicians' remarks in context for the audience. Viewers tend to place faith in them because of the aura of objectivity surrounding their work. Politicians, on the other hand, have only a single opportunity to put a statement on record and they are often captured on the run, at stressful moments, or while they are still in the process of formulating their positions. Television's requirement for instant reactions leaves little time for weighing answers to sometimes difficult or complex questions. Interviews are often designed to throw the subject off balance rather than elicit information. The battle is rarely fair.

Still, some politicians are acutely aware of the impressions transmitted to viewers by television and try to make the most of their situation. Peter C. Newman has described Lester Pearson's frustrations with the new medium.

> Expert after expert was given complete freedom to make him look as warm on TV as he was with small groups of friends. A voice coach was brought in from Toronto, and writers were hired to remove as many sibilants as possible from his scripts so that he could hide his speech problem. Toronto's MacLaren Advertising Company exhausted its considerable resources trying to improve his television manner. The TV manipulators tried a dozen different settings — intimate soirées, crowded scenes, living-room shots, interviews with academics — but nothing really worked. Lester Pearson emptied many a living room in his time. "They're trying to make me look like 'Danger Man' but I feel more like 'The Fugitive,'" Pearson complained to a friend about his TV advisors.[29]

Joe Clark reportedly gained considerable weight and changed his hairstyle after winning the Conservative party leadership in 1976 — so as to enhance his television presence. Pierre Trudeau, a man of relatively small stature, was rarely filmed beside taller rivals. His television consultants also advised him to rise slowly when answering questions in the House of Commons, to allow television cameras the opportunity to "frame" him.[30] René Lévesque, the master of television showmanship, knew how to create intimacy with television audiences by engaging his interviewers directly. For Lévesque, intensity and emotion seemed to work to his advantage. A CBC television reporter who covered Lévesque observed that "when the cameras were on he was on. When the cameras were off he was very different — he wasn't so charming."

There is little disputing that the prime minister's perceived importance has been enhanced by television. Some would see this as having contributed to the "presidentialization" of the office of prime minister. The medium's tendency to personify issues and to portray individuals rather than institutions as the prime movers behind policies and events has made the prime minister the main topic and symbol of government. Walter Stewart has noted that "he becomes the sole government spokesman on key issues."[31] This is especially evident during elections when party leaders are the electoral "breadwinners" for the party as a whole and the prime minister's performance can be the principal issue for the voting public. Coverage of party leaders accounted for forty-three percent of all election reporting on the CTV, and one third on the CBC networks, during the 1979 campaign. In the 1984 election, leadership, the results of public opinion polls and the debates among party leaders together consumed over fifty percent of television election coverage.[32]

Television's leader-centred coverage has had a profound impact on the party system. Before television, political parties played an important role as the meeting-ground between political leaders and the public. Citizens had to go to rallies staged by political parties to see important politicians. This function has been usurped by television. The medium reaches over the heads of the parties to link audiences to leaders directly. In addition, political power brokers like J.G. Gardiner and Alister Grosart, the products of party organizations, were turned to by prime ministers for advice because they had a grasp on the pulse of party and regional politics. Today, pollsters and advertising consultants can become important advisors and strategists without rising through party ranks.

Voters are conditioned by the media's devotion to the politics of leadership. Local candidates and M.P.s have become less important in voters' minds. In national elections, the fate of candidates for Parliament is decided largely by the perceptions of the national leaders, and local candidates are often rendered helpless as the tidal wave of public opinion sweeps across the country. Geoffrey Stevens of the *Globe and Mail* has described the frustration felt by local candidates:

> The role of the local candidate in an election now is if he's lucky he gets to introduce his leader, if his leader happens to come to his town. But if he does get to introduce his leader, he can be darn sure that he's not going to get on television; television isn't going to cover the introduction of the leader. Most of the time his job is simply to keep out of the way of the television cameras so he doesn't block the view of the leader and the band and the balloons.[33]

Even powerful cabinet ministers, once able to assure their elections because of their control over local party machines, are aware that their electoral survival depends on the prime minister's popularity, on the length of his coattails. If he can maintain broad public appeal, a prime minister has enhanced power vis-à-vis his party and Cabinet. Without a demonstrable popularity, his strength among party followers is greatly diminished and he is increasingly vulnerable to challenges. A good media image is the essential glue of party and cabinet control. Some would argue that the ability to perform on television has largely replaced the old requirements such as the dispensing of

patronage, elite recruitment, and the cultivation of a grass-roots party organization as the key element in successful politics.

CONCLUSION

The essential question is whether the media's values and priorities militate against prime ministers' enjoying balanced treatment. A former media manager at the *Toronto Star* has observed that despite the media's oppositionist tendencies, some political leaders have received favourable treatment for prolonged periods. He argues that if the prime minister appears to be pursuing important initiatives and moving rapidly to fulfill an exciting agenda, the media are likely to report these activities fully. When Trudeau moved decisively on the Constitution, and when he mounted his peace initiative, he received positive coverage. During his much-noted periods of reflection, he tended to do poorly in the media, because the media set the agenda according to their own priorities. This journalist's argument is that if leaders pursue substantive policies, and if their agendas coincide with those of the media, the chances of positive coverage increase. Inevitably, however, agendas and vocabularies are not synchronized for long.

The current situation is not without long-term dangers for the political system as a whole. The media's need for conflict and drama, their filtering of the prime minister's message, and their inherent cynicism and predilection to oppose can undermine the prime minister's capacity to use his or her position effectively. The need to survive in the media battlefield is not only becoming more time-consuming, it also threatens to become the key determinant of prime ministerial success. Ultimately the credibility of our highest office is diminished by a journalistic ethic that prizes criticism far more than praise, the sensational over the mundane and methodical, and personality over process.

Notes

All quotes not footnoted are from interviews conducted by the author in 1986.

1. This idea is developed most fully in Fletcher, "The Prime Minister as Public Persuader."

2. Zolf, *Dance of the Dialectic.*

3. Quoted in Cocking, *Following The Leaders,* p. 17.

4. Epstein, *News From Nowhere,* p. 215.

5. Fletcher, "The Prime Minister as Public Persuader," p. 99.

6. Gossage, *Close To The Charisma,* p. 154.

7. Fletcher, "The Prime Minister as Public Persuader," pp. 99-100.

8. Comber and Mayne, *The Newsmongers,* p. 13.

9. Ibid., p. 134.

10. Gossage, *Close To the Charisma,* p. 112.

11. Quoted in Cocking, *Following The Leaders,* p. 33.

12. Ibid.

13. Ibid.

14. Ibid., p. 31.

15. Gossage, *Close To the Charisma,* p. 24.

16. Quoted in West, "The Man in the Middle," p. 28.

17. Quoted in Cocking, *Following The Leaders,* p. 33.

18. Gossage, *Close To the Charisma,* p. 219.

19. Morton, "Television," pp. 43-44.

20. Quoted in Cocking, *Following The Leaders,* p. 139.

21. Ibid., p. 281.

22. Quoted in Fletcher, "The Contest for Media Attention," p. 134.

23. Comber and Mayne, *The Newsmongers,* pp. 131-132.

24. Martin, Gregg and Perlin, *Contenders,* p. 96.

25. Gray, "The P.M.'s office and the media square off."

26. Lichter, Rothman and Lichter, *The Media Elite,* p. 10.

27. Atkinson, *Our Masters' Voices,* pp. 175-6.

28. Meisel, "The Book-Tube Election," p. 175.

29. Newman, *The Distemper of Our Times,* p. 69.

30. Gossage, *Close To the Charisma,* p. 114.

31. Quoted in Fletcher, "The Prime Minister as Public Persuader," p. 88.

32. See Fletcher, "The Contest for Media Attention," and Frizzell and Westell, *The Canadian General Election of 1984.*

33. Stevens, "Prospects and Proposals," p. 102.

CHAPTER 5

The Machinery of Government: From Trudeau's Rational Management to Mulroney's Brokerage Politics

Peter Aucoin

INTRODUCTION

In his comparative study of the central executive systems of the United States, Britain and Canada, Colin Campbell describes the Canadian system of the early 1980s in the following manner:

> Turning to Canada, we find the most institutionalized system of cabinet committees. As well, the most highly differentiated central agencies support ministers' efforts towards collective decision-making. Thus the Canadian arrangements come much closer than the others to fulfilling the canons for institutionalized executive leadership.[1]

By 1985, however, this "most institutionalized system of cabinet committees" with its "most highly differentiated central agencies" had substantially changed in at least two major respects. First, a number of structural alterations had been made; parts of the system had been dismantled and some others had been simplified and streamlined. Second, there was a shift in power at both the political and administrative levels of the central executive system.

These changes resulted primarily from the entry of new prime ministers into office: first, John Turner as the Liberal party leader who replaced Pierre Trudeau, and, second, Brian Mulroney as the Progressive Conservative party

leader whose party defeated Turner's short-lived regime.[2] As Canadian and comparative studies on executive government have made clear, changes in the central machinery of government invariably follow changes in chief executive offices as new political leaders seek to mould structure and process to their personal philosophies of leadership and to their management styles and political objectives.[3] In some instances, changes in structure and process are minor and incremental; in other cases, they are major and substantial. These changes in policy are adopted in order to rearrange power and authority in the central executive system, and thus have an essentially political character. Questions of administrative efficiency and effectiveness need not be ignored in such attempts, but they are secondary considerations.

Following the departure of Pierre Trudeau, the Canadian machinery of government was subjected to a major assault on the executive system most clearly identified with his regime; that is, the PMO, the PCO, and cabinet committees. John Turner concluded that not only was his predecessor's system "too elaborate, too complex, too slow and too expensive," but also, and most importantly, that it had "diffused and eroded and blurred" the responsibilities of the ministers.[4] On the basis of this assessment, he took steps to dismantle and simplify it. He viewed these initial steps as just one part of a process of organizational change, a process that was interrupted by the electoral defeat of his government. However, these changes were not ignored by Brian Mulroney; his government took up the task of further consolidation, simplification and streamlining of the central executive machinery. In addition, and more significantly, Mulroney sought to alter the structure and processes of the central executive system in ways designed to enhance both the role of the prime minister and the functions performed by explicitly "political" officials within his government.

In some respects, the most important alterations of the Mulroney government are reminiscent of a number of developments initiated by Trudeau himself when he first came to power in the late 1960s. In others, however, Prime Minister Mulroney's philosophy of leadership, his management style, and his political objectives stand in sharp contrast to those of Trudeau. The latter's philosophy, style, and objectives of executive leadership constituted a "paradigm" of "rational management."[5] Mulroney's style, objectives, and philosophy are best described as a paradigm of "brokerage politics." Each of these paradigms has different organizational implications for the structure and process of the central machinery of government.

The purpose of this chapter is to describe these different paradigms, to examine their organizational implications, and to assess their respective usefulness for coping with the challenges to executive leadership inherent in the complex arrangements of our modern administrative state.[6] This examination of organizational change at the centre of our system of executive government illustrates not only the significance of the prime minister's prerogatives with respect to the machinery of government, but also the limits imposed by the very complexity that organizational change is meant to address. Two regimes are compared, one lasting a decade and a half, and the other in

office for just a short while. For obvious reasons, this analysis must be tentative in some important respects.

The basic features of a political regime in a parliamentary system of government are shaped by the organizational paradigm of the prime minister. While these can be subject to some evolution and adjustment over time, the evidence, both Canadian and comparative, indicates that change is first and foremost a function of political leadership. This conclusion is not surprising; at the same time, however, it makes clear the need for organizational analysis to be as precise as possible about the paradigms of political leaders and the relationship between them, the organizational design adopted by leaders, and the political and organizational context within which leadership is exercised.[7] The degree of precision that can be applied in organizational analysis is limited, of course, by a number of factors, not the least of which is the fact that the philosophies, styles, and objectives of leaders — their paradigms — are not easily defined as causal variables. But as with the effects of ideas in public policy analysis generally, to ignore what is not easily defined and measured is to ignore what are the most significant determinants of policy.[8]

THE TRUDEAU PARADIGM OF RATIONAL MANAGEMENT

As Bruce Doern noted in his initial work on the policy philosophies of Canadian prime ministers, the fact that Trudeau had written explicitly on his personal political theory prior to his entry into elective office made the task of identifying his philosophy of leadership much more simple than usual.[9] Trudeau professed a "rationalist" philosophy: reason, he argued, should take precedence over all forms of "emotionalism" in government. Within the framework of what he, along with several of his intellectual associates, considered to be a "functionalist" approach to politics, he advocated a non-ideological, even non-partisan, model of governance. His oft-quoted reference to a future in which the science of cybernetics would prevail captures this philosophy succinctly; in the "world of tomorrow," he wrote,

> the state... will need political instruments which are sharper, stronger and more finely controlled than anything based on mere emotionalism: such tools will be made up of advanced technology and scientific investigation, as applied to the fields of law, economics, social psychology, international affairs, and other areas of human relations; in short, if not a pure product of reason, the political tools of the future will be designed and appraised by more rational standards than anything we are currently using in Canada today.[10]

As several observers have stressed at length, this was not mere rhetoric; Trudeau did believe that knowledge would become the basis for political power. He was not alone in this belief, of course, either within his own provincial milieu of Quebec or within the more cosmopolitan setting of world affairs which he considered his intellectual home. His vocation, if not his profession, was that of political philosopher. As an elected politician in the late 1960s this may have made him unique among his peers, especially in Canadian party politics of that time, but he stood for both a major tradition in Western political thought and a trend then current in international politics and intellectual circles. His functional rationalism dovetailed with tenets of the technocracy of state planning in an era which posited the "end of ideology" in modern political life.

In and of itself, however, Trudeau's functional rationalism would not perhaps have had as profound an influence on his role as prime minister if his personal style of leadership had not also placed great emphasis on the essentially liberal concept of the interplay of ideas in the practical realm of decision-making. What functional rationalism was to the search for knowledge through political science, the interplay of ideas was to the application of knowledge in political practice. For Trudeau, as for other liberals, "the theory of checks and balances... translates into practical terms the concept of equilibrium that is inseparable from freedom in the realm of ideas. It incorporates a corrective for abuses and excesses into the very functioning of political institutions."[11]

This style of liberal leadership demands a collegial approach to political decision-making. The fact that it is easily incorporated within the cabinet system of executive government is essentially fortuitous. The style demands a collegial approach precisely because knowledge is best applied to practical concerns when ideas are freely expressed by more than one person; the interplay of ideas created encourages an equilibrium, thus avoiding the abuses and excesses resulting from of a monopoly of ideas by a single authority. The theory of checks and balances, however, requires collegiality primarily to conduct decision-making as an intellectual exercise. It presumes conflict, at least in the realm of ideas. As a style of management, advocated and practised by Trudeau, it does not seek consensus as a managerial norm or ideal. Rather, collective decisions are to be based upon rational debate wherein some ideas prevail and others recede. A consensus may be achieved as a matter of course, but is not sought as an end in itself. It follows, accordingly, that this management style is not that of a manager of a "team." In this sense, there was no obvious contradiction between Trudeau's collegial management style and the fact that "people management" was not his forte.[12]

The political objectives that Trudeau brought to his prime ministership were determined in part by his political philosophy and management style, and in part by his assessment of the prevailing practice of government. With regard to the latter, three situations, in his view, required attention. First, generally speaking, his government had to overcome the tendency to let public policy decisions be determined primarily by partisanship on the one hand and incremental drift on the other. Intense partisanship, as illustrated most clearly in the Diefenbaker-Pearson era, had to be mitigated by the injection of rationality into public policy debate. Incremental policy drift, on the other hand, had to be checked by a commitment to comprehensive policy planning and evaluation.

Second, the relative chaos in cabinet decision-making, in part a function of minority government which prevailed during the Pearson regime, had to be brought under control if a more rational approach to governing was to be implemented and if policy drift was to be checked. This required a greater stress on the collegial dimension of cabinet decision-making, requiring both an increased measure of corporate discipline and a greater formalization of the roles and responsibilities of cabinet committees. The abuses and excesses of individual ministerial autonomy had to be replaced by a rigorous system of checks and balances with the Cabinet as a collective executive.

Third, the influence of the bureaucracy had to be controlled, to ensure that the organizational interests of departments and agencies did not take precedence over required policy innovation and policy coherence. In part this was to be achieved by the assertion of the role of the Cabinet as a collective executive. As Richard French has noted, it was "the Prime Minister's often expressed conviction that the Cabinet is less easily captured by the bureaucracy than are ministers operating independently."[13] In part, as well, this was to be achieved by the expansion of bureaucratic "counterweights" in the form of the central agencies of the prime minister and Cabinet. Trudeau's objective in these two regards did not derive from partisan considerations. As a functional rationalist, he clearly supported the ideal of an expert, knowledgeable and professional bureaucracy as a prerequisite to effective and efficient public administration. As a Liberal prime minister coming to power in the late 1960s, moreover, he had little to fear in terms of "partisanship" in the federal bureaucracy. At the same time, he was well aware, given his

prior administrative and ministerial experience, of the degree to which bureaucratic mandarins were able to manipulate the decision-making system in the service of their own view of sound government. As a matter of general principle, as well as in the pursuit of several specific policy changes, Trudeau insisted on countering the influence of such bureaucratic forces in order to introduce a new perspective on national priorities.

It is the combination of Trudeau's philosophy, style and objectives that makes it possible and plausible to refer to a "paradigm of rational management." As Doern and others have noted, there was in fact a certain evolution in the executive machinery of government from Pearson to Trudeau. The latter's position, however, was that major, not incremental, innovations were required in this machinery; and this he set out to accomplish.

THE ORGANIZATIONAL INSTRUMENTS OF RATIONAL MANAGEMENT

Trudeau inherited from Lester B. Pearson a system of cabinet committees that enabled him to implement his paradigm of rational management without a great deal of structural alteration. Yet his approach to the actual operations and processes of decision-making did require significant change. First and foremost, the committee system had to be managed with a great deal more discipline. This meant increased formalization and more rigid rules and procedures. The primary rationale for such changes was not to use the committee system for the administrative purposes of increased specialization and delegation of authority, thereby reducing the scope of control of the full Cabinet (although each of these administrative purposes was also served). Rather, the intention was to effect a system of checks and balances in accordance with Trudeau's paradigm. This system of checks and balances was meant to ensure that individual ministerial autonomy would be offset by the collective authority of cabinet committees. In addition, the sectoral policy committees of Cabinet were themselves to be subject, on the one hand, to the direction of the Priorities and Planning Committee that was to provide overall integration and coherence, and, on the other hand, to the supervision of specialized co-ordinating committees such as the federal-provincial relations committee, the legislation and house planning committee and the Treasury Board. This matrix arrangement of committees, with its checks and balances and multiple reporting relationships, conformed perfectly to the principles of rational management.

Second, the cabinet committee system also had to be transformed from an arrangement that merely facilitated the processing of an increased volume of cabinet business to a forum for increased attention by ministers to policy planning. Policy planning was considered to be essential if policy drift was to be checked and the practice of disjointed incrementalism was to be avoided. This meant, of course, that ministers would have to spend an increased percentage of their time not only in committees but also in preparation for them. For this to occur, individual ministerial submissions to cabinet committees had to set out the policy alternatives for a given issue and provide comprehensive analyses of them. Ministers were to engage in policy planning; they were not simply to give or withhold final approval to the lone initiative of one of their colleagues. The design was meant as much to control the influence of departmental officials on their respective ministers as it was to control the individual ministers themselves.

In organizational terms, in short, the collegial character of cabinet decision-making had to be enhanced. Individual ministerial responsibility in the strict constitutional sense remained, insofar as the development and administration of departmental policies and programmes was concerned, but individual ministerial autonomy was to give way to an increased

diffusion of power and authority among ministers collectively, the Cabinet and its system of committees.

In order to support the increased attention given to the management of cabinet decision-making and planning processes, the roles of central agencies were expanded and their capacities strengthened.[14] Given the importance attached to the establishment of checks and balances within the decision-making system, it was logical that central agencies would have a critical role to play in providing the prime minister and Cabinet with independent analyses of the departmental proposals prepared for submission to cabinet committees. In addition, therefore, to the traditional secretarial functions required of central agencies, especially the Privy Council Office (PCO) and Treasury Board Secretariat (TBS), a greater emphasis had to be given to ensuring that departmental proposals were assessed in reference to the Cabinet's policy priorities and plans. Second, the importance attached to planning as part of cabinet decision-making demanded that central agencies manage the process of departmental submissions in a way that ensured that policy options were developed and analyses of them were provided. This required increased attention by central agencies to the substance of submissions for cabinet consideration. Finally, central agencies were expected to promote among departments a greater awareness of the need for interdepartmental co-ordination in policy planning and development. In this sense, they were to be among the chief promoters of rational management, with its emphasis on the integration of the total policy system.

This organizational design required that the capacities of the PCO and the TBS be strengthened. The PCO in particular was reorganized, to be better able to provide policy advice. An additional level of hierarchy was added to achieve this, an increased specialization of responsibilities was undertaken and a planning unit was created. A planning branch was also created within the TBS, and TBS management of the budgetary process was reoriented to focus more clearly on its relationship with other policy processes of the cabinet committee system.

In a similar fashion, the Prime Minister's Office (PMO) was strengthened and reorganized. The number of advisors was increased, greater policy specialization was introduced and regional responsibilities were differentiated by the creation of regional "desks." The PMO was also to co-ordinate the activities of the senior political staff of ministers in order to promote adherence to the political objectives of the government as a corporate body. In short, even these political or partisan functions were to conform to the paradigm of rational management.

These organizational instruments were among the most important in the redesign of the central machinery of government in the immediate aftermath of Trudeau's accession to power. The changes that took place in the context of a coherent organizational framework — coherent, that is, with respect to the principal elements of Trudeau's paradigm — prevailed over the decade and a half that Trudeau was prime minister. Although changes in structure and process were introduced as the system grew more elaborate, the central machinery of government in place at the end of his tenure as prime minister had not departed from the paradigm of rational management.

There were three major elaborations of this framework. First, there was the creation of a new type of co-ordinating portfolio and agency: the minister and ministry of state. Second, there was the closer integration of policy and budgetary decision-making through what is now known as the Policy and Expenditure Management System (PEMS). Third, there was increased organizational differentiation with the establishment of new central agencies.

Ministers and ministries of state were established as co-ordinating portfolios and agencies in order to provide both ministerial and admin-

istrative attention to what were called "priority problems": those that did not fall exclusively, or even primarily, within the scope of an existing portfolio, but cut across the mandates of several portfolios. Richard French and the present author described this organizational innovation:

> The ministers of state would be faced with a novel task. The organizations that would serve them would not be departments in any traditional sense, but rather ministries whose initiatives would inevitably and consistently involve the responsibilities of other ministers. Fundamental to the notion of a Ministry of State is the idea that the ideas of research and policy analysis can provide an adequate basis for successful policy formulation and coordination. The logic underlying such a ministry derived from the "knowledge is power" hypothesis: i.e. that research, information and analysis will carry the day in Cabinet and Cabinet committees against the traditional sources of political and bureaucratic power.[15]

The two portfolios and agencies first established according to this new design were the Minister and Ministry of State for Science and Technology and the Minister and Ministry of State for Urban Affairs.

The second and third organizational innovations of greatest significance were interrelated in an important way and also developed in part from the minister and ministry of state phenomenon. The increased integration of policy and expenditure budgets in decision-making developed in response to a number of factors, two of which were critical. On the one hand, the Planning-Programming-Budgeting System (PPBS) that was meant to relate policy and expenditure decision-making through the matrix of the sectoral policy committees of the Cabinet, the priorities and planning committee and the Treasury Board, and their respective central agencies, had not entirely lived up to the expectations of its designers. It had tempered the worst excesses of disjointed incrementalism, perhaps, but it did not eradicate the tendency of individual ministers and departments to independently pursue their own objectives and priorities. On the other hand, as recession and restraint took their toll on the Canadian economy and on government revenues, and thus expenditures, the deficiencies of the decision-making system became glaring. In the attempt to impose even greater discipline on the cabinet committee system, the machinery of government was refined further still in structure and process. The system that emerged was one in which the major sectoral cabinet committees were assigned the responsibility of allocating resources from sectoral expenditure "envelopes" at the same time as they approved policy proposals under PEMS, which replaced PPBS.[16] To assist these committees, new central agencies were created for the major sectors of economic development, social development, and foreign and defence policy. In the case of the first two sectors, new ministries of state were established and headed by ministers of state who chaired their respective sectoral cabinet committees. In the case of foreign and defence policy the secretary of state for external affairs was assisted by a group of central agencies lodged within the reorganized and enlarged portfolio of External Affairs.

The basic framework of this structure and process was put in place with the establishment of a cabinet committee for economic development, along with a minister and ministry of state for this sector, prior to the defeat of the Trudeau government in 1979.[17] The short-lived Conservative government of Prime Minister Joe Clark did not dismantle but rather further developed this innovation as the model for all sectors.[18] The elaboration of the system after Trudeau's return in 1980 provided the basis for the final addition to his "most institutionalized system." In 1982, a major reorganization included a redesign of the economic development sector to extend the responsibility for regional economic development to all ministers of the cabinet committee for economic development, and the creation, within the ministry of state which served this committee (the Ministry of State for Economic and Regional Development, or MSERD), of a system of regional offices in provincial capitals, headed by federal economic development co-ordinators. This "decentralization" of MSERD was a first for the system of central agencies in the federal government. As a consequence, the central agency role, heretofore confined to Ottawa, was now extended to the field, introducing an additional element in the complex matrix of authority and responsibility. These co-ordinators were to advise the cabinet committee served by MSERD, to assist the "regional minister" for their province, and, among other things, to facilitate co-ordination between the regional offices of line departments and agencies in the development and implementation of their policies and programmes.[19]

ASSESSMENT: RATIONAL MANAGEMENT IN PERSPECTIVE

In his assessment of Trudeau's "institutionalized executive leadership," Colin Campbell concluded that "the major difficulties with the Canadian system appear in the nature and organization of officials' support of the prime minister and the Cabinet."[20] In this regard he singled out in particular the following features of Trudeau's system: (1) the "access to cabinet committees enjoyed by Canadian public servants far exceeds that of their opposite numbers in the United States and the United Kingdom"; (2) the "proliferation" of central agencies "overly fragments support to the Cabinet in the very process that attempts to integrate and co-ordinate its efforts"; and (3) "the one explicitly political operation in the centre, the Prime Minister's Office, has yet to develop units that can play sustained independent roles in critical policy decisions."[21] Although Campbell suggested a number of ways in which these difficulties could be addressed, he neglected to point out that they were, to a significant extent, the logical consequence of Trudeau's paradigm of rational management.

Public servants enjoyed access to cabinet committees precisely because the committee system was by design "bureaucratic." When the prime minister wanted this system to work, paying close attention to its operation, it did work, and quite well. But when the prime minister did not provide the necessary leadership and discipline, one of two organizational pathologies tended to occur. On the one hand, some ministers would attempt "end runs" around the system, taking their proposals directly to the Priorities and Planning Committee and thus to the prime minister. On the other hand, the formalities of the process were observed, but departmental officials would end up carrying the ball for ministers who had found better things to do with their time than spending it in committee meetings. Innovations from 1978 onward, with the elaboration of PEMS, improved matters somewhat, because sectoral policy committees acquired important powers with respect to expenditure allocations.[22] Nonetheless, in the latter years of the Trudeau regime even these changes were undermined by several factors, the most important of which was the disintegration of cabinet collegiality as the race to succeed Trudeau took place.

The basic limitation inherent in the Trudeau design of cabinet committees was that, as organizational mechanisms to promote both checks and balances and collective ministerial planning, they depended greatly upon a strong prime ministerial presence. In some measure this was acknowledged. But it was also assumed that, because of the principle of collective responsibility which underlies the cabinet system of responsible government, the norm of cabinet solidarity could be transformed into a system of collegial decision-making wherein ministers would accept direction from other ministers in their own areas of responsibility, given the increased interdependence of government policies and programmes. It presupposed further that because ministers function within a corporate executive headed by a first minister who is more than a "first among equals," the prime minister could, in effect, delegate powers to certain ministers to effect the desired degree of control and co-ordination within cabinet committees.

The fundamental flaw in this design was that it counted on the collegiality of ministers; that is, it was too optimistic about their willingness, in the absence of a strong prime ministerial presence, to compromise personal objectives and departmental ambitions in favour of coherent corporate policies. Like any prime minister, Trudeau had a limited range of personal policy interests and thus his presence could not always be assumed. Within this context, accordingly, substantive priorities and the policies proposed to give effect to them were too often driven by individual ministerial and departmental ambitions. The structures and processes of rational management could not in themselves ensure that checks and balances and planning would satisfy the criteria of the prime minister's paradigm. Nor, in these circumstances, could the chairpersons of cabinet committees, even after the placement of ministers of state at the head of the major sectoral committees, fill the void. They could not function as deputies of the prime minister for their sectors simply because they had been given mandates to effect policy co-ordination. They required prime ministerial support and intervention to be effective. In many instances this was not available in the required degree.

The paradigm of rational management stressed the importance of policy advice and planning at the centre of the decision-making system, which meant that central agencies would be the focus within the Trudeau regime. The limitations of this paradigm would be most obvious at this level. In several respects, the influence of central agencies, wherein the "superbureaucrats" were housed, was significant. Central agency officials were able to frustrate the ambitions of individual ministers to a degree hitherto not witnessed. There were two reasons for this. First, the process of cabinet decision-making by its very character encouraged a greater bureaucratization of the Cabinet. The central figure most identified with the Trudeau paradigm, namely Michael Pitfield, Clerk of the Privy Council and Secretary of Cabinet, said it all when he stated: "My own view is that dealing with the governmental problems of which so many Canadians complain is a matter of process and machinery more than it is a matter of personalities and philosophies."[23] Given that ministers tend to focus on the latter set of factors and not the former, it is little wonder that central agency officials were able to exert considerable influence under Trudeau. Second, as noted, most ministers did not have either the time or the inclination to act collectively. Their natural inclination was to let their colleagues have their own way in their own portfolio domains, except in those circumstances where local or regional implications or ideological differences required them to seek either bilateral compromises or collective showdowns with their colleagues. In most instances, therefore, control and co-ordination, as much by default as by design, devolved upon central agency officials in the pre-cabinet committee process of inter-departmental relations, or within cabinet committees themselves, or both.

The flaw in this aspect of the design was that it depended too much on the capacity of an elaborate system of highly differentiated central agencies to provide integrated policy advice to the prime minister and cabinet committees. Although intended to serve as a counterweight to line-department bureaucracies, the complex system of central agencies also experienced competition from within. This was the case even before 1978, when the major contenders numbered only three — PCO, TBS and the Department of Finance.[24] After the creation of PEMS, three new major contenders were added — MSERD, the Ministry of State for Social Development (MSSD), and the reorganized External Affairs central staff — and the competition intensified accord-

ingly. In the absence of integrated or co-ordinated policy advice, ministers soon learned that they could more or less ignore most of the substance, if not the framework, of the strategic plans developed by these new central agencies even if they agreed to the general (and usually imprecise) set of priorities for their sector. As the system unfolded (or, as some would say, unravelled), Finance, because of its central role in setting the fiscal plan under PEMS, including the determination of major new expenditures, re-emerged as a major force. That it did so is in large part the result of the failure of the system of central agencies to provide for co-ordination among themselves. As one senior central agency official put it:

> It must... be noted that in a system dependent on different subsystems with different lead agencies, immense problems of coordination can arise. The result can be an apparent lack of overall direction in government policy, as if the government had jumped up on its horses and ridden off in all directions.[25]

Finally, it needs to be noted that the PMO, which at the outset of Trudeau's regime appeared to have taken on a major role, did not become the powerful political force in public policy-making that many had assumed it would. Its influence was significant throughout the Trudeau period, although it had its peaks and valleys, but three related factors kept its role a limited, albeit at times a strategic, one. First, in terms of its policy advisory functions, the size of its staff was limited to less than a handful, and it thus depended heavily on the personal capacities and stature of a very few individuals. Of necessity this meant a very narrow span of attention to strategic policy issues — strategic, that is, in terms of the prime minister's personal agenda. As a consequence, a large part of the ongoing agenda was given only limited attention. Second, throughout his tenure as prime minister, Trudeau relied on a number of key ministers whose political judgement on matters of policy he respected highly; he could therefore afford to have a minimal office staff. Third, as noted, Trudeau's Liberal partisanship was not of a kind that led him to distrust the mandarins of the public service on the basis of any perceived anti-Liberal bias. A strong PMO was thus not necessary to counter the bureaucracy with partisan analyses. And, in any event, Trudeau's paradigm stressed the importance of bureaucratic central agencies to provide a counterweight to the bureaucratic ambitions of departmental officials. For this reason, among his key policy advisors were officials from these bureaucratic central agencies, best exemplified by Michael Pitfield in the PCO and Michael Kirby in the Federal-Provincial Relations Office (the latter having also served previously in the PMO). Trudeau, in effect, obtained political advice from several quarters within government, only one of which was the PMO. The paradigm of rational management did not ignore political advice but it certainly downplayed purely partisan advice. For some Liberals this meant exclusion from the centre of power, as bureaucratic officials and a handful of party technocrats were able to control access to the prime minister.

THE MULRONEY PARADIGM OF BROKERAGE POLITICS

Although much press attention was paid to what was perceived to be a lack of specific policy objectives on the part of Brian Mulroney when he became prime minister, other than a general preference for restraint in government and a greater dependency on the private sector to generate economic growth, his philosophy of leadership was clear.[26] Mulroney's philosophy assumes that political leadership is about the accommodation of interests and not the interplay of ideas. Whereas Trudeau was most concerned with the role of knowledge and analysis in the pursuit of comprehensive planning and rational decision-making, Mulroney has a much more political conception of ideal government, namely the pursuit of compromise among competing interests. The differ-

ence, of course, is one of emphasis and degree, but it is critical insofar as it dictates different approaches to leadership. The rationalism of Trudeau made his leadership no less political for his focus on ideas, and the more explicitly political conception of governing that Mulroney brings to his leadership makes him no less rational. But what constitutes rationality and politics is obviously interpreted differently within these two perspectives.

It is important to note in this regard that Mulroney's philosophy of leadership, while it contrasts with that of Trudeau, is not simply or even primarily a reaction to it. Moreover, although both Mulroney's and Trudeau's philosophies owe something to the *zeitgeist* in which they became political leaders, each was developed as a personal perspective on politics. In Mulroney's case, his philosophy of leadership was clearly developed prior to the rise of neo-conservatism in Canada and internationally, increased skepticism about the efficacy of planning by government for state intervention, and the recognition of the limitations of the state in eradicating the clash of interests inherent in the political condition. However one interprets his ideological persuasion on a scale of conservatism or even liberalism, in the traditional understandings of these ideologies, it is clear that Mulroney, with his emphasis on the need to accommodate political, social and economic interests, upholds the tradition of both Robert Stanfield and William Lyon Mackenzie King in his philosophy of political leadership.[27]

It is not surprising, given this philosophy, that Mulroney's leadership style is transactional rather than collegial. His preference is to deal with people one-on-one rather than on a collective basis. The logic here, of course, is that this transactional style facilitates compromise among differing points of view much more than does the collegial process, where the checks and balances lead more readily to stalemates if different points of view are strongly held. The contrast with Trudeau is again obvious. Mulroney's philosophy, in comparison to

Trudeau's, assumes a greater degree of conflict over interests and thus implies a different priority to be given to their resolution. It follows that Mulroney's style seeks compromise and does not promote checks and balances.

The leadership style of Mulroney, with its emphasis upon personal transaction between the leader and his executive colleagues, does not imply that Mulroney does not value a consensus among his colleagues as a corporate executive. Indeed, as a strategy of management, consensus as an end in itself is given a high priority. In this sense Mulroney's style required that he be a leader of a "team" and, accordingly, that "people management" be among his main concerns as chief executive officer. As noted, however, the requirement does not demand collegial decision-making in the manner of Trudeau's design.

The political objectives which Mulroney brought to his prime ministership were in some measure determined by both his philosophy and style. They were also in part determined by his assessment of the current practice of government. At one level, the political objectives of Prime Minister Mulroney upon taking office were focussed on the need for political leadership to effect a "reconciliation," as it was termed, among the two orders of government in Canada on the one hand and major socioeconomic interests on the other. Mulroney's assessment of the legacy he inherited, an assessment widely shared, was that both federal-provincial relations and government-business-labour relations had deteriorated to the point where a major effort to reach new accords or accommodations was imperative. More specific to the structures and processes of governing, although related to his initial intentions, Mulroney's new objective required that his government take the initiative in determining ways and means to reach this reconciliation. Action rather than planning was to be the norm for political leadership, even if action was to involve much discussion with the affected parties. In some measure, of course, this focus on

"action" was political rhetoric, but so too had been Trudeau's focus on "planning." However, it was also more than simply rhetoric. This was evidenced by the effort of the prime minister and his cabinet colleagues to assert their authority over the administrative branch of government, including the "superbureaucrats" in central agencies.

"Bureaucracy-bashing" constituted a significant element in Mulroney's campaign for the leadership of his party as well as in the national election campaign of 1984. It was a function both of the perceived public opinion about bureaucracy that has become part of our contemporary politics, and of the fact that the Conservative party has played such a minor, almost negligible, role in the development of our national administrative state, especially in the staffing of the senior ranks within the federal bureaucracy. Because of this, there is an obvious similarity between what Trudeau and Mulroney, on assuming office, set out to accomplish with respect to political control of the bureaucracy. At the same time, however, Mulroney as a Conservative prime minister in the mid-1980s was in a very different situation from Trudeau in the late 1960s. Trudeau, as noted, did not confront a bureaucracy that was perceived to be an obstacle to the government in any partisan sense; Mulroney, in contrast, was confronted by a bureaucracy that was quite definitely perceived to be such an obstacle, if not in terms of party partisanship then at least in terms of policy partisanship. Whereas Trudeau simply wanted to overcome bureaucratic resistance to policy innovation per se, Mulroney's objective was to overcome bureaucratic resistance to "conservative" policy innovations, innovations considered not only contrary to the "liberal interventionist" preferences of the bureaucracy, but also counter to bureaucratic interests in "big government," with all that these entail for the personal rank and status of individual mandarins.

It is Mulroney's philosophy, style and objectives, then, that make it possible and plausible to refer to a "paradigm of brokerage politics." This is not to suggest that this paradigm is unique to Mulroney. But it is sufficiently different from that of rational management to require a radical change in the machinery of government.

THE ORGANIZATIONAL INSTRUMENTS OF BROKERAGE POLITICS

Prior to the 1984 national election that brought Brian Mulroney to office, John Turner presided as prime minister for several months. As noted earlier, he quickly proceeded to dismantle a good part of the machinery of government installed by Trudeau. In addition to a reduction in the number of ministers and cabinet committees, he eliminated the minister of state portfolios as chairs to two cabinet committees (Economic and Regional Development and Social Development), the central agencies (MSERD and MSSD) that served them, along with the central agency group in the Department of External Affairs that served the chairman and members of the cabinet committee on Foreign and Defence Policy, and the "mirror committees" of deputy ministers for each of these three committees. He also simplified the procedures of cabinet committees. It is clear that these steps would have occurred in any event with the coming to power of Brian Mulroney. Indeed, on assuming office, Mulroney immediately undertook a further rationalization of cabinet committees, a consolidation of the "envelopes" under PEMS and a further simplification of the procedures of the cabinet decision-making system.

These organizational changes have served to diminish what Doern, in describing the early Trudeau changes, characterized as "the differentiation and bureaucratization of roles and organizations in the executive arena" and which, he suggested, "may, in the long run, constrain the Prime Minister's power."[28] The Mulroney system, in reducing the "formaliza-

tion of policy organizations and procedures,"[29] downplayed the importance of the cabinet committee system. The need for the Cabinet to accommodate a variety of interests in public policy (in accordance with Mulroney's philosophy), his transactional style of executive management, and his objectives of reconciliation have each in their own way required the prime minister's freedom from tightly organized and collegial processes of planning and decision-making. Greater flexibility, and thus uncertainty, invariably enhance the power of the prime minister vis-à-vis his cabinet colleagues, thereby increasing opportunities for certain ministers to deal with pressing priorities without requiring that the initiatives be put through numerous hoops of collective decision-making.

The most important organizational implication of this approach is an increased concentration of power under the prime minister. With the largest federal Cabinet ever (forty members at the outset), such a concentration was in some respects inevitable. This has meant a relatively greater role for the Priorities and Planning Committee, chaired of course by the prime minister, as this committee constitutes the executive committee or Inner Cabinet, or, indeed, "the Cabinet" insofar as the strategic decisions of the political executive are concerned. Those ministers who are not members of this committee are simply part of the "ministry", notwithstanding their membership in the Cabinet. However, even with respect to the Priorities and Planning Committee as the executive committee, the prime minister requires a considerable degree of autonomy in order to negotiate on a one-to-one basis with his key ministers.

This change is, of course, relative, but by no means is it a minor one. The pre-eminence of the prime minister is inherent in our constitutional and political system, but the Mulroney paradigm of brokerage politics demands that the powers of the prime minister be exercised to the fullest. In this sense it involves more than simply prime ministerial presence to support collective decision-making. It also involves a significant personal intervention in those areas of priority for the prime minister and his government. The prime minister in this sense becomes the principal counterweight to ministerial ambitions that are not in accord with his policies, priorities or strategy.

To assist the prime minister in this role the position of Deputy Prime Minister has been enhanced. It was declared at the outset that the deputy prime minister would have "a substantial role and authority in the Ministry."[30] The first appointment to this position, Erik Nielsen, was made Vice-Chairman of Cabinet and the Priorities and Planning Committee, given responsibility for "government communications", and chosen to chair an ad hoc cabinet committee (called a ministerial task force) to review and assess all government programmes.[31] Nielsen was selected for this position as the minister most likely to be able to keep a firm hand on the behaviour of ministers. For a number of reasons, Nielsen proved unequal to the task. His successor, Donald Mazankowski, has not only proved to be more suitable but has demonstrated that the initial intention to have a deputy prime minister with "a substantial role and authority in the Ministry" could be a significant innovation in the executive system. In addition to his role as Chairman of the Communications Committee, Vice-Chairman of the Priorities and Planning Committee, and House Leader, Mazankowski chairs a quasi-formal cabinet committee on "operations" which includes the chairman of cabinet committees and which, as a de facto subcommittee of the Priorities and Planning Committee, serves as an executive management committee to direct and orchestrate the flow of cabinet business. In these roles the deputy prime minister receives support not only from the PCO but also from what is essentially a new office — the Deputy Prime Minister's Office. The DPMO constitutes an important constitutional manifestation of the expanded role given to the deputy prime minister as "chief executive officer." The

quasi-formality of this role in fact frees the prime minister from the necessity of performing many of these functions himself, reduces his reliance on the bureaucratic cabinet secretariat — the PCO — and maintains the flexibility of the system by minimizing its formality. In each of these respects, the objectives of the prime minister's paradigm are effectively secured.

The Mulroney paradigm has also meant that the PMO assumes an enhanced role at the apex of power. It was given the primary responsibility for managing the transformation of personnel under the new regime. All appointments made under the prerogative of the Crown were to be managed by the PMO. This centralization of appointments was to ensure close attention to the personal allegiances and partisan dispositions of those considered for appointment to key administrative positions as well as to federal government boards, commissions, councils, and the like. The PMO also played a central role in the selection of ministerial "chiefs of staff," an intended elevation of the rank of top ministerial political aides, in line with the objective that ministers receive advice from political officials who are sensitive to the priorities and concerns of the prime minister.

More importantly, the PMO was to assume a greater role in the decision-making process vis-à-vis the bureaucratic central agencies that support the prime minister and Cabinet. This happened not only because of the concentration of power under the prime minister, but also because his transactional style and his emphasis on negotiation as a critical leadership function demand a more active personal office, active, that is, in promoting the strategic policy initiatives of the prime minister as well as his partisan political concerns. Accordingly, the staff of this office was immediately increased by one third, with a budget over fifty percent higher than that allotted to it in Trudeau's final year in office. Of more significance, the number of "professional" staff concerned with policy advice, broadly defined, went from less than a handful to over a dozen.

This expansion of the PMO, it is now clear, was not simply the function of a new government coming to office, as it had been when Trudeau first assumed power. Rather it was, and continues to be, the organizational consequence of a different prime ministerial paradigm, one that extends to relations among all ministers and the public service bureaucracy. Its pervasiveness is evidenced by the new institution of the deputy prime minister's office and the elevated status of the "chiefs of staff" in ministers' offices generally. Although it would be inaccurate to suggest that relations among ministers (including the prime minister), their political officials and their public service advisors have been radically or fundamentally altered, there has been a relative change not only as regards the previous regime but in terms of the Canadian federal tradition. In some portfolios, to be certain, there has been little or no change; at the centre and not only in the PMO, however, political advisors have been given a greater role to play.

This relative "politicization" of the decision-making process, nonetheless, has not resulted in a politicization of the public service bureaucracy. Appointments below the level of deputy minister — the senior administrative position in departments and agencies — have remained "public service" appointments. Appointments to deputy positions, made by the prime minister under his prerogative powers as "order-in-council" appointments, have not departed from the Canadian federal tradition. Although a few external appointments have been made (external, that is, to the public service), this is not unusual and in no case has the appointment been regarded as either patronage or partisanship. From both a strategic and a symbolic point of view, the most crucial appointment to date has been that of the incumbent Secretary to Cabinet and Clerk of the Privy Council, Paul Tellier. Had this position, regarded as the most senior public service position, been given to someone regarded as politically partisan, as has in fact occurred in

some provincial government regimes, the traditionally non-partisan character of the PCO as Cabinet's public service secretariat and the prime minister's public service department would surely have been seriously undermined.

The appointment in 1986 of Dalton Camp, long-time *éminence grise* within the Conservative party, as a senior prime ministerial and cabinet advisor within the PCO did not, as might be feared, raise the spectre of politicization of the cabinet secretariat. This possibility was averted when Camp's position was clarified as "political advisor" sui generis. In one sense the designation sui generis is obvious, given the personality involved. In another sense, however, his appointment points up and helps to redress an obvious imbalance between the PMO and the PCO. The former serves the prime minister as party leader and head of the governing party. The latter serves the prime minister as head of the government; but it also serves the Cabinet as a collective executive. The PMO is involved in the business of Cabinet, but its structure and functions do not, for the most part, encompass the operations of the Cabinet in a way that matches those of the PCO. In short, "the capacity of the political arm of government", as a former Secretary to Cabinet put it, is not as "strong" as it should be.[32] Camp's position, as well as the office of the deputy prime minister, can thus be viewed as the strengthening of the "political arm of government."

The enhanced importance of the PMO and the enlargement of its policy capability was meant to have obvious implications for the roles of other central agencies, and in particular the Privy Council Office. With a less complex system and especially with less emphasis on planning, the PCO's role as a centre of administrative power has been downplayed. However, without the ministries of state and the mirror committees of deputy ministers which supported the three major policy committees, the PCO, as the "process" secretariat for cabinet business, does brief the Prime Minister and committee chairpersons on the policy issues before them. As a consequence, and especially since the PMO is meant to assist the prime minister in assuring that the policy proposals of ministers are in line with the prime minister's objectives and priorities, the PCO has become more highly structured in order to relate to the political staff in the PMO and ministers' offices. This increased formalization at the central bureaucratic level has been effected precisely because of the greater informality at the ministerial and political level that results from Mulroney's management style. This increased formalization of the structure of the PCO does not amount to increased clout within the centre, however; rather, it reflects an effort to cope with a greater diffusion of power at the centre, particularly in the direction of the political arm of government (the PMO).

The Department of Finance and the Treasury Board Secretariat have also benefitted from the elimination of the ministries of state which served as specialized central agencies to the sectoral policy committees of Cabinet. The former had in fact wrested back a good deal of power in the final two years of the Trudeau government, but with the elimination of the ministries of state, its position as chief financial and economic advisor to the prime minister, the Priorities and Planning Committee and the sectoral policy committees was strengthened. With a new Mulroney appointment to the deputy minister's post, the Department's position was enhanced even further. In large part, this latter factor has been critical because it has meant close relations among the senior Finance public servant, the Minister of Finance's political aides and senior advisors in the PMO. These close relations are crucial to the prime minister's approach in that the fiscal budget, as well as the expenditure budget, constitute central policy instruments of brokerage politics, with its emphasis on the distributive questions of who gets what. They must be subject, accordingly, to the active involvement of the prime minister and his office.

ASSESSMENT: BROKERAGE POLITICS IN PERSPECTIVE

Successful implementation of the paradigm of brokerage politics depends largely upon two related factors. The first is the capacity of the prime minister to retain his pre-eminence as a chief executive officer who can intervene effectively in the domains of other ministers in order to accomplish personal objectives. This intervention has been frequent and includes all major areas of government policy — fiscal, foreign, economic development and social. Mulroney's reach has not only been extensive, it has also taken at least some of the ministers by surprise. Given his personal style, however, such intervention is not surprising: his own policy agenda has been kept close to the vest, and "uncertainty," as Doern notes, "is part and parcel of this leadership style."[33]

This mode of prime ministerial intervention requires that the prime minister be able to keep his ministers, especially his senior ministers, on side. To date, Mulroney appears to have been able to do so, notwithstanding his and his party's decline in public support as measured by public opinion polls. There are two possible reasons for this. On the one hand, the major policy objectives of the party are being pursued, particularly with respect to fiscal and economic policies. Mulroney has not tried to change course, nor are there demands from within his Cabinet that he do so. On the other hand, the most senior ministers of Mulroney's Cabinet have been as perplexed as the Prime Minister by the degree to which "political" problems have overshadowed what they perceive to be the "policy" accomplishments of this government. In both these respects the Prime Minister has been able to secure Cabinet's solidarity for his personal objectives. His transactional style is obviously an asset, as it means that his efforts at intervention are managed at the level of individual ministers and not at the level of Cabinet as a collective.

Although the prime minister's paradigm of

brokerage politics remains essentially intact, the key to its effective functioning has revolved around the willingness of the prime minister to delegate important responsibilities to a select number of senior ministers. The Nielsen Task Force on Program Review was one such example. The restoration of the Foreign and Defence Policy Committee, chaired by Secretary of State for External Affairs Joe Clark, was another. Support for Finance Minister Michael Wilson's policies of fiscal restraint constitutes a third example, and the use of Deputy Prime Minister Don Mazankowski as "general manager" is a fourth. Such delegations do not depart from the prime minister's paradigm so long as he is able to play the role of chief executive officer with the discretion to intervene. The relative flexibility of this system of senior ministers serves to maintain this discretion.

In a related vein, the prime minister has reinstated the position and role of "regional ministers," part of a system that at the outset he tried to discourage. Its reinstatement was obviously a belated recognition of the limits of his own capacity to effect a national reconciliation of regional differences on the one hand, and the inability of his party — Cabinet and caucus — to resolve such differences simply on the basis of their pan-Canadian representation. The centralization of power under the prime minister, even with an overriding concern for the political dimensions of national policy, has its limits as a device for ensuring that the regional interests in national policy are well represented and, equally important, that they are seen to be well represented. As with previous governments, however, even a system of regional ministers, appended to the regular structure of ministerial portfolios, has its own limits, especially in terms of public visibility. Moreover, the strategic priorities of the Mulroney government, in both their political and policy implications, do not augur well for national reconciliation of regional differences, whatever their internal logic and coherence. Fiscal restraint,

free trade and private sector economic development policies have differential regional effects, especially for the "have-not" provinces.

The second factor that will determine whether the paradigm of brokerage politics is implemented successfully is the capacity of the Prime Minister's Office to provide not only political advice but also strategic policy advice. Both its enhanced organizational capacity and the support of the Prime Minister have enabled the PMO to extend its sphere of interest to include a wide range of policy areas. With the Prime Minister's blessing, for instance, the PMO was more intimately involved than usual in the preparation of the government's first budget. The PMO, and in particular the principal secretary, have covered policy as well as political issues relating to Quebec with a comprehensiveness that probably exceeds even the practice of the Trudeau regime, its overriding concern with the place of Quebec in the federal system notwithstanding.

The concentration of power under the prime minister cannot in itself ensure the effectiveness of the PMO as a central agency, however powerful it might be. Its record thus far is not much evidence that it has been able to manage and co-ordinate the decision-making system in ways that facilitate the prime ministerial leadership necessary for effective brokerage politics.[34] In most instances where Mulroney has intervened in the domains of other ministers, for example in fiscal, foreign and economic development policies, the intervention has been in reaction to ministerial or even cabinet decisions already taken and made public. This reactive interventionism may be indicative of a close monitoring of public opinion by the PMO, but it hardly speaks well of its capacity to either anticipate the political implications of policy decisions or to ensure that it is fully briefed on ministerial intentions.

In large part, the problems that have been experienced by the PMO are due to the fact that the policy agenda of the Mulroney government was so comprehensive at the start. A new regime inevitably overloads such a central agency, but in this instance the stress was especially great. This was compounded, of course, by the concentration of power under the prime minister, with its obvious implications for the PMO. In addition, the senior staff brought in by Mulroney were themselves new to government: the freshman prime minister had freshmen for advisors. The shuffle of his senior advisors in early 1987, after much public and private commentary on their capacities, including the appointment of a "chief of staff" from the permanent public service and the restructuring of the PMO, constituted a belated recognition of the deficiencies in the original design of the political-bureaucratic interface at the apex of power, especially considering the inexperienced individuals involved at this level.

It is now clear that Mulroney, despite the work of his transition team, had not carefully thought through just how to deploy the concentration of power in his position and his office in the operation of the cabinet decision-making process and the roles of bureaucratic central agencies which support it. The cabinet committee system can be arranged, it is clear, to serve a number of different purposes, depending on the prime minister's model of political leadership. Yet, it is also clear that the complexity of the national government obliges it to at least serve to process the tremendous volume of public business that must be addressed by ministers. In this sense, there are administrative requirements that demand an efficient committee system for cabinet government even when power is concentrated under the prime minister. Secondly, bureaucratic central agencies are crucial to these operations if they are to be managed effectively, even when the lead advisory role in policy is assumed by political officials in the Prime Minister's Office. On both of these counts, and they are obviously connected, the redesign of the central machinery of government, as undertaken during Mulroney's first two years in office, was faulty. The result has been, on the one hand, an overbur-dened prime minister and Priorities and Planning Committee, with a relatively inoperative cabinet committee system, and on the other hand, an overworked Prime Minister's Office with an underutilized Privy Council Office.[35]

CONCLUSIONS

The thesis advanced in this chapter is that the leadership paradigms of prime ministers — their philosophies of governance, their management styles and their political objectives — are the chief determinants in the organizational design of the central machinery of government. In the Canadian case, the prerogative powers of the prime minister are more than sufficient to change the executive organization inherited from a previous regime to fit a new paradigm. As noted, such change need only be minor or incremental, but when required it can be major or radical. The changes introduced by Trudeau in the late 1960s were clearly of the latter character. It has been argued here that Mulroney's leadership paradigm has introduced comparably major or radical changes in the structures and processes of the central machinery of government.

As also noted, however, the introduction of a new leadership paradigm by a new prime minister does not occur in an intellectual or political vacuum. However personal a prime minister's paradigm may be, it cannot help but be influenced by the intellectual and political environment in which a leader assumes office. The actual organizational design that is adopted to implement a new paradigm will therefore reflect in large measure the intellectual and political realities of the times. In the case of Trudeau, this was most evident when he assumed office. What is perhaps even more significant for the thesis advanced here is that his paradigm of rational management continued to be the driving force throughout his tenure as prime minister. Indeed, the organizational manifestation of his paradigm reached its zenith in his final design of 1982.

In the case of Mulroney, the intellectual and political environment when he assumed office in 1984 provided more than sufficient support for the replacement of the paradigm of rational management. What is less certain, however, is whether the paradigm of brokerage politics, especially Mulroney's version of it, is the most appropriate replacement. In some respects — its transactional management style and its objective of political control over the administrative state — it is clearly in tune with these neoconservative times. In other respects, however, it is more problematic. This is particularly the case in regard to its philosophy of accommodation, which gives priority to reconciliation of diverse interests and, in so doing, may undermine the perceived need for a major reordering of policy priorities away from the interventionism of the liberal welfare state. Accommodation and reconciliation, from the perspective of neoconservatism, can too easily lead to compromises of policy priorities. The experience to date confirms this tendency. In a number of important respects it is clear that Mulroney's paradigm is not entirely consistent with neoconservatism, and especially not with the version practised in the United States by Ronald Reagan, in Britain by Margaret Thatcher, or in British Columbia by Bill Bennett. Mulroney may not be a "red Tory" in the strict definition of this Canadian conservative tradition, but his philosophy of governance is certainly more populist than that of some of his neoconservative contemporaries.

The implications of all this for Mulroney and his government as they develop greater experience in the job cannot be stated with any great certainty, of course. Nonetheless, both Canadian and comparative studies would suggest that his basic paradigm and its design of the central machinery of government will prevail. As studies by Campbell and others have demonstrated, paradigms, and thus major organizational change, occur only with new leaders. At the same time, this does not preclude adjustments and modifications within a basic frame-

work of political and bureaucratic power. As noted, a more efficient and effective management of government requires that Mulroney make better use of both his cabinet committees and the central agencies of Cabinet, particularly the PCO. The ultimate test of his paradigm, however, will inevitably be his capacity and that of his office to provide coherent and co-ordinated political leadership and public policy. The final verdict on his regime's performance, of course, will depend upon a great deal more.

Notes

1. Campbell, *Governments Under Stress,* p. 351.

2. For a description of these changes, see Clark, "Recent Changes in the Cabinet Decision-Making System in Ottawa."

3. In addition to Campbell, *Governments Under Stress,* see Doern, "Recent Changes in the Philosophy of Policy Making in Canada"; and Seidman, *Politics, Position and Power.*

4. Office of the Prime Minister, Ottawa, *Release,* 17 September 1985.

5. See, for instance, Doern and Aucoin, *Public Policy in Canada.*

6. The analysis in this study is restricted to the paradigms of Trudeau and Mulroney. This is not to imply that the changes introduced by either Joe Clark or John Turner were not based upon their personal paradigms. On Clark, for example, see Doern and Phidd, *Canadian Public Policy.* By restricting the analysis to Prime Ministers Trudeau and Mulroney, however, it is possible to consider in some depth the relationships between their paradigms and their organization of the central machinery of government, and to do so within the limits of a single article.

7. The Trudeau regime has been analyzed extensively by students of Canadian politics and public administration. The treatment here draws upon these analyses. It is necessary, however, to consider the Trudeau regime at some length in order to look systematically at the effects of the three principal dimensions of

his paradigm, and to do so not only with hindsight but also in contrast to another major paradigm.

8. See, for instance, King, "Ideas, Institutions, and the Policies of Governments."

9. Doern, "Recent Changes in the Philosophy of Policy Making in Canada."

10. Trudeau, *Federalism and the French-Canadians,* p. 203.

11. Ibid., p. xxiii.

12. See Radwanski, *Trudeau.*

13. French, "The Privy Council Office," p. 365.

14. See Doern, "The Development of Policy Organizations in the Executive Arena."

15. Aucoin and French, *Knowledge, Power and Public Policy,* p. 12.

16. See Van Loon, "The Policy and Expenditure Management System in the Federal Government."

17. See French, *How Ottawa Decides,* pp. 120-32.

18. Clark's use and elaboration of this innovation, it should be noted, was not to refine collegial decision-making but rather to introduce greater control over government spending. As such, greater efficiency in government was to be achieved through control of the Cabinet and bureaucracy by his Inner Cabinet. See Doern and Phidd, *Canadian Public Policy,* pp. 194-96.

19. See Aucoin and Bakvis, "Regional Responsiveness and Government Organization."

20. Campbell, *Governments Under Stress,* p. 351.

21. Ibid., pp. 351-52.

22. See, again, Van Loon, "The Policy and Expenditure Management System in the Federal Government," and his chapter in French, *How Ottawa Decides.*

23. Michael Pitfield, Speech to the Empire Club, Toronto, 20 October 1983, quoted in Matheson, "The Cabinet and the Canadian Bureaucracy," p. 278.

24. See French, *How Ottawa Decides.*

25. Van Loon, "The Policy and Expenditure Management System in the Federal Government," p. 285.

26. See Simeon, "Prime Minister Brian Mulroney and Cabinet Decision-Making."

27. On the "accommodative" approach of King, see Smith, "Party Government, Representation and National Integration in Canada," especially pp. 20-25.

28. Doern, "The Development of Policy Organizations in the Executive Arena," p. 74.

29. Ibid.

30. Office of the Prime Minister, Ottawa, *Release,* 17 September 1984.

31. Ibid.

32. Osbaldeston, "The Public Servant and Politics," p. 6.

33. Doern, "The Development of Policy Organizations in the Executive Arena."

34. The most incisive analysis of the effectiveness of the PMO during the first year of the Mulroney government is provided by Simpson in "Problems in the PMO."

35. See Simpson, "The Missing System."

CHAPTER 6

Friends and Foes: Prime Ministers and Premiers in Intergovernmental Relations

Donald C. Wallace

One of the most notable features of Canadian politics is the political bargaining occurring between the federal and provincial governments over the past twenty-five years. This process, which Donald Smiley has called "executive federalism,"[1] is characterized by ongoing negotiations between elected and appointed officials of the two orders of government. Executive federalism developed as governments recognized the overlap of their jurisdictions, the differences between their legislation, and the extent of their interdependence. Although all federal systems must engage in some form of bargaining between various levels of government, few have such an extensive network of interaction, or such a reliance on intergovernmental mechanisms to resolve differences, as does Canada.

Over the years, co-operation has been required and a unique network of formal consultation, as well as joint co-operative programmes and fiscal transfers, have grown out of extensive negotiations. As these discussions embrace a larger number of issues, their most important format has been the federal-provincial conference, especially the First Ministers' Conference (FMC), where the prime minister and the ten provincial premiers tackle the country's more intractable problems. These conferences deal with the major policy issues,

including constitutional reform, and have been held with regularity since the 1960s. Yet the FMC is a curious institution. Governments come to FMCs with differing goals. Successive Quebec governments, for example, have regarded the FMC as the primary arena for pressing the province's case for an extension of its constitutional powers. Provinces aggrieved with the federal government are likely to use FMCs to gain allies and publicity for their cases. Many provincial premiers have sought the sympathy of their local electorates by vehemently pointing out the negative consequences of national policies. Such premiers will seize the opportunity of an FMC to remind constituents who is to blame for their problems: Ottawa. Similarly, premiers from the richer provinces will complain that the economy is being poorly managed by the federal government. First ministers must participate in several games simultaneously in order to retain their authority within Cabinet and caucus.[2] Given the frequency of elections in Canada, at least one of the eleven leaders is likely to be focussing on the electoral game at any given time.

The position of the prime minister in the face of such challenges from the provinces is a difficult one. He does not have recourse to the sorts of arguments advanced by the premiers; furthermore, the responsibility of chairing the conference limits the extent to which he can take issue at all with the claims of the premiers. Smiley observes that the prime minister is "at the same time chairman, head of a government with interests to defend, and the leader of a national political party."[3] The FMC is a graphic illustration of the fact that power in Canada is shared; *national* decision-making is perceived not as directed by the federal government but rather as the result of the federal-provincial process. For a number of reasons, provincial premiers over the last twenty-five years have come to regard themselves as the sole legitimate representatives of regional interests, and have increasingly sought to have an input in national policy-making.

In many ways, the provincial premiers have assumed the role of the opposition within the Canadian political system. Since World War II and particularly since 1960, the power of the federal government has declined, while that of the provincial governments has grown. It is this increased power, boosting the confidence and assertiveness of the provinces, which more than anything else has altered the balance of Canadian federalism. Provincial governments naturally have a constitutional place in the Canadian political system, but this fact has not prevented conflicts between the two levels of government; for example, in the late 1880s, Sir John A. Macdonald found himself at variance with the governments of Ontario and Quebec over the question of provincial rights.[4] While a federal constitution necessarily has a degree of tension built into it, which is in part a product of the distribution of legislative powers, and considered normal and constructive, conflict has been exacerbated, most notably since the Second World War, when the Constitution ceased to act as an accurate guide to the powers and responsibilities of the respective levels of government. The division of powers grants significant exclusive powers to each level of government, with the result that, in many areas, incentives to co-operate are lacking. In areas such as energy policy, both the federal and the provincial levels of government have impressive constitutional resources. Indeed, this is true of economic policy in general. In addition, constitutional authority is quite evenly matched by political power, so that it is difficult for either level to dominate policy.

A major reason for the ascendancy of the provinces in the federal-provincial system is the wide recognition which has been accorded to the provincial premiers. They are undoubtedly the best-known political figures in the country, after the prime minister, and have numbered many colourful individuals in their ranks in recent years. Once parochial officials whose interests rarely extended beyond the boundaries of their provinces, premiers nowadays exercise significant new powers, and have increased their influence in national as well as provincial arenas. Once intransigent foes of the federal government (e.g., Hepburn and Duplessis), premiers have become skilled negotiators and key players in the intergovernmental game. While in the United States the corresponding office of state governor is often a stepping-stone to national political office — the last two American presidents have been state governors — relatively few provincial premiers seek election to the federal Parliament. Not since 1967, when two provincial premiers contested the leadership of the federal Progressive Conservative party, have sitting premiers abandoned their significant power bases to move to Ottawa, and there is little likelihood of such a tradition arising, since some premiers have built their careers on a healthy measure of "fed-bashing."

The growth in the stature of provincial premiers can be observed from their crowded public agendas. Premiers devote themselves to a wide variety of social, health, educational, and economic concerns; matters such as the environment, transportation, women's issues, and consumer protection have been added in recent years. Simultaneously, provincial bureaucracies have matured greatly, especially in the larger provinces, and are now equipped with the resources necessary to challenge the federal government. As a group, provincial premiers are creative, forward-looking and experienced. This is a far cry from an era when premiers were insignificant individuals with little to attend to. Premiers have asserted their executive leadership in a time when overall confidence in the federal government has waned.

The story of governmental decision-making in Canada is one of sharing responsibilities. The most important dimension of that sharing is between the federal and provincial governments and among first ministers. A clear understanding of the key issues facing Canada cannot be achieved without reference to intergovernmental relations. This chapter focusses on the primary decision-making forum of federal-provincial relations — the First Ministers' Conference — and assesses the impact of the leadership style of recent prime ministers in the intergovernmental arena. The chapter concludes with a discussion of some of the factors which contribute to success in intergovernmental relations at the summit.

FIRST MINISTERS' CONFERENCES

The FMC has evolved into one of the most significant institutions not only of Canadian intergovernmental relations but of the entire Canadian political process. Many citizens do not fully perceive the importance of FMCs, believing that the key decisions are made in Parliament. Part of this misperception is the result of the modest appearance of FMCs. They occur irregularly and often long periods of time pass between full-scale FMCs. Not all FMCs are held in public in the glare of the television lights; even at televised conferences, most hard bargaining and important negotiating takes place behind closed doors. According to one veteran journalist, "public sessions of the conference are for show, the private lunches and dinners are for work."[5] Moreover,

FMCs lack any of the symbolism normally associated with parliamentary government. During the Trudeau years, most took place in the National Conference Centre, a converted railway station a short distance from the Parliament buildings. The conference room itself is a spartan, utilitarian television studio. Since Brian Mulroney has come to office, he has held some key FMCs outside of Ottawa, in order to create the impression that his government is more sensitive to regional feelings than were the governments of his predecessors. These latter conferences have taken place in nondescript hotel meeting-rooms. With the notable exception of the 1981 Constitutional Accord, FMCs have rarely produced monumental public statements or agreements readily comprehensible to the country at large. Communiqués released at the end of FMCs are vague documents pitched at the broad level of principle. They are usually the product of negotiations among officials taking place at the same time as discussions between the prime minister and the premiers, and are distributed to reporters after hasty photocopying.

While federal-provincial interaction takes place at all levels within the public services of both levels of government, it has long been accepted that important policy questions must in the end be dealt with at the top political level. The concentration of executive decision-making in the offices of prime ministers and premiers is perhaps even more pronounced in the federal-provincial arena than in other policy arenas. Richard Simeon noted some of the advantages and disadvantages of summit federalism more than a decade ago. In some cases, this "may make for easier resolution of conflicts because the political heads can make firm commitments [on behalf] of their own governments, but it may also mean that conflicts become much more sharply defined and therefore more intractable."[6] The increasingly central position of federal-provincial issues in the political system has led to greater reliance on FMCs.

Issues tend to be brought to the summit because they are difficult to resolve or involve high stakes. They tend to reflect the long-term interests of the provinces — economic or cultural — along with matters of central concern to all governments: jurisdiction, revenue, fiscal control, legitimacy, electoral success, and so forth. The desire for public attention — or politicization — can also be a factor. In addition, some essentially technical issues have come to the summit as central agencies have struggled to exert control over programme officials or to ensure that broader issues were considered in programme-oriented interactions. Once issues have reached the summit, the vested interests of governments play a major role, reducing the possibility that an issue can be framed in purely technical and objective terms. The organization of intergovernmental relations within governments themselves has become highly institutionalized in recent years. The prime minister has had the resources of the Federal-Provincial Relations Office (FPRO) to call upon since 1975. Van Loon argues that

> [the] FPRO has become an increasingly significant influence on policy decisions in Ottawa.... The prevalence of federal-provincial issues in almost any major policy area means that there is considerable leverage in the Office. As a result, if it retains strong leadership and staff and, most importantly, the trust of the Prime Minister, FPRO will remain a significant force.[7]

Many provinces have specialized departments or units to co-ordinate the intergovernmental activities of their governments. According to Bruce Pollard, "all intergovernmental affairs units, including those with a separate departmental structure and minister, have found that a substantial amount of work they do is directly for their premier or prime minister."[8] Smiley has criticized the role of central agencies for intergovernmental relations for their perceived deleterious effect on the conduct of federal-provincial relations. Specifically, he charges that officials in these agencies are more concerned with the preservation and

expansion of their government's jurisdiction — with enhancing provincial autonomy in the case of the provinces — than they are with sweetening federal-provincial harmony. In this way, officials of central agencies for intergovernmental relations inhibit agreements between governments, because they undermine the basis on which these agreements are concluded (shared professional and technical norms). He contends that

> the implicit and single-minded purpose of intergovernmental affairs managers at the provincial level is to safeguard and if possible to extend the range of jurisdictional autonomy, including of course the revenues that the provinces have under their unshared control.[9]

FMCs are held much more frequently than in the past. Christopher Armstrong notes that

> provincial barons had never to resort to open warfare to establish the conference of first ministers as the proper forum for the discussion of critical national issues. Seeking some institutional arrangement to express their views, they hit upon the interprovincial conference in the 1880s. Although ceremonial at first, in the course of time these conferences did become the place for making some important decisions.[10]

The years 1887 to 1941 saw six Interprovincial Conferences and ten Dominion-Provincial Conferences, an average of one every $3\frac{1}{3}$ years.[11] Table 6.1 summarizes the participation of the province of Alberta in meetings of first ministers from the mid-1970s until the early 1980s. (Alberta is the only province to publish comprehensive figures of its intergovernmental dealings. It is also one of the more active provinces on the federal-provincial stage.)

The bulk of encounters between first ministers in which Alberta Premier Peter Lougheed was involved between 1974 and 1983 were multilateral gatherings or FMCs (62.1 percent). Stated another way, in an average year, the Alberta premier would participate in two multilateral meetings, and one bilateral meeting (with the prime minister). By way of compari-

Table 6.1 — Alberta's Participation in Meetings of First Ministers 1974-1984, by Category

Year	Bilateral	Regional	Multilateral (FMCs)	Total
1974	1	0	3	4
1975	2	0	2	4
1976	0	0	3	3
1977	1	0	0	1
1978	0	0	3	3
1979	3	1	2	6
1980	1	0	2	3
1981	1	0	1	2
1982	n.a.	n.a.	n.a.	3
1983	1	0	2	3

n.a.: not available

SOURCE: Alberta, Department of Federal and Intergovernmental Affairs, *Annual Reports, 1974-75 to 1983-84.*

son, there would be approximately 40 ministerial-level federal-provincial conferences in which Alberta would participate during an average year, 70 percent of them multilateral. David Milne has found that Prime Minister Trudeau averaged five bilateral or multilateral meetings with provincial premiers during each year of his tumultuous 1980-1984 term of office (compared with an average of 82 ministerial federal-provincial meetings a year). In the first year of the Mulroney government, a vastly increased rate of consultation can be observed, with four multilateral meetings involving the Prime Minister and the premiers, and nine bilateral meetings between the Prime Minister and provincial premiers (compared to a whopping 353 ministerial-level sessions).[12]

There is little doubt that FMCs have been the inspiration of many important measures which have affected the Canadian population. National health insurance and the Canada Pension Plan are two of the more notable products of FMCs in the 1960s. However, where meetings of first ministers used to be concerned almost

exclusively with discussions of fiscal and economic questions, the scope of FMCs has widened, especially since the late 1960s. In 1968, constitutional affairs joined finance to become a central issue on the agendas of FMCs. Between 1968 and 1981, fourteen FMCs were devoted to the Constitution, and some of these conferences were televised. These meetings were not evenly spread across this period. The Constitutional Review process, begun at the interprovincial Confederation of Tomorrow Conference in 1967, took up several meetings in a four-year period, breaking down after the June 1971 Victoria Conference. Three FMCs in 1980 and 1981 produced the Constitution Act, which included an amending formula and the Charter of Rights and Freedoms. That process also authorized a series of four constitutional conferences to deal with the issue of aboriginal rights. These meetings also included representatives of the major Native organizations in the country. Constitutional conferences in 1987 both brought Quebec into the constitutional process, from which it had been absent since 1981, and mandated annual FMCs to deal with the issue of Senate reform. Energy also has found an important position on the agendas of first ministers, and there were FMCs on the issue in January 1974, April 1975 and November 1979. Since that time, it has been addressed largely in a bilateral context between Ottawa and the energy-producing provinces in the West. The November 1986 FMC on the economy dealt with federal transfer payments to the provinces, the federal deficit, regional economic development, free trade negotiations, and the softwood lumber dispute with the United States. Since Brian Mulroney has come to office, portions of the major FMCs have been televised. In summary, there is at least one FMC a year, occasionally more. Even with the repatriation of the Constitution in 1982, the pace of conferences seems undiminished, although the majority of them are now devoted to the economy.

FMCs provide an opportunity for Canada's leaders to set priorities for the country and to formulate policies which seek to reconcile divergent federal and provincial points of view. In one forum, all government leaders are drawn together and all governments share equally the right to be heard.[13] Yet many observers doubt whether FMCs are an effective instrument. Garth Stevenson contends that

> despite all the advance preparation, expense and ballyhoo, the record of First Ministers' Conferences in reaching agreements or solving problems is exceedingly poor. Consensus among eleven leaders representing different regions, political philosophies and jurisdictional interests in rarely possible, and decisions by majority vote may serve little purpose.[14]

FMCs on the economy particularly serve to underscore the federal government's difficulties in dealing with the enormous problems in the economy. The past few FMCs have done little to reduce regional tensions despite the early promise of the Mulroney government.

One common feature of the Trudeau and Mulroney years is the fact that the FMC remains the preferred arena for provincial premiers to defend their interests in front of the entire country. As FMCs have become more frequent and visible, they have received greater public attention; consequently, expectations for success have risen. The very presence of eleven leaders around one table leads many observers, especially in the media, to hope that differences will be overcome and satisfactory policies agreed upon. In reality, formal FMCs have become theatre more than anything else. When problems cannot be resolved, the tone of the meetings becomes shrill and aggressive, and the first ministers play broadly to the television audiences back home. It is little wonder that during a controversial period in federal-provincial relations Prime Minister Trudeau was reluctant to call an FMC: "I would rather have no meeting if...the premiers will use the next meeting...to make ten speeches on television blaming the federal government for all the evils for the nation."[15]

In the long run, the federal government faces serious risk in such an adversarial environment. The impulse, particularly among media observers, is to declare a winner and a loser. The federal government is likely to appear divided, indecisive, or incapable of solving the country's problems under a barrage of provincial criticism. At the same time, no other institution offers much of an alternative to the FMC. Parliament, as a result of party discipline and other factors, has been unable to take account of regional questions even within the federal government apparatus. Senate reform has foundered over the past two decades. Roger Gibbins concludes that despite any shortcomings, the FMC will remain an important institution in Canadian politics:

> Provincial governments will continue to have an important stake in national economic management, and will demand a stage upon which provincial opinions can be heard. For its part, the national government will continue to need to bring provincial governments onside if it is to pursue effectively its management of both the economy and social programs.[16]

At the strictly housekeeping level, FMCs have adopted a roughly consistent pattern since the late 1960s, under the auspices of the Canadian Intergovernmental Conference Secretariat. The first ministers usually sit at desks arranged in an oval shape. There is one seat beside each premier for a minister and one seat to each side of the prime minister for his cabinet colleagues. Other members of delegations including officials are seated in rows behind the main players. The occupants of the ministerial chairs rotate according to the issue under discussion and occasionally ministers will be called upon to address the conference, especially when the results of ministerial-level meetings have to be reported to the full FMC. This game of musical chairs often has symbolic connotations. Orland French observed that the session on women's issues at the November 1986 FMC combined

> tokenism and showmanship.... Cabinet ministers and advisers vacated their seats to allow

lower echelon women to sit next to their premiers. Television screens were filled with tokenism. But it must be said, in their defence, that the first ministers were unanimously in support of women's rights. Not one opposes equality for women. And that was that. Performed for show, it's a disposable issue.[17]

The organization of delegations has also followed a standard arrangement. The federal government sits at the head of the table and the provinces are arrayed in order of their entry into Confederation, beginning with Ontario and Quebec on the prime minister's right and left respectively. This order also prevails in the opening and concluding statements that characterize FMCs, especially the ones which are televised. These speeches rarely contain significant proposals or relate in a concrete way to any negotiations likely to take place at the conference; they are long on rhetoric and aimed at home audiences more than at the assembly at hand. In general, the first ministers dominate discussion, and participation by others is infrequent. Exceptions to this fact have occurred when a premier has been absent (Premier René Lévesque occasionally staged dramatic walkouts from FMCs for political reasons of his own) and during the series of FMCs on aboriginal rights when Native leaders were allowed to participate. Officials usually do not speak in plenary sessions, and almost never at open FMCs. Briefings from officials, notably the Governor of the Bank of Canada and Canada's free trade negotiator, have taken place behind closed doors.

The fact that the prime minister holds exclusive authority to call an FMC is a matter of concern, because it means that the institution is likely to be used for advancing his own political agenda. Some prime ministers have resisted provincial calls for FMCs for fear of giving premiers' criticisms national attention or of allowing them to seize hold of the national political agenda. There is enormous variation in the degree of consultation which precedes FMCs and the conditions under which they

have been convened. In some instances, the prime minister has met individually with each premier to solicit or explore agenda items, and to investigate the potential for agreement on a particular issue. On other occasions, the scheduling of an FMC has more to do with developments within the federal government itself. Smiley worries that FMCs do not have a formal constitutional basis. He points to a number of difficulties caused by the absence of established procedure:

> How is the agenda to be determined? Are conferences to be open or closed? Should communiqués issued at the end of conferences make reference to unresolved differences among governments? Is it reasonable to expect first ministers to commit their administrations at conferences or are there circumstances where such a commitment can appropriately be delayed? Is it appropriate for governments …to introduce new proposals into conferences without prior consultations with other jurisdictions?[18]

Even the May 1987 Meech Lake Accord, which pledged the entrenchment of the annual FMCs devoted to the economy and the Constitution (Senate reform), does not address these concerns. One of the realities of FMCs is that they are intensely political events. The fact that the political convictions of the governments around the conference table are all different is a given of the process. It is interesting to note that there were no provincial Liberal governments in the country in the last few years of the Trudeau government, but that since the election of the Mulroney government, Liberal administrations have been elected in the two largest provinces as well as in Prince Edward Island and New Brunswick.

For some time the tendency for federal-provincial agreements to be made with little or no reference to legislative bodies has been contentious. In many cases, such agreements can be implemented without legislation. Even when legislation is forthcoming, governments are generally unwilling to make changes in hard-won agreements in order to satisfy legislators.[19] While there have been examples of effective legislative scrutiny of proposed agreements, mostly at the federal level (such as the constitutional reform package), there is consensus among observers that executive federalism, with its requirement of unanimity (or near-unanimity for some types of constitutional change established under the rules for repatriation) distributes power among eleven governments but helps to concentrate it in the executive of each government.[20] Van Loon and Whittington comment on the "startling lack of attention paid to federal-provincial relations in either Parliament or the provincial legislatures,"[21] noting that legislators have little input across jurisdictional lines, and that only ministers play any role in federal-provincial bodies. Members of opposition parties are nearly always completely locked out of the process.

There is little doubt that the practitioners of federal-provincial bargaining prefer secrecy. As Simeon put it some time ago:

> The emphasis on *in camera* discussion, so evident among the Canadian decision-makers, seems to imply a belief that the decision-makers themselves share many more common interests that do their constituents, since it is believed that if the conferences were public the participants would be given to public posturings rather than constructive discussion.[22]

Subsequent experience with open (and televised) meetings has done little to change the minds of most practitioners. Indeed, grandstanding is now a recognized function of open FMCs. The prospect of having to justify compromises — to bargain and make political points at the same time — appears to daunt most first ministers.

LEADERSHIP STYLE

The personal style of the first ministers participating in the intergovernmental arena can have a substantial impact on the tone and substance of federal-provincial relations. It is often easier for premiers than it is for the prime minister to put a distinctive stamp on their governments, since they are at the head of more compact bureaucratic apparatuses and in a better position to influence policy development. At the federal level, though, the personal style of the prime minister has had a profound effect on the operation of the process. In some instances the strategy of the prime minister can set the tone for the operation of the entire federal-provincial system. In many ways, the era of cooperative federalism in the 1960s was identified with the leadership style of Prime Minister Pearson. Coming from the world of diplomacy, Pearson was dedicated to the resolution of disputes, the avoidance of controversy and the solving of problems. According to Simeon, Pearson's style was "low-keyed and flexible, dedicated above all to reaching agreement and avoiding conflict and dissension."[23] Richard Gwyn noted that

> it is the hallmark of Pearson's style of government that...achievements have come, not through any preconceptions or commitments to fixed positions, but through an endlessly flexible series of individual responses to individual problems.[24]

Pierre Trudeau's impact on federal-provincial relations was momentous. It is not an exaggeration to suggest that his performance in the 1968 FMC on the Constitution established his reputation. According to one observer, the "constitutional debates...were the ladder Pierre Elliott Trudeau used to climb to power. If there had been no constitutional crisis in the fall of 1967, making national figures of the proponents of each option, and no constitutional conference in February 1968, it is doubtful that Trudeau would [have become] anything more than Minister of Justice."[25] The early perception of Trudeau's participation in the intergovernmental process was that he was more analytical and abstract than Pearson and possessed enormous capabilities. But from the beginning, Trudeau seemed less willing to deal than Pearson, if it meant compromising on a point of principle. Trudeau was also uncomfortable with the ad hoc nature of Pearson's style and set about to introduce greater planning and rationalization into the governmental process. The early Trudeau years were given to decentralization of power, with the provinces receiving new authority, new responsibilities and new resources. Ironically, in light of his later reputation as a centralist and his attack of the Meech Lake Accord as a giveaway to the provinces, Trudeau was prepared to sign a constitutional deal in 1971 which would have seen a substantial transfer of power to the provinces. Trudeau's dominance of the process quickly became apparent. He neutralized his regional ministers so that they could not compete with the provincial premiers as spokespersons.

Even in the beginning, Trudeau's style was confrontational. He delighted in attacking opponents — including provincial premiers — always confident that he would emerge victorious. Indeed, he went so far as to label two Western premiers "enemies of Confederation" because of their demands for enhanced provincial powers in the Constitution. In Smiley's view, Trudeau contributed greatly to an increasingly ideological tone in federal-provincial relations:

in the polarizing process it is almost impossible to exaggerate the personal influence of Pierre Trudeau with his penchant for debating even the most particularized matters within the framework of generalized concepts about the nature of the Canadian Confederation and his demonstrated capacity to keep federal questions at or near the top of the Canadian political agenda.[26]

As a consequence of Trudeau's approach, the atmosphere of federal-provincial relations became one of constant bickering. Richard Gwyn described Trudeau's performance at FMCs in the following terms:

watching Trudeau dominate the premiers at First Ministers' Conferences, immobile, sphinx-like, but puissant, at the head of the horseshoe table, evokes James Morris's marvelous description of [George Nathaniel] Curzon among the Indian princes and British generals, "slightly sneering...dominating the room with an astringency, a sheathed cleverness, that inhibited all but the most self-confident.[27]

Yet it is probably unfair to place the blame for the unsettled state of federal-provincial relations entirely on Trudeau's shoulders. If Trudeau was a champion on the federal side for a number of causes, René Lévesque and Peter Lougheed were willing to challenge Trudeau on Quebec's place in Confederation and energy issues respectively. Put simply, the 1970s were marked by a clash in perspectives between an Ottawa-centred view of Confederation and a province-centred one. This contrast can best be seen in two statements made at the September 1980 FMC on the Constitution. According to Trudeau, the national interest transcended regional or provincial concerns and Canada was greater than a sum of its parts. In his view,

Canadians believe there is a national interest. They do want a strong country, and they do believe that we are more than a collection of provinces, more than a community of communities. Canadians...have a desire that there be national institutions and a national government capable of acting on behalf of all of them.... Provincial governments are not constituted to do that. This is not what they are elected for.

The provincial perspective was put by Premier Allan Blakeney of Saskatchewan:

I do not believe that the national interest is represented by a consensus of all provincial governments. The federal government has a role to play. It is not a creature of the provinces. This is not a confederation. Nor, however, do I believe that the national interest is ascertained by the majority will of Canadians. This is something more than a collection of citizens.... The essence of Canada is therefore that on major matters we need a double majority. We need the majority of citizens as expressed by the popular will in the House of Commons and we need the majority, however defined, of the regional will. That is the essence of a federal state.

Upon his re-election in 1980, Pierre Trudeau launched an offensive on a number of issues:

the Constitution, energy policy, social programmes, economic development, and Western Canada. Underlying his approach was a
distinct nationalist and interventionist philosophy, one bound to clash with the provinces.
According to Smiley, "with the Trudeau Liberal
restoration to power in 1980, there was a
reassertion of federal power and purpose and
in 1980-81 a period of federal-provincial conflict of a virulence unprecedented in Canadian
history."[28] After proclaiming that co-operative
federalism was dead, Trudeau summarized his
attitude to the provinces at a news conference
on February 25th, 1982:

> I think we have tried governing through consen-
> sus; we have tried governing by being generous
> to the provinces, you will recall, even in the
> constitutional area; and we have tried governing
> in 1979 by offering a rather massive transfer of
> powers to the provinces, and that was never
> enough. So, we have changed that and we have
> said on the constitution, as we are doing on the
> economy, there is not much point...[in] shifting
> powers and resources to the provinces because
> there is no stop. The pendulum will keep swing-
> ing until we end up with a community of com-
> munities or...a confederation of shopping cen-
> tres, or whatever it is, and that is not my view of
> Canada. I thought that we could build a strong
> Canada through co-operation. I have been disil-
> lusioned.

During this period, the federal government
stuck insistently to its demands for a higher
profile in intergovernmental programmes, and
was toying with the idea of more direct involvement in several sectors. In sector after sector,
Ottawa chose to follow a strategy of unilateralism, to reach around the provinces to deal
directly with Canadians more than in the past,
to impose its wishes on the provinces, and to
rebuild a national political base for itself.

The Trudeau era was characterized by intense federal-provincial conflict and tension. In
one of his final speeches as prime minister,
Pierre Trudeau neatly summarized his perceptions of Canadian federalism:

> In order for Canada to survive and prosper in
> the future, it will have to pursue more effec-
> tively than it is now doing two complementary
> objectives which are equally essential to the
> country's harmonious existence and
> development:
>
> — To maintain a central power strong enough
> to reflect our desire to live as one people,
> settle conflicts of interest between provinces
> and regions with unquestioned political au-
> thority, and speak on behalf of all Canadians,
> both at home and abroad; and at the same
> time,
> — To develop better means for co-ordinating
> the efforts of the two levels of government
> and for ensuring that provincial government
> involvement in the affairs of the nation is
> substantial enough to make them feel full-
> fledged members of the federation, and thus
> inclined more and more to plan their devel-
> opment within a broadly Canadian perspec-
> tive.

The assessment of Pierre Trudeau's performance in federal-provincial relations is mixed.
Most observers credit him personally with re-
patriating and obtaining the entrenched Charter of Rights and Freedoms. Others wonder
about the price of these achievements. Upon
his retirement, the *Globe and Mail* remarked
that he had "redefined the very nature of this
country" but continued that "he was not, in
fact, a great or noble player of the political
game. He preferred to fight with provincial
premiers rather than stroke them, and Western-
ers in particular came to feel, probably correctly, that he had little understanding of the
provinces."[29] The *Vancouver Sun* called the
Constitution and the entrenched Charter of
Rights and Freedoms Trudeau's "crowning
achievement"[30] but the *Winnipeg Free Press*
observed that Trudeau had "launched an un-
principled effort to force a new constitution on
the country before the courts could rule on the
propriety of the process."[31] The *Toronto Star*
noted that his political mission had been
achieved: "he indelibly made his mark on our
future by accomplishing the main goal he had
set for himself in politics: to make sure that

Quebec wouldn't leave Canada through separatism, and to make sure that Canada wouldn't shove Quebec out through narrowmindedness."[32] The *Edmonton Journal* concurred:

> Trudeau had a historic mission that was his alone, and he fulfilled it: breaking down two solitudes that existed between Ontario and Quebec; setting Canada free of its ties to Britain with a constitutional amending formula and Charter of Rights that fundamentally altered the nature of our parliamentary system.[33]

It is difficult to provide a detailed assessment of Joe Clark's impact on federal-provincial relations since his tenure was so short, but there is no doubt that his downfall can be attributed partly to the actions of provincial premiers of his own party. The Clark victory in 1979 seemed to herald the beginning of a decentralist trend, by giving up certain federal powers to the provinces and increasing consultation among governments. Clark embodied his view of federal-provincial relations in the vague phrase "community of communities" and promised to reduce the intergovernmental tensions which characterized the government he had replaced. However, Trudeau's charge that Clark was acting as a "headwaiter" to the provinces stuck. Moreover, Clark relied on the fact that seven of the premiers were Conservatives to rebuild trust.

Clark's pledge to improve federal-provincial relations foundered on the energy issue. Negotiations between Ottawa and the producing provinces in the West, especially Alberta, proved difficult. Excluded from this process was the key consuming province, Ontario, which perceived that Clark was caving in to Alberta Premier Peter Lougheed's demands. Premier William Davis of Ontario neglected no opportunity to slam the federal government for threatening to raise energy prices. As Warner Troyer put it:

> in trying to stay friends with both Alberta's Peter Lougheed and Ontario's Bill Davis — the former chasing glory via rapidly escalating oil prices, and the latter struggling to maintain Ontario's

industrial hegemony and, to that end, lower oil prices — the neophyte P.M. was bound to end up looking like a rookie cop who'd been assaulted by both husband and wife after trying to settle a domestic dispute.[34]

Ron Graham viewed Clark's treatment at the hands of the premiers as "mean-spirited and greedy."[35] Jeffrey Simpson suggested that "Clark learned a lesson a more experienced Prime Minister would have understood. In federal-provincial relations, premiers are colour-blind when the vital interests of their provinces are at stake."[36] Even a prime minister who had strong inclinations toward enhancing provincial powers and rights ended up mauled by several provincial premiers for his troubles.

Ottawa's relations with the provinces began promisingly under the tutelage of Brian Mulroney, soured for a period, but recovered with the 1987 Meech Lake Accord. A change in tone in the conduct of federal-provincial relations was clearly evident from the beginning of the government's mandate. In a 1984 election speech, Brian Mulroney characterized this new approach as follows: "The Liberal philosophy has been replaced by a new philosophy. To me, the Canadian federation is not a test of strength between different governments. Federal power is more than that of a policeman whose nightstick happens to be bigger than those of the others." For the new prime minister, the opportunity shone golden. Most provincial premiers welcomed his election (even though the group of seven Conservative premiers was soon reduced to four) and would prove powerful allies in the initial days of the government. An early imperative for Mulroney was to restore peace in federal-provincial relations and to avoid the intergovernmental conflict perceived as so unproductive by the voters. Although many suspect that, like Trudeau, he is something of a centralist, early indications pointed in the opposite direction. Mulroney seemed to embrace the principles of co-operative federalism and tried to signal his good faith with the premiers. The Atlantic and Western Accords tried to settle long-standing problems, even if they proved to be only temporary expedients. These agreements did not prevent the premiers of Alberta and Newfoundland from attacking the federal government for not doing enough for their regions. The Meech Lake Accord saw significant powers go to the provinces: participation in the appointment of Supreme Court judges and senators, authority over immigration, limits on the federal spending power, and changes in the amending formula for the Constitution, which would allow any province to veto certain constitutional amendments.

With a new generation of leaders taking office at about the same time as Mulroney, there came a fresh approach to the national political agenda, partly because Mulroney made national reconciliation and renewal such a high priority. In his book *Where I Stand,* Mulroney argued that Canadians had to throw off the "black mood of pessimism and despair that grips our national consciousness.... Let us not blame any one group, including governments, for our problems, although it is tempting to do so."[37] At the same time, first ministers were no longer consumed with the momentous questions of separatism and constitutional reform. Moreover, there was a widespread sense that the intense conflict which had characterized Canadian federalism since the mid-1970s was no longer appropriate. The new premiers did not bring different values to political life; they brought with them, however temporarily, a new style and a strong desire to reinstitute co-operation in federal-provincial relations. As early as 1985, however, storm signals appeared on the horizon, including the recalcitrance of some provinces regarding free trade discussions with the United States, federal transfer payments to the provinces, and interregional squabbles. Although there was no doubt that the tensions of yesteryear had been substantially diminished, few were willing to wager that there were not provocations of significant dimension capable of touching off a federal-provincial row. Taken together, these new faces

represent a transitional phase in federal-provincial relations and, if the past is any guide, many of them will be in place into the 1990s.

Although Mulroney is not likely to echo Trudeau's sentiment that federal authority is the only legitimate instrument of national development, he is also not likely to participate in the wholesale dismantling of federal power. Mulroney has been inclined no less than Trudeau to undercut regional ministers in favour of appeasing the premiers. According to Ron Graham,

> Mulroney was hoping that an atmosphere of trust, conciliation, and consensus could go a long way in resolving the centrifugal tensions in the federation. Like Clark and Turner before him, Mulroney assumed that the confrontations of the early 1980s had more to do with the personality of Pierre Trudeau than with the dynamics of the system.[38]

Others have observed that in a country such as Canada intergovernmental conflict and competition are not only inevitable but healthy. Changes of personality did not bring radical shifts in policy, and the country's regional differences remained like the rock of the Canadian Shield. Mulroney's first FMC in 1985 was widely described as a "love-in" but it was followed some months later by another at which proposed federal reductions in transfer payments effectively ended the federal-provincial honeymoon. It remains to be seen whether the Mulroney propensity to favour certain regions, especially Quebec, for partisan reasons, will set certain provinces against him.

In the final analysis, Canadians may perceive that prime ministers who appear to give in to the demands of the provincial premiers are weak leaders. Although it is too soon yet to judge long-term effects, the Meech Lake Accord was an immediate triumph for Mulroney. According to one columnist, the agreement "was a dramatic, measurable success for Brian Mulroney. He fulfilled his election promise to bring Quebec into the Constitution. He demonstrated his negotiating skills. He proved himself capable of statesmanship."[39] The contrast with Trudeau was striking. Mulroney had never been closely identified with a particular constitutional perspective, and behaved in a conciliatory manner. Trudeau was well known for his constitutional views and it was always difficult to get him to retreat from his hard-line positions. At Meech Lake, and a month later, into the wee hours of the morning in the Langevin block, Mulroney closeted himself alone with the premiers with a definite and limited agenda until all the participants could agree. The resulting agreement was a masterful combination of an understanding of the national agenda with pure political tactics. The Accord became controversial during the long period of ratification by Parliament and the provincial Legislatures. Critics, including former Prime Minister Pierre Trudeau, argued that Mulroney had paid too high a price for securing provincial agreement. By mid-1987, it was far from clear that the Meech Lake Accord was a Mulroney triumph.

FACTORS LEADING TO AGREEMENT IN INTERGOVERNMENTAL RELATIONS

There are a number of external factors which can affect the capacity of first ministers to reach agreement, and they tend to fall into one of two categories: type of issue and the nature of the interests mobilized. With respect to type of issue, agreements are most likely to be reached when the issues are: (1) relatively uncontroversial and of common concern to all or most governments, (2) framable in ways which permit splitting the difference and avoiding winners and losers, and (3) limited in scope and specific. Thus negotiations involving the provision of services have proven easier to conclude than those involving regulation, since it is easier to split a difference in cost-sharing than in jurisdiction. When it comes to reducing conflict, there are clear benefits in narrowing

issues to manageable proportions and in articulating them in terms of sharing. It must be noted, of course, that failure to reach agreement on many issues in the 1970s was not simply a function of the greater involvement of summit decision-makers. Stevenson has argued that functional or co-operative federalism is unable to "deal very successfully with conflicts that originate outside the governmental or bureaucratic milieu and that result from more fundamental antagonisms."[40] The frequency of disagreement in the 1970s, he suggests, resulted from the emergence of deeper issues and not from the shift from functional to executive federalism.[41] In fact, of course, summit meetings have some major agreements to their credit.

With respect to interests mobilized, matters are less clear-cut than for the type of issue discussed above. For the many routine intergovernmental interactions that make the system work, even in time of crisis, it seems clear that absence of publicity facilitates agreement, for with attention and controversy, the political concerns of the governments come into play, as well as other interests, and agreement is often made more difficult. On the other hand, widespread public and/or media demand for action can also bring issues into focus and facilitate agreement, as long as there are no major regional differences in policy preference. The impact of politicization — or publicity — therefore depends upon the specific pattern of interests mobilized. (Publicity surrounding actual negotiating sessions appears to promote symbolic combat and impede compromise.) The issues which pose most difficulty are: (1) those upon which there are major differences in cultural or economic interest among the provinces, (2) those with a high level of symbolic content, especially if there are probable electoral implications, and (3) those which touch fundamental questions of ideology, community, or support of the regime.

Certain issues, such as fiscal policy and economic development (especially industrial strategy), are highly problematic in the federal-provincial arena because they require both long-term planning and a co-ordinated programme design covering many sectors, and because they are complicated by deep regional divisions. There is an inescapable tension between the logic of planning and the logic of federalism, which deals most effectively with specific, short-term issues,[42] and the conflicts inherent in the Canadian federal system have made agreement on matters of fiscal policy and economic development extremely difficult.[43] The logic of federalism reflects its origins in a period of limited government. The intergovernmental mechanisms which evolved in the post-1945 period were designed to cope with the relatively moderate forms of government activism reflected in the development of the welfare state, from federal government leadership through exhortation to expenditure programmes (shared-cost arrangements). As the form of government intervention shifted to regulation and public ownership, there was a quantum increase in intergovernmental conflict.

The attitudes to intergovernmental negotiations adopted by the first ministers are also important. Certain tactics are clearly less conducive to harmonious interaction than others. Simeon laid out several rules which prevailed in the federal-provincial system in the early 1970s, including "don't attack other provinces," stay "reasonable, realistic and modest," "don't rock the boat," and "don't throw your weight around."[44] Most of these rules are still in place, albeit in modified form. Another important rule suggested by Simeon — "don't be a localist"[45] — has been more difficult to observe. In the harsh reality of federal-provincial relations, premiers cannot always resist the impulse to make special pleas for the interests of their constituents. Premier Brian Peckford's February 1987 campaign to convince the Mulroney government to abandon a controversial cod treaty with France is merely one of the more blatant examples.

At the midpoint of the mandate of the Mulroney government, the mood of national reconciliation gave way to a series of regional demands, including the international banking centres controversy, the CF-18A maintenance contract, free trade discussions, and Western dissatisfaction over federal support for the resource industry.[46] Although he acknowledges other factors were partly to blame, Jeffrey Simpson argues that "the Mulroney government tried to play brokerage politics, making promises about 'inflicting prosperity' on every region, and is now being hoist [by] its own rhetorical petard."[47] Yet this brokerage style paid off handsomely for Mulroney with the Meech Lake Accord. The prime minister was able to play off the particular demands of Quebec for that province to be declared a "distinct society" against Alberta's demands for senate reform by incorporating a process to explore the latter, and by agreeing to appoint senators from provincial lists in the interim. He brought the other provinces on board by giving to them, too, all the powers Quebec had been seeking.

Nevertheless, there will always be certain circumstances where it pays for a provincial government to attack Ottawa, especially when the federal government is perceived as weak. Many a premier has ridden to re-election by targeting the federal government. On the other hand, premiers will find some difficulty in challenging a popular federal government or a highly regarded federal initiative. With the Meech Lake Accord, the impulse to "bring Quebec into the constitutional process" was a powerful one.

Simeon argues that these norms or rules are not the only factors limiting available tactics in the federal-provincial sphere. He reasons that political resources and constraints have a significant impact:

> Political support and other political resources may be seen as providing the actors with incentives to undertake some kinds of action and not to undertake others. The actor will tailor his tactics to the kinds of resources he feels he has. If he has political support, he will exploit that.[48]

In addition, Simeon reviews the personal style,

moves and counter-moves (e.g., persuasion, cajolery, convincing, calling upon allies, etc.) employed by participants to achieve their aims. In this way, federal-provincial relations are similar to other bargaining situations. Strategies can include "divide and conquer," confrontation, alliance-building, or threats to withdraw from the process. A common strategy in federal-provincial relations is to raise issues to an ideological level. Mundane discussions about freight rates become impassioned arguments about Western alienation. The equalization issue is almost always construed in terms of the appropriate regional distribution of resources.

The emphasis on bargaining in intergovernmental relations is largely borrowed from the study of international politics. This perspective is valuable in many ways since it does not reduce our analysis to the areas of conflict, and demonstrates that co-operation exists as well. However, the bargaining metaphor is limited for a number of reasons. In the first place, the multiplicity of actors necessitates detailed and complex calculations. Most bargains (e.g., labour relations) are struck on a bilateral basis rather than among eleven delegations. Even nominal allies might disagree in the midst of a major transaction. Second, the bargaining concept implies that everything is negotiable. Even though Canadians have been accused of being a highly pragmatic people, willing to compromise on almost any issue, it must be acknowledged that conflict is a standard feature of intergovernmental relations and that some element of disagreement is a healthy phenomenon, symptomatic of differences in principle. Third, the bargaining model tends to simplify the process and ignore the interactions within each government.[49]

Some strategies lend themselves more easily to intergovernmental relations. One example is making alliances with outside actors. In some cases these outsiders can be interest groups mobilized by one participant against the other. In energy negotiations, the resource industry has often pressured the federal government to adopt the provincial position. In 1981, a speedy mobilization by women's and Native groups after an FMC convinced several recalcitrant provincial premiers to include reference to their issues in the new Constitution. In other instances, alliances are formed with important political leaders who are not in government, or with incipient participants in the federal-provincial process. In the months preceding his election in December 1985, Quebec Liberal Leader Robert Bourassa toured capitals in other parts of the country, spelling out his terms for Quebec's entry into the constitutional process. Although he was not the head of a government, Bourassa was widely seen as a sure bet to defeat the Parti Québécois. Early in 1984, then Opposition Leader Brian Mulroney announced the signing of the Atlantic Accord — an "agreement" on offshore resources with Newfoundland Premier Brian Peckford which closely resembled a deal that had fallen through between Newfoundland and Liberal energy minister Jean Chrétien in 1983. Although the agreement carefully avoided any reference to the contentious aspect of ownership, it was widely viewed as a brilliant stroke on the part of the Conservatives. Not only were the Liberals upstaged and held up as antagonists to federal-provincial harmony, but the Conservatives had effectively claimed many elements of the 1983 near-deal as their own. When the Conservatives were elected later in the year, the Atlantic Accord was one the first agreements put in place by the new government. Most importantly, Premier Peckford had made use of partisan connections with his federal party even though it was not in office, and forced the hand of the incoming prime minister.

Some strategies can be quite costly and should be used only in extreme circumstances. Withdrawing from the process falls into this category. Part of the Quebec government's strategy to protest its exclusion from the November 1981 constitutional accord was to withdraw from all federal-provincial conferences save those on the economy. This position

ences save those on the economy. This position proved very difficult to maintain and was eventually abandoned when ministers of intergovernmental affairs were changed. When Premier Lévesque announced that he would participate in the February 1982 economic summit, he generated considerable tension with one of his provincial colleagues. In a strongly worded letter to B.C. Premier Bill Bennett, Lévesque contended that, contrary to tradition, Quebec could not accept the last host of the annual premiers' conference as the spokesman for all the provinces, and that Quebec's silence on certain issues did not imply that his government had been willing to attend the first ministers' meeting.[50] In late January and early February, newspaper reports began to appear which indicated that Quebec was risking considerable financial loss — between $38 and $80 million according to federal estimates — by not participating in the federal-provincial process.[51] Premier Lévesque consistently challenged the value and legitimacy of the process, but his government grudgingly began to attend conferences again.

There are three factors common to successful negotiation: (1) the existence of a clearly defined and stated objective supported by all key units of the initiating government (usually the federal government), (2) consultation at the early stages of proposal development, and (3) flexibility.[52] Even where there is considerable disagreement about programme structure, cost-sharing, and other central concerns, the existence of a shared commitment to resolve the issue generally leads to an agreement. While the emergence of rational planning at both levels of government has promoted distinctive approaches to common problems and increased the likelihood of disagreement, early consultation and the involvement of programme specialists appear to facilitate compromise. Also, an incremental approach — seeking resolution of specific issues one by one rather than tackling more general disagreements head-on — has been found to be effective.

Dupré also suggests that making federal-provincial summits a regular practice will contribute to successful intergovernmental relations. He suggests that the purpose of routine annual summits would be to

> make summit interaction a commonplace event.... Their informal atmosphere would stress consultation and exchange, not negotiation. Emphasis on the fundamental routine nature of the events would contain public and media expectations. It should involve an undertaking among first ministers that routine meetings do not include televised proceedings, or invite pre- or post-conference posturing by the participants.[53]

The Macdonald Commission recommended that FMCs be entrenched in the Constitution and that first ministers meet annually on a fixed date.[54] The Meech Lake Accord enshrined annual FMCs on two areas: the economy and the Constitution.

The increase of bilateral negotiations has obvious benefits in certain cases. For example, bilateral interaction avoids the complexities of multilateral negotiations simply because there are fewer actors and therefore fewer interests to be accommodated. They permit a focus on issues of specific interest to both parties, reducing the prospect that provincial governments with little involvement in the specific subject matter will bring in other issues of more interest to them. In addition, the reduced number of participants permits tradeoffs between the two governments on a broader range of issues than can be handled easily in multilateral negotiations. It is also true that bilateral meetings are generally unpublicized, lessening the likelihood of extraneous political factors entering the picture.[55] Bilateralism also holds promise as an instrument for breaking deadlocks. Willingness on the part of first ministers to provide general direction to other bodies or to leave details for bilateral bargaining might also be helpful in this regard.

Summit federalism will also work effectively when the issues come to the summit clarified with room for tradeoffs. Adequate preparation clearly is crucial, as is a degree of trust and a sense that to compromise is not to lose. The new rules developed during repatriation — more public involvement and less emphasis on unanimity (with some exceptions spelled out in the Meech Lake Accord) — may promote resolution of some of the less thorny issues. Nevertheless, FMCs will still have to deal with the hard issues and an inability to achieve consensus should not be seen as a failure of the system. The series of FMCs on aboriginal rights has introduced a new element at the conference table, namely the participation of outside groups. The presence of additional actors complicates the possibility of agreement but does ensure that certain groups have direct access to the country's key decision-making forum. The participation of other groups will perhaps allow for a more accurate determination of regional needs, though such a move would probably be resisted by some provincial governments.

Many FMCs will not take place in public. There is little doubt that many governments will insist on retreating behind closed doors for important discussions and that some degree of secrecy will always be necessary. Key agreements — including the 1981 and 1987 constitutional agreements — were concluded behind closed doors. When it comes to open FMCs, it would be desirable to reduce the importance of the mass media, to eliminate the media circus atmosphere. A sensible reform would limit the agenda of any one conference to a number of specific questions. In this way, governments could prepare positions on the issues under discussion, rather than participating solely when their region was affected. Advance notice of the questions to be discussed could facilitate effective pre-conference consultation and allow governments an opportunity to reflect on their positions. In this way, agreements might be easier to achieve.

The author would like to thank Dean Tom Traves, Faculty of Arts, York University for providing a research grant in support of this chapter, and Brandi Dickman for her capable research assistance.

Notes

1. Smiley, *Canada in Question,* 3rd edition, Chap. 4 and Smiley, *The Federal Condition,* Chap. 4.

2. Simeon, *Federal-Provincial Diplomacy,* p. 130.

3. Smiley, *Canada in Question,* third edition, p. 100.

4. See Armstrong, *The Politics of Federalism* and Cook, *Provincial Autonomy.*

5. Orland French, "Media Like a Tool That's Used," *Globe and Mail,* p. 24, November 1986.

6. Simeon, *Federal-Provincial Diplomacy,* p. 144.

7. Van Loon, "Planning in the Eighties," p. 177.

8. Pollard, *Managing the Interface,* p. 34. See also Wallace, *Provincial Central Agencies for Intergovernmental Relations.*

9. Smiley, *Canada in Question,* third edition, p. 113.

10. Armstrong, "Ceremonial Politics," pp. 142-3.

11. Ibid., p. 143.

12. Milne, *Tug of War,* p. 222. These same figures are cited in Kernaghan and Siegel, *Public Administration,* p. 386. In 1986, Pollard (*Managing the Interface,* 34) reported that since 1867 there have been 61 FMCs, 41 since 1960.

13. It must be remembered that the first ministers are accompanied by large delegations of ministers and officials at FMCs. Kernaghan and Siegel (*Public Administration,* p. 386) report that 269 ministers and officials attended the FMC on the Economy in Halifax in November 1985.

14. Stevenson, "Federalism and Intergovernmental Relations," p. 386.

15. House of Commons, *Debates,* 14 December 1982, p. 21569.

16. Gibbins, *Conflict and Unity,* p. 253.

17. French, op. cit.

18. Smiley, *Canada in Question,* third edition, pp. 99-100.

19. Simeon, *Federal-Provincial Diplomacy,* pp. 279-80.

20. Van Loon and Whittington, *The Canadian Political System,* pp. 543-544.

21. Ibid., p. 542.

22. Simeon, *Federal-Provincial Diplomacy,* p. 311.

23. Ibid., p. 239.

24. Gwyn, *The Shape of Scandal,* p. 168.

25. Sullivan, *Mandate '68,* p. 236.

26. Smiley, *The Federal Condition,* p. 97.

27. Gwyn, *The Northern Magus,* p. 272. Curzon was Viceroy of India at the turn of the century and later became British Foreign Secretary.

28. Smiley, *The Federal Condition,* p. 189.

29. 1 March 1984.

30. 1 March 1984.

31. 1 March 1984.

32. 1 March 1984.

33. 1 March 1984.

34. Troyer, *200 Days,* p. 149.

35. Graham, *One-Eyed Kings,* p. 58.

36. Simpson, *Discipline of Power,* p. 204.

37. Mulroney, *Where I Stand,* p. 71.

38. Graham, *One-Eyed Kings,* p. 397.

39. Carol Goar, "Constitution: Last Piece in Place," *Toronto Star,* 2 May, 1987.

40. Stevenson, *Unfulfilled Union,* p. 190.

41. Ibid., pp. 191-2.

42. Banting, *The Welfare State,* pp. 77-78.

43. Smiley, *Canada in Question,* third edition, pp. 185ff.

44. Simeon, *Federal-Provincial Diplomacy,* pp. 229-233.

45. Ibid., p. 230.

46. Carol Goar, "Is Mulroney Era of 'National Reconciliation' Over?" *Toronto Star,* 10 February 1987; Graham Fraser, "Learning How to Live With Gang of 10," *Globe and Mail,* 10 February 1987; and Andrew Cohen, "Fish Dispute Turns Focus on Provinces' Discontent," *Financial Post,* 16 February 1987.

47. *Globe and Mail,* 27 February 1987.

48. Simeon, *Federal-Provincial Diplomacy,* p. 235.

49. Schultz, *Federalism, Bureaucracy, and Public Policy,* 1980. See also Smiley, *The Federal Condition,* p. 90.

50. *Montreal Gazette,* 9 January 1982.

51. *United Press Canada,* 30 January 1982 and *Presse canadienne,* 5 February 1982.

52. Jenkin, *The Challenge of Diversity,* pp. 104-105.

53. Dupré, "Reflections," p. 26.

54. Royal Commission on the Economic Union, *Report,* Vol. 3, p. 265.

55. Van Loon and Whittington, *The Canadian Political System,* p. 547. See also McRoberts, "Unilateralism, Bilateralism and Multilateralism," pp. 71-129.

CHAPTER 7

Prime Ministers and Their Parties: The Cauldron of Leadership

Leslie A. Pal

The contemporary prominence of political leaders, magnified by the media's preoccupation with prime ministers and premiers, encourages the casual observer to dismiss the importance of political parties. To the vast majority of Canadians for whom casting a ballot is the full extent of their political engagement, parties are not much more than labels for different policy positions, or logos beneath a leader's beaming photograph. The party is, sometimes justifiably, reduced in the minds of many to its parliamentary rump — the handful of M.P.s or M.L.A.s who carry the party banner between elections.

The three major Canadian political parties consist of much more than this, of course. They consist of thousands of volunteers scattered over every region, in every city and town. Our prime ministers, while they must ultimately present themselves before the "many-headed Caesar," or electorate, need first to be elected leaders by their parties. Parties formulate policies (often ignored), and aggregate interests (usually difficult). They meet periodically to consider the highest matters of government, but also organize picnics at the constituency level. It is true that Canadian political parties are not of the all-embracing variety one sees in Western Europe, but they do perform a bewildering array of tasks.

Our interest here is in the relation of leaders, especially prime ministers, to their party. As

Weller puts it, "parties are the foundations on which prime ministers must build. There the transactional link is most obvious. Prime ministers hold their position because they lead the elected majority in the popular chamber. That majority is maintained by party discipline."[1] But surprisingly little information exists on what should, after all, be a crucial link in modern democratic politics.[2] Several reasons might explain this. First, party activity is often tedious and pedestrian. It is scattered across the nation in every constituency, large and small. Outside of leadership conventions, which have the virtues of drama and concentration, party routine is rarely exciting enough to attract the media. A second reason is that, despite their public purpose, political parties are actually private organizations. Moreover, they are engaged in a struggle for power with each other and against other parties. Accordingly, they prefer some secrecy, or at least discretion, on sensitive matters. The details of their relations with leaders are confidential in the extreme, rarely open to systematic study. Finally, parties are amorphous and shifting. Between elections they wither as volunteers drift away.

Aside from a few outstanding efforts, our knowledge of prime ministers in the party arena is almost entirely anecdotal, or else based on the perhaps atypical phenomenon of leadership conventions. Thus it is really not much more than a series of *aperçus* — of brief but unconnected illuminations which cast light on the parts without revealing the whole.

THE PARTY ARENA: TEN *APERÇUS*

1. Political Parties as Coalitions

There is possibly no more venerable truth about political parties than that they aggregate interests. Their aim is to fight and win elections, but a democratic system demands organization in every capillary of the formal political system. In presenting a platform, political parties present a national agenda. They must therefore be able to muster troops at the constituency level as well as to demonstrate that they truly represent the nation and its interests. It is important to remember, however, that individual groups and interests within the party will never allow themselves to be entirely submerged in some collective party personality; they will assert themselves in a process of internal decision-making. Parties are therefore in fact loose coalitions of various interests bound either by the enjoyment of power (if they are in office) or the desire to gain it (if they are not).

In a country like Canada, the most salient divisions are regional and linguistic. The major parties have had to deal with reconciling East and West, Quebec and the rest, within their own ranks. This generates sometimes unbearable tensions. The Conservative party has traditionally had difficulty with Quebec, and only long years of patient work by Joe Clark, capped by the appeal of Brian Mulroney as a native son in 1984, succeeded in expanding the party's base there. During the 1976 Tory leadership campaign, various factions were known to support either the Western candidates (e.g., Jack Horner and Joe Clark) or the Quebec candidates (Claude Wagner and Brian Mulroney).[3] When John Turner became leader of the Liberal party, his main rival was Jean Chrétien. Pierre Trudeau was seen by some Western Liberals as preoccupied with the problems of Quebec and

central Canada.[4] These internal tensions go back to the days of Macdonald and Laurier, and are a basic fact of political party life.

In recent years, other sociological groups have begun to visibly claim their rightful place in party affairs. Most notable among these are women and youth, though ethnic groups (especially among the Liberals) are emerging as well. Women's and youth caucuses were established in each major party in the 1960s and 1970s, and women's policy issues are now debated separately and at length. Women, now more active in political parties, are increasingly expressing their frustration with the so-called old boys' network which often excludes them from key leadership roles.[5] When Flora Macdonald ran for the Tory leadership in 1976, she was seen by many as "the women's candidate."[6] The 1984 general election had a separate leadership debate on women's issues.

In addition to these sociologically defined interests, each party contains clusters of politically defined constituencies. Former leaders, current premiers, senators, M.P.s, party executives, and an odd assortment of "backroom" types make up what is often referred to as the Establishment. Sheila Copps, for example, claims that when she ran for leader of the provincial party, the Ontario Liberal Establishment failed to back her, mobilizing instead behind David Peterson.[7] Sean O'Sullivan complained of the Tory Establishment's attempts to control the party's youth wing.[8] In normal times, between elections, this Establishment exercises substantial influence. During leadership conventions, though easily outnumbered by grass-roots delegates, its members often act as synapses in the collective consciousness of party, passing critical information, processing demands and providing cues.[9] They are by no means united, and swirl in shifting coalitions, depending on issues at hand.

2. The Party and Ideology

Some sort of glue is needed to bind this rag-tag coalition. One adhesive element is ideology, or a shared vision of current problems and future prospects. It is by no means the only bonding agent, nor is it the most powerful. Yet parties are obliged by their public purpose to demonstrate a belief in some sort of coherent vision. The vision itself may be difficult to articulate, in part because it arises from the various constituencies mentioned above, but a vision there must be nonetheless.

Perhaps, however, calling a shared vision of this kind an ideology is not appropriate. It may explain the contortions political analysts suffer in pigeonholing parties by ideology.[10] Are the Liberals liberal, and the Conservatives conservative? To some degree one can find echoes of ideology in party platforms, but they are difficult to identify clearly. The two main parties are noted for this infidelity. It may be more accurate to say that political parties have *ico*nologies rather than *ide*ologies. Icons are symbols of complex and often inexpressible things, and an iconology may be defined as an eclectic collection of powerfully charged symbols. They do not make a system, nor do they necessarily compel policy conclusions, but they do define a shared, characteristic discourse which can clearly distinguish one party from another.

The Tories and Liberals each, for example, carefully nurture the icons of past leaders. Macdonald, Diefenbaker and, increasingly, Stanfield are symbols, in the Tory mind, of the traditions and practices of greatness. Laurier, Mackenzie King, St. Laurent, and Pearson, on the other hand, are icons of Liberal vision, compromise, competence, and internationalism. The Tories have a complicated visceral allegiance to the concepts of free enterprise and competition, while the Liberals vigorously embrace the idea of cultural and economic sovereignty. Internal dissension among Tories has a long history, but is mitigated by the belief that Conservatives are principled and hence prepared to do battle for what's right. Among Liberals, the long party tradition of compromise and consensus has instilled the dread of

self-destruction by attacks on the leader. The extraordinary attention paid in 1986 to criticisms of John Turner's leadership betrayed the extreme Liberal sensitivity on this issue.

Senator Keith Davey has been involved in Liberal Party politics since 1949, but is apparently not able to define a Liberal in terms other than a list of icons. A Liberal likes the *Toronto Star,* bilingualism, John Turner, Pierre Trudeau, David Peterson, Canadian content, Air Canada, and multiculturalism, among other things, but hates Ronald Reagan, Margaret Thatcher, sacred trusts, foreign control, Doug Fisher, and separatism.[11]

While the lack of a clearly articulated ideology is a commonly noted fault of party leaders, it is certain that without a firm grasp of the party's iconology, no leader can hope to succeed. Brian Mulroney, despite his lack of parliamentary experience and apparent absence of ideology when he became leader, was able to skilfully tap key party icons, using their energy for his own purposes. His connections to Diefenbaker and his articulation of the party's resentment at losing power in 1980, when it had been within its grasp, were brilliant examples of how would-be leaders can invoke symbols in their own behalf.[12]

3. The Party and Elections

In the first essay in this section, David Taras outlined the strategic importance of the media in modern politics. They bring leaders into our living rooms, revealing foibles with an electronic intensity completely beyond the grasp of print journalists. The media game has special rules which a prime minister must master. The phenomenon of "tagging," whereby leaders are quickly labelled as "strong and arrogant" (Trudeau), "wimpy" (Clark), or "untrustworthy" (Mulroney), makes immediate mastery a major priority for every leader. Parties now routinely employ media consultants who drill leaders on the rituals and tactics of media combat.

Despite their clear and growing influence in focussing our political attention on leaders, the media have by no means completely expunged the importance of party. It remains a fact that elections, while they are increasingly fought *in* the media, are fought *with* party machines.[13] Parties remain important as instruments of political success and as the training ground for future politicians. In Canada it is simply inconceivable that someone should aspire to political leadership without reasonably close ties to his or her party. As in most things, Prime Minister Trudeau was the exception to this rule, a man who within only four years of joining his party became its leader. But of the other leaders of the two main parties — Mulroney, Clark, Stanfield, Diefenbaker, and Drew; Turner, Pearson, St. Laurent, and Mackenzie King — all had long associations with the organizations they eventually led. Election of leaders by party convention has eroded the connection to some degree, since almost anyone with the right organization can contest the leadership. But plausible candidates must at least be of the clan, if not necessarily in the family.

Parties are political instruments as well, indispensable to fighting and winning elections. At the federal level, there are almost 300 seats or constituencies that require candidates. Parties perform the nominating functions at the grass roots. They handle the routine of local campaigns, and are critical to "getting out the vote." No amount of clever media hype will budge voters from their sofas — indeed, *too* clever a media campaign may dispose voters to stay home, comfortable in the knowledge that their party will win. This is the moment at which ordinary party organization can make the difference — the reminders to vote, the personal phone calls, the offers to provide transportation to and from the polls — mundane as they are, these efforts may often make the difference between winning and losing. Sheila Copps, for example, recounts how she lost her first election by 15 votes out of 20 000 cast: "In almost any local or provincial election, especially in urban areas, more people stay at home than vote. And those stay-at-

homes can make or break a candidate."[14]

Beyond offering these mundane election services, political parties are increasingly important as organizations in the soliciting of campaign contributions, a long-standing feature of Canadian politics, especially to parties in power. In the past, these contributions were solicited by a few notables or functionaries within the party, and usually somewhat discreetly. However, since the 1974 Election Expenses Act, party financing has become big business, and political parties have become increasingly sophisticated in encouraging donations.[15]

4. The Party and Purpose

This brings us to the reiteration of a fundamental if somewhat obvious truth about political parties. Their *raison d'être* is to win elections. All of their other activities ultimately must square with this goal and its reward, power.[16] Several simple corollaries accompany this fact.

First, parties are not policy-making or generating machines. In order to win elections, of course, one must be able to present a platform, some reasonably coherent vision of the party's public purpose. However, as this volume has stressed, prime ministers and premiers are increasingly the focal point for the Canadian policy process. As a focal point, they must balance their activities over a wide range of arenas. The party as a machine or instrument remains indispensable in mobilizing voters at the constituency level, but policy matters have to be addressed simultaneously in all arenas. Policy conventions have grown in popularity in recent years among political parties, but leaders continue to treat any resolutions agreed to by these conventions as advice and not instruction.

Second, if winning power is the primary function of the party, it is not surprising that most leaders eventually neglect the party between elections. The machine gets rusty, volunteers drift away, meetings become infrequent. Once elected to its head, most leaders see the party, outside of its electoral role, as a nuisance. Mackenzie King, for instance, allowed the Liberal party to atrophy drastically during World War II, and then realized, to his chagrin, that the 1945 election would be unwinnable without the Liberal organization.[17] Pierre Trudeau is sometimes blamed for having won power at the expense of his party. He believed in appealing directly to the voters over the heads of the party, and quite deliberately allowed the Liberal organization (especially in the West) to decline.[18] He loathed the normal duties of the party leader among the faithful: appearances at local events and meetings with constituency executives.[19] John Turner, upon assuming the leadership, promised to revitalize the party at its roots. His efforts were a response to the drubbing the party had received in the 1984 election. Turner's atypical attention to the party between elections is clearly linked to his judgement that the party had lost its effectiveness as an electoral weapon.

Finally, the fact that parties are in business to win elections helps explain the special character of their relationship to the leader. The leader, in service of the led, must be seen to further the party's electoral goal. As long as he remains successful in that quest, the party will follow. But should he falter and stumble, his followers are often quite prepared to trample him underfoot in their stampede to appoint a new champion. Party members therefore have, to use Burke's phrase, a dignified obedience, a proud submission to their leader which retains, even in servitude, a terrible potential of retribution should the leader fail. The Conservatives have been noted for exercising this punishment upon leaders who lose: Diefenbaker,[20] Stanfield,[21] and especially Joe Clark[22] all felt the sting of rejection. Indeed, the "leadership review" which eventually forced Clark out in favour of Mulroney proved so painful that the party has now limited its use. The Liberals are also cautious about formal review mechanisms, but John Turner clearly felt the intense heat of party disappointment after the 1984 electoral

debacle. Two years later, with party fortunes still ambiguous, he had to defend himself against criticisms by the "old guard" of Trudeau supporters in the party.

5. The Party and Its People

In some ways, prime ministers would be better able to handle their parties if they had only to deal with paid personnel. While the paid staff of all Canadian political parties has grown substantially in the last ten years, the vast majority of party members and workers are still volunteers. They receive no direct benefit or reward other than the party's success as a whole, or perhaps the success of the individual candidate they have supported.

The demographic profile of party members is what one would expect. For both Liberals and Conservatives, they tend to be drawn disproportionately from the middle- and upper-income groups, with higher levels of education. Women play a prominent role at this level, in sharp contrast to their under-representation in candidacies and executive functions. Party members are more ideological than the average citizen, meaning that they are capable of articulating a reasonably consistent political position on a wider range of policy issues.

Why do they join and contribute their time this way? Surely it is not for the intrinsic rewards of envelope-licking and doorbell-ringing. Their motives are complex, but can roughly be organized into three categories. The first, and most benign, is a simple desire for camaraderie and social intercourse. As Jean Chrétien has put it: "Politics is a game of friends."[23] Political parties are like massive clubs, and party members often enjoy the opportunity to meet a wide range of different people and build up social contacts, as well as the satisfaction of working with others for a common goal. The second category of motives is more clearly political. People with convictions on certain political issues are prepared to fight for the victory of those convictions through the medium of a political party. They believe, in short, in "the cause" and are prepared to advance it as best they can.

These first two categories help us understand the support that political parties may draw upon when they are out of general favour. The NDP, the Tories, and recently the Liberals need volunteers with conviction, who are prepared to give of their time and energy for little or no direct compensation. It would be foolish, however, to ignore the fact that over time, even the most selfless volunteer may begin to yearn for a more tangible recognition of his or her sacrifices. This is the third type of motive for political involvement. The most tangible rewards are appointments or perks doled out by government, so that political success becomes a sine qua non of party survival. Brian Mulroney, when he ran for the Tory leadership, made it quite clear that upon election, his government would ensure the bestowal of patronage on Conservatives.[24] For party supporters who had endured almost twenty years in the political wilderness, and who had briefly gained control and then lost the government under Joe Clark, it was an irresistible promise.

Donald Johnston has put the issue graphically:

> Separating the powermongers and the patronage-seekers from the dedicated is a chronic problem of political parties. This process is easier following defeat when hard work rather than a place at the public trough is the only reward. When the beast is dead, parasites migrate to another warm body.[25]

The motivational reality which underlies party support suggests a number of key prime ministerial strategies. A prime minister will always have to retain some degree of control over the patronage system, and will have to use that system to proffer incentives when appropriate.[26] Senatorships, Royal Commissions, obscure boards and agencies — the deliberate and judicious distribution of these and other plums will keep the spirit of self-sacrifice from flagging. As important, if not more so, is the need to provide *symbolic* rewards. Most party volunteers crave nothing more than respect and acknowledgement. These can be provided in various ways: the leader can solicit advice, compliment the work of volunteers, proclaim the importance of party democracy, and appear at local functions.

6. The Selection of Leaders

Before 1919, Canadian political parties followed British practice in electing their leaders from within the parliamentary wing. The caucus elected the leader. Since 1919 (1926 for the Tories) the parties have selected their leaders by open convention.[27] Delegates from all the ridings, members of the parliamentary party, and others specially designated arrive by the hundreds to select, by run-off ballot, the new leader. This selection process has several consequences for the relations of leader and party.

First, the leader, once elected by the party, can plausibly claim national and broad party support. The run-off system assures that the leader must be elected by a majority, however slim, and since no provincial breakdowns of the votes are given, there is no chance of discerning an imbalance in regional support. Since the leader is elected by *all* of the party, he or she may claim a moral and symbolic power of representation which would simply be unavailable under a different, more restricted, system.

Second, the dynamics of convention elections reduce the importance of parliamentary experience among leadership aspirants. The hallmark of a parliamentary career is skill in the parry and thrust of debate, but modern Canadian politics places relatively little emphasis upon it. Question Period is often a revue of theatrical accusations and denials, and media image matters as much as, if not more than, parliamentary substance. Convention delegates know this, and so a long career in formal politics is no longer regarded as crucial for leaders. Brian Mulroney, Joe Clark, and Pierre Trudeau are proof of this new reality. Some substantial connection with the party is still important, however, as the Clark and Mulroney examples show.

Finally, the convention process can create difficulties for the new leader. Defeated rivals may nurse a grudge, or protest a specious loyalty while they plot anew. In some instances, as happened with Joe Clark, the new leader is under constant threat of revolt and must use every resource just to maintain control of the party. In other cases, as with Mulroney and perhaps Turner, the wounds heal more rapidly. But the smoothness of this process will in part reflect on the leader's abilities. Possessing the prime ministership is the leader's key weapon: grudges and dissension will eventually evaporate in the face of the resources and prestige available to the prime minister.

7. The Leader's Power in the Party

In an essay earlier in this volume, I have argued that we need a different concept of power to fully grasp what it is that leaders do, and what they are capable of doing. Leaders are plugged into pre-existing and ongoing political and social processes, and their leadership consists of an ability to harness these various processes in the service of a single vision. It is wrong, therefore, to conceive of the leader's power as something "possessed" or imposed; it is rather the use of strategic intervention to alter and direct flows of power in other arenas that defines the leader's influence.

In these terms, a leader's power in the party which elected him may be reduced to waiting for opportunities and nurturing the resources available for intervention. In formal terms, the leader of each of the major parties has few opportunities to direct party affairs. Each party has a national executive, of which the leader is a member, to oversee party affairs. The nomination and selection of delegates is controlled by the local riding. The leader may try, of course, to influence those processes informally or use prestige to encourage certain outcomes, although not on a regular basis.[28]

In formal terms, then, the leader has in fact relatively few opportunities and resources to intervene in party processes.[29] Informally, however, the scope is much wider. A key asset in this regard is his symbolic role as leader, though if he also occupies the prime ministership he obviously has more tangible instruments at his disposal. He can work behind the scenes to encourage his supporters to outflank his foes, he can use his platform as leader to alter or amend terms of debate on key issues, he can force issues as "tests" of his leadership, he can, over time, demonstrate capacities of moral leadership which attract new support for his position, he can encourage coalitions and discourage alliances. None of these means is immediate or necessarily direct, which helps explain those awkward episodes when party leaders seem at war with their own supporters. Tories, who have been out of power much longer than the Liberals, have been afflicted by this more frequently.

8. The Prime Minister as Leader

A central fact which helps explain both the opportunities and constraints faced by prime ministers is that they are simultaneously leaders of a *party* and of a *government*. The contrasts, indeed the contradictions, are sharp: (1) the party is partisan, while the government is in the broad public interest; (2) the leader can only influence the party, whereas he may command the government; (3) party loyalty is to his person, government loyalty to his position; (4) the party is most alive during elections, the government is most alive between them; (5) the leader is elected by his party, but the government is elected by the people. There are other contrasts, but these reveal the tensions which all prime ministers face — in effect, the tensions in managing the dynamics of two related yet often conflicting arenas.

As party leader, the prime minister is expected to be concerned with partisan advantage and party affairs. The reward of the party faithful through patronage may extend from obviously partisan appointments to the awarding of contracts to loyal ridings. Partisanship means stirring up the troops occasionally with attacks on opponents. And yet, as government leader, the prime minister must preserve the fiction that he is above mere partisan concerns and is engaged in furthering the public interest. Appointments should be made on merit, contracts awarded on the basis of efficiency, and ad hominem attacks should be avoided in favour of principled debate.

The tensions between party and government are reflected further in the loyalty which the leader may demand: in the party it is a loyalty to his person as one of them, to his qualities and abilities. To appear prime ministerial is to appear distant and aloof. Every leader must somehow balance the dignity and distance of his role as prime minister with the familiarity and openness expected by party followers. His influence over his party comes from his formal role as prime minister, but he can never forget that as party leader he heads a voluntary organization quite jealous of its autonomy; as government leader he has a much greater ability to issue formal commands and assume obedience. In part, the temptation of power is to embrace the formal role since, superficially at least, it is an arena of recognized authority. Since the party may to some degree be safely ignored between elections, the temptation can seem sweet indeed. But as stated earlier, parties are indispensable weapons in electoral struggle, and the true challenge for any leader is to play all these arenas and their demands. Pierre Trudeau appeared to embrace his formal prime ministerial role to the disadvantage of his party role; Prime Minister Mulroney is perhaps doing the reverse.

9. The Party and Voters

In their struggle for power, political parties must of course appeal to voters. They must either play on a pre-existent loyalty, diminish a lingering doubt, or activate neutrality. Looked at from this perspective, political parties are really just the nodal point for a vast, shifting and temporary coalition of voters. The party must hammer together, by election day, a plausible coalition of socio-economic constituencies which ordinarily might be opposed to each other. This is the aggregating and integrating function of parties writ large.

In modern politics the media expect the leader to articulate the party's national profile. In doing this, the leader may initiate subtle yet far-reaching changes in the sociological base of a party. This role was not lost on the pre-television generation of party organizers. In the 1930s, for instance, a belief grew among some Tories that their party was perceived as being too right-wing; accordingly, John Bracken was recruited to the leadership in the early 1940s and brought with him a change in the party's name to *Progressive* Conservative.[30] Pierre Trudeau was an attractive leadership candidate in 1967 because, in part, he could be counted on to appeal to Quebeckers as well as to women and youth. In his second bid for the Tory leadership, Brian Mulroney had a tremendous advantage in being able to plausibly claim that he could "deliver Quebec."

In retrospect, those leaders whom we designate as great are often the ones who, whatever their reputations while in office, have managed to forge, on behalf of their parties, new and enduring coalitions. Macdonald created a coalition of Quebec and Ontario; Laurier's coalition was built of Quebec and the West. Pierre Trudeau changed the sociological profile of his party to include many more ethnic Canadians.

10. Leaders, Parties and Policy

These preceding glimpses or *aperçus* lead to some tentative conclusions on political parties, their leaders, and public policy. Perhaps most important is the realization that party and government are very different arenas which demand different skills and behaviour. The demands they make on the prime minister are often contradictory. Many observers have attempted to deal with these arenas as two stages: *first* the leader arises in the party, *then* the leader assumes the prime ministership. It is much more fruitful, however, to remember that these arenas operate simultaneously, and hence may tug the prime minister in different directions.

Political parties are not machines, however often that analogy may be used for them. They are ragged coalitions of many interests, centred around a few key ideas and, more often, icons, aiming to win power but having to rely largely on volunteers. Prime ministers are easily and understandably distracted by their governmental responsibilities, but the very fact of prime ministership gives them certain leverage over the party. The prospect of patronage is extremely effective in welding together disparate party factions. The power over cabinet appointments and some parliamentary perks helps discipline the caucus. Modern elections focus on the leader, and leaders who lose risk the wrath of the followers. By the same token, however, leaders who win power, especially those who do so regularly, attain an almost unrivalled authority over their followers.

The fact remains, however, that prime ministers are also party leaders, and the forces described above place constraints on their actions. M.P.s, for example, may toe the line in the Legislature but are quite prepared to vent their views in caucus. No prime minister can completely disregard these internal caucus debates, though he can try to channel them. Parties can also have a cherished commitment to certain policies that no prime minister may reject with impunity. It is not that they are unable to reject the policies or practices, only that they must be prepared to carry the party with them. In this regard, as in others, Pierre Trudeau seems to have been an exception. His solitary decision in 1978 to cut $2 billion from federal expenditures not only departed from government policy but was made without the consultation of key ministers.[31]

It is clear from the preceding review that political parties have a modest role in policy formation. The dynamics of parties demand that leaders give a respectful hearing to party policy resolutions, but the discipline of power requires that these resolutions be considered guides and nothing more. However, the party's informal policy role can be strategically important. The prime minister, as leader, needs to secure party support from among its many factions and coalitions. A process of anticipating reactions can thus occur, whereby the party does not *formally* determine policy, but informal and potential responses may affect policy design. As well, no leader can ignore the iconology of the party — it contributes a vocabulary of symbols and concepts whereby policy is shaped in a party's image.

Ultimately, a prime minister's success depends on adroitly playing these various arenas, and that often demands a politics of position rather than of principle. Principles matter, of course, but they need to be translated into terms appropriate to each of the key arenas. This in turn requires a sensitivity to the dynamics and opportunities that arise independently in the political process. In the 1984 election, for example, Brian Mulroney capitalized brilliantly on the patronage issue: it echoed the resentment of his party against those who had so long enjoyed the fruits of power, it expressed a fundamental principle of good government, and it could be clearly articulated in the media. Good political issues do not simply arise; they are made. Their fabrication requires a measure of luck, but ultimately depends on the successful, and often instinctual, exercise of strategic leadership.

Notes

1. Weller, *First Among Equals,* p. 18.
2. See, for example, the skimpy treatment of this issue in the leading textbooks on Canadian politics: Van Loon and Whittington, *The Canadian Political System,* Chap. 10; Jackson et al., *Politics in Canada,* pp. 465-73; Gibbins, *Conflict and Unity,* pp. 306-309.
3. Brown, Chodos and Murphy, *Winners, Losers.*

4. For an amusing description, see Gwyn, *The Northern Magus,* Chap. 16.

5. On women in politics, see Bashevkin, *Toeing the Line.*

6. Brown, Chodos and Murphy, *Winners, Losers,* p. 72.

7. Copps, *Nobody's Baby,* p. 41.

8. O'Sullivan, *Both My Houses,* pp. 34-35.

9. Senator Keith Davey is the backroom politician extraordinaire. See his autobiography, *The Rainmaker.*

10. See for example Christian and Campbell, *Political Parties and Ideologies in Canada.*

11. Davey, *The Rainmaker,* p. 327.

12. Martin, Gregg and Perlin, *Contenders.*

13. For instance, televised leadership debates have relatively little impact on election outcomes; Leduc and Price, "Great Debates."

14. Copps, *Nobody's Baby,* p. 18.

15. Stanbury, "The Mother's Milk of Politics."

16. See Winn, "Elections."

17. Whitaker, *The Government Party,* Chap. 4.

18. Johnston, *Up the Hill,* p. 57.

19. As described in McCall-Newman, *Grits,* p. 340.

20. Newman, *Renegade in Power,* Chaps. 24-25.

21. Stevens, *Stanfield,* Chaps. 12-13.

22. Simpson, *Discipline of Power.*

23. Chrétien, *Straight From the Heart,* p. 23.

24. Martin, Gregg and Perlin, *Contenders.*

25. Johnston, *Up the Hill,* p. 135.

26. Prime Minister Trudeau ended his time in office with a barrage of appointments. Having held them vacant for so long may have enhanced party discipline.

27. For background, see Courtney, *The Selection of National Party Leaders,* Chaps. 1-2.

28. When Don Johnston mentioned to Pierre Trudeau that he was interested in running for office, Trudeau was encouraging. "[There] was little he could do to help, however, since it would have violated Party convention for him to give the nod to any particular person in a Liberal nomination race." Johnston, *Up the Hill,* p. 31.

29. See McMenemy, Redekop and Winn, "Party Structures and Decision-Making."

30. Morton, *The Progressive Party in Canada.*

31. As described in Chrétien, *Straight From the Heart,* pp. 117-118.

CHAPTER 8

The Discipline of Democracy: Prime Ministers and Economic Policy

Robert Malcolm Campbell

> *Politics is a strong and slow boring of hard boards. It takes both passion and perspective. Certainly all historical experience confirms the truth — that man would not have attained the possible unless time and again he had reached out for the impossible. But to do that a man must be a leader.*
>
> Max Weber[1]
>
> *It still makes an extraordinary political difference if a government...is prepared to take steps to try and reduce unemployment from 10 percent to 8 percent, perhaps with a sacrifice in inflation or other indicators of performance.*
>
> Bruce Doern[2]

The question of leadership and economic policy in Canada engenders skepticism and ambivalence, if not outright despair. On the one hand, it is easy to recite the familiar litany of constraints on national economic policy: international conditions, foreign ownership, the deficit, federalism, the bureaucracy, the uncertainty of our times, a multitude of vested interests, capitalism itself. On the other hand, governments are expected to ensure stable economic circumstances, reduce inflation and unemployment, improve economic capacity and productivity, protect the dollar, and promote fairer economic distribution. In debating economic policy, we are happily inconsistent. We ridicule politicians for trying to accomplish the impossible — yet we are indignant when they fail. Depending upon whether we are wearing our descriptive or prescriptive "hats," we see political leaders' acceptance of constraints and reality as a sign of either maturity or expediency, and their attempts to change reality as either naïve or courageous.

Is political leadership an independent variable in the economic policy equation? The first two sections of this chapter will set out the concepts necessary for discussion, and suggest that leadership is indeed possible and necessary. The third section is an accounting of the resources for, and constraints on, political leadership in national economic policy-making in Canada. The fourth section will present a series of case studies, examining C.D. Howe, John Diefenbaker, Walter Gordon, and the Trudeau and Mulroney eras.

CONCEPTUAL ISSUES

Discussion of leadership and economic policy is complicated by two recent but opposing intellectual and social tendencies: (1) scholarly analysis of economic policy has become sophisticated and arcane, focussing particularly on aggregates and macrostructural variables and conditions; and (2) strong ideological currents have arisen against technocratic styles and approaches to policy-making, condemning their failure to make good their promises, as well their apparent lack of purpose or goals. These tendencies are difficult to reconcile in the present discussion, for the first seems to trivialize human agency in economic policy, while the second appears to cry out for it.

Parallelling these two currents are two of the most famous characterizations of political leadership. Joseph Schumpeter[3] (1883-1950) was concerned that an "ineffective" democratic system would ultimately be replaced by an "effective" non-democratic one. In devising his "elite theory of democracy," he argued that the legitimacy of liberal democracy could be sustained only in the realization of three conditions: (1) the limitation of the area of political decision-making, (2) the exercise of political self-restraint, both within Parliament and in society at large, and (3) the existence of capable leadership and a well-trained bureaucracy. For Schumpeter, effective political leadership involved setting strict boundaries for political activity, to ensure that democratic politics would be effective within these bounds. Political leaders had also to keep expectations in check in order that democratic politics should not be swamped by potentially unrealizable demands. In addition, political leaders were to insulate the technical experts in the bureaucracy from political and ideological pressures, to allow them to manage the economy success-

fully. In sum, Schumpeter saw political leadership as a disciplinary agent whose purpose was to help ensure the economic stability and security that would sustain liberal democracy's effectiveness and legitimacy.

Max Weber[4] (1864-1920) was also concerned about the future viability of liberal democracy. He anticipated that advances in science and technology would create an ever more bureaucratized world, one in which experts and rationality would dominate the management of human life. Weber feared that the values of science and rationality would replace human norms and values in society. In the process, the mass public would become increasingly enervated politically, leaving the major decisions about how to live to the experts, seemingly competent and able to deliver the goods. For Weber, political leadership entailed a critical political role as a democratic antidote to the threats of bureaucratic and technological dominance. The importance of "charismatic" leadership for Weber was its capacity as a countervailing force against science and rationality. The political leader has the responsibility of translating technological issues into debatable human and normative terms, while keeping the mass public democratically alive, alert, and anxious to discuss these issues. In sum, Weber saw the role of political leadership as similar to a preacher's, with the ultimate responsibility of sustaining democracy's vitality and humanity in the face of bureaucracy and technology.

The Schumpeterian notion of political leadership contains expectations, while the Weberian model excites them. In the former, the leader is a disciplinarian, in the latter, a preacher. These models reflect, in broad terms, the ambivalent attitude most people have towards leadership. One directs us to hard realities and constraints; the other points us to goals and opportunities. One places a premium on effectiveness and rationality, the other fears an exclusive reliance on these goals and places a premium on human norms and values.

This chapter will explore leadership as a

synthesis of these two models. Three ingredients will be analyzed in the calculation of political leadership: means, ends, and accomplishments. The first refers to the array of resources available to, and the constraints on, political leaders in the policy process. In the abstract, leaders certainly have power, influence and opportunities for action. But they also face political, bureaucratic, and socioeconomic checks on this power. An accounting of resources and constraints will be made in Section III. For now, one can say that political leaders have a capacity for action that is real but not unlimited. "Ends" refers to the use of resources or the exploitation of opportunities for particular purposes or goals. This is perhaps the essence of leadership. "To take a stand, to be passionate," wrote Weber, "is the politician's element, and above all the element of the political leader."[5] Finally, political leadership comprises the use of political capacity to realize results or "accomplishments" in accordance with the leader's vision.

The above ingredients suggest that political leaders have "space" to manoeuvre. This space is defined by political resources and constraints. As for the multitude of possible political objectives, the choice is determined by the leader's personal values. Political leadership thus implies the maximum use of resources, understanding and perhaps neutralizing or transforming constraints, and the selection of an objective or combination of objectives.

Political accomplishments depend on more than the exercise of raw power or the labelling of winners and losers. First, politics comprises an almost limitless array of conflicting goals. The leader's choice of objectives might involve the redefining of political life, the setting of priorities, and the legitimizing of new policy options. In this, the leader may be transforming constraints into opportunities and, if successful in striking a resonant public chord, the "symbolic" leader may increase the resources available for action. Second, one must evaluate results according to the reality of resources and

constraints, as well as according to the coherence of the objectives chosen. Resources can be well or poorly used, constraints can be well-judged or underestimated, goals may be reasonable or create false expectations. The successful leader requires "warm passion and a cool sense of proportion."[6] Third, results are seldom attained all at once or in the first attempt. Here again, Weber is instructive. "The final result of political action," he warns, "often, no, even regularly, stands in completely inadequate and often paradoxical relation to its original meaning."[7] Unintended results may not reflect poorly on the leader's actions. Circumstances can change, technical calculations may be wrong; the world is usually more complicated and unyielding than it seems. Effective leadership requires patience, the "slow boring of hard boards." "Only he has the calling for politics who is sure that he shall not crumble when the world from his point of view is too stupid or too base for what he wants to offer."[8]

Fourth, political leadership can be assessed by the extent to which leaders engage and animate the public in the discussion and evaluation of values and goals. The public is a potential resource in the leader's attempts to realize certain objectives. The modern politician is sometimes caricatured as a timid, cautious leader, poring over public opinion-poll results, afraid of tampering with opinion and the chance of re-election. This is internalizing and being inhibited by public opinion, instead of engaging it. In this way, the absence of political leadership is potentially a threat to democracy, particularly as bureaucratic and technological imperatives limit the scope of human choice.

THE CONTEXT OF ECONOMIC POLICY

Given our conceptual sense that leadership must be assessed in terms of the space allowed by resources, constraints, and goals, it is important to indicate the extent to which the context of economic policy has changed drastically over the last two decades. The postwar period can be divided into two eras: the Keynesian era, from World War II to the early 1970s, and the post-Keynesian era, from the early 1970s to the present. Each era produced its own policy style and concept of political leadership. The former was marked by Schumpeterian leadership, while the latter demands a more assertive style.

The Keynesian Era

Economic policy in this era occurred in the following conditions:

- The quarter-century after World War II was marked by a ''long wave'' of economic expansion which produced economic stability, growth and prosperity. Postwar reconstruction, the application of technological innovations, cheap resources, and the liberalizing of the international economy provided substantial opportunities for private economic activity.[9]

- The economic policy of this period can be summed up in the Keynesian countercyclical paradigm. In broad terms, the government would act to smooth out the business cycle by incurring budget deficits to inject demand when economic downturns threatened, and budget surpluses to withdraw demand when inflationary pressures developed. Ironically, the policy approach was not used to any great extent, given economic conditions and other factors. In any event, the Canadian version of Keynesianism was market-oriented, with a marginal, passive and disciplinary role for the state.[10]

- There was a high degree of consensus about how the economy worked, what policies to use, what (limited Keynesian) goals to pursue. Policymakers faced a relatively certain and simple world.

- As goals were limited and state expansion minimal, there was little proliferation of economic departments or agencies. The Department of Finance dominated a simple policy process, though the occasional strong minister made his presence felt.

The Post-Keynesian Era

Economic policy-making since the early 1970s, on the other hand, has taken place in a very different context than in the Keynesian era.

- The postwar ''long wave'' of economic expansion came to an end in the late 1960s. The pace of economic growth slowed considerably; as resource prices grew, the ''old'' technology's possibilities were fully exploited and the tasks of reconstruction were completed. A new economic phenomenon — stagflation — developed as individuals, groups, corporations, and the state acted to protect themselves from the impact of economic decline.

- Economic uncertainty was not neutralized by theoretical innovation. While conventional wisdom was incapable of explaining what was going on in the economy, no victor emerged from the variety of theories contending to replace Keynesianism. Since the early 1970s, there has been no policy consensus on how to conduct economic life.

- Once economic circumstances declined, there was immense pressure placed on the state to sort out economic difficulties. Myriad new objectives and issues were placed on the political agenda: regionalism, foreign ownership, supply-side issues, productivity, resources and the environment, etc.

- These were issues previously sorted out in the market, and now to be dealt with by the state. Political goals and objectives increased, with a spate of new economic departments and agencies. The provinces returned to economic policy-making with a vengeance. With departmental proliferation came a weakening of the Department of Finance's policy dominance. The new multiplicity of goals and bureaucratic fragmentation made policy co-ordination difficult, and efforts were launched to systematize and make rational this complex policy process. The result was an unwieldy and complicated policy milieu.[11] Ironically, the early postwar era afforded governments substantial opportunity for initiatives, but the policy style called for a passive and disciplinary state. The recent era is marked by economic uncertainty, multiple goals, less policy and technical consensus, and more policy players; it demands leadership, but the opportunities have diminished and the constraints have increased.

LEADERSHIP CAPACITY — AN ACCOUNTING

This section reviews the resources for, and checks on, political leadership in economic policy.

Resources

Compared to more consensual or fragmented political systems, the Canadian parliamentary system provides considerable space for manoeuvre. The policy process is dominated by the prime minister and Cabinet, as a result of executive-legislative fusion which concentrates power in their hands. This power is relatively stable and certain, given prime ministerial control over election timing and over the hiring and firing of cabinet ministers, and given also Canada's idiosyncratic electoral system, which translates plurality support into majority government for four to five years. The prime minister dominates the use of this concentrated power, personifying as he does "the government." This is the result of media-dominated election campaigns, which focus on the prime minister, making him the star attraction and allowing him to appeal directly to the public. Underlying this development is the fact that the deferential, passive Canadian public feels quite comfortable with strong leaders. Election campaigns focus on the leader, and party platforms are soft and warm; the prime minister settles into office with few constraints from a policy platform. This has been reinforced recently by the phenomenon of the prime minister as "outsider," unsullied by past political activity and free of the debts incurred over a lifetime of political compromise. It seems that there is considerable institutional space for the prime minister to manoeuvre in.

The prime minister may have little interest in economic affairs, but can place his or her stamp on the area through appointments (e.g., Minister of Finance, Governor of the Bank of Canada, head of the Treasury Board, Chair of the Economic Council of Canada). Appointment of deputy ministers is a prime ministerial prerogative as well. The finance minister, in turn, has considerable resources, including the tradition of secrecy and the glamour of the budget, considerable control over fiscal resources, key access to decision-making points, a capable bureaucracy with a deep sense of tradition and importance, and the mystery and complexity of economics itself.

The prime minister cannot reasonably be thought to have much influence on the mechanics of formulating and executing economic policy. Potential leadership in economic policy comes with the P.M.'s prerogative to define the political agenda and set political and economic priorities, and to have these reinforced through appointments. It is worth remembering that politics is as much about ideas as it is about power. The prime minister can inject new ideas or even redefine the economic situation, thereby tilting the policy process in a certain direction and reorienting public attention. Of course, this cannot be done in all areas at once, lest political resources be spread too thin. In all of this, the prime minister plays a kind of symbolic role, and acts as a policy initiator and even "preacher" about policy.

While lacking the power to directly control the mechanics of policy-making, the prime minister can alter the character and direction of the policy process through government reorganization. This can range from inventing new departments to rearranging the Prime Minister's Office (PMO) to changing the rules of the policy game. Successive executives have recently attempted to increase political control over the bureaucracy, resulting in innovations like the cabinet committee system and the Policy and Expenditure Management System, and the recasting of the roles of the Treasury Board and the PMO. Overall, the policy process has become rather Byzantine, collegial and cumbersome, reducing individual ministerial power while apparently increasing the prime minister's and the Cabinet's control. The prime minister is clearly pre-eminent, assigning ministers as he sees fit to various committees, including the crucial Priorities and Planning Committee. He is in the best bargaining and levering position, controlling the agenda of government and the timing of consideration of issues. He may also delay addressing awkward issues. More often than not, crucial and far-reaching decisions are taken in times of "emergency" or "crisis," where the prime minister has immense authority and capacity to act in the "national interest" or to do what is "technically" necessary.

There are a number of broad environmental factors which give political leaders room to manoeuvre, of which only two of the most important can be noted here. First, one cannot understate the extent to which the Canadian public is politically passive and inexperienced, and willing to accept strong political leadership. This is partly a result of the relatively small and weak labour force in Canada. Organized labour lacks the institutional position or the moral force necessary to veto, or to threaten to veto, a policy proposal. This allows leadership considerably more space than if organized labour had an institutional role to play in economic policy-making, or if it could ensure that all economic proposals were debated in class terms. Economic issues in Canada rarely take on "us versus them" class character, although this is in part the result of the federal system, which regionalizes economic issues. Second, while obvious economic constraints exist, economic policy in Canada is constructed on a reasonably healthy and viable base. Canada is an immensely rich country, with abundant raw materials, a well-educated work force, a fully developed economic infrastructure, an abundance of economic expertise, and considerable economic opportunities.

Constraints

Despite the fusion and concentration of power, the prime minister faces a variety of institutional constraints:

- Policy *initiation* is not identical to policy *formulation* and *implementation.* In these latter areas, the permanent bureaucracy commands considerable resources, including access to information and technical economic expertise; in addition, it has the advantages of permanence, a strong sense of purpose and goals, and numerous potential points at which it can delay and veto.

- Given the peculiarities of Canadian Cabinet-making, the prime minister often faces a wide range of political and ideological opinion in key areas. Policy integration and prioritization may be impossible with intense infighting and controversy, and threats of ministerial resignation can be inhibiting.

- Similarly, there may be little or no unity in the caucus on key or controversial matters, as it, like the Cabinet, also contains wide ideological diversity and cleavages. If the latter cannot be resolved, policy initiatives can be delayed or even shelved.

- As discussed in another article in this volume, national policy-making faces a federal reality. In economic areas, jurisdictions overlap, and national policy has provincial spin-offs and implications whose impact is monitored and scrutinized by the suspicious and assertive provinces.

- The prime minister faces the inevitable prospect of seeking re-election, and this reality may ultimately conflict with his personal ideas and aspirations as election time draws near.

- A proliferating bureaucracy and a more collegial, systems style of policy-making make life complicated for the prime minister and key economic agencies like the Department of Finance.

All of these constraints essentially present tests of leadership for the prime minister.

There are also three serious environmental constraints on political leadership in economic policy. First, Canada is a liberal, democratic, capitalist country, and there are two competing "systems of authority" where economic matters are concerned.[12] Private property confers authority in economic matters to corporations and business, whose opposition can undermine the legitimacy of leaders' economic goals and policies. Governments must therefore retain the confidence of this sector, for electoral financing as much as because the Canadian public acknowledges corporate authority in economic matters. Even the Canadian labour movement rarely challenges corporate authority in any significant way.

Second, new political leaders usually inherit less-than-optimal economic conditions; these can seriously limit the space for manoeuvre. Economic conditions over the last decade have been uncertain, and there has been little analytical or policy consensus either. This uncertainty has been exacerbated by the bewildering pace of technological change and the increasing internationalization of economic activity. A change in a Third-World country's debt policy, a shift in political conditions in the Middle East, or the use of more efficient industrial machinery in the newly industrializing countries can alter the economic picture very quickly and dramatically.

Third, Canada's political economic system has some constraining peculiarities. For example, Canada is a trading nation which is quite dependent on foreign markets and capital. Private corporate decisions are made, to a considerable extent, outside of the country, as a result of high degrees of foreign ownership. Canada's proximity to, and dependence on, the United States affects Canada's tax, monetary, and trade policies. The economy is unevenly developed, both sectorally and regionally. Leading sectors (e.g., finance, energy) absorb resources and expend influence, unbalancing the policy agenda. The manufacturing sector is weak and truncated. The economy is balkanized around the resource and economic bases of different regions, which makes national consensus on economic matters all but impossible.

Finally, the prime minister's pre-eminence also makes him or her a clear target. With the assumption of office, expectations are pumped up by the media about the "new regime," whose performance must inevitably fall short. The ensuing disappointment, sense of betrayal and criticism are as intense as the previous degree of support, and come to act as an effective constraint on the leader. This is the direct result of interest-group politics. Leadership normally involves innovation or assertion on one or two fronts, and those interests not part of the chosen few feel let down. If the leader acts to make everyone happy, he appears to lack principles or purpose, and risks spreading resources too thinly. In all of this, the political leader confronts the real, messy, disappointing world of politics — a world of limited budgets and inherited commitments, of multiple objectives and competing interests, of departmental competition and political rivalries, and of short-term political pressures conspiring against the realization of long-term goals.

What is the balance of resources and constraints in economic policy? These considerations are all abstractions whose impact depends on political personality and historical circumstance. Moreover, they rarely act all at once. On balance, it appears that the prime minister and his delegates have considerable symbolic and institutional power, and a genuine capacity to shape the policy agenda. They are also well-positioned to exploit opportunities should they arise, and use the mystique of economics or declare an emergency to their advantage. However, the constraints on economic policy are formidable and limit leadership capacity; they cannot be underestimated, and the political leader must exercise considerable patience and skill in pursuing his agenda for action.

POLITICAL LEADERSHIP IN ACTION

This section will present brief historical sketches of leadership in economic policy, following the ideas and considerations presented up to this point. Two exceptionally interesting economics ministers — C.D. Howe and Walter Gordon — will be assessed, and three economic policy "eras" will be reviewed — the Diefenbaker, Trudeau and Mulroney administrations.

C.D. Howe

C.D. Howe is remembered as a strong, assertive and active minister,[13] who had space in which to manoeuvre and place his stamp on economic policy in the 1940s and 1950s. There were three factors which allowed for this. First, neither Mackenzie King nor Louis St. Laurent were prime ministers especially interested in economic matters, and they delegated great authority to Howe. This authority was continuously renewed as he accumulated a vast store of information, experience and contacts in heading a number of critically important economic departments, both during the war and in peacetime. Many of these departments were new ones (e.g., Munitions and Supply, Reconstruction, Defence Production), with few inhibiting traditions or interests and with a wide scope for action. Others were dormant (e.g., Trade and Commerce) and easy to mould. To the extent that his policies were successful, his authority and stature grew. Given majority governments, federal dominance, fusion of power, cabinet support and a simple policy process, Howe was well positioned to shape economic policy.

Second, Howe was able to move into a "policy vacuum" created by the dominance of the Canadian version of Keynesianism. The Keynesian state's role in general — that of the Department of Finance in particular — was to be relatively passive, manipulating aggregate demand to ensure an economic stability in

which private enterprise could prosper. The Department of Finance was content with its monopolization of demand-side considerations and continued to adopt a relatively laissez-faire attitude to the economy. Economic development and technological change were ready to be assumed by an assertive and able minister. Ironically, then, even though Howe was never Minister of Finance, the Keynesian era provided a context in which he had few institutional or bureaucratic constraints.

Third, environmental factors favoured the exercise of leadership. The economy was healthy, particularly after 1947. The federal government emerged from the war as the dominant partner in the Canadian federation, and provincial constraint was weak. The Canadian public expected strong postwar leadership, and so tolerated the extension of wartime emergency powers which were available to Howe for a decade.

These conditions would have amounted to little if Howe himself had been a moderate, passive or disinterested minister. But he was a doer, an engineer by training and temperament, who liked pursuing big projects and enjoyed using political power to realize his goals. He remained in politics because he felt that there was more "action" in Ottawa than in the private sector.

Howe's major accomplishment was in shaping the direction and character of postwar Canadian economic development. As World War II was drawing to a close, tremendous pessimism prevailed and a postwar depression seemed inevitable. For many, this implied the necessity of extending into peacetime the massive state economic intervention of the war years and the establishment of economic planning and the welfare state. Howe was all but alone in his optimism about postwar economic prospects. His personal vision embraced free enterprise, and he argued against public investment, state economic controls, and a massive welfare state. He effectively neutralized the pessimism that was taking the policy process in a certain direction, and reoriented the government to a policy which emphasized decontrol and initiatives to the private sector. Prime Minister Mackenzie King, fearing the electoral consequences of such a narrow postwar economic focus, did ensure a modicum of social security measures, but there would be little expansion of the welfare state between 1945 and 1957.

Howe was undoubtedly the symbolic leader in postwar economics, embodying the optimistic, confident, growth-oriented mood of the time. He struck a resonant chord in the Canadian public, which appeared anxious for opportunities after years of depression and war. That he seemed able to deliver the goods increased his authority and stature. He repeatedly identified business interests with the public good. He enjoyed a symbiotic relationship with the "other" (i.e., besides the government) authority system — the capitalist world — which he regulated and patronized simultaneously.

The major postwar economic policy initiatives and innovations were Howe's. Overall, he ensured that Canada's would be a free-enterprise economy, not a state-regulated one. He effectively neutralized concerns about American investment and ownership, although King derailed the free-trade talks of the mid-1940s. An array of Crown corporations was sold to the private sector, at attractive rates, and business was offered generous tax advantages and subsidies. King encouraged economic development and grand projects in a number of areas (e.g., airline, pipelines), and used the tax and tariff system imaginatively to regulate and encourage investment. For example, he initiated a system of "double depreciation" after World War II and during the Korean War to direct investment funds and materials into areas of priority. During the 1947 exchange crisis, Schedule III of the Emergency Exchange Conservation Act discouraged imports and encouraged exports of certain American goods which could be manufactured in Canada.

Regardless of one's views about postwar economic development, one can conclude that

Howe made good use of the scope afforded him to realize his goals, although, admittedly, he did not face serious constraints until the end of the Liberal era. At this time, concerns about American influence and the Liberal style of government created an effective opposition. This was a leadership test for Howe, and here he failed, because he was impatient with opposing views and ideas, and misread the public's attitudes towards these claims.

The Diefenbaker Era

John Diefenbaker[14] was allotted all of the institutional resources noted in Section III, as a result of acquiring the largest majority of seats in Canadian history. He was the star attraction as the classic Weberian charismatic leader. On the one hand, he seemed to be a political outsider, a small-town Western lawyer with a fresh reform program. He also symbolized a reaction against the disciplines and inhibitions of Canadian Keynesianism, with its bureaucratic and technocratic character. Foreshadowing the neoconservative surge of the 1970s, he struck a resonant public chord in asserting the authority of politics and passion over rationality and technique.

His major political accomplishment was to redefine and reorder the political economic agenda to include and prioritize those issues which had been neglected in the Keynesian approach. The postwar "losers" or marginal elements — farmers, the elderly, and certain regions and sectors — were the source of his political strength and were spotlighted on the policy agenda. He resurrected ideological concerns about the economy in criticizing three negative implications of the Liberals' alleged laissez-faire approach: uneven regional and sectoral economic development, American dominance of the economy, and technocratic dominance of the policy process. He presented an alternative vision, one which gave the state the lead role in ensuring regionally and sectorally balanced national development, with greater manufacturing activity and less dependence on the United States.

This vision was not translated into reality to any great extent. Diefenbaker had inherited a weak and uncertain economic situation which, despite his avoidance of Keynesian measures, resulted in substantial, and growing, budgetary deficits which, in turn, constrained the possibilities for government spending. The environment closed down the political space for manoeuvre. More importantly, though, Diefenbaker's paranoia about the "Liberal bureaucracy," his ideological distrust of "experts," and his antipathy to the use of coercive means to implement goals blinded him to the fact that the realization of his vision required state planning and the sophisticated and substantial use of all of the state's powers. Economic policy was hesitant, amateurish, ad hoc — and not terribly successful. He was politically irresponsible in the sense that his goals or vision were never clearly articulated or defined, the constraints faced were underestimated, and there was insufficient consideration given to the means required to realize the ends.

Diefenbaker's leadership has left a policy legacy influential to this day. Governments since then have confronted a more extensive policy agenda, one not exclusively related to demand-side and management issues. His actions legitimized the idea that the national government was responsible for regional and sectoral economic balance, and supply as well as demand conditions. Tentative measures were taken, such as the Productivity Council, Roads to Resources, the Atlantic Development Board, work-force training, and tax incentives in the Fleming supply-side budgets of 1960-1962. His administration also generated political momentum to fill out the welfare state and give the provinces more fiscal and economic elbowroom.

Walter Gordon

As Finance Minister in the first Pearson administration, Walter Gordon enjoyed a brief period with considerable room for manoeuvre.[15] First,

the prime minister was not particularly interested in economics, and so delegated economic authority to his close friend. Second, Gordon had prime ministerial, party and caucus support as a result of the immense task he had accomplished in rebuilding the Liberal party after the 1958 electoral debacle. Along with Maurice Lamontagne and Tom Kent, he played a strategic role in proposing policy for the "reformed" Liberal Party. Third, he enjoyed considerable economic authority, thanks to his business background and the reputation he had developed in working with the public bureaucracy in wartime, and later on a number of Royal Commissions. He was the symbolic leader of a Liberal management team which exuded competence, professionalism, and experience.

Gordon used his advantages to redefine the political economic agenda. While he initiated and supported development in the area of regional, industrial, and social policy, his real political passion was the "national question." He rejected the Howe model of Canadian economic development, with its reliance on American funds and know-how, resulting in American ownership and dominance. At the first opportunity, in his 1963 budget, he produced a number of nationalist economic measures, including a withholding tax on dividends paid to non-residents and a takeover tax on foreign purchases of Canadian companies. Committed to getting the kind of budget that he wanted, Gordon chose to do a policy end run around the permanent bureaucracy, and hired three consultants to formulate and write this budget.

Reaction to the budget was so overwhelmingly critical that Gordon offered up his resignation to Pearson. Gordon was criticized for using outside consultants and for imposing a tax on manufacturers' equipment (in order to balance the budget). More importantly, though, the nationalist policy measures were assailed by the business community. These measures were dropped, and no similar action was attempted in Gordon's next two budgets.

Why was Gordon so unsuccessful? First,

expectations for the budget had been high, as it was the first real action of the government in its self-declared "Sixty Days of Decision." Gordon probably tried to do too much. Second, as a minority government, the Liberals lacked political leverage. An anxious prime minister, Cabinet and caucus did not rally to Gordon when trouble arose. Third, Gordon failed to take careful enough stock of the situation and to properly define his goals. The policies were poorly conceived and weak in detail, and their impact was not properly calculated. This was the result of acting in haste, which in addition led him to misjudge the degree of support for the measures. The nationalist plank in the party platform was not particularly strong. He risked all of his political resources in this one action, instead of using his position to nurture business, popular, and party opinion. Fourth, he underestimated the constraints involved, particularly the views of the business community. Fifth, he used outside consultants in order to act quickly and with intended effect. In the process, he alienated his own department, whose advice and expertise were hardly used in the formulation of the budget, and whose support therefore was not forthcoming in its defence.

Once Gordon's budget initiatives had been challenged and undermined, and his political resources weakened, his image as competent professional was tarnished, and he lost his room for manoeuvre. He and his reform colleagues did manage to produce substantial policy innovations, including the creation of the Department of Industry, the Economic Council of Canada and the Municipal Loan Fund, as well as the expansion of the welfare state (Canada Pension Plan, Medicare). These reform items seemed to be much more in tune with public opinion than were his nationalist initiatives, which continued to be unsuccessful (e.g., Canada Development Corporation). Nonetheless, even after he left the Ministry of Finance and the government, he continued to exert political pressure. The Watkins Report on foreign ownership in Canada, which has influenced academic and political discussion for a generation, was a product of his lobbying efforts.

The Trudeau Era

Characterizing leadership in economic policy during the Trudeau era is difficult for two reasons.[16] First, Pierre Trudeau was not particularly interested or well-versed in economic matters. Second, he was anxious to initiate a "rational" policy process, and policy successes or failures in this period suggest more about the new policy system than they do about leadership.

Trudeau's political authority rested on an odd mixture of charisma and rationality. He was always the star attraction, speaking directly to the people, particularly in his first and last administrations. While there was always an irrational aspect to his relationship with the public, he was also admired for his intellectual abilities and competence. He always seemed to enjoy the image of the "outsider," above the political fray, which provided him with considerable room to manoeuvre. Despite his Weberian charismatic qualities, he was by no means a politician of "passion." Driven by the pursuit of the rational, and distrustful of the permanent bureaucracy, Trudeau accelerated the movement towards more systematized and co-ordinated policy processes. In the fully developed cabinet committee system, the prime minister's leverage in the policy process was strengthened, and he commanded considerable political resources in the PMO and PCO. The whole process was slow and cumbersome, and weakened the role of individual ministers and the permanent bureaucracy in establishing policy.[17]

When so inclined, Trudeau could use his resources to affect the economic policy agenda. For example, national unity (a Trudeau priority) was seen to be a function of regional economic balance. Regional economic policy was given a high priority and profile in his first administration: a new department was estab-

lished; its first minister was the prime minister's trusted friend Jean Marchand, and its first
deputy minister, the influential Tom Kent, and
it was assigned a healthy budget.[18] Similarly,
after the 1980 election, Trudeau's two most
trusted political allies — Allan MacEachen and
Marc Lalonde — were named Ministers of Finance and Energy, respectively. The administration was determined to assert a federal presence in politics, especially with respect to the
West, energy, and economic development. Using the confines of budget secrecy, the National
Energy Program emanated from a very closed
policy circle, and was more or less imposed on
the country.[19] These were two examples of the
Prime Minister tilting the policy process
through establishing his priorities and using the
resources at his command to realize them.

But the "rational" policy process was designed to automatically generate and set priorities. One example of this was industrial policy
in the 1970s, which was pushed hard as a
policy idea in the cabinet committee system.
Despite continuous efforts, only one Minister
of Industry, Trade and Commerce (Pépin) was
ever really interested in the idea of an industrial
strategy for Canada. After elaborate consulting
exercises and a flurry of sector-by-sector and
national reports, only one substantial result
was achieved by the late 1970s — the short-
lived Board of Economic Development Ministers.[20] The rational systems approach was designed to make better policy. However, as Max
Weber wrote, "politics is made with the head,
but it is certainly not made with the head
alone."[21] This system had no goals or motives
propelling it, other than the rational production of goals. The limits of this approach were
cruelly exposed in the infamous priorities exercise of 1974-75, which managed to produce a
priority list that omitted the obvious issue of
the day: inflation. An elaborate and expensive
exercise was undermined by one public opinion poll and one political resignation.

The irony of this period is that assertive and
confident action was often taken, but in "emer-

gency" situations outside of the normal policy
process. The indexing of personal taxes and
social security, the development of FIRA and
Petro-Canada, the initiation of a social security
review and a new national oil policy, and the
choice to deal with unemployment rather than
inflation all occurred in the highly politicized
context of a minority government. Wage and
price controls were developed and applied in a
matter of weeks. Massive government spending
cuts were announced without warning by Trudeau after the Bonn economic summit in 1978.
Granted an unexpected and probably final political opportunity, the Trudeau team put together the National Energy Program in a way
that avoided the elaborate and cumbersome
rational policy process.

There are other accomplishments of the
Trudeau government to point out, like regional
policy and post-1980 energy and economic
development policy. But these assertive actions
were not so much demonstrations of leadership as acts of power and domination. The
manner in which the policies were developed
and applied ensured that there would be little
long-term support for them. The cynical application of wage and price controls weakened
the possibilities for a post-controls consensus
about new economic approaches. The National
Energy Program had no roots in public discussion, and weak constituency support, which
made dubious its chance of staying the course.
Government economic policy in the late 1970s
was schizophrenic, inconsistent and confusing,
and at a time of uncertainty and instability,
failed to provide the type of economic leadership for which the public was crying out.

The Mulroney Era

The Mulroney government will provide a remarkable case study of the potential for political leadership in economic policy. Mulroney
and his associates are attempting to resurrect a
Schumpeterian approach to political economy,
with leadership to play a disciplining role. In
the emerging neoconservative style set by

Reagan and Thatcher, the Mulroney team has redefined the political economic agenda. Reacting against both economic decline and the previous administrations' political style, the government is seeking to revitalize the economy through encouraging individual economic initiative. This is to be accomplished by direct incentives, deregulation and privatization, narrowing of the social security system, lightening the tax burden, cutting government spending, reducing the deficit, and encouraging market economic predominance via free trade. Political leadership is directed towards reinvigorating the market system and limiting the state's role in the economy.

This approach has been successfully placed on the political agenda and has acquired — in the abstract, at any rate — a certain degree of legitimacy. Mulroney won a strong electoral mandate in 1984, which provided considerable political space for manoeuvre. The test of his leadership will be the extent to which he will be able to solidify and carry out the policy strategy in a politically acceptable way, to confirm that his electoral mandate was indeed for this overall policy purpose. He faces formidable obstacles. His conciliatory style has, in the first instance, softened the harsher edges of the strategy, but may turn out to be a serious liability. As decisions are made, interests and supporters are affected unevenly. For example, the free trade initiative has generated concern among the provinces about the probable impact on their economies. The review of social security by the Nielsen task force and the discussion about universality led to strong reactions from pensioners and other recipients of social assistance. There have been widespread expectations created by Mulroney that the strategy could be carried out with minimal costs and dislocations, but there will obviously be winners and losers. Second, there are a variety of factors over which the Prime Minister has little control. For example, while he has legitimized — to an extent — the free trade option, he cannot control American leaders' reactions,

demands, and performance in the talks. Third, he heads an unwieldy government and caucus of great political and ideological diversity. He will have to juggle goals and actions in keeping all, or most, groups happy. Unanticipated political problems, like the spate of recent scandals, drain political resources and energy and make even more difficult the pursuit of policy goals. Fourth, and perhaps most importantly, the strategy comprises a huge agenda and an immense number of particular policies. If the government moves on all fronts at once, it may be swamped by the sheer volume and complexity of the task, and will make mistakes. But, if it moves too cautiously or incrementally, it may be chastised for compromising its principles. There are signs that the government may already be too preoccupied with opinion-poll results.

To this point, it appears that the government will opt for caution over haste, and attempt to renew its political resources for a second term.[22] There has been a mix of substantial, symbolic and incremental actions. The NEP was dismantled, a half-million-dollar lifetime capital gains exemption was initiated, and a general fiscal move has been made towards encouraging investment and corporate activity. A considerable number of Crown corporations have been privatized (e.g., de Havilland, Canadair, Canada Development Corporation, Teleglobe), but some of the more substantial ones remain in the public domain (e.g. Air Canada, Petro-Canada). The deficit has declined, but perhaps not as far as may have been anticipated, and even this accomplishment has been more the result of tax increases than spending cuts. There has been, though, a qualitative shift in spending away from energy and social programs and subsidies, through there was much less "wasteful" spending to cut than had been maintained. FIRA has been replaced by Investment Canada.

Towards the close of Mulroney's first term, one can comment that he continues to attempt to legitimize this neoconservative economic orientation and reorient the public to this way of thinking about economic matters. After a bumpy beginning, the government has been a touch more cautious and patient in the pursuit of its overall objective. But it is clear that political and interest-group reactions to each particular policy innovation will generate substantial obstacles which the government will have to overcome. The leadership opportunities are there, but so are the constraints. As has been seen in the previous case studies, the persistence or success of a particular policy approach is based on the leader's ability to ensure that policy objectives are set and realized in an effective way, thereby re-establishing the legitimacy and predominance of that particular policy. The legitimacy and staying power of the neoconservative approach will be determined by the skills of Mulroney and his team in initiating policy and convincing Canadians of the appropriateness of their actions. If goals are inadequately specified and expectations created are false, if constraints are underestimated or resources squandered, if accomplishments are meagre or non-existent, then the legitimacy and logic of this policy approach will be undermined and will be replaced by a competing vision. But, whatever the government manages to accomplish, it is hard to imagine that the political economic agenda will not have been affected for years to come.

CONCLUSION

As a result of economic and policy uncertainty, political leadership in the 1980s and 1990s will consist largely of competing efforts to legitimize broad, paradigmatic approaches to economic policy. Within this setting, there will be opportunities to initiate and realize particular policy goals, and these will be legitimate accomplishments. But, as this chapter has illustrated, the obstacles to, and checks on, political leadership in economic policy are real and formidable. Policy accomplishments are by no means simply a matter of assertively exercising

political will. Patience, an understanding of constraints, the best use of resources, and the clear definition of goals are all critical variables in the leader's effort to realize objectives.

As seen in the case studies, the most substantive accomplishment of political leadership in economic policy is the setting of priorities and the tilting of the policy agenda in a certain direction. Politics is about ideas as well as about power. In the Weberian sense, the politics of "vision" and "passion" matter very much. There have been substantial swings in economic policy orientation since the Second World War, informed to a considerable degree by normative and ideological debates. Of course, policy swings reflect structural changes. But it is political leaders and political debates which shape our perception of the meaning of these structural changes, thereby influencing what will emerge as the legitimate and specific policy response to these changes.

Two styles of political leadership can be identified in this regard. In the Schumpeterian model, structural changes and their rational, scientific management are seen to be inherently positive and logical, and not to be interfered with on political or ideological grounds. The political leader's role is to ensure that these issues remain off the political agenda, lest democracy be swamped and a less-than-optimal economic development create doubts about democracy's effectiveness and legitimacy. In the Weberian model, structural changes due to some sort of disembodied technological rationality are not beyond human judgement. The political leaders' role is to animate democratic discussion of structural changes from the perspective of human norms and values, lest a technologically determined and expert-run world eliminate individual and social choice.

In Canada, as elsewhere, these two models of political leadership have competed. Periodically, the Weberian style emerges as the dominant form, when political leaders incite Canadians to consider both the costs and benefits of technological and economic progress. Leaders then raise issues such as foreign ownership, regional economic imbalances, economic distribution, and the overall character of the Canadian economic experience. These exhortations do not necessarily result in concrete policy changes, for the various reasons noted in this chapter. But the fact that these issues appear on the political agenda is evidence of the "competitiveness" of the Weberian leadership style. On the other hand, the Schumpeterian style is presently dominant in Canada. The Mulroney government is pursuing a neoconservative economic strategy, which includes dampening public expectations about what the state will do in the economy. Major economic issues will be returned to the private sector. In this way, the government aims to have structural and economic changes determined by corporations, technological processes, and the market in an "impersonal" way. Thus we can conclude that political leadership is an important variable in the economic policy equation.

Notes

1. Weber, "Politics as a Vocation," p. 128.

2. Doern, "The Politics of Canadian Economic Policy," p. 92.

3. Schumpeter, *Capitalism, Socialism and Democracy,* pp. 289-96.

4. Weber, op. cit.

5. Ibid., p. 95.

6. Ibid., p. 115.

7. Ibid., p. 117.

8. Ibid., p. 128.

9. Lamontagne, *Business Cycles in Canada,* Chap. 5.

10. Campbell, *Grand Illusions,* especially Chapter Two.

11. Phidd and Doern, *The Politics and Management of Canadian Economic Policy.*

12. Lindblom, *Politics and Markets,* Chap. 13.

13. Bothwell and Kilbourn, *C.D. Howe.*

14. Campbell, "The Diefenbaker Years Revisited."

15. Smith, *Gentle Patriot.*

16. Gwyn, *The Northern Magus;* McCall-Newman, *Grits.*

17. Doern and Phidd, *Canadian Public Policy,* Chap. 7.

18. Savoie, *Regional Economic Development,* Chaps. 3, 4.

19. Doern and Phidd, op. cit., Chap. 16.

20. Gillies, *Facing Reality,* Chap. 4; French, *How Ottawa Decides,* Chap. 6.

21. Weber, op. cit., p. 127.

22. Prince, "The Mulroney Agenda."

CHAPTER 9

Political Leadership and Foreign Policy: Trudeau and Mulroney

Kim Richard Nossal

In few other policy fields can one find such scope for prime ministerial leadership and policy initiative as in foreign affairs. The prime minister's position in the foreign policy-making process in Canada is usually characterized as so central and commanding that no other official, not even the foreign minister, rivals his ability to shape Canada's foreign relations.[1] The burden of fashioning Canada's general approach to international politics, of deciding on specific responses to international issues of the day, and of conducting diplomatic relations with other powers, both great and small, rest largely on the prime minister's shoulders. Indeed, so distinct and enduring is the mark left by a prime minister that eras in the history of the country's external policy are inevitably tagged with his name.

The purpose of this chapter is to examine more closely the dominant assumptions about prime ministerial influence that pervade the literature on foreign policy-making in Canada, and to argue that the assumptions cannot be sustained without considerable qualification. It will be argued that the prime minister does indeed dominate the foreign policy-making process. However, it will also be shown that one cannot take for granted a relationship between pre-eminence in the policy process on the one hand and leadership and policy initia-

tive on the other. In fact, the possibilities for any prime minister to introduce significant change in Canadian foreign policy are quite limited. Domestic and international systemic factors are more potent in the shaping of policy than is a prime minister's ability to dominate the decision-making process.

THE CONVENTIONAL VIEW

Prime ministerial influence is a dominant theme in the literature on foreign policy-making in Canada. James Eayrs's examination of government and foreign policy in Canada flatly states at the outset that in Canada, foreign policy is the prime minister's prerogative,[2] an assertion that he demonstrated vividly in his five volumes of *In Defence of Canada*.[3] Likewise, C.P. Stacey, in the second volume of his history of Canada's external relations, *The Mackenzie King Era,* noted how impressed he was with the "overmastering importance" of the prime minister's personal preferences in the making of Canada's interwar foreign policy.[4] It is thus perhaps not surprising that contemporary analyses of the role of the prime minister have tended to reflect the judgement of historians.[5] Indeed, so pervasive is this view that not even those whose general analytical approach tends to downplay the importance of personality in foreign policy-making appear able to avoid focussing on individual leadership. Thus in their sketch of five distinct "eras" in Canada's postwar foreign policy, David Dewitt and John Kirton implicitly, if unwittingly, acknowledge the impact of individual prime ministers. They attach to each era a jargonistic and depersonalized label (for example, the period 1957 to 1963 is termed "the era of competitive fragmentation"), but in fact, each period matches precisely the tenures of Louis St. Laurent, John Diefenbaker, Lester Pearson, and the several incarnations of Pierre Trudeau.[6]

The literature provides, broadly speaking, a not inaccurate depiction of the impact of the prime minister on the making of foreign policy in Canada. In particular, it gives us a fairly clear idea of opportunities for the exercise of leadership and possibilities for strategic intervention by the individuals at the apex of government. First, it stresses the power and influence of prime ministers, both contemporary and historical. For Canada developed a tradition of domination of foreign affairs by the prime minister long before the formal creation of a foreign affairs portfolio in 1909, and well before the de jure independence in foreign policy achieved by Canada in 1931. Such dominance resulted from, but was also reinforced by, the statutory provision dating from 1912 that the prime minister would automatically be the Secretary of State for External Affairs. This lasted until 1946, when Prime Minister Mackenzie King devolved some of the responsibilities of the portfolio to a separate minister. But having a separate minister in the portfolio did not lessen the desire or the ability of Canada's postwar prime ministers, without exception, to interpose themselves successfully into the foreign policy process.

The literature also recognizes the prime minister's ability, through the power of appointment, to determine who will occupy the policy-making positions at the apex, and thus to anticipate the nature and quality of advice on international issues that he will receive. No prime minister has been able to avoid the consequences, both salutary and otherwise, of his particular appointment decisions in the sphere of foreign policy.

Finally, the literature accurately reflects the importance of the role of individual leaders in summit diplomacy. For it is the prime minister, not the members of the Cabinet, who is called on to engage in summitry in a wide range of bilateral and multilateral forums. A prime minister's performance at Commonwealth Heads of Government meetings, at the annual Economic Summit, at the regular bilateral summits held with the president of the United States, or in a variety of other forums, can be critical to the development of Canadian foreign policy.[7]

Most importantly, however, the potency attributed to the prime minister by academics appears to have been taken to heart by most of Canada's postwar leaders. Diefenbaker, Pearson, Trudeau, and Brian Mulroney all took office with the firm belief that they could impose their own special stamp on Canada's course in international affairs, and in particular, reverse what were seen as inappropriate policies pursued by their predecessors. In short, all saw the possibilities for leadership in foreign affairs inherent in the position. And yet the foreign policies of each of these prime ministers over the course of their years in power show remarkable continuity, as well as considerable resistance to the kind of policy change desired by the incumbent at the outset. A focus on two leaders — Trudeau and Mulroney — demonstrates why, for all of the potential of prime ministers to dominate the policy-making process, and regardless of their leadership skills, they tend to eventually pursue very traditional courses in international politics.

TRUDEAU'S FOREIGN POLICY

When in 1968 Pierre Elliott Trudeau secured the leadership of the Liberal Party, and hence the prime ministership, he brought with him into office the firm desire to alter Canada's role in international politics. He was dissatisfied with the content of foreign policy, as well as the process by which it was made, and set out to change both.

The policy process was relatively easy to tackle. Trudeau came to office dissatisfied with the style of decision-making he had witnessed during his three-year apprenticeship in the Pearson Cabinet. He believed that the process of deciding policy, not only in foreign affairs, but in other areas as well, was too resistant to new ideas and debate, too dominated by a single minister and his or her departmental bureaucrats, too elitist, and, ultimately, deficient in rationality. Almost immediately, Trudeau initiated a set of dramatic reforms of the way that policy decisions were made by the federal Cabinet — reforms that would inevitably affect foreign affairs.[8] These efforts to increase rationality at the ministerial level were mirrored by comparable reforms at the bureaucratic level: Trudeau oversaw a sixteen-year process that attempted to make the foreign affairs bureaucracy more rational.[9]

But it was on the content of Canadian foreign policy that he fixed his sights at the outset of his tenure. Trudeau's critique of policy inherited from Pearson has been termed by Dobell "self-confident and almost naïve,"[10] but it was fundamental. Pearson's policies, Trudeau argued, no longer served Canadian national interests. First, Trudeau contended that Canada's external relations were being overly circumscribed by defence commitments to the North Atlantic Treaty Organization (NATO) and to the North American Air Defence Command agreement with the United States (NORAD). Were these military alignments, forged during the Cold War in the decade after 1945, entirely necessary in a world of relaxation of tensions between the two superpowers, and growing multipolarity? Judging by his speeches, and the initial actions of his government, Trudeau felt that NATO and NORAD, and the extensive commitments and obligations they imposed on Canada, were no longer as crucial to Canadian

security as they had been in the years immediately after the Second World War.

Second, Trudeau was of the view that the Pearsonian tendency to try to moderate international tensions had by the late 1960s become entirely outdated. What may have been appropriate for the mid-1950s, when Pearson's masterful diplomacy as Canada's Secretary of State for External Affairs during the Suez crisis earned him the Nobel Peace Prize, was now seen as a fruitless expenditure of Canadian effort, energy, and scarce resources in order to secure foreign policy objectives that were, at best, intangible. The Canadian government's propensity to excessive concern with its role as a middle power in world affairs — scornfully derided as "helpful fixing" — was declared to be both outmoded and distinctly unhelpful to Canadian interests.

Trudeau had a different vision for Canadian foreign policy. Termed by Peyton Lyon the "Trudeau doctrine,"[11] this vision was for a foreign policy that would serve Canadian interests more directly. The world by the late 1960s was looking more tranquil, and there was little prospect that the superpowers would engage in war. The United States and the Soviet Union were negotiating over arms control; thus, there seemed less need for emphasis on alliance and military spending. However, the issues of massive hunger and underdevelopment remained pressing, and threats to the environment continued. It seemed clear that a more sophisticated foreign policy was required. Trudeau wanted a foreign policy that was more concerned about Canada and Canadian interests.

Trudeau's dissatisfaction led the government to undertake what the prime minister termed a "severe reassessment" of foreign policy — a review that took two years to complete. The result was the publication in the summer of 1970 of a white paper on foreign policy. Its French title, *Politique étrangère au service des Canadiens,* captured the essence of the change much better than the ambiguous English *Foreign Policy for Canadians*. The blueprint for foreign policy outlined in the document matched perfectly Trudeau's wide-ranging critique of the Pearsonian tradition.[12] Gone was the equation of Canadian interests with international peace and order, and with it the idea that it was always in the Canadian interest to attempt, by diplomatic means, to defuse or moderate conflict in the international system. Instead, the white paper called for an essentially narrower definition of Canadian national interests, one that would focus on promoting economic growth, defending Canadian territory, battling threats to the environment, and establishing more extensive international relations to countervail the powerful attraction of the United States.

The review of the late 1960s and the white paper that resulted from it provide an excellent example of political leadership in foreign policy. The prime minister's intervention was ambitious, in that Trudeau presented a very different way of looking at Canada's role in the world and the possibilities for Canadian diplomacy. It was bold, in that Trudeau's view seriously challenged the bureaucratic establishment's *Weltanschauung* and turned what had become an established "understanding" about foreign policy in Ottawa on its ear. It was also oddly naïve. For the underlying belief of both the review and the white paper was that the international system could be made to serve Canada's purposes, and that other states would be either supportive of, or at worst indifferent to, the goals laid down in 1970.

This, of course, was not to be the case. Canada's NATO allies were hardly indifferent to what was seen as a selfish freeloader's attempt to garner the benefits of alliance membership without contributing to the costs. At first they were dismayed, and then mightily annoyed, by Trudeau's disparagement of the usefulness of the Atlantic alliance, his unilateral troop reduction in 1969, and the cuts introduced in the defence budget.[13] Nor did Trudeau find the international system itself as benign as he, and others, had so breezily assumed in the late

1960s, for the period of détente and the relaxation of tensions between the superpowers proved to be unhappily fleeting. Likewise, the problem of nuclear weapons continued to dominate the international agenda: the technological refinement and expanded deployment of strategic and tactical weapons systems continued apace despite the successful conclusion of the first round of SALT, or Strategic Arms Limitation Talks. Various regional conflicts and wars continued to complicate the relations of the superpowers, and little sustained attention was paid by the international community to the continuing problems of underdevelopment.

As a result, Trudeau, having recorded his ideas about international politics for posterity in *Foreign Policy for Canadians,* spent the remaining years of his long tenure as prime minister ignoring, contradicting or reversing the main tenets of the white paper. Underlying the Prime Minister's many foreign policy initiatives after 1970 was the discovery (or the rediscovery) of the usefulness of traditional patterns of postwar foreign policy for the protection of Canadian interests, in particular of middle-power internationalism and also of the role of "helpful fixer" that had been the object of such derision in the late 1960s.

There were many reasons for the changes in Trudeau's foreign policy after 1970. First, the Trudeau government recognized, albeit slowly, the essential rationality of military spending and concrete participation in alliances: military expenditures were critical to successful Canadian statecraft. That realization did not dawn until the mid-1970s, when Trudeau was trying to negotiate an economic agreement with the European Community as part of his counterweight strategy.[14] Confronted directly with European anger at Canada's military unilateralism, Trudeau initiated a slow but steady rehabilitation of the NATO alliance. (To be sure, it can be argued that the realization had come too late: by that time, Canada had considerably damaged its reputation as a trustworthy ally, and consequently its influence within alliance circles.)

Second, Trudeau quickly discovered the utility of peacekeeping. For a prime minister who began his tenure in the firm belief that peacekeeping missions were essentially irrelevant to Canada's international interests, his government was an extraordinarily active participant in international peacekeeping and truce supervision.[15] Throughout the sixteen years of his tenure, Trudeau maintained Canada's costly contribution to the UN peacekeeping force in Cyprus. His government agreed to participate in the face-saving truce supervisory commission that allowed the Nixon administration to end U.S. intervention in Vietnam.[16] Indeed, when it appeared as though Canada would not be included in the peacekeeping force established in the aftermath of Israel's Yom Kippur War of 1973, Ottawa protested loudly. Likewise, in the spring of 1984, the Trudeau government tried to bolster the Contadora process in Central America by offering to help in the design of a truce supervisory commission for the region. And while Allan MacEachen, then Canada's Secretary of State for External Affairs, was quick to add that helping design an effective truce supervisory commission did not imply Canadian participation,[17] it is unlikely that, had the United States asked Canada to participate, the Trudeau government would have refused.

Third, in his own way, Trudeau became a firm practitioner of the "helpful fixing" tradition in Canadian diplomacy. On numerous occasions in the fourteen years after the publication of the white paper, the Prime Minister actively played the role of interlocutor, mediator, or in some other way inserted himself and his ideas into key issues in international politics. For example, he recognized at the Meeting of Commonwealth Heads of Government held in Singapore in 1971 that the divergence between Britain and the non-white members on the question of arms sales to South Africa was again threatening an international association greatly valued by Ottawa. Like King in the late 1940s, Diefenbaker in 1961, and Pearson in

1966, Trudeau was to play the role of mediator between opposing groups, pressing for compromise and in the process helping sustain the association.[18] Likewise, on the issue of nuclear arms, Trudeau was outspoken about the need for greater progress on arms control: for example, in 1977 he used the United Nations General Assembly as a platform to lobby for a "suffocation" of nuclear weapons.[19]

However, Trudeau's two most sustained efforts at "helpful fixing" came during his last four years in office: his North-South initiative of 1980-81, and the peace mission that concluded his tenure as prime minister. The North-South initiative was an eighteen-month attempt to rally the support of other leaders for a greater commitment to the problems of global hunger and underdevelopment. Spurred by the report of the commission headed by his friend, former German chancellor Willy Brandt, Trudeau tried to convince other states, particularly those in the capitalist First World, to enter into a new round of global negotiations on the issue of underdevelopment. For his efforts, he was appointed co-chairman of the North-South summit held in Cancún, Mexico in October 1981, but in the end the initiative proved unsuccessful: the meeting was inconclusive, and much of the momentum that had led to the summit was lost.[20]

The peace mission that capped Trudeau's career as prime minister was motivated by concerns about the level of international tensions in the early 1980s, and the obvious hostility of Soviet-American relations. But, by the fall of 1983, following the shooting down of Korean Airlines (KAL) flight 007 by Soviet fighters, Trudeau was sufficiently alarmed by what he later termed the "parlous state" of East-West relations that he decided that he could not stand by silently. In October he launched a personal and unilateral diplomatic effort to reduce the tensions had been building since the early 1980s. Between October 1983 and February 1984, Trudeau visited the capitals of all the major powers, urging on their leaders both moderation and negotiation, and putting forward a ten-point plan for defusing East-West hostility.[21]

Thus, by the time he resigned on February 29th, 1984, Trudeau had come full circle in foreign policy. While he had started his tenure as prime minister convinced that the internationalist approach to world politics held little relevance for Canadian interests, Trudeau's many interventions in foreign policy were in fact fundamentally Pearsonian in intent, if not in style.

MULRONEY'S FOREIGN POLICY

Like Trudeau, Brian Mulroney came to the prime ministership with his own critique of foreign policy as pursued by his Liberal predecessor; like Trudeau, he was able to dominate the process of decision; like Trudeau, he embraced a number of personal initiatives in foreign policy. And, like Trudeau, Mulroney was to discard most of the foreign policy positions he had brought to office, and revert to a more traditional course in foreign policy.

In the last months of Liberal rule, the focus of the Progressive Conservative critique of foreign policy was on the deterioration of Canadian-American relations in the early 1980s. That deterioration had resulted from a number of factors. First, many of the Trudeau government's domestic policy initiatives — notably the National Energy Program — were seen by the Reagan administration as fundamentally unacceptable to American economic interests. The NEP in particular sparked a nasty dispute between Ottawa and Washington in 1981,[22] in which the Reagan administration, in an unusual departure from traditional American policy towards Canada, used the blunt instrument of economic threats against the Trudeau government. The effects of this dispute were still being felt at the end of Trudeau's tenure.

Second, the relationship had been soured by an escalating dispute over the issue of acid rain. Canadian expressions of concern about the effects of acid precipitation from the United States were met in Washington by claims that more research was needed before any concrete action on the issue could be taken. In response, Ottawa became increasingly strident. Canadian diplomats in the United States gave distinctly undiplomatic speeches accusing the Reagan administration of stalling on the issue; Canadian politicians made only the scantest efforts to disguise their feelings about the environmental policies of the president; even American tourists visiting Canada were greeted by propaganda tartly reminding them that their country was ruining the Canadian environment.

Finally, the bilateral irritants were seriously aggravated by the considerable divergence between Trudeau and Reagan on issues of global policy. Trudeau rarely bothered to hide his belief that Reagan's policies on a variety of international issues were simply wrongheaded. On American interventionism in Central America, on martial law in Poland, on the KAL 007 incident, on Grenada, on nuclear strategy, or on relations in general with the Soviet Union, the gap between Trudeau and the President was obvious — and wide. For his part, Reagan and his advisors had little use for Trudeau's perspective, or his international initiatives.

Brian Mulroney seemed determined to change both the tenor and the substance of the Canadian-American relationship. In particular he wanted to "refurbish" the relationship by removing the irritants that had plagued relations between Reagan and Trudeau, particularly on global issues.

The policy initially embraced as the means to achieve this end was the alignment of Canadian foreign policy more closely to that of the United States. As Leader of the Opposition, Mulroney had adopted a very simple pro-American, anti-Soviet approach to foreign policy. His reactions to the shooting down of the KAL airliner and the United States invasion of Grenada in the fall of 1983 virtually mirrored American policy. During the election campaign of 1984, Mulroney's rhetoric confirmed his desire to shift Canada's traditional international stance. His anti-Soviet posturing on the hustings was complemented by his persistent promise to improve relations with what he called Canada's four traditional allies — the United States, Britain, France and Israel. Canada under a Conservative government, Mulroney promised, would spend more on defence. It would be less critical of the global policies of the United States. It would give Washington the benefit of the doubt in its global initiatives. In short, Canada would be a "super" ally. Moreover, Mulroney promised that he would bring a "new era of civility" to the bilateral relationship. Bilateral conflicts between Canada and the United States would be settled amicably, with a minimum of carping and hostility.

To be sure, Mulroney's statements during the summer of 1984 must be put in context, for the gap between rhetoric and reality is stretched considerably during election campaigns. Moreover, the Progressive Conservative party has a well-established tradition of using foreign policy issues to woo votes from ethnic groups. Thus Mulroney's repeated assertion that Israel was one of Canada's great traditional allies bore no relation to historical reality, but, like Joe Clark's 1979 promise to move the Canadian embassy to Jerusalem, may have been calculated to win Jewish votes. Likewise, Mulroney's anti-Sovietism reached a high pitch during the election campaign. At an international convention of Estonians in Toronto, he roundly denounced the Soviets, describing the world as "half slave and half free." He reminded them that John Diefenbaker's criticism of Soviet domination of Eastern Europe had prompted Khrushchev to bang his shoe on the table at the United Nations, and that he, Mulroney, would do no less than Diefenbaker for the cause of Eastern Europeans.[23] But Mulroney was not only perpetuating a disingenuous Conservative myth (for Diefenbaker had not even been in New York during the shoe-banging episode), he was also perpetuating an electoral tactic that

had effectively served Diefenbaker. On the other hand, it should not be forgotten that underlying the often overblown rhetoric during the campaign was a genuine desire for a substantial change in policy direction, particularly an improvement in Canadian-American relations.

Once in power, Mulroney, like other prime ministers, placed his personal stamp on the decision-making process, confirming — yet again — the pattern described in the literature.[24] However, he also spent his first two years as prime minister either discarding or downplaying the ideas about foreign policy he had initially brought to office. In particular, Mulroney dropped his overt pro-Americanism, and began pursuing a more traditional internationalist course. Mulroney was to find himself thrust into an international dispute over South Africa that was to pit Canada against two of its "great traditional allies" — Britain and the United States.

Canada under the Conservatives did not in fact become a "better" ally than it had been under Trudeau. While Canadian troops in Europe were augmented marginally after 1984, and while the Conservatives were generally less dismissive of the military than the Liberals, defence spending under the Conservatives did not increase substantially. This was because the Mulroney government was unwilling to choose among the limited options available for substantial and real increases on defence spending: increasing the federal deficit, or redirecting expenditures from social programs, or increasing taxes. Moreover, as Michael Tucker has cogently argued, most of the increases in spending under the Conservatives were on behalf of commitments undertaken by the Trudeau government.[25]

Nor was Mulroney as supportive of United States foreign policy — or as critical of the Soviet Union — as his pre-prime ministerial rhetoric would have suggested. On relations with the Soviet Union, Mulroney maintained a delicate balance: on the one hand, he made clear Canada's continuing concerns over human rights issues; on the other hand, Ottawa's general relationship with the USSR remained cordial. On nuclear weapons and arms control, both the Prime Minister and his Secretary of State for External Affairs, Joe Clark, often distanced Canada from the United States. Most importantly, by refusing to participate in the Strategic Defense Initiative, Mulroney effectively denied the Reagan administration the political endorsement for SDI that Washington was seeking from its allies. And both Mulroney and Clark were quite vocal on other nuclear issues. For example, they openly called on the United States to abide by the provisions of the Anti-Ballistic Missile Treaty and the unratified provisions of SALT II.

Likewise, Mulroney was distinctly unsupportive of American policy towards particular regional conflicts. The Reagan administration's policies in Central America drew considerable and outspoken criticism from both Mulroney and Clark. The government refused to join in American economic sanctions against Nicaragua; while he criticized the Sandinistas for human rights abuses, Mulroney continued to embrace a moderate view. Similarly, Mulroney made little effort to disguise his belief that Reagan's approach to South Africa was short-sighted. One of the few clear instances of support for a United States regional initiative came in the wake of the American bombing of Libya early in 1986. On that occasion, Mulroney, at some political cost domestically, declared his support for Reagan's actions. It might be noted, however, that this declaration of support came on the eve of a crucial vote in the United States Senate on the Canada-United States free trade negotiations.

Finally, Mulroney's assumption of office coincided with the renewed outbreak of widespread violence in South Africa, and on this issue, the Prime Minister eventually abandoned any predisposition to side with the United States and Britain. Apartheid had not been a focus of Mulroney's foreign policy pronounce-ments prior to the 1984 elections, and as civil unrest in South Africa grew that fall, the new government in Ottawa said and did little. Indeed, throughout 1985, the economic sanctions adopted by the Mulroney government against South Africa were cautious measures seemingly designed to mirror the punitive measures being adopted by the United States. However, by the fall of 1985, the South African issue was threatening the unity of the Commonwealth, as it had on numerous occasions in the past. Mulroney's rhetoric on the South African issue became considerably harsher and at the biennial meeting of the Commonwealth Heads of Government in Nassau, the Prime Minister found himself at the centre of a major mediating effort between Margaret Thatcher of Britain, who was adamantly opposed to sanctions, and the rest of the Commonwealth. Indeed, Mulroney's performance at Nassau, and his active diplomacy on this issue during 1986 and 1987, which pitted him against both Thatcher and Reagan, was an unlikely role for a leader who had in 1983 and 1984 cast himself as a "super" ally of Britain and the United States.

In conclusion, by the time the Progressive Conservatives celebrated their second anniversary in power, those who had welcomed (or feared) a pro-American shift in foreign policy under Mulroney had cause for disappointment (or surprise). For by 1986, continuity in Canadian diplomacy was more evident than change. Once in power, Mulroney demonstrated that he was as concerned over the American approach to East-West relations, nuclear weapons, and global peace as Trudeau, Pearson, Diefenbaker, and St. Laurent had been. The immoderacy of United States policy in the case of Nicaragua concerned Mulroney no less than Poland had concerned Trudeau, Vietnam had concerned Pearson, Cuba had concerned Diefenbaker, or China had concerned St. Laurent. And in his mediatory diplomacy in the Commonwealth on the issue of South Africa, Mulroney was following a path well-trodden by every prime minister from Diefenbaker to Trudeau. In fact,

Mulroney proved to be a great deal more active than all of his predecessors in trying to reduce Britain's isolation in the Commonwealth by prompting a change in London's traditional policy of de facto support for South Africa. In short, by his actions, Mulroney established that his government's foreign policy was firmly in the mainstream of the traditional patterns of postwar Canadian statecraft.

CONCLUSION

Pierre Trudeau and Brian Mulroney each came to office with very different ideas about Canada's proper role in international politics. Trudeau sought to have the Canadian government embrace policies radically different from the internationalist traditions of Louis St. Laurent, John Diefenbaker and Lester Pearson. For his part, Mulroney believed that the proper course for Ottawa was to align Canada more closely with its principal allies, notably the United States. Yet both ended up pursuing policies marked by moderation, a predilection for compromise, and an abiding concern for systemic peace and order — the classic hallmarks of the internationalist tradition that dominated Canadian foreign policy in the two decades after 1945. How can one best account for the distinct difference between the policy ideas enunciated by Trudeau and Mulroney at the outset of their respective terms as prime minister, and the foreign policy eventually adopted?

Certainly one cannot point to the position of the prime minister in the policy-making process. Both Trudeau and Mulroney were able to dominate the process of decision-making, and to play a pre-eminent role both in shaping the foreign policy agenda and in carrying out personal initiatives. Both used the prerogative of inserting themselves into particular policy issues which they considered important. In particular, both used the opportunities afforded by international summits to inject their own views and personalities into the diplomatic sphere. In short, a survey of Trudeau's sixteen years in

power and of the first two years of Mulroney's prime ministership reveal what the literature leads one to expect: a portrait of prime ministerial pre-eminence.

Nor can one account for the change that both prime ministers underwent by attributing it to a failure of political will or political leadership. Both men demonstrated, albeit in very different ways, leadership on key political issues of their time. Trudeau's pursuit of a new Constitution and Mulroney's pursuit of a new trading arrangement with the United States are examples of such a capacity for leadership. Likewise, in foreign policy, Trudeau's numerous personal initiatives — from his intervention at Singapore, to his exercise of personal diplomacy in Europe to secure an economic link with the European Community, to his North-South initiative and his peace mission — confirm both his will and his leadership. Mulroney's foreign policy initiatives have been less sustained, but his Commonwealth diplomacy over apartheid suggests comparable skills.

The above brief sketches of foreign policy under both Trudeau and Mulroney suggest that neither prime ministerial pre-eminence in the foreign policy decision-making process, nor the more intangible qualities of leadership in international diplomacy, are likely to significantly alter either the international systemic or domestic political constraints and imperatives within which any prime minister of Canada must work.

The conditions of the international system itself are relatively unchanging: Canadian governments in the 1970s and 1980s could scarcely have less interest in global peace than did their predecessors in the 1950s or 1960s. For the same basic threat to all that Canadians value remains, and Canadian governors have come to recognize that either remaining indifferent to the rivalry of the superpowers, or actually encouraging hostility and bellicosity by simplistic alliance partisanship, are unlikely means of protection against the outbreak of war. Rather, given Canada's status as a middle power between the United States and the Soviet Union, while linked to the United States by a web of economic and cultural ties, a more rational approach is the encouragement of moderation and compromise, the adoption of an activist interest in the settlement of regional conflicts, and an equally activist involvement in global issues within the context of the alliance. It would appear that simply being an allied middle power inexorably demands an abandonment of indifference, and its replacement by the kind of activism that Trudeau came to embrace. On the other hand, being an allied middle power also requires the abandonment of a simplistic attachment to the alliance leader's approach to international politics;[26] Mulroney has discovered that what is at stake for Canadian interests is too important to compromise by giving the United States automatic and unqualified support.

The domestic environment both reflects and reinforces the systemic influences on policy. The political preferences of Canadians, upon which the electoral fortunes of governors and would-be governors ultimately depend, demonstrate an uneasy ambivalence about Canada's role in world politics. On the one hand, it would appear from their behaviour that most Canadians remain fundamentally content with Canada's general alignment in international politics. Thus, those who propose withdrawing from NATO or NORAD, or suggest that Canada become Finlandized, neutralized, or non-aligned, are consigned to the fringes of Canadian politics. Likewise, there appears to be a general preference for harmonious relations with the United States, over and above the recognition by the vast majority of Canadians of the relationship between their wealth and economic links to the United States.

On the other hand, Canadians have demonstrated distinct uneasiness about superpower hostility. Thus it is not surprising that they tend to support governments which try to reduce international tensions: the massive and non-partisan public support in Canada for Trudeau's peace mission clearly shows this. Despite a basic acceptance of the idea of nuclear weapons as a deterrent to systemic war, Canadians are also concerned about each successive change in strategic doctrine and each new generation of nuclear weapons, as is indicated by the national debates over Bomarc in the early 1960s, the cruise in the early 1980s, and the SDI in the later 1980s. Likewise, Canadians may endorse the country's membership in NATO and NORAD, but the mythology of Canada as an unmilitary society is firmly entrenched. Thus there is little groundswell for massive increases in expenditures on conventional defence. Finally, while Canadians may accept American alliance leadership, there appears to be little support for a policy of sycophantism in global affairs. There is a well-established view in Canada of many American global policy initiatives as overly zealous, excessively militaristic and generally immoderate, and a concomitant desire that governments in Ottawa not support, by silence, such policies.

Denis Stairs has argued that an internationalist posture fits well with Canadian political culture.[27] Canadians appear to be most supportive of governments in Ottawa which stress prudence, moderation, and compromise in international affairs, which mirror the public's ambivalence on military security issues, and which maintain a distance from the alliance leader that is sufficiently discreet without prompting a rupture in relations between Ottawa and Washington. In short, internationalism is also good politics.

It can thus be suggested that both Trudeau and Mulroney, once in power, were affected by the influences of the domestic and the international environments in one of two ways. On the one hand, it is possible that both prime ministers were stricken with inertia and incrementalism: confronted with domestic and international environments that stubbornly refused to embrace their notions about international politics, Trudeau and Mulroney may have simply tired of trying to translate their idiosyncratic preferences into policy, and lapsed instead into the less arduous and taxing posture of doing what had been done in the past. On the other hand, given their embrace of many of the tenets of traditional internationalism, it is more likely that both prime ministers came to appreciate the domestic and international virtues of the traditional approach they had begun by rejecting.

In conclusion, a focus on the contexts in which prime ministers must operate provides a compelling explanation for the abandonment by both Trudeau and Mulroney of their initial conceptions of Canada's proper role in world politics, and their adoption instead of a more traditional internationalist course. It also serves to put into clearer perspective our understanding of prime ministerial pre-eminence in foreign policy. The prime minister is usually portrayed as so powerful in foreign policy decision-making that it may appear, at first blush, that all that is needed is purpose, will and leadership to effect significant change in foreign policy. By contrast, a focus on the domestic and international settings of Canadian foreign policy provides a sobering reminder that there are larger forces that impel and constrain prime ministers, forces that often remain impervious to the initial intentions and visions of those who assume power.

Notes

1. Eayrs provides the classic description: *Art of the Possible,* pp. 3-4.

2. Eayrs, *Art of the Possible,* p. 4; also Eayrs, "Foreign policy of Canada."

3. For example, see Eayrs, *In Defence of Canada,* Vol. 3: *Peacemaking and Deterrence,* pp. 3-28.

4. Stacey, *Canada and the Age of Conflict,* Vol. 2, p. ix.

5. Farrell, *Making of Canadian Foreign Policy;* Thordarson, *Trudeau and Foreign Policy;* Thordarson, "Posture and policy";

von Riekhoff, "Impact of Prime Minister Trudeau"; Nossal, *Politics of Canadian Foreign Policy.*

6. Dewitt and Kirton, *Canada as a Principal Power.*

7. For a general discussion of these factors, see Nossal, *Politics of Canadian Foreign Policy,* pp. 74-103.

8. Doern and Aucoin, eds., *Public Policy in Canada,* Chaps. 2-3; also Thordarson, "Posture and policy."

9. Nossal, *Politics of Canadian Foreign Policy,* pp. 133-43.

10. Dobell, *Canada in World Affairs,* p. 416.

11. Lyon, "Trudeau doctrine."

12. This was no coincidence: when the Trudeau Cabinet rejected initial drafts of the white paper prepared by the Department of External Affairs as overly conservative, DEA assigned an official to draw from Trudeau's speeches and writings an exact indication of the prime minister's views as a guide for further drafts of the white paper. The product of this exercise, put up to the ministers, was, not surprisingly, adjudged acceptable. Thordarson, *Trudeau and Foreign Policy,* Chap. 5.

13. Ibid. Also, Dobell, *Canada in World Affairs,* pp. 140-41.

14. Bothwell, "The Canadian connection"; Tucker, *Canadian Foreign Policy,* pp. 126-33.

15. Ichikawa, "Helpful fixer."

16. Ross, *In the Interests of Peace;* Taylor, *Snow Job.*

17. Lemco, "Canada and Central America," pp. 12-13.

18. Redekop, "Trudeau at Singapore."

19. von Riekhoff, "Impact of Trudeau"; Tucker, *Canadian Foreign Policy.*

20. Nossal, "Personal diplomacy and national behaviour."

21. Gwyn and Gwyn, "The politics of peace," Bromke and Nossal, "Trudeau rides the 'third rail'," Tucker, "Trudeau and the politics of peace," von Riekhoff and Sigler, "Trudeau peace initiative," and Pearson, Mackinnon and Sapardanis, "'The world is entitled to ask questions'".

22. Clarkson, *Canada and the Reagan Challenge,* Chap. 1.

23. *Toronto Star,* 13 July 1984, quoted in Taras, "Mulroney's foreign policy," p. 40.

24. Kirton, "Managing Canadian foreign policy" and "Foreign policy decision process."

25. Tucker, "Canadian security policy."

26. For a most cogent discussion of the requisites of "alliancemanship," see Holmes, *Life with Uncle,* pp. 83-104.

27. Stairs, "Political culture."

SECTION III

Leadership in the Canadian Provinces

Comparing prime ministers to premiers is a difficult task because the office of premier varies among provinces and regions. Daniel Latouche reminds us that Quebec's premier has become a societal leader as well as a political leader. The premiership in Prince Edward Island has often been a jumping off point for those with federal cabinet ambitions. The Ontario premier presides over a governmental system that is large and complex and a Legislature that has a reputation for being the most boisterous and unruly in the Commonwealth. In Alberta, where one party, although not the same party, has always dominated, political life has focussed around the management of the province's natural resources. The job of premier in some provinces has become "prime ministerized"; the premier is expected to dominate in many arenas of power, co-ordinate many roles, and wear many hats. In other provinces, particularly in the "small worlds" described by Jennifer Smith, the premier can, without straining, have a finger in all relevant pies.

What is presented in these essays is a physiology of the office of premier in different settings. Each author has described the relationships that premiers have had to party, Legislature, government, and society. Jennifer Smith, Daniel Latouche, and Nelson Wiseman link the development of the office and political styles to the evolution of distinct provincial political cultures. Graham White and Neil Swainson demonstrate how individuals have shaped the office to suit their own needs and purposes.

CHAPTER 10

Ruling Small Worlds: Political Leadership in Atlantic Canada

Jennifer Smith

In comparison with the other Canadian provinces, the two outstanding facts about the Atlantic provinces are that they are small and economically weak. Looking first at population, we find Nova Scotia at the top, with roughly 900 000 residents, followed by New Brunswick with some 720 000, Newfoundland with about 580 000, and tiny Prince Edward Island just reaching the 125 000 mark. Metropolitan Toronto includes more people than all four provinces combined. A similar picture emerges in terms of geographic dimensions. The Island, sometimes fondly termed "The Garden," is less than 6000 km² in area; Nova Scotia and New Brunswick are larger, but still only 55 000 km² and 73 437 km² respectively. Newfoundland is by far and away the largest of the four at 404 520 km², about one quarter of which is the island, and the rest Labrador on the northeastern boundary of Quebec. Corresponding figures for Ontario offer a sharp contrast: a population of over 8.5 million within an area of 1 068 600 km². Geographically Quebec is one third as large again, with a population of 6.3 million.

On the economic front, the Atlantic provinces perform worse than the others on most indices. The unemployment rate in the region, for example, is normally higher than it is in other parts of the country. Newfoundland's, invariably the worst of all, is currently running at just over 20 percent.[1] The per capita income is generally at the low end of the scale, Newfoundland again distinguishing itself with the lowest in the country.[2] Between 40 and 50 percent of the population, depending on the province, lives in rural areas. The provincial economies are not highly diversified, relying as they do on combinations of four primary industries: agriculture, fishing, forestry, and mining. One consequence of all this is that the provincial governments have but limited fiscal resources of their own. They are dependent on federal transfers for almost half of their annual revenues.[3]

In this chapter I propose to examine how small size affects political institutions, and the impact of weak economies on political leadership in Atlantic Canada. Small size and economic weakness are inescapable and persistent features of political life in the region, and operate as ever-present constraints on the conduct of provincial premiers. They take on particular significance when we consider the relationship between size and the general concern for economic well-being. Alexis de Tocqueville offered an account of this relationship in his two-volume study of American life. *Democracy in America,* which I would like to examine briefly before turning directly to my theme.

SIZE AND THE CONCERN FOR ECONOMIC WELL-BEING

Tocqueville's account appears in his discussion of the advantages of federalism. The federation has the advantages of being large and powerful while allowing its smaller constituent states to preserve their integrity. Under the umbrella of the federal state, these are not only protected, but in that protection are free to contribute to the whole, as well as to pursue their own interests. Tocqueville mentions three politically significant results — diversity, freedom and economic well-being — not all of which are of the same order. For example, diversity, a healthy counter to the pressure towards conformity, is to be expected in the federal state, simply by virtue of the fact that it is a collection of smaller states. Political freedom is of the same order in the sense that their inclusion diffuses power and thereby promotes freedom. But there is more to it than that. While acknowledging that tyranny, because of its terribly pervasive nature, is "more galling" in a small state than in a large one, Tocqueville argues that on the whole, assuming some sociological conditions, freedom is the "natural state of small communities." This is because small communities have little to offer the ambitious. Pursuit of their meagre prizes is an "empty pursuit of glory." What takes the place of glory in a small state? According to Tocqueville, the desire for well-being: "the ambition of the people being necessarily checked by its weakness, all the efforts and resources of the citizens are turned to the internal well-being of the community."[4]

The concern for economic well-being, then, is characteristic of small communities. The intimate setting, the common knowledge of everyone's economic needs and wants, the fact that each state government is "in immediate relationship with the citizens" and "daily apprised of the wants that arise in society" all serve to encourage it. Tocqueville places special emphasis on this point within the context of federalism: federalism intensifies the passion for well-being within the small states because it removes their need to worry about self-defence. Free of this care, both public authority and private individuals devote their energies to the pursuit of prosperity, an activity "less refined and less dangerous" than the "imperialistic pursuits in which large nations are wont to indulge."[5]

If Tocqueville's argument has any application to Canadian federalism, surely it is most appropriate in connection with the smallest provinces. In the large and populous provinces like Ontario and Quebec, it might be suitably applied to the municipal, as opposed to provincial, level of government. But in the Atlantic provinces, municipal government is not as well-rooted or powerful as its counterparts elsewhere. Indeed, at the time of Confederation, it hardly existed at all, which made it difficult for Maritime proponents of legislative union to argue their case.[6] As Rand Dyck reports, today it is "rudimentary" in Prince Edward Island, where almost every matter is dealt with at the provincial level.[7] In Newfoundland and New Brunswick, municipalities have only recently been charged with the provision of basic residential services such as roads, water, and sewage disposal, and they have no jurisdiction in the areas of social services and administration of justice.[8] Nova Scotia's system of municipal government took a long time to establish (because of citizens' concerns about higher local taxes), but it is the most developed of the four. On balance, the provincial governments dominate, and their energies are consumed by efforts to create prosperous economies. Small size and the problems posed by marginal economies intensify this preoccupation, a fact that is abundantly clear when we consider the impact of size and economic concerns on the office of premier.

SIZE AND POLITICAL LEADERSHIP

The provincial governments in Atlantic Canada, like their counterparts in the rest of the country, possess the parliamentary institutions of responsible government. In practice, this means an executive or Cabinet composed of some of the members of an elected legislative assembly, who together command the support of a majority of this same assembly. Responsible government is also party government. The party — that is, the disciplined party system characteristic of the federal and provincial levels of government in Canada — is the key mechanism in responsible government. Thus the legislative majority which a Cabinet needs to maintain itself in office is ordinarily a party majority. Even this brief account of the system, which omits all of its complexities, suggests the degree to which it is governed by convention. The same is true for the office of premier.

The Premier and Legislative Institutions

Premiers are leaders of governing parties and it is not an exaggeration to say that they are normally the most powerful political individuals in the provinces. In part, this results from their position as heads of Cabinet and therefore leaders of the government. As heads of Cabinet, they possess in practice the power to appoint and dismiss its members, as well as the final say on when to dissolve the Legislature and call an election. There is nothing remarkable about any of this in the case of Atlantic Canada's premiers, until the size of the legislative institutions with which they work is considered. In Prince Edward Island there are sixteen dual-member constituencies, which means a Legislature of thirty-two members, the smallest in the country. The Cabinet, at least since the mid-1960s, has consisted of about ten members, or almost one third of the membership of the assembly.[9] Given the Island's traditional two-party system, a closely contested election can produce a governing party with more members in the Cabinet than out of it.

Cabinet positions are among the most valued prizes a premier has to offer, and the selection process is difficult and sensitive no matter what the size of the pool of aspirants.

The small caucus setting makes it particularly tricky because it is relentlessly personal. It is obviously much harder for a premier to exclude from the Cabinet individuals he cannot help but know very well than individuals he hardly knows at all. Moreover, for ministerial aspirants, exclusion when the pool of candidates is so small is a grim and potentially embarrassing matter. And since premiers, unlike prime ministers, have little in the way of consolation prizes to bestow, such as important committee chairs, parliamentary secretariats or even whip offices, there are fewer opportunities for caucus backbenchers to fashion satisfying legislative careers and gain status or a public profile independent of the Cabinet. The option of legislative renegade, discouraged in any event by the conventions of party discipline, is even less likely when those conventions are reinforced by personal intimacy afforded by the smaller scale. The conventions of responsible government have always favoured premiers' control of their caucuses, and small size encourages it further.

To stay for a moment with the admittedly extreme Island example, it would appear easier for a premier to contend with a Cabinet of ten than with one of twenty or more. Force of personality becomes more of a factor while organizational devices seem less necessary. On the other hand, such devices, precisely because they are impersonal, offer surer possibilities of control. Today larger Cabinets are increasingly organized into elaborate and hierarchical committee systems designed to ensure, among other things, effective prime ministerial control. In the other three Atlantic governments, Cabinets have grown to the point where they are twice the size of the Island's, and it is not surprising to find that they exhibit some of the marks of current cabinet organization.

Nova Scotia is organized into fifty-two single-member constituencies. The government has remained in the hands of the two traditional parties, while the NDP maintains a small but growing third-party presence. The present Conservative government of Premier John Buchanan attained office in 1978, at which time Buchanan formed a fourteen-member Cabinet. It now consists of twenty-two members, which with a forty-one-member caucus, favours cabinet control of caucus. Other mechanisms reinforce this control. Cabinet ministers regularly sit on legislative committees, and the most important, the Law Amendments Committee, is chaired by the Attorney General.[10] The Cabinet, dominated in turn by the premier, includes a Management Board, a Policy Board, and Boards of Social and Resource Development. The premier is served by an office of six officials plus secretarial staff, minuscule by comparison with the PMO in Ottawa, but formidable from the point of view of ordinary members of the assembly, whose research and administrative resources are minimal. Staffing of this kind in the premier's office is a relatively recent development. Buchanan's Conservative predecessor, Robert Stanfield, ran a very lean office, initially making do with a staff of three, which included his private secretary and a stenographer. The addition of an executive assistant later raised the number to four. Meanwhile, during his eleven years as premier (1956-1967), Stanfield was his own Minister of Education and, for the first six years, Provincial Treasurer as well.[11]

New Brunswick's institutions are comparable in scale to Nova Scotia's. There are fifty-eight seats in the Legislative Assembly, usually shared between the traditional parties in a classic, alternating two-party system that has only recently been disturbed by the NDP. The Cabinet of Conservative Premier Richard Hatfield, who formed his first government in 1970 and held office until 1987, ultimately included some twenty members drawn from a government caucus of thirty-nine. The cabinet committee system, developed during Hatfield's administration, included an Executive Committee, which he chaired, a Management Board and committees on economic and social policy and programmes. In Newfoundland, Conservative Pre-

mier Brian Peckford heads a Cabinet of eighteen drawn from a caucus of thirty. Like its counterparts in Nova Scotia and New Brunswick, it is organized on a committee basis, and features a Planning and Priorities Committee chaired by the premier, a Treasury Board, and committees on social and economic policy. By contrast, Newfoundland's first post-Confederation premier, Joey Smallwood, presided for almost twenty years over Cabinets whose only organizational principle was the energetic, diminutive figure of the premier himself.[12]

The trend towards relatively large Cabinets and the accompanying cabinet committee systems is common to all the provinces, although in the Atlantic provinces it did not take hold until the early 1970s. It is attributable to a number of factors, among them the need for effective administrative support during a period of prolonged and extensive federal-provincial negotiations on constitutional and economic issues. In the Atlantic provinces, the trend is particularly striking when considered in relation to caucus size. By strengthening their executives in ways that the institutions of responsible government permit, that is, larger Cabinets, more elaborate cabinet committee systems and larger premiers' offices, the premiers in Atlantic Canada have benefitted from the fact that their provinces, however small, are endowed with the full array of the institutions of responsible government. Meanwhile the Legislatures loiter far behind. Non-ministerial government members and opposition members possess little in the way of administrative and research support. More importantly, their opportunity to sparkle in the limelight is limited. In Nova Scotia the legislative session is short and held normally once a year in late winter and early spring. Newfoundland's is of comparable length, the Island's even briefer. New Brunswick, with lengthier sessions, is the exception.

The Premier and the Bureaucracy

From the point of view of a political leader, the ideal bureaucracy is responsive to the executive, administratively sophisticated, resourceful and a fund of sage advice sympathetically offered. In the case of the federal bureaucracy, doubts have been expressed from time to time about its responsiveness and political neutrality. This criticism has come from members of Conservative governments.[13] In both instances they were raised by members of Conservative administrations. It is commonly supposed that difficulties arose out of the longevity of federal Liberal governments in this century and the resulting close rapport that developed between Liberal politicians and senior civil servants. While there is some truth to this supposition, the question of scale must also be considered. The federal bureaucracy is vast, immense by comparison with the provincial bureaucracies of Atlantic Canada, and it is a rich reservoir of expertise. Thus it has the capacity to resist or at least undermine changes in policy direction. In the Atlantic provinces, however, the issue rarely arises. Policy-making is said to be highly "political," meaning that the politicians are in charge. If there are problems on the bureaucratic front, they have been with small size and lack of expertise. In response to the expansion in provincial government activity, much accelerated after the Second World War, premiers have sought to strengthen their bureaucracies. They have not worried about controlling them. Much of this is attributable to scale, and the effect of scale, in turn, on bureaucratic modernization.

The bureaucracies of the three Maritime provinces remained small and patronage-ridden until well into this century. So too did Newfoundland's under Smallwood's lengthy administration. The temptation to reward party workers with civil service positions, particularly in depressed economic conditions, was too great to resist, and the tradition has persisted, despite occasional displays of reform. Thus, Murray Beck writes that in Nova Scotia the appearance of the Civil Service Act of 1935 merely enabled the government of the day to continue its habit of patronage appointments under the guise of a different intent.[14] The merit

principle would not come into its own for at least another decade. Indeed the assumption of power by Robert Stanfield's Conservative administration was considered to be the first to put an end to the widespread turnover of civil servants that had marked change in party in the past. But some of the old ways persisted. Geoffrey Stevens writes that the highways department reverted to tradition, although it confined dismissals to party-time employees of the opposing partisan persuasion.[15] The push for greater bureaucratic expertise came a little later, when the same government, intent on economic development, found it required a more sophisticated backup.

The pattern in Nova Scotia was repeated in the other provinces. New Brunswick established a Civil Service Commission in 1938, but its effect seems to have been to enlarge the civil service rather than to ground it in the merit principle, since successive governments continued to make their own appointments. Moreover, its quality was such that Louis Robichaud, Liberal premier from 1960 to 1970, was forced initially to turn to expertise outside the civil service for advice on his economic and social policy initiatives.[16] In Newfoundland the period of expansion and professionalization came a little later. Its Civil Service Act of 1926 had made virtually no inroads into a thoroughly patronage-based appointment system, a failure for which the province paid dearly during the Smallwood administration. Smallwood almost single-handedly pursued economic opportunities, not on the sustained advice that a strong and professional bureaucracy might have offered — for the province did not have one — but in the company of sharp promoters and outside "experts" of dubious origin.[17] Under the Conservative administration of Premier Frank Moores (1972-1979), a new Public Service Commission was established, effectively transferring control over internal recruitment to the service itself. In Prince Edward Island, official adoption of the merit principle was some time in coming. A Civil Service Commission was not established there until 1963, too late, in hindsight, to transform the existing bureaucracy into an organization that would be equipped to deal a few years later with Premier Alex Campbell's ambitious modernization programme, the Comprehensive Development Plan. Since the federal government practically funded the entire Plan, it was keenly interested in its administration and not entirely happy with what the province had to offer in that respect. In fact, it insisted on the establishment of a new Department of Development, staffed mostly by experts brought in from outside.[18]

The modernization of the bureaucratic organization does not appear to have undermined the prominence or the powers of Atlantic Canada's premiers. On the contrary, it may well have reinforced them. The provincial bureaucracies, though still modest in size, offer greater expertise and have better managerial capabilities. At the same time, the change has not been without some effect on political leadership. S.J.R. Noel has examined political leadership in the provinces through the concept of "clientelism," a concept based on observations on the relationship between patrons and clients. As Noel describes it, the forms of that relationship, itself one of reciprocal benefit, vary according to the economic context. Thus, in its simplest form, it is a direct relationship between a local notable with real benefits to bestow and less notable individuals with loyalty and services to offer. When the economic context, the rural society of small producers, shifts to the more complicated array of economic transactions characteristic of industrialization, the relationship between patron and client often attenuates, and the intermediary or broker appears in between. In political terms, the "in between" is the organized political party which bestows benefits in return for political support. When governments equipped with modern bureaucracies assume an active role in the economy, the bureaucracy comes to displace the political party in the role of broker or even patron. The patron-client relationship remains but now it is

the "patron bureaucracy" with which individuals as clients must deal, for the bureaucracy comes to control many of the resources previously at the disposal of the parties.[19]

Noel does not suggest that communities move distinctly through these stages. The different forms of the patron-client relationship may coexist at any one time. However he does suggest that the third and most current form of the phenomenon represents a threat to political leadership. This is because the patron bureaucracy, unlike the patron political party, does not have the same concern for support for the leadership. It has its own preoccupations, among them maintenance of its position and importance. The leadership is then faced with the task of persuading people with whom it does not deal directly that they are benefitting from programmes it has initiated. If the modern form of the relationship now prevails, the threat it implies must prevail as well. But as Noel remarks, it does not wholly obtain in any province, and in my view, it obtains less in the Atlantic provinces than anywhere else, mainly because of their smaller and more traditional economies and societies.[20] The political parties, more precisely, the government parties, still control important sources of patronage, including government advertising contracts, untendered purchases of various goods and, important in the more rural parts, the use of trucks in road construction and maintenance. Added to these is an array of economic development programmes, some administered from within the bureaucracy, others not. The upshot is a system in which premiers are served by bureaucracies that are more efficient and professional that they used to be, and by useful sources of patronage that have considerable impact in small communities.

The Premier and the Political Party

Each of the Atlantic provinces has a system featuring the two traditional parties. Each has experienced periods of one-party dominance, Nova Scotia being the most notable in this respect.[21] A third party, the NDP, is active in all four provinces, particularly in Nova Scotia, where it now holds three seats in the Legislative Assembly. Almost all observers agree that the traditional parties do not view themselves in ideological terms. During election campaigns they claim to be better managers than their opponents and occasionally make vague suggestions on what they might do to remedy particular ills. They rarely clash on larger questions of public policy and in one notable instance, the Nova Scotia provincial election in 1984, the incumbent premier caused a mild stir by saying there were no issues at all in the campaign. Consistent with the absence of ideological differences between the two parties is traditional voter loyalty.[22] In Prince Edward Island it is particularly strong. Since parties there can balance their dual-member tickets with Protestant and Roman Catholic candidates, and since the ethnic background of the population is homogeneous, religion and ethnicity are not reliable indicators of the vote. Family is the strongest indicator. Frank MacKinnon has described Island elections as the "politics of acquisition"[23] and Murray Beck has argued that one of their main purposes is to determine which party will dispense the limited but all-important patronage resources. "The intimate contact between politician and citizen in a small community," Beck writes, "both produced this tendency and ensures its continuance."[24]

In Nova Scotia, New Brunswick and Newfoundland, where the traditional parties continue to dominate, voting patterns are not quite as stable as in PEI, as indicated by the fortunes of the NDP. In Nova Scotia, until recently the CCF/NDP rallied most of its support amongst workers in industrial Cape Breton. But in the 1984 election, the NDP's growing appeal to voters on the mainland finally produced a Halifax seat for its leader and another seat in the Annapolis Valley, both important firsts for the party. A more impressive change in traditional voter loyalty has taken place in New Brunswick, where religion and ethnicity combine to influence the vote. In this century the Acadian, Catholic vote in the poorer northeast section of the province moved to the Liberal party while the English-speaking, Protestant vote in the more prosperous southeast has favoured the Conservative party. Hence the famous diagonal line dividing the province into two voting publics. However, under Richard Hatfield's leadership, the Conservative party managed to make inroads north of that line. By championing the cause of bilingualism (federally as well as provincially) and responding constructively to Acadian concerns about lack of power and influence in the province's political life, Hatfield made his party a credible alternative for the Acadian community's support. He also demonstrated the traditional parties' characteristic capacity to accommodate and mediate cultural conflict. The NDP is active, but there is no indication that it has influenced political debate in the direction of class issues. The traditional parties, indistinguishable in terms of their party platforms, continue to dominate in New Brunswick and their politics is the politics of pragmatism in a community where religious and linguistic divisions are important. The Tories' loss of every seat in the 1987 provincial election was due more to the personal unpopularity of Premier Richard Hatfield than to dissatisfaction with the party itself.

A non-ideological party system operating in small and economically depressed communities offers advantages to a premier, chief among them control of the available sources of patronage. Judiciously dispensed, patronage helps strengthen the government's reputation in local constituencies. In Atlantic Canada, it is often practised during elections in the form of straight vote-buying — or "treating," as it is euphemistically termed. Beck asserts that in Nova Scotia it continues "almost undiminished." Referring to a critical by-election in Guysborough in 1973, he observed that "the value of a vote rose to a level unparalleled in the province's history."[25] The practice prevails par-

ticularly in the rural areas of all four provinces, for the simple and obvious reason that it is an effective vote-getter in small communities with serious and ongoing economic problems. But it does not always work. Richard Gwyn recounts an incident from the first post-Confederation provincial election in Newfoundland in which Smallwood is alleged to have promised the voters in Ferryland "not one red cent" of governmental largesse if they declined to return his candidate. They declined, and Smallwood appointed the defeated candidate to the chair of the province's Liquor Board.[26]

Patronage is also an effective means of keeping party members enthusiastic and loyal. Smallwood operated through a loose network of friends as opposed to a formal party organization and looked after his supporters very well. His patronage-dispensing capacity was unusually broad since it extended to Liberal nominations in federal as well as provincial elections. Indeed, in some of the outport constituencies his imprimatur meant a sure win, thus enabling him to treat these areas rather in the manner of "rotten boroughs."[27] The more common uses of patronage extend to appointments and tendering procedures. In his account of the patronage practices of the Stanfield administration, Stevens describes a system that served effectively to reward party supporters, albeit in a more discreet manner than that employed by previous administrations. On the tendering front, for example, suppliers were not required to pay to do business with the government. However, those who supported the Conservative party were favoured so long as their bids were competitive. And while major purchases were tendered, the tender system was by invitation, not public advertisement.[28]

Aided by small scale when it comes to controlling legislative institutions, the bureaucracy and party organization, an Atlantic premier appears to enjoy an enviable position. The problem is that small size is not always an advantage on the economic front, for two reasons. One is simply that tiny populations

inhabiting regions with limited natural resources cannot easily generate prosperous economies; rather, they generate marginal economies. The other reason is that everyone knows about everyone else's economic straits. It is not possible for political leaders to ignore, or distance themselves from, the economic consequences to citizens of decisions they might be required or want to take. As a result, premiers in Atlantic Canada are faced with the distinctly unenviable task of pursuing economic strategies of which the results are visible to everyone. Moreover, the very factors examined above that enable them to take charge of their governments also ensure that they are relentlessly identified with, and held responsible for, the economic state of affairs in general. This is especially so in an age that demands an active government presence in the economy. If, as Tocqueville surmised, small communities are preoccupied with the pursuit of material well-being, it is not surprising to find that the pursuit of economic development is the preoccupation of the region's premiers.

THE ECONOMY AND POLITICAL LEADERSHIP

Before the Second World War, the preoccupation with economic development, shaped by assumptions about the limited possibilities of government intervention in the economy, took the form of efforts to extract better financial terms from Ottawa. It was rooted in the growing recognition that the Maritime economy, far from deriving any economic benefits from Confederation, was rapidly becoming an uneconomic adjunct to it. The federal government's National Policy, in place by the 1880s, was designed to protect and develop the nascent industrial sectors of Ontario and Quebec. It was indifferent to the requirements of Maritime economies.[29] As a result, Maritime premiers expended considerable energy attempting to persuade Ottawa of the need to rectify inequities of income, often through detailed briefs to royal commissions.[30]

By contrast, the postwar premiers have operated within a very different climate of opinion that, until recently at least, has favoured government-sponsored economic development. They have undertaken initiatives of their own, primarily to attract businesses to the region, and they have worked with the federal government in order to take advantage of federal development initiatives. Occasionally, as in the case of Premier Brian Peckford's jousts with the Trudeau government over the development of offshore resources, they have been in conflict with Ottawa. What is noteworthy is the extent to which they have assumed personal leadership in the sphere of economic development, identifying their administrations with their efforts and inevitably risking their political careers over them. The political risks have been magnified by the constraints they invariably face. These constraints arise from the constitutional limits on their economic powers, the region's political decline within the nation as a whole, and the disadvantages peculiar to the small bidder for the attention of private industry.

As far as constitutional limits are concerned, provincial governments in Atlantic Canada, like all provincial governments, do not operate the controls affecting national economic policy. Those controls, however unreliable they may be, are in Ottawa's hands. In addition, and unlike some of the other provinces, the Atlantic provinces have little influence over the direction of national economic policy. This is simply a function of numbers. Since Confederation, the proportion of seats in the House of Commons assigned to the Maritime provinces and, since 1949, to Newfoundland, has declined steadily, while the proportion assigned to Ontario and Quebec has increased to eventually account for two thirds of the total. As a result, the federal governing party, the caucus of which will reflect these proportions to some extent, has every political reason to pay close attention to the economic interests of the central provinces. Finally there is the problem of being the smallest and weakest bidder for industrial development. In that game, the Atlantic provinces play from a weak hand because they have much more to gain than they have to offer. The recent case of Litton Systems, an arms manufacturer, is instructive. Ottawa awarded Litton a defence contract on condition that it build the production facility somewhere in the Maritimes. That sparked an intense bidding war among the three provincial governments that enabled the company to win a variety of concessions. In the end Prince Edward Island's Premier Joe Ghiz decided the province could not afford to deal, and the plant went to Nova Scotia, which offered the most attractive "incentives package."[31] This is a classic example of how easily companies can take advantage of provincial governments desperate for new development.

Despite these constraints, the Atlantic premiers have made strenuous efforts to encourage economic development in the hope of lessening their provinces' reliance on the financial benevolence of the rest of Canada. Each province has produced among its premiers a pioneer who has served as a model for his successors, if not in method or direction, then at least in vision. In Newfoundland, Smallwood pursued direct foreign investment, often for spectacular projects with doubtful prospects.[32] His successors, who have been left to salvage what they can from some of these efforts, notably the oil refinery at Come-by-Chance, have concentrated on resources indigenous to the province, primarily fish, oil and hydroelectricity. In Peckford's case, development strategy in relation to offshore mineral resources has been linked to a concerted effort to assert ownership of those resources and, failing that, control of their development. Despite the shift in direction, both Peckford and Frank Moores before him have followed Smallwood in personally and visibly taking charge of development initiatives, with all the attendant responsibilities and political risks that that entails.

In Nova Scotia, Robert Stanfield put economic development at the top of the premier's

agenda and it has remained there ever since. The same is true for Louis Robichaud in New Brunswick and Alex Campbell in Prince Edward Island. Their names are associated with planning strategies as well as attempts to attract new industries. Stanfield experimented with the notion of voluntary economic planning, relying on the assistance of local entrepreneurs; Robichaud pursued an ambitious Equal Opportunities programme in the fields of education, health and social welfare, with assistance from the federal government; Campbell, again with the aid of Ottawa, chose the vehicle of a Comprehensive Development Plan. In all three provinces, premiers, responding to changing conditions and changing opportunities, have continued to assume the mantle of economic leadership during a period in which government initiatives are more welcome than ever; indeed, they have come to be expected. Neither the record of projects that have turned into expensive disasters, nor the fact that the Atlantic provinces are as dependent as ever on federal largesse, have lessened the pressure on premiers to concentrate on economic development. They have only served as arguments for changing tactics.

CONCLUSIONS

I have argued that the two central facts affecting Atlantic Canada's premiers are the economic conditions of their provinces and the small scale of their political institutions. The provincial economy sets an Atlantic premier's agenda and the scale of his government means that he actually controls it. The result in the postwar period has been a preoccupation with economic development. How else would a premier in this region make a mark? In what other way would he try to succeed? Let us recall that in his account of the reasons for the overriding concern of small states with material well-being, Tocqueville points out that they cannot emulate the aggressive, imperialistic pursuits of large states. They turn inwards instead, transforming private regard for well-being into the substance of their politics. From this perspective he argues that the federal structure, by shifting the business of defence from the combining states to a central government, allows them to retain their economic preoccupations. It also means that they can continue to offer only meagre prizes to the ambitious. They offer no avenues for statesmanship. In terms of Canadian federalism, what statesmanlike role can an Atlantic premier play? Premier Hatfield of New Brunswick is the exception that proves the rule. He tried to pursue the statesman's role, particularly in relation to constitutional questions where the province's concerns bear some similarity to the nation's. But Hatfield never set the national agenda on the Constitution. Only the premiers of Ontario and Quebec can compete effectively with the federal government for that distinction.

Notes

1. Statistics Canada, *Labour Force Annual Averages, 1975-1983,* pp. 367-77.
2. Dyck, *Provincial Politics in Canada,* p. 34.
3. Ibid., p. 28.
4. de Tocqueville, *Democracy in America,* Vol. 1, p. 165.
5. Ibid., p. 169.
6. Browne, ed., *Documents on the Confederation of British North America,* p. 123.
7. Dyck, *Provincial Politics in Canada,* p. 85.
8. Ibid., p. 46.
9. Ibid., p. 85.
10. Laundy, "Legislatures," p. 285.
11. Stevens, *Stanfield,* p. 112.
12. Gwyn, *Smallwood,* p. 132, p. 282, p. 286.
13. MacDonald, "Ministers, Civil Servants, and Parliamentary Democracy."
14. Beck, "An Atlantic-Region Political Culture: A Chimera," p. 3.
15. Stevens, *Stanfield,* pp. 121-22.
16. Sparrow, "Royal Commissions: A Study of Five Provinces."

17. Gwyn, *Smallwood,* p. 141, p. 241.

18. Dyck, *Provincial Politics in Canada,* p. 90.

19. Noel, "Leadership and Clientelism," p. 208.

20. Ibid., p. 209.

21. Two of the Liberal party's longest periods in office were 1882-1925 and 1933-1956.

22. Bellamy, "The Atlantic Provinces," p. 13.

23. MacKinnon, "Prince Edward Island: Big Engine, Little Body," p. 247.

24. Beck, "Elections," p. 181.

25. Beck, "An Atlantic-Region Political Culture: A Chimera," p. 4.

26. Gwyn, *Smallwood,* pp. 125-26.

27. Noel, *Politics in Newfoundland,* p. 284.

28. Stevens, *Stanfield,* p. 123.

29. Alexander, *Atlantic Canada and Confederation,* pp. 51-54.

30. Ibid., p. 52; Smiley, *The Rowell-Sirois Report,* Book I, pp. 154-55.

31. *Maclean's,* 4 August 1986, pp. 13-14.

32. Alexander, *Atlantic Canada and Confederation,* p. 21.

CHAPTER 11

From Premier to Prime Minister: An Essay on Leadership, State and Society in Quebec

Daniel Latouche

Prime ministers, chancellors, presidents, and general secretaries are often described as sitting at the apex of political power. Descriptive as it is, this metaphor of Olympian localization has come to distort our perspective of these privileged pinnacles. Even the most cynical of political scientists does not approach such magic places without deference. But reverence, if it breeds good manners, does not necessarily ensure good analysis. To correct their vision, observers have developed defence mechanisms in order to view these godlike figures as mere mortals after all.[1]

THE STUDY OF GODS, POLITICAL AND OTHER

Semantic similarities (the president, le président, il presidente) have created a false sense of comparability across political systems.[2] The fact that blame and responsibility cannot be shovelled any farther up the line — "the-buck-stops-here" syndrome — has come to obscure the very real difference in size of the buck, how quickly it moves, how decisively it is stopped, and more importantly, how the buck is handled once it reaches the desk of final appeal. As they all strive to glow with the utmost vigour, it is not easy for political analysts to distinguish one god from another. We have come to expect the functions of ministers, state secretaries and assistant-deputy-director-generals to be more differentiated across systems because their hierarchical position is defined both from above and below. In the case of prime ministers or presidents, there is no "above" to which they can climb and from which they can receive orders and admonitions. They are gods, and by definition all gods are equal.

Being at the top of the political order makes these leaders less and not more suitable for comparative analysis, although the latter is a tempting strategy to the scholar confronted with a paucity of information and the magic aura of leadership. The mystery is maintained by the fact that in Westminster-style democracies, constitutional documents — the sacred texts — rarely mention prime ministers. Furthermore, since the chief executive is a single office, it presents quantitatively oriented scholars with the insurmountable problem of making use of a sample of one. Comparisons across time and geographic barriers are often the only way out. So far, little has been gained by such comparisons, except generalities about leaders' school and party antecedents.[3] In the worst case, comparisons have resulted in the imposition of an inappropriate framework derived entirely from one system, as when leadership changes in the Soviet Union are judged along the lines of American presidential transitions and inaugurations.[4] Occasionally, even inspired comparative analysis leads to conclusions such as "it is necessary to be aware of the actual situation to understand what prime ministers do."[5]

Scholars of leadership have derived satisfaction from uncovering paradoxes, from which they have found it difficult to extricate themselves later on. The *altitude paradox* is well-known to mountain climbers and business entrepreneurs alike. As you near the top, the air gets almost tangibly cleaner, purer and more precious. But it also gets quite rare and this makes breathing at the same time intoxicating and more difficult. So it is also with political leadership.[6] As you move to the top of the pyramid, power gets more concentrated and more precious, but also more difficult to see and more complicated to use. Too little, you die; too much, you get dizzy! Indeed, upon reaching the top most politicians cannot refrain from expressing their distress: "But where has the power gone?"[7]

Most arguments about "apex political leaders," not unlike conversations among climbers, have to do with the exercise of power as if this were the only commodity to which they had access. For prime-minister-watchers, the power-related questions are plentiful. Has prime ministerial power increased in recent decades and have prime ministers become more "presidential" in their behaviour and self-image?[8] Do they really exert power, or are they manipulated by their staff? Where does this power reside? In their use of the media? In their capacity to articulate issues? Does it really make a difference who rules?

The nature of this high-level political power is rarely defined, and the various paradigms — elite, pluralist and class — usually associated with the study of political power find little resonance among students of top political leadership. In industrial democracies, power is said to be balanced, fused, centralized, fragmented, distributed, organized, or limited, but rarely is the specific role of the prime minister within this web examined in any detail.[9]

And then there is the *uncertainty paradox.* As you win control of the highest office in the land, you take all including, paradoxically, the possibility of losing all.[10] As you sit on top of the pyramid, you can see for long distances in all directions, including the one in which political gravity will eventually take you: down! As many analysts increasingly see presidents and prime ministers only as likely candidates for ruin, identifying the first signs of a political downfall and its consequences has with them become an obsession. As particles in quantum physics, prime ministers are seen as being simultaneously "there" (at the top) and "not there." Everything about apex leaders has become larger than life: the uncertainty, the risks, the pitfalls, the stress, the rewards, the downfall and, almost as a consequence, the difficulties encountered by merely mortal scholars in their efforts to demystify such offices.

In the end, the paradoxical nature of a job where so much is possible and so little is accomplished is constantly reaffirmed by observers even as they wonder at the successes of those few who have done reasonably well. When analysts are not searching for the magic mix of qualities which make "great" presidents possible,[11] they are looking for what it is that "apex leaders" do and what they do best in their job as political gods. What is the exact nature of their contribution to the political process? How do they get other people to recognize that they are gods? How does a god get things done and why is it that most of the time things do *not* get done? Where does authority begin and influence stop? Do gods contribute directly or indirectly to the policy process? What management techniques should they use?[12] Should they get involved in details? How should they use their staff?[13]

These are important questions. They can be answered in various ways. One way is to set down job descriptions, compare responsibilities and pick apart personalities. In this approach, apex leaders are most often seen removed from the political context which is supposed to give sense to their presence. They are said to be in charge of everything, though this "everything" is nowhere in sight. Another approach to leadership studies seeks to bring back to empirical and theoretical life the forgotten concept of the state and statesmanship. But even in this approach, while leaders are present in the form of elites, bureaucrats and revolutionaries, their contributions are depersonalized. The process which provides the state with autonomy and capacities is deemed to happen aside from these actors, who at best are seen as just so many markers of the transformations of the modern state.

Studies of state-making and nation-building make little scrutiny of political leadership, either in autocratic or democratic terms.[14] Similarly, social mobilization is described by analysts as a process where, as if by magic, thousands of individuals overcome their inertia and engage in collective action, most often with the leaders watching from the sidelines.

At times, individuals do step in to influence the development of the modern state. Marx has described in vivid detail how the intrusion of specific individuals could be orchestrated, using as an example the case of Louis Napoleon. But, ultimately, Louis Napoleon's success in convincing the bourgeoisie to forfeit the Crown to save the Purse is to be understood essentially through a class logic. Described as a caricature of his great uncle, he is given almost no freedom of action and is treated as a prisoner of his providential role as chairman of the bourgeoisie's executive committee.[15]

In the end, those who focus on the leaders and their very particular tasks, and those, on the other hand, who choose to ignore them in favour of the autonomous state each end up presenting only one half of the picture. Clearly, if the state is autonomous, then its highest leader and his personal antecedents and particular management style must have something to do with it. Similarly, if power at the top is

difficult to manipulate, it must be because of the ways in which society, the ultimate object of any leadership exercise, has organized itself vis-à-vis the state.

The rest of this chapter will sketch the outlines of the triangular relationship between state, society and political rulership as it has developed historically in Quebec. As can be inferred from the preceding paragraphs, our concern is not with a job description, management techniques and organizational structures. Rather, we choose to view the premiership in a historical and global context, as one manifestation of the phenomenon of leadership, and as the result largely of patterns of state-society relationships. As exhilarating as the top of the political pyramid may be, leadership is more than this.[16]

POLITICAL AND SOCIETAL LEADERS: THE SEARCH GOES ON

Politics, at least in theory, is about order and coherence. The provision of guidance by leaders is necessarily an important element in this process. As the state became the privileged framework in which societies sought to achieve this purposeful rationality, "governments," in their executive, legislative and administrative capacities, rapidly became the major source of this collective guidance. In turn, prime ministers and other apex political leaders succeeded in absorbing much of the responsibility for governmental guidance. But their executive primacy, so central in modern governments, depends on their ability to exert effective control over the legislative and administrative apparatus, and to a lesser extent, over the judiciary body. Effective political rulership requires a dominant presence in every corner of the government. Establishing this presence has not been an easy task.

Although armies, religions and social movements also offer the necessary organizational and symbolic resources, political parties remain the preferred means of achieving a position of executive leadership. Thus, political rulership has a dual dimension: governmental and partisan. Prime ministers and presidents are both government heads and party leaders even if their combination of the two roles varies greatly across systems. The two are distinct but interpenetrated and the balancing act which is required of political leaders constitutes the bread and butter of electoral politics and the test of effective political leadership.

On the other hand, to provide any given society with what it needs most, that is, the capacity to act as a whole, is what societal leadership is all about.[17] No society as a whole has ever, without an able leader, defined a direction which it wanted to take, an idea which it wanted to see implemented and a self-image with which it felt comfortable.

Thanks to the diversity of Canadian culture, formal organizations of all sizes and natures (e.g., parties, corporations) have come to dominate the offering of directions, ideas and images to society, and for a while it was thought that they would succeed in eliminating competition from informal identities based on sex, age, ethnicity or class, and even from individuals, however talented and resourceful.

But with the rise of mass society and media culture the tendency to uniformity has inspired new life in those social actors which could claim to be different. The push for homogenization has helped resurrect groups in the form of ethnic minorities, racial movements, and religious sects, not to mention groups defined by generations or age, and sex or sexuality.[18] The rise of the "showbusiness society" leaves little doubt as to the place of individuals in the shaping of modern society.[19] Football heroes, soap opera divas, sex therapists, convicted criminals, rock stars, royal bachelors, and talk-show hosts all contribute more than their share of societal leadership.[20]

Every day new individuals and groups step forward to offer their most recent proposals as to what our society is all about. Over the last few decades, much attention has been directed at the state and its capacity to impose its own preferences, but in fact, it is society's level of autonomy which has been increasing. Societal leadership, although more ephemeral and often very sectorial, has been able to constantly rejuvenate itself. Fashions, fads, cycles and crazes have perhaps deprived society of any sense of permanent identity, but they have also made it possible for the state to captivate and dominate a given society.

But what do political and societal leaders do when they lead? To lead a party is to strive for the control of governmental institutions and ultimately to employ the capacities of the state to preserve the interests of those socio-economic groups, including social classes, in whose name the party is said to act and speak. As conditions of electoral competition and functions of political parties are transformed — notably with the advent of modern communication technologies — so are the tools available to party leaders.

But the increased complexity of the party and governmental leadership jobs should not be exaggerated. To "lead" a party of one million voters and a government with a $100 million budget is not intrinsically different from leading a ten-million party and a one-million budget. For both the party and the government leader, the task remains the same: steering an organization through bureaucratic rules, hierarchic sanctions, group pressures, definition of routine tasks and emotional investments. In this sense, political leadership is not different from other forms of organizational leadership, as the effective leader is the one who succeeds in inducing human efforts in pursuit of the organization's goals.[21]

Societal leadership is not "above" politics and in this sense those who pretend to speak for a given social group or for the entire society necessarily speak with a voice grounded in experience of the cleavages and confrontations of the time. But political parties, state institutions and electoral politics are not the central ingredients in societal leadership. If political leadership is more instrumental and action-oriented, then societal leadership tends to be preoccupied with the provision and effective management of *meaning*. Societal leaders work at defining the reality of their society. The articulation of tactics, strategies and methods is of secondary importance to them.

The task of providing a collective definition is constrained by the objective reality of the group — its size, nature (ethnic, religious), status (minority or majority) — but all social leaders seek to provide meaning by identifying the "problems" faced by the group, the core elements of its identity, its world-view, and the system of values which should be shared by all, as well as the direction which change should take. Societal leadership is based first and foremost on a diagnosis which has to "make sense" if it is to be shared.[22]

Societal leadership remains a fragmented phenomenon, conducted among the clamour of many, sometimes conflicting, voices. Indeed, the cacophony is indispensable if a given society is to exist. Party and governmental leadership on the other hand is an exclusive process, with little tolerance for dissent and multiplicity. Its logic is one of exclusion rather than inclusion. It demands one voice above the babble. While societal and party leadership can coexist, they can rarely cohabit.

POLITICAL RULERSHIP IN A STATELESS SOCIETY, 1608-1867

Can Quebec as a polity and French Canada as a society claim a specific tradition of political and societal leadership because of their French colonial antecedents? As a complete history of the French administrative apparatus in New France has yet to be written,[23] myths and counter-myths still provide the dominant answers to what is undoubtedly the most perplexing question in the study of Quebec's political development. One school of thought stresses the lack of representative institutions and democratic expression. This negative perception has given rise to another school, presenting the counter-image of the freethinking *habitants,* reluctant to accept any form of authority, preferring retreat to the woods to submission to the directives of the French *intendants*.[24]

Both interpretations emphasize the fact that New France was the creation of the greatest absolutist power of the time. France, it is thought, could not conceive of anything else but to recreate in a colony the well-structured authoritarian pattern of its own central government. The artificiality of this rational colonialism, with its clearly defined chain of command and its neatly-drawn rectangular *seigneuries,* has been well documented.[25] New France in reality had nothing to do with its official version as defined on maps and in royal instructions.

The failure of the French rationalist vision had little to do with the so-called independent spirit of the inhabitants of New France; nor can it be ascribed to any inherent "backwardness" among them. It was ordained simply by the size of the territory, the harshness of winter and the dispersion of the population. In short, political rationality was never really given a reasonable setting in which to succeed or fail.

The transplanted society of New France was part of a colonial institutional order whose importance remained more symbolic than real. In New France, the dominant rationality was domestic and private rather than public and collective.[26] Even the idea of the colony as a totality remained only that, an idea, whose time would in fact never come. Society, inasmuch as it needed to, organized itself outside the realm of politics. Nevertheless, the political superstructure of New France was well developed, and probably more complex than was required for a string of settlements totalling less than 70 000 inhabitants. With an *intendant,* a governor general, local governors, a Sovereign Council and a bishop, the "entry points" in the system, the checks and balances mechanisms and the feedback possibilities were numerous enough to accommodate societal inputs and produce policy outputs. It is true that elections were non-existent and that public meetings could be held only with special permission. But it is equally true that there was little to decide and few issues worth a long journey to attend a meeting. While various private requests could be directed to a Council, which usually acted on them favourably, such requests remained rare and concerned the most trivial matters.[27]

The history of New France has not preserved the names of any local agitators, heroic bandits, peasant leaders or urban conspirators. Justice records reveal a low and declining level of criminality and civil disputes throughout the period. Between 1700-1760, only four individuals were accused of sedition, among them one who had refused to take to sea during a violent storm. For the entire French period, only 181 *habitants* were accused of crimes against the public order, the most frequent of which were non-payment of fines, resisting arrest and counterfeiting.[28]

Revolt was unheard of and public disturbances remained isolated incidents, for example, the 1733 "revolt" following the request by the Montreal governor that the good citizens of Longueuil participate in the reconstruction of the Montreal fortifications. Blows were exchanged as the governor and his escort retreated across the river. No charges were laid and certainly no legends arose out of the incident, as they later would about the *patriotes* of the 1837 Rebellion.

Although injustice, nepotism and corruption were rampant in the colony, they were never seized upon as the pretext for revolt. Contrary to Boston and Philadelphia, where the standard of the ideal Quaker and Puritan colony, respectively, prevailed, New France had no ideal to live up to or to compromise, engendering distemper. In the absence of any such ideal, mediocrity could not be identified and stigmatized as such.[29] When Colbert made it clear that, unlike in France, colonial public offices could not be bought, there was no outcry from merchants and aspiring *bourgeois* as there was little money to spend for rapid advancement, and little worth buying anyway.[30]

The peaceful nature of New France's internal order has often been taken as a sign of the non-democratic and obedient nature of its inhabitants. The absence of turmoil has been taken to mean that the *Canadiens* would obey any authority, however unjust, as long as it was legitimate. Occasionally, though, it has been argued that the *Canadiens* did revolt by individual and silent resistance. Was the internal order of New France simply the manifestation of a contented society?[31]

More bluntly, we suggest, if only as a hypothesis, that throughout the French regime, society had little to revolt against and the state had little to impose. In a stalemate of mutual incapacity and laissez-faire between the *Canadien* society and the French state, local leaders, political and societal, had little opportunity or reason to emerge.[32] They could be party leaders but could not count on governmental resources to achieve their objectives. They could become religious martyrs or military heroes, but had little chance to propose alternate directions and visions for the colonial society.

Only when the geopolitical circumstances are such that politics seem to make sense, i.e., when mobilization can be expected to provide individual rewards and improve collective goods, is political leadership likely to emerge as a distinct force. This was the case between 1830-1850 and again during the Quiet Revolution.

The patriation of the French administrative class after the 1760 Conquest, the rejection of the American Revolution and the decision of the new British authorities not to directly confront the *Canadiens* all contributed in preserving the non-conflictual nature of the state-society relationship. For military and geopolitical reasons, the British did not immediately attempt to impose more than a minimal state presence. The most important contact zone between the *Canadiens* and the new order, the legal system, was left relatively intact.

This hybrid normative system was amenable

to all possible compromises and adjustments.[33] In such an under-defined regime, injustices were difficult to document and reports rarely coalesced into collective protest. As in New France, local society required little rulership and indigenous political leaders had no ground on which to build followings. For different reasons, neither the French nor the British colonial order made much difference to the people themselves, and so could not be used as a basis upon which to develop organizational support, or as a force against which to assert a legitimate claim to authority.

The 1791 Constitutional Act modified the political landscape and crystallized for decades to come the geography and internal articulation of the new Canadian state order.[34] For the first time, *Canadien* society could no longer ignore a state which the new English settlers intended to use to counterbalance their demographic inferiority, and maintain their integrity, vis-à-vis the United States. Suddenly, politics became relevant as party leadership and governmental rulership became very real possibilities both for individuals in terms of personal careers and for society in terms of collective choice.

The next 40 years witnessed a multiplication of aspiring leaders as well as successful heroes and martyrs. In the process, *Canadien* society gave itself original instruments for collective action. The *Parti patriote* was not only the first political party in the British North American colonies, its high level of organization prefigured similar parties both in Europe and America.[35] The surprise created by this new party and some of its novel techniques, including economic boycott, best explain the initial successes of the 1837 Rebellion.

Louis-Joseph Papineau was the first "apex" political leader of French Canada. His ultimate failure is often explained through weaknesses of his personality, or his own confusion as to the ideological and political objectives of the Rebellion. The debate on his precise contribution to the 1837 debacle has not ended[36], but moving beyond the clichés, we find in Papi-

neau the first concretization of the dilemmas and constraints under which all apex political leaders in Quebec have had to function. He was expected to be both a party and a societal leader, and reconcile the exigencies of the two positions. But not only are the audiences very different, but the leadership "skills" and even the purpose of collective action are different in the two cases.

Papineau was the first to have to deal with this leadership confusion. Much was expected of him and for a short while he actually was able to fulfill his leadership roles on both the societal and political fronts. As a party leader, Papineau was expected to seize control, either electorally or militarily, of the existing state apparatus and put an end to the dualist (Upper Canada, Lower Canada), colonial and undemocratic nature of the political institutions. On the other hand, while many of his followers hoped he would reaffirm the traditional vision of the *Canadien* society, others were hoping for a radical redefinition of the same society. In the end, Papineau's failure was not so much the result of his leadership shortcomings as of the existence of contradictory expectations of what the party should do and what the society should be.

The full-blown nature of the revolt made the emergence of a single leadership impossible. The military imbalance between the *patriotes* and the British made the particular contribution of leadership an irrelevant question. And so, one is tempted to conclude, it has been ever since.

POLITICAL LEADERSHIP IN A WEAK STATE: 1867-1905

Much has been said about what the Fathers of Confederation really had in mind in 1865, and about how French Canadians perceived the constitutional settlement. These considerations are important if we are to make sense of the subsequent evolution of the initial agreement.[37] A telling fact is the ease with which the new formula, in sharp contrast with the acrimonious parliamentary debates of only a few months before, was finally accepted in Quebec. Could it be that it simply did not matter much?

In Quebec, unlike in other provinces, Confederation was not an important issue during the first post-1867 provincial elections. French-Canadian elites did not rush to occupy the newly created provincial state, and made relatively few demands for jobs and special policies. Three years after its creation, the provincial administration still had only ninety-two full-time employees.[38] Not unlike the artificial bureaucratic structure of New France, the new administration offered little to fight over. Little was asked of it, except to serve as a transmission belt to and from Ottawa.

Nowhere is the inconsequential nature of the new provincial state better expressed than in the composition of its apex government structures. Until the turn of the century, close to 40 percent of the provincial Cabinet, and 25 percent of the Legislative Council, were made up of English-speaking representatives. But unlike similar situations only a few years before, this over-representation created little turmoil and the issue was rarely mentioned.

Two English-speaking representatives and two unelected members of the Legislative Council even served briefly as premiers without any protest that this was contrary to the natural order of things or was establishing a precedent. At the time, more attention seemed to be attracted by the Montreal mayoralty than by the Quebec premiership.[39]

From 1867 to 1900, eleven individuals occupied the position of premier, two of them twice. Only Chauveau, appointed as part of the 1867 settlement, served for more than five years. Electoral defeats, scandals, federal appointments and federal pressures tended to take care of most careers. This rapid turnover is remarkable, considering that the Conservative Party was in power during most of this period. The premiership was but a brief interlude in a career which included more important stopovers in the federal Cabinet, the Senate, the

Legislative Council, the Courts, and if one was fortunate, the Office of Lieutenant Governor.[40] It would seem that during these years nobody really wanted the job!

The office of premier was not as important as that of the specialized portfolios which the premiers retained for themselves. Two premiers, Ouimet and Mercier, were forced to resign amidst accusations of corruption, though the accusations exclusively concerned their ministerial responsibilities. Apparently, the premiership offered little opportunity for dishonesty to flourish.

As a rule, the federal Cabinet, especially its French Canadian members, had as much to say in the selection of provincial cabinet members as the premier himself. Little was made of the fact that in 1897 and again in 1900 the new Liberal premiers felt obliged to submit their cabinet list to Laurier for approval. In 1886, specific instructions were sent from Ottawa for the Lieutenant Governor to appoint J. Ross as premier, although his party had been narrowly defeated in the general election. Even the final decision of who should be included or excluded from the Cabinet had none of the dramatic quality so prevalent today. As a rule, Quebec premiers selected their own ministers on strictly electoral grounds with little regard for any ideological or even geographic representation.[41] Family ties were more important than programs or styles. For example, Premier Mousseau was the grandson of a well-known Lower Canadian representative, had a brother in the House of Commons, a nephew in the Legislative Council, a father-in-law and a cousin in the Quebec Legislative Assembly (as well as, eventually, André Laurendeau as a grandson). H. Mercier, for his part, was the father-in-law of L. Gouin, a future premier, while S.-N. Parent had immediate family ties to four active politicians in Toronto, Ottawa and Quebec City.

Much has been said of the exclusive control of the anglophone community over certain cabinet appointments, notably Treasury and

Table 11.1 — Quebec Premiers: 1867-1905

P.-J.-O. Chauveau	Conservative	1867-1873
G. Ouimet	Conservative	1873-1874
C.-E. Boucher de Boucherville	Conservative	1874-1878
		1891-1892
H.-G. Joly de Lotbinière	Conservative	1878-1879
J.-A. Chapleau	Conservative	1879-1882
J.-A. Mousseau	Conservative	1882-1884
J.J. Ross	Conservative	1884-1887
L.-O. Taillon	Conservative	1887
		1892-1896
H. Mercier	National	1887-1891
E.J. Flynn	Conservative	1896-1897
F.-G. Marchand	Liberal	1897-1900
S.-N. Parent	Liberal	1900-1905

Justice. But such portfolios were of little importance in the strategic calculus of this most privileged minority. Favours were indeed obtained, especially for those involved in building regional railways, but on no occasion were such favours made possible only because of an ethnic connection. All railway promoters benefitted from government handouts and all members of Cabinet were anxious to share in the distribution of rewards.[42] For both the French majority and the English minority, Ottawa, not Quebec City, was the centre of political power.

Except for Mercier, no premier considered himself anything other than premier of a provincial government "just like the others." On no occasion did a premier take the lead in a campaign against Ottawa or for French Canadian rights. None of them spoke "eloquently" about Quebec being the homeland of the French-Canadian nation.

Honoré Mercier briefly found himself in a multiple leadership position as a result of Louis Riel's execution in 1885. He succeeded in using the crisis to transform a rag-tag Liberal party, including a few dissident conservatives and some ultra-Catholic elements, into a winning electoral coalition. But Mercier failed to transcend his basic roles as party leader and provincial premier. He could not transform the temporary nationalist outcry around Riel into a permanent platform or effectively change the course of federal-provincial relations. Ontario premiers and the Judicial Committee of the Privy Council were more effective in this regard than any Quebec premier.

Re-elected in 1891, Mercier was forced to resign because of a corruption indictment. The rapidity as well as the circumstances of his downfall only confirm the fragility of his leadership. Much has been made of Mercier's attempt to establish a strong provincial state and use it to promote economic and social development.[43] But in 1896, the Quebec civil service still consisted of less than 200 full-time employees and had yet to develop an interest outside the provision of state subsidies to railway promoters and agricultural developers.

Often singled out as the forerunner of a new breed of Québec premiers, interventionist and nationalist, Mercier left only negligible traces, as if to point out that the traditional qualities associated with political leadership — vision, self-assurance, dedication, shrewdness and willpower — are neither sufficient nor necessary conditions for the establishment of an effective leadership. In the period from 1850 to 1900, 500 000 Québécois left for the United States to work. As successive governments were left impotent when confronted with an issue of such magnitude, the Church provided Quebec society with a coherent vision of the world and of itself, as well as the leadership and institutional structures necessary for its survival. From 1850-1900, membership in the religious orders went up from 893 to 8612 as the Church became the dominant organizational, economic and ideological force in Quebec.[44] With 3380 clerics serving outside the Quebec borders, the Church even succeeded in transforming a threatening population drain into a challenging collective enterprise, that of catholicizing North America and serving as a civilizing vanguard in Africa and Asia.[45] It could provide all the necessary candidates and supply

Table 11.2 — Quebec Premiers, 1905-1960

L. Gouin	Liberal	1905-1920
L.-A. Taschereau	Liberal	1920-1936
J.-A. Godbout	Liberal	1936
		1939-1944
M. Duplessis	National Union	1936-1939
		1944-1959
P. Sauvé	National Union	1959
A. Barette	National Union	1960

them with the necessary organizational and symbolic resources to effectively monopolize most opportunities for societal leadership in Quebec.

RULERSHIP IN A FRANCHISED STATE, 1905-1960

Until the turn of the century, Quebec premiers were obviously at a disadvantage both as party and as societal leaders. The underdeveloped Quebec state offered few resources which they might transform into permanent political advantages.[46] Nor could they compete with the societal leadership offered by the Church. In short, they were expendable and the replacement of one premier by another, an abrupt resignation, a forced retirement and even being fired by the Lieutenant Governor was of little consequence. The high turnover in the office best illustrates how, in effect, "irrelevant" Quebec premiers were on all counts.

The situation obviously changed after 1905 as three premiers — Gouin, Taschereau and Duplessis, held the job for forty-nine of the next fifty-four years. Could it be that the job of premier had suddenly become more important? Of course, such long careers have often been taken as an expression of an authoritarian streak among French-Canadians and a low level of commitment to democracy which was supposedly characteristic in Quebec before the Quiet Revolution. But we will look elsewhere for an explanation of these striking instances of political longevity.

Reconsiderations of pre-1960 Quebec politics have yet to address the issue of leadership.[47] Twenty years after his death, the spectre of Maurice Duplessis still haunts Quebec. Attempts to move away from the first wave of biographies, critical or defensive, have still not led to a more balanced assessment, not so much of his personality and practices — for no amount of reinterpretation could turn him into a radical progressive — but of the insertion of his particular mode of political leadership into the general context of politics and societal conditions during those years.

The authoritarian personality of Duplessis has been diagnosed variously as the result of his small-town, middle-class upbringing, of his aristocratic aspirations, his ultra-conservative ideas, his nationalism, his personal life (he remained a bachelor, a "*vieux garçon*" all his life), his alcoholism and his 1940 electoral defeat.[48] Or maybe it is, as *Saturday Night* once observed, simply the result that both Duplessis and Hitler were born on the same day (April 20, 1890).[49]

The fact that Duplessis personally approved the installation of telephone lines in key offices, would hand out scholarships to sons of political supporters and keep track of all but the most insignificant of government contracts is often taken as an indication of the dictatorial and corrupt nature of his regime. But it also points to the fact that the premier had little to do besides fuss over minor matters and had both the time and the resources to exert a personal control over the administration. This clientelistic relationship tells us not so much about the premier's personality or about the so-called disposition of French Canadians towards personalized rule, but of the particular nature of the premiership throughout this period. To worry about details and take minute decisions was apparently a very successful way to operate an office which had suddenly become much more relevant.[50]

The replacement, after a revolt of his caucus, of Premier Marchand by Lomer Gouin in 1905 marked the end of the political subjugation of the structure of Quebec party leadership to Ottawa. Angered by Marchand's willingness to transform the office into an electoral machine for Laurier, a group of ministers, led by Gouin, staged what amounted to a coup d'état by forcing the newly elected premier to resign. Although then at the height of his popularity, Laurier could do little for his protégé. After that unprecedented event, the road to party leadership became exclusively Quebec's, with little interference from Ottawa.[51] Quebec party leadership was perhaps still not a very important political job; nevertheless, it was a legitimate one.

After 1905, one can no longer dismiss Quebec as a non-existent state. Legislative activities, administrative complexity, the size of the budget and the number of civil servants all grew after this date. In all areas — education, welfare, health, culture, economic development, the Quebec state adopted, though, it must be said, very slowly, new responsibilities; occasionally this new activism led to serious clashes with the federal government.

But this new activism took place in a haphazard and purely reactionary way, so that J. Gow has coined the concept of the "dilettante state" to refer to this period.[52] In such a state, new ministerial departments are rarely established, and when they are, bureaucratic activism by a minister, or personality conflicts between two ministers are usually the cause. No mention is ever made of the need for overall administrative reorganization and marginal administrative adjustments are rarely accompanied by a new set of programs or activities.

Between 1944 and 1959, Maurice Duplessis created only three departments: Hydroelectric Resources, Youth and Transportation. There was little intention of using them as the cornerstones of any governmental economic strategy. All new responsibilities were handled on an ad hoc basis and gave rise to little debate within the government. During the Liberal interlude of 1939-1944, Premier Godbout set up a num-

ber of central administrative apparatuses either to increase efficiency and depoliticize the administration (Civil Service Commission, Labour Relations Board) or to provide the embryo of a neocorporatist infrastructure (Cooperative Council, Labour-Management Advisory Council, Economic Council). These institutions had so little credibility that when re-elected, Premier Duplessis had no difficulty in either disbanding them formally, or "forgetting" to make the necessary nominations, or using them to reward friends and allies. They also disappeared from the Liberal program almost as if no one in the Liberal electorate coalition had ever really needed them.

Between 1940 and 1960, the Treasury Board, whose formal responsibilities included the control and authorization of public expenditures, could not find the time to meet. Special funds were the preferred budgetary vehicle and, on the average, 45 percent of all public expenditures were not specifically authorized by the Legislative Assembly. This often led to budgetary shortfalls. As deficits were less important than today, such instances of financial malpractice were of little consequence.

After its election in 1939, the Liberal government succeeded in replacing 60 percent of all full-time and part-time civil servants (3817 out of 6365!). This massive purge was achieved with minimal administrative chaos and when Duplessis came back in 1944, he in turn decided not to conduct a new purge and to accommodate himself to the predominantly Liberal civil service. More important to the re-elected premier was to ensure that certain individuals would not find any job anywhere in Quebec. Again, the attention to detail! Until 1959, the government did not know the exact size of its payroll and no classification of tasks existed. Had it existed, such knowledge would have served no purpose.

Between 1944 and 1960, the number of civil servants increased from 11 000 to 25 000 while para-public employees went up from 13 000 to 28 000. But this remarkable growth was mainly the result of an equally remarkable patronage system whose logic and systematic character far outweighed that of the state.[53] Once more the consequences, except for the democratic costs, appeared to have been minimal.

During those years, Quebec premiers, convinced as they were that only massive foreign investments could ensure the province's development, acted as managers of a franchise state. Their role was that of intermediaries between foreign capital and Quebec society. As pointed out by Boismenu, what is surprising is the ease with which the premiership's tasks could be accomplished, as they required only minimal institutional support.[54] More important was the extent of personal contacts linking the premier and the foreign business community.

No one was better prepared for this role of premier as middleman than Louis-Alexandre Taschereau, who collected as many board memberships as he could possibly handle. With little difficulty, he was able to transform accusations of conflict of interest into electoral advantages; his biography reveals that his close ties with the lumber barons, paper companies and utility trusts were indeed the basis on which he made decisions.[55]

Under Duplessis, the Premier's Office provided all the decision-making which was required to keep the various components of the National Union coalition in line. Under both Duplessis and Taschereau, interest groups of all kinds (including the Church) rarely went outside the premiership to press their case. They could talk to the boss directly.

All decisions were made on an ad hoc and case-by-case basis. This form of personalized rule was particularly suited to the kind of decisions which needed to be made in such a franchise state. No need to balance the interests of one region against the other, of one interest group against another or of one "strong" minister against an equally strong colleague. Electoral calculations counted for little, as first the Liberal Party and then the National Union

could count on powerful party machines to sweep them back into power. As suggested by Boily, the Union Nationale is to be understood purely as an electoral machine, as a "*partito-cratie*," with little linkage to the interests of its class supporters.[56] It did not need to respond to such interests.

This personalized form of rulership corresponded not so much to a French-Canadian predilection for authoritarian rule as to a certain vision of the role of the state which was shared by all Liberal and Union Nationale governments of the 1905-1960 period, and best exemplified by Maurice Duplessis. Without claiming any specific causal relationship between the two, one is nevertheless struck by the correspondence existing between certain aspects of this personalized mode of rulership and certain aspects of the dominant mode of state intervention in society.

In addition to its shortcomings on the democratic front, personalized rulership was also limited by its very restricted amplitude. Being the central and often the only focus of the entire decision-making chain, the premier had not only to be made aware of the issue, but also had to formulate possible solutions, find the necessary support for his decision, select a course of action, see to its implementation, and follow it through. In such a context, only a limited number of decisions could possibly be made and those decisions which could count on precedents and which entailed little complexity were necessarily favoured. This form of rulership was thus particularly appropriate in a situation where the government saw itself as a last-minute intervenor and as providing only the most basic services.

In a sense, Duplessis and Taschereau, within the limits of their abilities, gave the Quebec government all the helmsmanship which such a franchise state required. All of their energy was given to their role as party leader, inasmuch as the party was a more important instrument of political rule than the Cabinet.

Personalized rulership made for an ad hoc

pattern of intervention whose disjointed nature corresponded closely to a similar vision of the role of the state and of government. Much has been made of the reactionary and pro-business attitudes of the Taschereau and Duplessis regimes. While such attitudes were real, their pervasiveness and their insertion in an overall ideological program should not be exaggerated. One should be careful not to assign to these governments mirror-characteristics derived from the Quiet Revolution. Only a post-facto reconstructed logic can discern a rationale, class or ideological, behind each case.

Because decisions were most often made by the premier in secret and communicated confidentially to the interested party, they could easily be reversed or supplemented by a subsequent decision. This form of personalized rulership was particularly suited for those decisions which could be simplified to the extreme, as when Duplessis was called upon to determine the royalty charged for Quebec's iron ore. Personalized rule calls for and thrives on such simply structured decisions, which can be communicated personally, and the effects of which are immediately perceptible. Personalized rule needs this visibility.

Labour relations served these paternalistic rulers with their most formidable leadership challenges. Again, much has been said of the renowned anti-labour policies of Duplessis. Apparently, he hounded labour unions with a vengeance, sparing no tactic to eliminate them. His animosity is said to have been fuelled by the progressive policies and emancipatory practices put forward at the time by Quebec unions, which had to be crushed for fear of setting a bad example for newspapers, intellectuals, students — and all who were silent out of fear.

Duplessis's anti-labour reputation is well deserved, but the unions' radical image owes more to a romantic vision than to a close study of the labour agenda.[57] Duplessis's obsession with unions had more to do with his inability to understand, much less accept, social organizations whose raison d'être was essentially to create conflict. His objective was not to eliminate all traces of a labour presence — he even lowered from 60 to 50 percent the percentage of "signatures" required before a certification by a government labour board could be granted — but to contain labour within the range of his personalized rule so that he could offer "his" civilized and well-behaved unions as another comparative advantage to foreign investors.

In Duplessis' vision of rulership, there was no more room for business organizations than for labour ones. True, every year he personally attended the annual presentation of a brief by the *Association professionnelle des industriels,* but on no occasion did he follow up on any of their suggestions. In 1949, 1954, 1955 and 1957, he acted as a guest speaker at their annual convention, only to deliver on each occasion the same speech, word for word.[58] Labour and professional organizations, because of their representative structure and their high visibility, simply had no place in Duplessis' approach to rule.

The equilibrium between the demand and supply of political leadership was contrasted in the society by an effervescence rarely encountered in Quebec history. As industrialization and urbanization came to break the Church's monopolistic position, a multitude of groups rapidly emerged to fill the void. In the thirties and early forties, *Le Devoir,* the *Ecole sociale populaire,* the *Action nationale,* the *Jeune Canada* and the *Nation* multiplied the proposals for the reorganization of French Canadian society. Although they differed in the details of their plans, they unanimously agreed on the need for French Canada to find its survival "outside" of politics, and on the absolute necessity of a *chef* to emerge.[59] André Laurendeau, later to become co-president of a Royal Commission of inquiry on bilingualism and biculturalism wrote some of the most eloquent words on this quest for the ultimate leader:

> Nous demandons à la Providence de nous envoyer cet homme qui nous tirera de notre désarroi social et national, qui nous arrachera d'entre

les trusts accapareurs. Il nous faut un vrai
Canadien-français, cent pour cent, qui aime sa
patrie et la sauve. Pour le chef, nous consen-
tirons tous les sacrifices et quand il apparaîtra,
nous le reconnaîtrons, nous nous mettrons sous
ses ordres car nous serons prêts à lutter et
avancer.[60]

Similar appeals have been taken as a sign of
the helpless state in which Quebec society
found itself when it discovered that its traditional social and political leaders could not
rescue it from economic depression.[61] The rise
of a small fascist movement is usually taken as a
definite proof of this sense of general confusion. We prefer to see this ideological and
organizational agitation as a manifestation of
the extreme fertility and resilience of French
Canadian society in response to a political
leadership completely overcome by events. But
in a reversal of the situation of the thirties, the
leadership confusion was now to be found in
the societal camp as the exuberant societal
leadership failed to make its junction with the
political order.

FROM PREMIERS TO PRIME MINISTERS, 1960-PRESENT

On the surface, one cannot imagine a more
diverse collection of individuals than the six
politicians who have served as Quebec premiers since 1960. What common features are
there in the personalities, management styles
and ideologies of Jean Lesage, Robert Bourassa
and René Lévesque?[62] Lesage was perceived as a
"grand seigneur," aloof, convinced of his inherent capacities as a leader, imbued with his
mission as "father" of the Quiet Revolution,
trying his best to keep his star ministers (Lévesque, Kierans, Laporte and Gérin-Lajoie) under
control without giving any group too much
power. Robert Bourassa, for his part, has been
described as having no sense of mission at all,
preoccupied exclusively with the daily management of governmental and party affairs,
incapable of saying no, image-oriented and

Table 11.3 — Quebec Prime Ministers,
1960-1987

J. Lesage	Liberal	1960-1966
D. Johnson	National Union	1966-1968
J.-J. Bertrand	National Union	1968-1970
R. Bourassa	Liberal	1970-1976
		1985-
R. Lévesque	Parti Québécois	1976-1985
P.-M. Johnson	Parti Québécois	1985

easily influenced. As for Lévesque, his unpre-
dictability and disorganization contributed to
his image as the reluctant manager, indifferent
to administrative details and preoccupied almost exclusively with moving Quebec along
the road to sovereignty.

Such differences in style and vision are no
doubt real and very much the product of these
premiers' different personalities. But once
again, a process of post-facto reconstruction is
probably at work so that each premier is provided with a management style and a rulership
vision corresponding to what is perceived to
have been his party's contribution to Quebec's
political development.[63]

For example, Jean Lesage, because of his
presumed role as "father" of the Quiet Revolution, is often attributed with a *pater familias*
management style which bears little resem-
blance to reality. In the process, he has been
transformed into an ardent Quebec nationalist,
a highly ethical politician with sincere social-
democrat and progressive views. In fact, his
previous membership in the St. Laurent Cabinet had shown him to be a centralist and anti-
nationalist minister. His opposition to measures
such as the establishment of a provincial department of education and reform of the social
services and his initial refusal to support the
1962 hydroelectric nationalization plan make
him at best a reluctant "father" of a Quiet
Revolution which occurred for the most part
outside of his realm of influence and in some
instances despite his intentions.

Many decisions which were in his exclusive

sphere as premier turned out to be close to catastrophic. Many had to be withdrawn and others were termed successful, but for the wrong reasons. For example, the snap decision to hold a 1962 election had more to do with a last-ditch attempt to prevent a cabinet split than with any desire to rewrite Quebec economic history. As for the Liberal victory, it also had much less to do with the central issue in the campaign — hydro-electric nationalization — than with a high level of popular satisfaction.[64] In 1966, under the best of electoral circumstances, his campaign style as well as his refusal to face up to the new issues of labour militancy and nationalism precipitated the Liberal defeat.

Similarly, Lévesque is presumed to have been undisciplined and lacking in the rationality of Trudeau's management style because he is seen essentially as a movement leader. Nevertheless, he holds the record for the greatest number of cabinet shuffles, ministerial reorganizations and dismissals of ministers by a Quebec premier.[65] Contrary to his bohemian and casual image, he spent considerable time and energy balancing and counter-balancing the political, regional and personal mix of his Cabinet, at the same time sending signals as to his own ideological orientation. Under Lévesque, cabinet committees achieved unprecedented power as they were put under the responsibility of "activist" ministers who had a personal stake in promoting sectoral co-ordination. Between 1976 and 1982, the management performance of Lévesque was nothing short of exceptional, considering the strains imposed by the presence of militant, activist ministers, a referendum campaign and a federal government dedicated to destabilizing the "separatists."

CONCLUSIONS

Between 1960 and 1985, Quebec premiers saw their role redefined as they became increasingly absorbed in responsibilities of governmental leadership. As the presence of the Quebec state grew more pronounced on all social, economic and cultural fronts, and as the level of autonomy enjoyed by the Quebec polity reached an unprecedented level, so too did the responsibilities of the premiership.

The rise of executive federalism, the ongoing process of constitutional negotiations, recent international exposure and the almost absolute separation between Quebec political parties and their federal counterparts (when they exist) has provided Quebec premiers with diplomatic, partisan and governmental responsibilities comparable to those of the prime ministers. As Québécois continue to identify more closely with their provincial government, perceived as being more "important" than Ottawa in their daily lives, the Quebec premier has become known, in French at least, as the other *premier ministre*. But this new status has been an unstable one as Quebec *premiers ministres* have found it increasingly difficult to fulfill their role of societal leaders. As the autonomy of the Quebec political system increases, so also do the expectations put on this system.

In Quebec as elsewhere, party and societal objectives rarely coincide and Quebec's case is no different from the Hungarian, Black American or Danish one. But only in Quebec does one find such a close correspondence between the boundaries of a subnational political system and that of a national community. Quebec premiers cannot escape the fact that more is expected of them than basic management of a provincial government or the winning of an election. When the integrity of the society or its political system is threatened, or when the relations between the two are radically transformed, Quebec premiers are expected to be both political and societal leaders. This unique position offers them accrued capacities which they work to transform into electoral benefits. It also seriously limits their effective ability to impose their own vision, as both the civil society and the political realm have their own performance requirements.

The identity and the boundaries of state and

society have never been simple in Quebec's case, and compound the complexity of the matter. Not only do the federal and provincial state intermix, but both have tended to produce their own leadership structure. Because Quebec is part of the overall Canadian political system, a number of individuals can lay claim to be political ruler of Quebec: the premier, the federal prime minister (if he happens to be French-speaking or Quebec-born), and his "lieutenant."[66]

As for the society in question, should it be defined as the French Canadian, the Quebec, the French Quebec or the francophone society? Over the years, the interests of these constituent "societies" have increasingly diverged as each "society" has tended to produce its own leaders. The recent development of Quebec into a "*société globale*" has again multiplied the candidates for societal leadership.[67]

Beyond these stylistic differences, real and imaginary, all post-1960 prime ministers share certain traits, notably the extremely fragile nature of their party leadership. Four premiers were defeated while in office (Lesage, Bertrand, Bourassa and P.-M. Johnson), while one died (D. Johnson) and the other was "convincingly" pushed out (Lévesque). One premier (Bourassa) was defeated twice in his own riding. No premier has succeeded in winning three consecutive electoral terms and none has managed an electorally successful transfer of power. Finally, all premiers faced serious leadership challenges while in office and three had to resign (Lesage, Bertrand, Bourassa) after an electoral defeat. None was able to successfully resist a challenge to his authority.

These difficulties will undoubtedly be interpreted as reflecting the indomitable character of the Québécois or the inherent difficulties associated with ruling "*La Belle Province.*" We prefer to view them as reflecting, at an even higher level, the leadership confusion first identified and described in the case of Papineau. The rapid expansion of the Quebec state has provided the premier with unprecedented

advantages to establish pre-eminence as Quebec's major political ruler. On this front, the victory has been complete but rarely lasting.

Most of the difficulties premiers have encountered do not stem from their personalities or from the management tools at their disposal but from a confusion as to what it is they are supposed to be ruling. Over the years, Quebec prime ministers have availed themselves of the instruments necessary to exercise efficiently their multiple leadership roles. Their personal staff now reaches close to fifty, as assistants and advisors of all sorts have multiplied. The stringent rules for party financing have "forced" all Quebec political parties, not just the Parti Québécois, to become efficient political machines. The captive nature of the French media market has provided them with a ready-made audience. To borrow from a well-publicized image, Quebec prime ministers have gone presidential, even more so than their federal counterparts.

But there is something artificial behind this transformation. Rulership in New France, as well as later on in Lower Canada, Canada East and Quebec, has always had a theatrical quality imposed by the make-believe nature of the polity. The most important responsibility of political leadership in Quebec has always been to ensure that the "show" did in fact go on!

Much has been made of a so-called "Papineau syndrome" which supposedly has come to haunt all French-Canadian leaders, i.e. stumbling on the most insignificant details after drawing the most grandiose of plans.[68] This schizophrenic personality has been said to be in tune with a congenital tendency of modern-day Québécois to react with ambivalence to everything involving the exercise of political power. Nowhere has this so-called trait of collective character been put to more extensive use than for explaining the attitude of the Québécois towards their political leaders as well as the leadership style of their various premiers and prime ministers. For example, the simultaneous reigns of Trudeau and Lévesque are often taken to reflect the two conflicting sides of the Quebec political personality: one, extremely rational, intellectual and well-organized; the other, emotional, instinctive and always late![69]

But this is not so much of a case of split personality as the result of the complex configuration in which Quebec political leaders and Quebec society both have to operate. As is often the case in medicine when schizophrenic patients are absolutely justified in feeling threatened, maybe it is similarly "rational" in this case for both the leaders and the led to feel a bit confused.

Notes

1. Of course, in Canada the sense of awe is less pronounced. Except when they run across the country, or play hockey, heroes are a rare resource and first ministers rarely qualify (on either count). Nevertheless, the study of top political leaders should begin, here as elsewhere — if only to serve as an exorcism of our misconceptions with a list of caveats.

2. Even the best of comparative works fall into this trap and usually end up offering advice to improve the presidential or ministerial regimes by amalgamating the best of all systems. See the articles in Rose and Suleiman, eds., *Presidents and Prime Ministers.* For an interesting attempt to compare presidents, governors and mayors in the American system, see Herzik, "The President, Governors and Mayors."

3. See Blondel, *World Leaders.* On the concept, in a comparative perspective, of political leadership, see Edinger, "The Comparative Analysis of Political Leadership"; Dion, "The Concept of Political Leadership." Except for a burst of interest in the early seventies, Dion's call for a more strictly political concept of leadership has remained unanswered. See Edinger, *Political Leadership in Industrial Societies;* Paige, *The Scientific Study of Political Leadership.* The most comprehensive study of political leadership remains that of Burns, *Leadership.*

4. See Bunce, *Do New Leaders Make a Difference?*

5. Weller, *First Among Equals.* This sweeping diagnostic should somewhat be tempered as the literature, especially on American presidents, is so vast as to include all possible quality levels. For an extensive review and a well-formulated plea for more comparative research, see Rockman, *Presidential and Executive Studies;* Prindle, *Towards a Comparative Science of the Presidency.*

6. As will soon become clear, no serious attempt has been made to distinguish leadership, rulership, premiership, high offices or apex leaders.

7. For a Quebec version of this politician's primal scream, see the incisive memoirs of the Ministre de la condition féminine in the first Lévesque government, Payette, *Le pouvoir? Connais-pas!* Three other ministers who left the Lévesque cabinet in disgrace also contributed memoirs; Charron, *Désobéir;* Tremblay, *Le Québec en crise;* Léger, *Ce n'était qu'un début.*

8. For an extensive review of the literature on British prime ministers, and a few trenchant comments, see King, ed., *The British Prime Minister.* While prime ministers are said to be on the move to become presidents, president-watchers are worried about the presidency becoming more "imperial." It would seem that even in heaven, there is a pecking order of sorts. In Canada, the presidentialization theme has become a permanent fixture ever since the Trudeau government. See Hockin, ed., *Apex of Power;* Matheson, *The Prime Minister and the Cabinet;* Punnett, *The Prime Minister in Canadian Government and Politics.*

9. For a recent presentation of the three power "schools," see Alford and Friedland, *Powers of Theory: Capitalism, the State and Democracy.* In all fairness, it should be said that power-watchers have also given little attention to the specific contribution of top leaders except to point out that the personality or socio-economic background of the U.S. president "clearly" confirmed his membership in the ruling elite, that his incapacity to get his way on all issues was typical of a pluralist equilibrium, and that his appointment of private bankers demonstrated the class basis of his policies.

10. Lowi has pointed out that the very real possibility of losing all is the natural counterpart to the

extremely high expectations which are put on the job and perhaps constitute our best protection against abuses of power. Lowi, *The Personal President.*

11. The "right-stuff" approach to political leadership includes a vast literature. The classic statement remains Barber, *The Presidential Character.* For an extreme but fascinating case of psychology, see Iremonger, *The Fiery Chariot.* Her vision is criticized with equal passion in Binington, "Review Article: The Fiery Chariot: British Prime Ministers and the Search for Love."

12. Some scholars have come close to suggesting the establishment of leadership schools where future rulers could be trained in the best of modern management techniques. See Dror, *On Improving the Performance of Rulers.*

13. For an interesting study of executive offices, i.e. one that stays away from the management and strategic planning perspective, see Hamilton and Biggart, *Governor Reagan, Governor Brown.*

14. See Tilly, *The Formation of National States in Western Europe;* Eisenstadt and Rokkan, *Building States and Nations.* Bendix, *Kings or People,* has examined the conditions under which societies went from a kingship and aristocratic mode of political authority to a more democratic and people-oriented one. But again, he is not strictly speaking concerned with the contributions of leaders and types of political leadership to this transformation.

15. See his *The Eighteenth Brumaire of Louis Napoléon.* The leadership strategy of the emperor is described in more details in Zeldin, *The Political System of Napoléon III.* Still, Zeldin refuses to interpret these strategies outside of class logic.

16. Evidently, the provincial status of the Québec state and government and the multiple identities — nation, minority, people, group — applicable to Quebec society seriously limits generalizations. In this sense, Québec is an exceptional case, but no more exceptional as all other cases be they cities, provinces, nation-states, regions or lands.

17. This action-oriented definition of society is part of a long sociological tradition. See Linton, *The Study of Man;* Touraine, *Sociologie de l'action.*

18. This process has been well-documented in the case of the "new" ethnicity. See Smith, *The Ethnic Revival in the Modern World;* Rotschild, *Ethnopolitics.*

19. The French have been particularly productive in dissecting the new jet-set society. See the "situationist" analysis of Debord, *Society of the Spectacle,* as well as Schwartzenberg, *L'Etat spectacle;* and Clouscard, *Le capitalisme de la séduction.*

20. Their symbolic rather than organizational form of leadership has been well documented in Klapp, *Heroes, Villains and Fools: Symbolic Leaders, Public Dramas and Public Men;* Jennings, *Anatomy of Leadership: Princes, Heroes and Supermen.*

21. On this concept of organizational leadership, see Miner, "The Uncertain Future of the Leadership Concept."

22. The concept of "management of meaning" is borrowed from Smirich and Morgan, "Leadership: The Management of Meaning."

23. This return to the French regime should not be taken as proving a deep sense of continuity in the social and political development of Québec. On this very important question of continuities and discontinuities, see Paquet and Wallot, "Sur quelques discontinuités dans l'expérience socio-économique du Québec."

24. The most eloquent presentation of this Davy Crockett vision of the *habitants* is found in Monière, *Le développement des idéologies au Québec.*

25. See in particular Bureau, *Entre l'Eden et l'utopie.*

26. On this idea of a prefabricated society, see Diamond, "Le Canada français au XVIIIe siècle."

27. On the administration of New France, see Lanctôt, *L'administration de la Nouvelle-France;* Hamelin, *Economie et société en Nouvelle-France;* Vachon, *L'administration de la Nouvelle-France, 1627-1760.* Their vision is representative of the "absolutist" per-

spective. Trudeau was to elaborate his entire vision of Québec on this "absolutist" original sin. See his "Some Obstacles to Democracy in Québec" originally published in English in 1958 and reprinted in Trudeau, *Federalism and the French-Canadians.* L. Hartz and S.M. Lipset have done much to popularize this vision of French Canada as a fragment of absolutist France. See Hartz, *The Founding of New Societies,* and Lipset, *Revolution and Counterrevolution.* For an updated version of the thesis see his "Historical Traditions and National Characteristics."

28. See Lachance, *Crimes et criminels en Nouvelle-France.*

29. Frégault has elaborated on this theme in his "Politique et politiciens."

30. Dechêne, *Habitants et marchands de Montréal au XVIIe siècle.*

31. This romantic vision is best expressed in Rioux, *Les Québécois;* and Meyer, *Québec.*

32. It is only because of a desire to emulate, at least minimally, the revolutionary spirit of the American colonists that the natural points of friction between French and local-born settlers are usually blown out of proportion.

33. For a detailed study of the normative context of the period and its impact on state developmetns, see Fecteau, "Prolégomènes à une étude historique des rapports entre l'Etat et le droit dans la société québécoise, de la fin du XVIIIe siècle à la crise de 1929."

34. See Tousignant, "Problématique pour une nouvelle approche de la Constitution de 1791."

35. See the interesting article of Bernier, "Le Parti Patriote, 1827-1838." To some extent the party was over-organized for its objectives. It had numerous youth wings, both English and French, a Central Committee, regional sections and newspapers.

36. The new historiography of the 1837-1838 Rebellion, preoccupied as it is almost exclusively with identifying the prevailing social forces and their relationships with the level of economic development, has somewhat forgotten Papineau. No studies exist of the leadership and the strategic decisions made during the Rebellion. See Bernard, *Les rébellions de 1837-1838.* Only Ouellet has examined Papineau's leadership and his portrait of a divided, cowardly and incompetent leader is much in tune with his general presentation of the Rebellion as a reactionary cry for help on the part of a society incapable of adjusting to change. Nevertheless, see his *Papineau: Textes choisis.*

37. Events of the time are often judged through contemporary lenses. For example, it has been argued, quite convincingly, that Confederation was sold to French Canada as a formula which provided them with a state which they could claim as their own and whose government responsibilities were such that it could pretend to equal in importance a federal government whose dependency towards London was almost equivalent to that of the provinces on Ottawa. See Silver, *The French-Canadian Idea of Confederation, 1864-1900.*

38. On the first years of the Québec provincial government, see the fascinating account of Hamelin, *Les premières années du parlementarisme québécois, 1867-1878.*

39. See Bourassa, "Les élites politiques de Montréal: de l'aristocratie à la bureaucratie."

40. Joly de Lotbinière even served as Lieutenant Governor of British Columbia from 1900 to 1916.

41. See Hamelin and Beaudoin, "Les Cabinets provinciaux, 1867-1967." Occasionally, entire regions, including the Montréal one, were left without representation.

42. No one has ever attributed the inferior position of French-speaking *Québécois* to a lack of initial control over the provincial state. See Clift and Arnopoulos, *Le fait anglais au Québec;* Caldwell and Waddell, *Les Anglophones du Québec;* Young, *Promoters and Politicians;* Hamelin and Roby, *Histoire économique du Québec, 1851-1896.*

43. Mercier was the first premier to successfully make use of nationalism. But his was a temporary success achieved because of the Riel Affair which evaporated rapidly. His vision for Quebec did not prevent him from being one of the outstanding corrupt premiers during a period which had set exceptional standards of immo-

rality. For a sympathetic biography, see Charbonneau, *Le projet québécois d'Honoré Mercier.*

44. The role of the Catholic Church in Quebec has given rise to numerous interpretations and contradictory assessments. Our intention is only to point out that it is after Confederation, when the Church could benefit from a stable political climate and had to face a weak provincial state, that its predominance became overwhelming. See the various volumes in Hamelin and Gagnon, *Histoire du catholicisme québécois.*

45. This is not to say that the state and the Church are two sides of the same coin, each representing a supposedly deeply-ingrained desire of the Québécois for outside guidance. For a well-formulated presentation of this thesis, see Laforest, "Le sculpteur collectif et l'Etat pastoral."

46. There is a long-standing controversy as to the extent and the reasons for this absence. Some have argued that the low level of economic development and the traditional class structure prevented the state from emerging as an important actor. Others have stressed the importance of ideology and the permanent suspicions towards the state from nationalist intellectuals for whom a more active state could only mean a more active Canadian state. The classic study of the pre-1960 vision of the role of the state remains that of Brunet, "Trois dominantes de la pensée canadienne-française; l'agriculturisme, l'anti-étatisme et le messianisme."

47. This reinterpretation is taking place on all fronts. See Coleman, *The Independence Movement in Québec, 1945-1980;* Behiels, *Prelude to Québec's Quiet Revolution;* Roy, *La marche de Québécois: Le temps des ruptures (1945-1960).*

48. Among the more positive visions on Duplessis, see Rumilly, *Maurice Duplessis et son temps;* Black, *Duplessis;* Roberts, *Le Chef.* Others are less enthusiastic: Quinn, *The Union Nationale;* Saint-Aubin, *Duplessis et son époque.*

49. Quoted in Nish, ed., *Québec in the Duplessis Era, 1935-1959,* p. 151.

50. Heintzman has suggested that it was part of the political culture. See his fascinating article, "The Political Culture of Québec, 1840-1960."

51. Except for the New Democratic Party, until recently an irrelevant political force in Québec, no provincial political party has felt the need to "coordinate" its program and leadership with that of its federal counterpart.

52. Gow, *Histoire de l'administration publique québécoise, 1867-1970.*

53. The Union Nationale patronage system has been the object of numerous studies, and quite surprisingly for a subject of that nature, these studies are both empirical and theoretical in their orientation. See Hardy, *Patronage et patroneux;* Lemieux and Hudon, *Patronage et politique au Québec, 1944-1972.*

54. Boismenu, *Le Duplessisme.*

55. Vigod, *Québec before Duplessis.*

56. Boily, "Les hommes politiques du Québec, 1867-1967."

57. Tremblay, *Le syndicalisme québécois.* For the romantic vision, see David, "La grève et le Bon Dieu."

58. This relationship between Duplessis and organized interest groups is very well described in Roy, *La marche des Québécois.*

59. This depoliticization of Québec ideologies has been extensively documented by Bélanger, *L'apolitisme des ideologies québécoises.*

60. *Le Devoir,* 28 February 1935, p. 2, quoted in Bélanger, *L'apolitisme des ideologies québécoises,* p. 287.

61. Not to mention the usual interpretations of a so-called profound desire to be "led."

62. There is a vast literature on the post-1960 Québec prime ministers including memoirs, biographies and "Where-I-stand" books: Daignault, *Lesage;* Thomson, *Jean Lesage and the Quiet Revolution;* Lesage, *Jean Lesage s'engage;* Godin, *Daniel Johnson;* Gros d'Aillon, *Daniel Johnson;* Johnson, *Egalité ou indépendance;* Murray and Murray, *De Bourassa à Lévesque;* MacDonald, *From Bourassa to Bourassa;* Bourassa, *L'énergie du Nord* and *Le défi technologique;* Fraser, *René Lévesque and the Parti Québécois in Power;* Desbarats, *René: A Canadian in Search of a Country;* Pontaut, *René Lévesque;* Provencher, *René Lévesque;* Lévesque, *An Option for Québec* and *Memoirs.*

63. On the styles of the various Québec premiers, see O'Neil and Benjamin, *Les mandarins du pouvoir;* Benjamin, *Comment on fabrique un premier ministre;* Baccigalupo, *Les grands rouages de la machine administrative québécoise.*

64. Two surveys taken at the time throw some doubt on the traditional vision of the Quiet Revolution as a widely based social movement. See Groupe de recherche sociale, *Les électeurs québécois,* and *Les préférences politiques des électeurs québécois en 1962.*

65. This analysis is undoubtedly tinted by the author's short stay in René Lévesque's office. See my "The Organizational Culture of Government Myths." On cabinet shuffles in Quebec, see Desrochers, *Les remaniements ministériels au Québec.*

66. Little has been written on this most peculiar leadership structure of the Québec Lieutenant. See English, "The French Lieutenant in Ottawa," in Carty and Ward, eds., *National Politics and Community in Canada.*

67. Who is "in charge" in Québec and which group holds power have become a perennial exercise in self-diagnosis almost as if to confirm that a distinct Québec society must indeed exist if it is the object of such a takeover by its very own power-seekers. On this question see Assimopoulos et al, *La transformation du pouvoir au Québec.* In recent years, the clergy, the new middle class, the intellectuals and the politicians have been dethroned in favour of the "economic elites." On the new Québec elites, see Dufresne and Jacques, *Crise et Leadership.*

68. Popular culture has retained this image of the arrogant, pompous and tragi-comical political leader. In Québec, to say of someone that he is "une tête-à-Papineau" is no compliment.

69. All biographies and films (as in the National Film Board, *The Champions*) about the two men have stressed the love-hate relationship of all Québécois with these two individuals. Unfortunately, this dualistic interpretation does not resist analysis as the electoral studies of P. Drouilly have shown. The same individual voters did not vote for both men although both were often supported by the same socio-economic categories. See his *Le paradoxe canadien.* For a thorough presentation of the dualist thesis, see Bergeron, *Notre miroir à deux faces.*

CHAPTER 12

Governing from Queen's Park: The Ontario Premiership

Graham White

Reflecting on his experiences in comparison with those of Leslie Frost, who was premier of Ontario in the 1950s, former Premier William Davis expressed the view that in Frost's day, the process of governing Ontario was "more manageable." Cabinet meetings were less frequent, media scrutiny of the premier was far less intense, the Legislature sat for only a few weeks a year, and most fundamentally, the scope of government and its scale of operations were much more limited.[1] Accordingly, Frost could personally oversee all the important political and administrative decisions to a degree no longer possible today.

Despite the acknowledged importance of provincial premiers as heads of governments which have great impact on our daily lives and as the "feudal barons" of Canadian federalism, little has been written about their policy roles and management styles. This chapter attempts to remedy the deficiency by examining the evolution and operation of the premiership in Canada's largest province. Following a brief review of the social characteristics of Ontario's premiers, the chapter offers some comparisons between the Ontario premier and the prime minister; examines the constraints and the opportunities facing the premier of Ontario in his roles as head of government and as party leader, with particular emphasis on his sources of advice and his influence on the policy-making process; and looks briefly at the pre-

mier's relationship with the Legislature. The empirical focus of the paper is the record of the five most recent premiers, Leslie Frost (1949-1961), John Robarts (1961-1971), William Davis (1971-1985), Frank Miller (1985) and David Peterson (1985 to date), with particular emphasis on Davis and Peterson.

As elsewhere, the first minister in Ontario stands at the centre of a complex web of influences, information and political processes. Not only does he make the critical decisions and set the direction of the government, but he must also manage his Cabinet, his political advisors, the bureaucracy, and his party, as well as dealing with the media, interest groups and the Legislature. Each premier must establish a patterned relationship with each of these in order to be able to act effectively. As government has become more complex, these patterns have evolved substantially; a central theme of this chapter is the degree to which the Ontario premiership has become institutionalized in recent years in response to the increased scale and complexity of government. Yet the transmission of complexity in the political and bureaucratic environment into an institutionalized premiership is by no means straightforward. First ministers' personal styles and philosophies clearly affect institutions.[2]

Related to this is the question of whether it may still accurately be said of Ontario that "provincial government is premier's government"[3] — that the premier dominates all facets of provincial government and that he enjoys significantly greater authority in running his government than does the prime minister.

Germane to this question are the implications of the degree to which time has become a serious constraint on the premier. The business of government in Ontario has become so extensive that no one person or office could hope to be knowledgeable on more than a small number of current issues, and the relentless pressure of business has rendered the premier's time a scarce, much -sought-after commodity. As Oliver Mowat's three-month vacations to Britain and Europe attest, this was not always so. In less complicated times, premiers had sufficient time to keep for themselves such senior portfolios as Attorney General (Macdonald, Mowat, Hardy and Whitney), Treasury (Ross, Hepburn and Frost), Education (Ferguson, Drew and, briefly, Robarts) and Agriculture (Hearst and Kennedy). Davis and Miller served only as premiers and although Premier Peterson held two portfolios, Intergovernmental Affairs and (as an interim measure) Northern Development and Mines, they did not represent significant extra burdens (since inevitably all premiers are personally involved in questions of federal-provincial relations anyway). The tendency of recent premiers to serve only as premier is an important institutional refinement signalling a less dominant role in provincial affairs than that enjoyed by earlier Ontario first ministers who retained powerful portfolios (especially the Treasury).

This chapter focusses on the premier as head of the government rather than as head of the party and does not discuss in any detail at least two important topics. First, the ideological stances of premiers are not considered. Successful Ontario premiers have generally been perceived as moderates, and as cautious reformers, but a thorough analysis of this question might well demonstrate that this is an overly simplistic view. Secondly, although any Ontario premier necessarily is a central figure in federal-provincial relations, no exploration of his role in

this arena is attempted here. Clearly, given Ontario's weight within Confederation, a wide range of roles is open to its premier: the statesman, as personified by John Robarts' dealings with Quebec; the behind-the-scenes broker, typified by Bill Davis' contribution to the 1981 constitutional agreement; and the vociferous opponent of federal schemes, in the mould of David Peterson's criticism of the Mulroney government's policy on trade with the United States.

PREMIERS' SOCIAL CHARACTERISTICS

Do differences in premiers' governing styles reflect different backgrounds, or must we look elsewhere for explanations of such variations? A review of their social characteristics reveals a marked homogeneity among Ontario's twenty premiers. All of course until now have been male, a fact which should occasion little surprise. The typical premier comes to power in his forties or fifties: only two assumed office before they turned forty and only two had passed their sixtieth birthday; their mean age on becoming premier is 51.6 years. Given the early predominance of persons of English, Irish, and Scots stock in Ontario, it is perhaps to be expected that few with any other ethnic heritage should attain the premiership, yet it is surely noteworthy that in multicultural Ontario, only one has. Except for David Peterson's Norwegian forebears, no Ontario premier's roots have been other than Anglo-Celtic. A further indication that Ontario premiers all tend to be drawn from the same community is the fact that only one was born outside Ontario.

Related to the premiers' ethnic background is their religion: save Sandfield Macdonald, who was Catholic, every Ontario premier has been Protestant in religious affiliation. However, the premier's religious conviction probably is of little consequence in modern Ontario, as is suggested by Premier Peterson's public admission that he is not a regular churchgoer.[4]

Thirteen of the men who have held the

Ontario premiership have been lawyers. This is striking enough, but when account is taken of the non-lawyers, such as Harry Nixon, T.L. Kennedy, and Frank Miller, who held the office only briefly, the astounding result is that of the 121 years since Confederation, there have been only 25 when Ontario did not have a lawyer as premier. Whether this is merely happenstance, the preference of the electorate, or a conspiracy by the Law Society of Upper Canada remains to be established.

In some ways, perhaps the most telling of premiers' social characteristics is that there has never been a premier from Toronto. A handful have had Toronto connections but they could not really be considered to represent the city.[5] This may well reflect an important political reality, namely that Ontario's political leader must bring to his task an understanding of the province that is wider than the somewhat narrow horizons of the typical Torontonian. To be sure, Toronto offers a much wider range of experience than do smaller centres, but the citizens of London, Kemptville and Morrisburg are much more sensitive to the fact that Ontario is rather more than Toronto writ large. Not for nothing did Frost speak of viewing Ontario politics "from the barber's chair in Lindsay"; Davis liberally sprinkled his speeches with references to his experiences in "the great community of Brampton."

Analysis of premiers' social characteristics can be instructive about the society they represent and its citizens' preferences in a leader, but one should be wary of hard-and-fast conclusions. After all, the Conservative leadership convention of January 1985 came within 77 votes of electing as premier Larry Grossman, who is Jewish, the grandson of Polish immigrants, and quintessentially Torontonian.

THE ONTARIO PREMIER: A SCALED-DOWN PRIME MINISTER?

At first blush, it would seem reasonable to presume that most observations which could

be made about the prime ministership would apply with equal validity to the Ontario premiership, given minor modifications for the smaller scope. All first ministers of Westminster-style democracies must be essentially of a piece. Moreover, the differences in size are of degree rather than of kind, for, after all, Ontario has a gigantic landmass and a population greater than that of many European countries including Sweden, Denmark, and Switzerland. Yet, while it is unquestionably true that the two offices are far more alike than not, important differences can be discerned.

The scale of operations does matter. First, Ontario is small enough that its premier is able to become personally involved in most significant issues, whereas the prime minister necessarily must give short shrift to matters that on a provincial level could expect to receive the premier's personal attention. Conversely, though both are constantly beset with all manner and variety of problems, the prime minister is not required to be familiar with and knowledgeable about everything happening across the country, while the premier of Ontario is generally expected to be aware of all events and developments throughout the province. Whereas few would fault the prime minister for ignorance of a factory closing in a small Nova Scotia town or of the repercussions of a bad harvest in the Okanagan, woe betide an Ontario premier without a personal knowledge of a significant layoff in Kenora or the plight of the province's tobacco farmers.

Secondly, as one respondent with inside knowledge of both Ottawa and Queen's Park maintains, because government is so much larger and more complex at the federal level, established ways of doing things are much more ingrained, and the policy process is much more impervious to change. Related to this is the significantly greater ease, at the provincial level, of getting all the key players together on short notice when crises develop. In other words, the Ontario premier finds himself in a substantially less institutionalized setting than does the prime minister.

Another important difference is the prime minister's role in foreign affairs. Except for leading an occasional trade mission, and periodic consultations with governors of nearby states, the premier of Ontario has little involvement in foreign policy, which for the prime minister is, of course, a major preoccupation. Conversely, the prime minister has little to do with local municipalities, which are of substantial import for the premier. Aside from the obvious differences of content — the concerns of the mayors of Cornwall, Strathroy, and Sudbury are not those of the leaders of the European Economic Community — other differences are evident. Municipal politicians, who are beholden to the province for grants, approvals, and the like, tend to be deferential in their dealings with the province, yet their concerns are of immediate political and electoral importance. The reverse is true of the federal government in its relations with foreign nations. In short, though both consume substantial time and energy, the prime minister's responsibility for external affairs and the premier's involvement with local municipalities raise qualitatively different problems and require very different approaches.

Like all Canadian first ministers, the premier of Ontario must be mindful of regional considerations in putting together his Cabinet. And while a province as large and diverse as Ontario is analogous to the amalgam of regions that constitutes Canada, nothing so clearly defined as interprovincial boundaries delineates Ontario's regions. This leaves the Ontario premier with a much freer hand in seeing to regional representation in selecting ministers. By way of illustration: should New Brunswick lose its minister in Ottawa for any reason, it is unquestioned that another must be appointed from the ranks of New Brunswick M.P.s. In Ontario, it is equally plain that Eastern Ontario must be represented in Cabinet, but not at all clear whether Eastern Ontario begins at Belleville, Kingston or Brockville, and whether Ottawa

should be counted as part of the region. Regional imperatives in Cabinet-building are thus less constraining for premiers than for prime ministers. In another way, though the prime minister has a wider choice for his Cabinet, since recent national Cabinets have included between one fourth and one fifth of a caucus of roughly 130 to 210 members (plus occasional senators), whereas the premier of Ontario must choose for Cabinet at least a third, perhaps half, of his 50- to 80- member caucus.

One final difference highlights an important feature of the Ontario premiership. Ontario premiers have been less inclined to take on a "public persuader" role[6] than have various prime ministers and other provincial premiers No Ontario premier has ever commandeered a province-wide television hook-up to announce policy, or to exhort or comfort the electorate in the way that recent prime ministers have on numerous occasions. This points up the degree to which Ontario premiers are (and are expected to be) *managers* more than *leaders*. Perhaps because of its traditional prosperity, Ontario has preferred premiers who were solid, competent managers rather than visionary leaders with clearly set out programmatic goals. It is by no means coincidental that only one premier — Mitchell Hepburn — could be described as charismatic and that his premiership was arguably the most disastrous in provincial history.

ADVISING THE PREMIER: THE PREMIER'S OFFICE

One of Premier Peterson's first actions was to establish a clear division between the Premier's Office and the Cabinet Office, along the lines of the PMO and the PCO in Ottawa. This may appear routine housekeeping, but in fact it marked a change of fundamental importance, as indicated by one senior official's reference to it as "separating church and state". The Ontario premiership — past and present — cannot be understood without an understanding of the development of these two key offices.

Only in the late 1940s did a rudimentary Cabinet Office emerge in Ontario, with a formal civil service position of Secretary to Cabinet; previously, the organization of cabinet business had fallen mainly to the Provincial Secretary, a cabinet minister.[7] Shortly after assuming office in 1949, Leslie Frost expanded the cabinet secretary's duties to include the position of Deputy Minister to the Prime Minister. This arrangement, which remained through Frost's term in office, is a clear example of his penchant for centralization of authority. Particularly given the limited size of the premier's staff, the question of distinguishing a formal Premier's Office from a formal Cabinet Office never arose.

Robarts inherited "a skeletal staff barely adequate for routine administrative functions,"[8] and ordered a revamping of the organization. The result was a certain division of labour, with the establishment of distinct Cabinet and Premier's Offices, though they remained united in a single Department of the Prime Minister, reporting to the same administrative head. Throughout the late 1960s, a duopoly existed at the top of the premier's staff. Malcolm McIntyre, the Secretary to Cabinet and deputy minister, was the nominal head, though increasingly ministers and senior bureaucrats came to recognize Keith Reynolds, the chief executive officer in the Premier's Office, as the principal conduit to Robarts.[9] With McIntyre's retirement in 1969, Reynolds assumed formal responsibility for the entire operation and effectively merged the staff of the Cabinet Office and the Premier's Office.[10]

One of the few areas not examined by the mammoth Committee on Government Productivity, which set the stage for wholesale restructuring of the Ontario executive in the early 1970s,[11] was the organization of the premier's staff. Thus during the Davis administration, the fusion of the Cabinet and Premier's Offices continued. This fusion did not mean that the career civil servants in the Cabinet Office engaged in partisan activities or were responsible

for the sort of political analysis that the political advisors in the Premier's Office supplied. It did mean, however, that some senior staff who were unquestionably Conservative partisans, such as Hugh Segal and John Tory, held appointments in the Cabinet Office and were technically civil servants. Perhaps of greater significance, both offices reported to the premier through one person: Dr. Edward Stewart, a career civil servant.[12]

While both Frost and Davis may have had just one person heading both the Premier's Office and the Cabinet Office, the consequences were very different. Under Frost, the size and scope of government was limited and the premier could personally attend to important issues, but by the 1970s the range and complexity of problems facing government had expanded exponentially so that the position occupied by Dr. Stewart was far more influential than it ever had been in the 1950s. Not only was the position inherently powerful, the personal relationship between Davis and Stewart greatly intensified its importance. Dr. Stewart came close to being the premier's alter ego, and those knowledgeable about government recognized that approval from him was tantamount to approval from Davis, not because Stewart controlled the premier but because he understood him so well, could predict his reactions so accurately, and enjoyed his complete trust. Not surprisingly, Stewart became the focus of sharp criticism from the then Liberal Opposition (and to an extent from the Tory caucus), who thought it improper that the province's top civil servant should have such political clout. The Liberals also looked upon the political links between the Premier's Office and the Cabinet Office as symptomatic of an unhealthy politicization of the public service, the so-called "blue tinge", which they were convinced had developed after four decades of Tory rule.

Accordingly, the Liberals' decision to rigorously separate the Premier's Office from the Cabinet Office owed something to a belief in the principle that civil servants' administration of government policy should be entirely divorced from partisan politics, and also something to a very pragmatic refusal to entrust their political life to anyone but a party person, or to expect that anyone from outside government (that is, a non-party person) could have sufficient knowledge of the bureaucratic machine. Moreover, Premier Peterson's personal style of seeking advice from a host of sources would not have meshed with a system predicated on funnelling so much through a single person.

To replace the old organization, Peterson created a three-part structure, each part with its own head, each head reporting to the premier. The Cabinet Office was retained, along with most of those in it, as the civil service secretariat to the Cabinet: the cabinet secretary is the most senior civil servant, through whom all deputy ministers and other civil servants report. The Premier's Office is divided in two: the Principal Secretary (Hershell Ezrin) has responsibility for policy, legislation and communications; largely, that is, the governmental side of the premiership. Under the Executive Director (Gordon Ashworth) come office administration and operation, including travel arrangements and correspondence, as well as party liaison, order-in-council appointments, the premier's constituency, and liaison with community and ethnic groups; in the main, the party side.

Three important counter-arguments were advanced against hiving off the bureaucratic from the political in this fashion. First, the suggestion was made that at the level of the premier, any distinction between governmental and political aspects of issues is arbitrary and artificial, and that the organization around the premier must recognize this fact. Secondly, it was feared that civil servants would attempt so-called end runs by appealing to the principal secretary if they were turned down by the cabinet secretary. This has not occurred, due largely to the principal secretary's avoidance of involvement in bureaucratic matters. The final

and most fundamental concern was that, without flawlessly clear communication between the two offices, major foul-ups could develop as problems fell between the cracks. By and large, communication has not been a problem, in part as a result of the daily meeting Premier Peterson holds with his senior staff, including civil servants, in which problems and ideas are thoroughly canvassed, and in part because the premier's executive assistant (Vince Borg), who reports only to the Premier, devotes a good deal of his time to dealing with potential "between-the-cracks" issues. It could be argued, though, that the serious difficulties over ministerial conflict of interest which bedevilled the government in the summer of 1986, culminating in the resignation of two ministers, reflect inaccurate assumptions by both the political and bureaucratic elements that the other side was looking after the situation.

Direct comparisons between the size of the Premier's Office under Premiers Davis and Peterson are not possible, since, under the Liberals, the correspondence unit was transferred to the Cabinet Office and the personnel and accounting functions were taken over by the Ministry of the Treasury. On balance, the current staff of thirty-one is roughly of the same magnitude as that which tended to Premier Davis' political needs. The estimated cost for running the Premier's Office in 1986-87 was $1.9 million.[13] Aside from the division between the principal secretary and the executive director, the main structural and substantive change in the Premier's Office has been the establishment of a small policy unit to oversee policy development from a political viewpoint: ensuring that emerging policies square with party principles, election promises, statements made while the party was in opposition, and the like. Staff from the policy unit sit in on cabinet committee meetings, and will sometimes follow Cabinet Office staff in briefing cabinet committees, making explicitly political presentations. Representatives of the policy unit are frequently present when the premier meets with interest groups.

In view of the premier's formidable power, his limited time, and the range and complexity of the issues confronting him, his sources of advice assume critical importance. Patrick Weller has argued that in the countries he examined, including Canada, the existence of a prime minister's department did not fundamentally alter the fact that "the prime minister's main advisers are ministers."[14] In Ontario, many would argue, this observation does not hold. The press, the opposition and even Conservative backbenchers regularly complained that Premier Davis ignored the views of his Cabinet, preferring the advice of a small tightly-knit group which came to be known as "the Park Plaza Breakfast Club," after the hotel near Queen's Park where it met most Tuesday mornings. A few senior ministers usually took part, but they tended to be outnumbered by staff from the Premier's Office and Cabinet Office and by Davis' long-time party associates, such as Eddie Goodman, Hugh Macaulay, and Norman Atkins. Davis argues that it is essential for a premier to be able to call upon a group of advisors, with a broad network of contacts, "who are supportive in a general sense but who are not reluctant to be critical."[15] Frank Miller agreed, and in effect continued the Park Plaza breakfasts, though he changed the venue and the day. Top Liberal officials proudly proclaim that the days of a "Park Plaza in-group" are over; nevertheless, among the advisors on whom Premier Peterson relies most heavily are three or four senior ministers, and a greater number yet of personal staff.[16] This balance may shift, however, as the Peterson Cabinet gains experience.

Premier Peterson's staff insist that, in keeping with his promise on the day he was sworn into office to conduct a government "without barriers or walls," he is much more accessible to a much wider range of people, and cultivates much more diverse sources of ideas and advice than did Premier Davis. The claim has some validity to it, though the differences in the two regimes are in some measure reflections of the differing ways in which premiers solicit advice and use staff.

In comparison with his predecessor, who was said to prefer working with a select few advisors, Davis was described as needing "a wider circle, both because he liked to receive information from a variety of sources and because by not giving his ear exclusively to one group he could maintain his authority."[17] This early assessment remained fundamentally accurate, though as time went by Davis often preferred to have ideas from the wider circle distilled by trusted confidants rather than hearing them first-hand. Those beyond the "inner circle" did not often have direct access to him. Davis was renowned as a consummate listener, who might say little in response to the ideas put to him and who rarely gave much indication of his own thoughts; by this technique, he promoted wide-ranging discussions and avoided being told what his advisors thought he wanted to hear.

By contrast, Peterson revels in freewheeling discussions with anyone he believes has something interesting to say. When confronted with a problem, his style is to call in whoever knows about it or has interesting ideas, regardless of status — Peterson is not averse to personally telephoning middle-level bureaucrats — or whether he or she works for government or has any Liberal connections. On occasion, as many as thirty people, some of whom were clearly "outsiders", have crowded into his office to thrash out an issue — an approach Bill Davis would never have taken. In soliciting advice from any of these sources, Premier Peterson is not overly troubled by protocol; by way of illustration, he once brought a deputy minister into Cabinet to debate a key policy issue with a minister — and the minister and the deputy were not even from the same ministry.[18] Similarly, he is quite prepared to go outside the regular bureaucratic process for solutions to problems. To a certain extent, this uninhibited style is a matter of individual personality, but it may also reflect the fact that, unlike Frost, Robarts and Davis, Peterson came to the premiership directly from the opposition and had not, as had they, served an apprenticeship as a cabinet minister. The opposition style tends to be somewhat haphazard and opposition leaders are necessarily open to more unconventional sources of advice than cabinet ministers who are accustomed to formal bureaucratic decision-making processes. Those who have been ministers are naturally inclined to model their premierships on that experience, whereas premiers whose previous experience has been in the opposition will tend to be less structured in their approaches.

In his first term, Premier Davis unwisely allowed himself to be somewhat isolated by his advisors from the political rough-and-tumble, and turned into a technocratic decision-maker.[19] However, the ability of the premier's staff to impose a rigid bureaucratic regimen on the government was limited: "the premier's deputy, James Fleck, ordered that his office should vet all speeches by Cabinet ministers before they were delivered. Most ministers... simply ignored this."[20] One closely involved observer contends that Davis's basic mistake lay in not relying on his own best judgement and listening instead to others' notions of "how a premier should act." It was widely believed that the Tories' political insensitivity, spawned by the premier's isolation from Cabinet, caucus and indeed, the world outside the Premier's Office, almost cost them the 1975 election. The emphasis during the resulting minority government was on adroit political manoeuvring, and Premier Davis developed a substantially different approach, becoming, as one writer has argued a first minister must be, "the arbitrator of the advisory process that serves him."[21]

Most significantly, perhaps, he came to trust in his own formidable political instincts, but he also continued the changes begun in his office and in his sources of advice before the election. He created the position of Principal Secretary, who was to combine policy advice and political acumen at the very highest level in the Premier's Office. Davis instituted regular quarterly policy conferences, usually held outside Toronto, to reflect on the government's performance and to sketch out ideas for future directions. Those invited included some, but not all, ministers, selected backbenchers, senior public servants, party officials and people from outside government. As well, Davis created an Economic Advisory Group, composed mainly of business leaders, but with a sprinkling of top labour officials and academics, which convened monthly. One of Davis' senior ministers contends that these various advisory bodies and conferences were great political and public relations successes, but had little influence on the Premier's thinking or on government policy; Davis avers otherwise.[22]

As had been the case at the outset of the Davis era, key figures on Frank Miller's staff isolated him from diverse sources of political advice.[23] Once he became premier, Miller was surprised and disappointed that people whose judgement he had come to value no longer seemed to be around; in turn, these former allies found that they were denied access to Miller, and felt discarded. Unlike under Davis, though, the motivation seems to have been less a faith in a highly bureaucratized premiership than an attempt to aggrandize personal influence. Not surprisingly, then, Miller's view is that the greatest pressure on a premier comes from those jockeying for position around him, and that staff "will usurp power in your name if they think they can get away with it."

An important distinction relating to the operation of the premier's staff is that between advice and implementation. Even a premier such as David Peterson, who readily takes advice from a great many people, some of whom he knows only slightly, will trust only a select few to implement a decision once it is taken. In concert with the unlimited access to the premier that a handful of senior staff will enjoy, this means that it is all but inevitable that a small group of people around the premier will wield enormous power and influence. The significance of these advisors is underlined by the fact that in recent years even incoming premiers of the same political stripe have moved quickly to replace the top staff in the Premier's Office with their own entourage. In part this assures loyalty, but more fundamentally, it reflects the premiers' recognition that their ability to put their own mark on the office depends on the people closest to them.[24]

THE PREMIER AND THE POLICY PROCESS

Ontario cabinet ministers describe the premier as "the 51 percent shareholder" and "the guy who breaks our 5-to-5 ties". If, as in other Westminster-style systems, the premier of Ontario has the unquestioned power to decide any point of government policy, as a practical matter, he must be selective in personally intervening in issues and in exercising his prerogative of overruling ministers. Like any other first minister, the Ontario premier must be sensitive to the political ramifications of interfering too directly and too frequently in his ministers' business. Premiers must worry that highly able ministers in senior portfolios will not tolerate being kept on a short leash for long.

Still, the premier's personal style of governing can make for great variation in the extent to which he retains power in his own hands. Hepburn used to secure the Cabinet's approval for important decisions by circulating to individual ministers for their signature "walking orders," which indicated their presence at fictional meetings. "By the use of this device," writes F.F. Schindeler,

> the Premier could carry on the functions of government without the niceties of cabinet meetings, and he could insure the unopposed implementation of his will by the judicious selection of the ministers to whom he would send each walking order for signature.[25]

Such legerdemain would not be possible today. Leslie Frost was renowned for his highly centralist, interventionist approach to running the government; as one of Frost's ministers put it, he "ran a one-man show and would brook no interference from anyone...it was common knowledge that senior civil servants in the departments often reported directly to him and not to their ministers."[26] By contrast, John Robarts allowed his ministers considerable free rein, though he tightened his control after the Bill 99 fiasco.[27]

Bill Davis tried to refrain from constantly looking over his ministers' shoulders. One of his senior ministers described Davis as a "total non-interventionist" and recounted that although he had expected to be upbraided for particular mistakes, he never did hear from the Premier. Indeed, Davis stated that when ministers were not performing satisfactorily, they could gauge his reaction "quite often by what I didn't say [rather] than by what I did say".[28] Through Ed Stewart, Davis kept in close contact with the deputy ministers as a means of monitoring situations in the ministries, though he was careful not to allow this link to undermine the ministers' authority.[29] Ministers understood that important or controversial decisions were to be cleared first with the Premier, who depended on ministers' judgement to bring potential problems to his attention; "no surprises" was the operative philosophy. More insecure ministers were more likely to submit their proposals for the Premier's personal attention, though even senior ministers might rely heavily on his advice with particularly tricky problems.

Frank Miller is not the only person who contends that over time, as a premier continues in office, a gradual accrual of power occurs towards him personally.[30] Not only does he have experience behind him, he also eclipses his leadership rivals, and the ministers who owed their elevation to Cabinet to the last premier are supplanted by his appointments. Davis was clearly a first minister who could control Cabinet because he had "been around for so long, either as prime minister or as a senior minister."[31] By the late 1970s only two of Davis' ministers had served in Cabinet before he became premier, and by the 1980s most ministers hadn't even come into the Legislature until he had been premier for some years.

David Peterson was effectively in the same position as Davis from the outset. Only two of his ministers had served longer in the House, and half of his initial Cabinet were utter rookies looking to him for direction. Because the Cabinet was so inexperienced, it was imperative that the Premier personally take a firm hand in guiding the new ministers. As his press secretary put it, in the early days "there were some very green, inexperienced cabinet ministers. The premier kept decisions to himself; he couldn't let them [cabinet ministers] out on their own."[32] As ministers began to prove themselves, control from the centre was slackened, though Peterson showed few inhibitions about reimposing controls when they seemed warranted; a senior Premier's Office official has described his management style in the following terms: "to give people all the rein they need, and to yank it back whenever they're going too far, too fast"[33]

The premier's involvement in policy-making entails more than his relations with individual ministers; he must also deal with Cabinet as a collective entity. This raises two subthemes: the premier's role in the cabinet committee system and his style of running cabinet meetings. Cabinet committees had been used sporadically through the 1950s and 1960s, but they were generally not of great import. The Committee on Government Productivity reforms of the early 1970s were built around an extensive cabinet committee system to which much of the detailed work of Cabinet was delegated.[34] The centrepiece of the system was a Policy and Priorities Board of senior ministers chaired by the premier, which had some elements of an Inner Cabinet. "P. and P." is the only cabinet committee that the premier regu-

larly attends, though he is kept well informed of developments in the other committees and his approval is necessary for items to move from the committees to the agenda of the full Cabinet. David Peterson almost never attends other cabinet committees, but Davis and Miller appeared intermittently, especially if important delegations were scheduled before a committee or if the matter up for discussion had important intergovernmental overtones. Both, however, recognized that extensive involvement in the cabinet committee system not only was a poor use of their time, but would undercut the usefulness of the committees.

Premier Davis tended not to use P. and P. as a central decision-making or even priority-setting body, beyond having it assume the lead role in determining financial allocations within government. He had no qualms about circumventing the established routes for policy proposals through the committee system; roughly half the time the normal policy process was "short-circuited." Usually this meant putting an item directly on the cabinet agenda without its having been discussed in the cabinet committee. On occasion ministers went directly to the premier for a decision without seeking Cabinet's approval. These end runs by ministers required the premier's sanction, which was by no means always forthcoming. Ministers did not have to take cabinet committee decisions as the final word, for "despite the bureaucratic and political processes in place, every minister sensed that he or she had a direct line of appeal to cabinet and to the Premier personally".[35] In the words of one of his key advisors,

> Davis moved in the direction he felt right without relying in any detailed way upon the various committees, policy fields and structures of his own administration... [he used cabinet committees] in a fashion that was responsive to his own personal agenda and to the agenda which he believed, with cabinet, was essential to his government.[35]

Since the question of whether or not the usual rules for the decision-making process would apply was settled by the Premier in an essentially unpredictable fashion,[37] the net result was a formidable concentration of power in the premier at the Cabinet's expense.

This context is relevant to the accusation that on major issues Davis ignored his Cabinet or forced a decision upon it in dictatorial fashion. The two most notable occurrences were the Suncor purchase in 1981, when the government of Ontario paid $650 million to acquire a 25 percent interest in a Canadian subsidiary of an American oil company, and Davis's announcement in June 1984 that Ontario was reversing its long-standing refusal, which Davis had reaffirmed in 1971, to extend full funding to Roman Catholic separate schools. Although plans for the Suncor acquisition were known to several top ministers, the matter was not discussed in Cabinet, in part for fear that leaks about the government's intentions might inflate the price. The separate schools decision has been described by one of the ministers present as follows:

> The Progressive Conservative Cabinet was told at 11:00 a.m. that Mr. Davis was going to announce the extension of funding to separate schools. It wasn't a proposal — no cabinet submission was ever presented — it was an order. It was clear that little discussion would be tolerated. A similar charade took place at a Progressive Conservative caucus at 1:00 p.m. prior to the 2:00 p.m. announcement in our Legislature.[38]

Other ministers have privately given similar accounts. Davis, however, adamantly maintains that such interpretations are quite inaccurate:

> Cabinet was very definitely involved. They were informed. It had been discussed informally for years... [all ministers were thoroughly conversant with the issue]... they may have been surprised at the particular date, but they knew it was all going to come at some point... When it was brought I was frankly surprised at the measure of support for it... if the majority of Cabinet had said there's no way, we wouldn't have done it... it was not forced upon Cabinet at all.[39]

Resolution of these contradictory yet honestly held assessments may be sought in two ways. First, one must recognize the nature of the immense power accruing to an experienced, well-entrenched first minister. Such leaders' power lies not so much in the undoubted prerogative to impose a decision over the objections of Cabinet, but in a more subtle and thereby more significant dynamic. When ministers perceive that a policy ranks as a very high personal priority for the premier, they are naturally reluctant to register disagreement, especially when they expect that dissent would be futile; and when such a matter is placed before them without formal notice, any possibility of organized opposition developing in time to be effective is precluded. While the premier is doubtless aware ministers will be somewhat reticent about voicing objections in such circumstances, he may well not recognize the extent to which ministers defer to his views. Secondly, since the circumvention of the formal decision-making process at the premier's whim has become routine, there can be little grounds for objecting that the process is improper or inadequate. Since the rules are so ill-defined, ministers cannot know when abstract musings about issues in Cabinet are just idle chatter or when they might be taken by the premier as support for a specific policy position. This interpretation can also be applied to conflicting accounts of the imposition of rent control in 1975; the two ministers whose departments were most involved claim they were not even consulted about the decision. Davis disagrees, arguing that the matter came before Cabinet several times.[40]

Paradoxically, considering that he only inherited the system that Davis had instituted, Peterson has required his ministers to be much more faithful to the cabinet committee process, and somewhat constrains himself through his commitment to abide by its rules. He uses the Policy and Priorities committee to give an overall direction to government, similar to the way in which the prime minister employs the Priorities and Planning Committee in Ottawa.[41] End runs by ministers around the cabinet committees directly to Cabinet or the premier are infrequent; Peterson believes that the cabinet committee process must be followed so as to keep all ministers informed and involved in a wide range of policy development.[42] At the same time, Peterson does not allow the structures to dictate the process, and will on occasion supplement rather than circumvent the cabinet committee system. By way of illustration, he referred the question of rent control to all cabinet committees so that every minister could take part in the formative stages of what he considered a critical issue. Alternatively, he will sometimes place an item on the cabinet agenda before it goes to cabinet committee, so as to encourage a wide-ranging general discussion, untrammelled by considerations of detail.

The premier's individual style of conducting cabinet meetings probably is less significant in determining actual policy outcomes than it is in either fostering or discouraging among ministers a sense that they have a genuine role in the process, which in turn builds cabinet support for the eventual decision. A comparison of Davis's and Peterson's techniques points up important similarities as well as differences. Both turned the chairing of the formal, routine proceedings of cabinet meetings over to a Chairman of Cabinet (indeed, in the later years Davis often skipped this part of Cabinet), but effectively took control of the meeting when important new business came to the fore.[43] Both were said to be very good listeners who would encourage the expression of a broad spectrum of opinion. Davis tended not to make his own views known (though seasoned ministers could often tell where he was headed) until a consensus emerged or until he could propose a course that met with general approval; if this was not possible, he would hold a decision over for another meeting, perhaps weeks later. This approach had an element of seeking resolution of problems through discussion and an element of guiding the debate and waiting until general agreement was possible along the lines

desired by Davis. Peterson is much more forthright about stating his preferences and about admitting when he is uncertain about what to do. He is not averse to deferring a decision to a future meeting if more information is required; however, if, after all points of view have been thoroughly aired, no consensus is evident, he will usually proceed to settle the matter immediately. Related to this is the Premier's approach to resolving disputes between ministers. Davis frequently avoided tackling such conflicts himself, preferring to assign someone, frequently his Treasurer, to arbitrate the matter;[44] Peterson's style is to bring the ministers together in his office to work out a solution.

Whether or not one subscribes to the view popularized in the British television series "Yes Minister" that civil servants run the world, the premier's relations with the bureaucracy, particularly with the deputy ministers, are of unquestionable importance. As elsewhere, deputy ministers are appointed directly by the premier and owe an important loyalty to him.[45] Deputies often accompany their ministers to meetings with the premier, but it is fairly rare for deputies to meet the premier without their ministers, though recent premiers have made it clear that they are welcome to do so. The more usual channel of communication from deputy ministers to the premier is via the Secretary of Cabinet. Premier Davis held bi-yearly meetings with the deputies, not so much to develop policy as to keep up morale and maintain lines of communication. When deputies were coming up for reappointment, they would meet briefly in private with him to discuss their performance.

Before David Peterson could develop similar routine mechanisms for dealing with deputy ministers, he was faced with the critical task of dispelling the suspicion between the first non-Tory ministers in over four decades and the senior bureaucracy. To this end, shortly after coming to power, he arranged a highly successful evening at a Toronto hotel for the ministers and the deputies to socialize and break down barriers. Early in his term, he also met individually with each deputy minister to express his confidence in the civil service and to seek a long-term policy agenda for each ministry. His approach, premised on an expectation of civil service professionalism and non-partisanship, quickly won the confidence of the bureaucracy, without which his government would certainly have been incapacitated. Once established in office, he continued to build links to the Ontario mandarinate by giving it a more active role in policy development and by paying special attention to its concerns, as typified by his gathering nearly 600 senior executives to personally announce plans for revamping the province's management of senior personnel.[46] One seasoned observer commented that during the Davis years a good deputy minister was one who didn't bother the Premier and Ed Stewart too much, whereas under Peterson, the good deputy is the one who keeps the Premier informed and involved.

One of the most difficult tasks facing a first minister is long-term planning and policy development. Given the crush of routine business and the constant diversions into crisis management, how can the premier afford the luxury of serious thought about the direction of his government for two or three years ahead, let alone about the nature of Ontario society a decade or more in the future? In part the answer rests with individual premiers' approaches to setting the government's agenda for the medium and long term. The contrast here is between Bill Davis, who was mostly content to allow ideas to percolate up through the bureaucracy and through his advisors, responding to them as they emerged, and David Peterson, who prefers to "drive the policy agenda," that is, to take the lead in setting his staff and senior bureaucrats to work on ideas and policies he thinks should be developed. This activism appears in other ways as well: as the secretary to Cabinet put it, "Premier Davis liked his ministers and officials to reach a consensus before they came to him for a decision. Premier Peterson likes to direct the consensus-building himself."[47] Of course, the initial policy directions of the Peterson government were largely determined by the provisions of the Liberal-NDP "Accord" which brought the Liberals to power in the summer of 1985. Apparently, Peterson has made a more concerted effort than his predecessors at coming to grips with long-range issues, including occasional sessions with analysts of future social trends, special retreats to contemplate the role of government into the next decade, an early instruction to deputy ministers that he wanted from them a ten-year prospectus of their policy priorities, and a heightened emphasis in the Cabinet Office on long-term strategic planning. As yet, it is too early to judge the effectiveness of such techniques.

THE PREMIER AND THE PARTY

Compared with other jurisdictions, the constraints placed upon the Ontario premier by the fact that he also serves as leader of his party[48] are minor. Of course, party business consumes a substantial proportion of his time. During his first year in office Premier Peterson spent between 15 and 25 percent of his time on party matters, according to his senior staff, and the expectation was that this would increase as election time approached. In terms of ideology and policy, however, it is invariably the case that by his actions and statements the premier determines the party programme; former Premier Davis's indication that one of his most important party-related duties was explaining government policy to the party is telling.[49] While in office, both the Liberals and the Conservatives have been non-doctrinaire, brokerage parties, harbouring a broad spectrum of political beliefs; moreover, neither party feels committed to implementing policy resolutions passed at party conventions in the way that the NDP does. This affords the premier great latitude in setting his policies. Though he must take care to develop policies appealing to all shades of party opinion, the premier dominates the party so thoroughly as to be able to unilaterally impose even policies opposed by large segments of the party. Both Premier Davis' 1981 decision to purchase Suncor and his separate school funding announcement were anathema to great numbers of the Tory faithful, yet there were, beyond general mutterings, no significant attempts to reverse them.

This dominance stands as both cause and effect of the improbability of party revolt against a premier. Opposition leaders may face openly rebellious factions within the party (as former Premier Miller found out on becoming leader of the opposition), but no modern premier has ever had to deal with any serious organized opposition from within his party. This reflects the premier's sensitivity to party opinion as well as a reluctance on the party's behalf to take on the premier (or for that matter, the impossibility of its doing so — for the constitution of the Conservative party makes no provision for a leadership review unless the party is out of power).[50]

As with all other aspects of the premiership, relations with the party have become more complex. Leslie Frost entrusted virtually the entire running of the party to one man, the legendary A.D. McKenzie,[51] while John Robarts delegated most party business to Ernie Jackson.[52] By the 1970s, however, the Conservative party apparatus had become much larger and more professional and Premier Davis came to rely for party liaison not on a single person but on a sizeable group — the vaunted "Big Blue Machine".[53] Similarly, David Peterson's leadership of the Liberal party is effected through a substantial number of people, some in the Premier's Office, some in the party bureaucracy. Any premier's exercise of his party leadership is less a matter of formal mechanisms than of maintaining good relations with individuals, notably the members of the party executive and key organizers. Even here, however, substantial institutional differentiation is evident from the days when the premier, along with

one trusted confidant, could run the party himself. For David Peterson the most important principle in dealing with the party is avoiding the temptation to try to run the party out of the Premier's Office.[54]

Recent premiers have focussed their attention on organizational rather than policy matters: membership morale, candidate selection, finances, and the maintenance of an effective election machine. Even at that, they have been generally content to leave the details of administering the party apparatus to the party professionals. Personalities and styles naturally make a difference in enthusiasm for and diligence in party work. Robarts was said to be much more interested in running the government than in attending to the party, and Frost, Robarts and Davis were all criticized for having let party organization run down in their last years.

In his comparative study of first ministers, Patrick Weller observed that Canadian parties are tied together by patronage far more than are their Australian and British counterparts.[55] Patronage has traditionally been of fundamental importance to the governing party in Ontario and the premier is very much at the centre of it (though John Robarts preferred to avoid personal involvement in patronage).[56] Ontario's labyrinth of agencies, boards and commissions entails several thousand order-in-council appointments, many of which are given to party supporters.[57] The premier's approach to patronage has evolved considerably since the time that Whitney's house in Morrisburg was besieged with favour-seekers the morning after the 1905 election.[58] During the Davis administration, a Premier's Appointment Advisory Committee, composed mainly of party people but chaired by Ed Stewart, met regularly to review names for upcoming appointments.[59] (Early on, a substantial number of important appointments, for example the Chairmanship of the Ontario Arts Council, were identified as being "the premier's prerogative" even if they were nominally made by ministers.) Dr. Stewart would take the committee's recommendation

— usually it was one name rather than a list — to the Premier, who normally agreed with it. Most of the minor appointments, though reviewed by his office, were not personally approved by Davis.[60]

While in opposition, the Liberals were scathing in their attacks on Tory patronage; once in office, however, they firmly linked the appointment process to the party. Although several high-profile, well-paid positions, such as Chairman of the Workers' Compensation Board, Head of the Ontario Film Review Board and the Chairman of the Commission on Election Finances, went to prominent Conservatives and New Democrats, the party faithful have been rewarded with a good many of the less noteworthy, though often locally important, positions.[61] The Premier's Office plays a prominent role in these appointments. Two of its staff (one of whom is Premier Peterson's sister-in-law, who has extensive experience and contacts in the party) work almost exclusively on appointments. Some 1010 of roughly 4750 order-in-council appointments are considered to be the premier's prerogative.[62] In light of the notoriety of patronage in recent years, Premier Peterson has been careful to review personally a large proportion of appointments, and often prefers to choose from a list of candidates. For the less significant appointments, the role of the Premier's Office tends to be one of prodding the ministers in charge of regional patronage to do the work, and monitoring their suggestions.

THE PREMIER AND THE LEGISLATURE

The premier's role in the province's most important political forum has changed markedly in the last two or three decades. Drew, Frost, Robarts at least in his first years, and many of their precedessors personally dominated the Legislature. If one of Frost's ministers or backbenchers was not performing as well as the Premier might want, he would rise, take over the floor from his member with a dismissive

wave, and make his point — all quite contrary to the rules of the Legislature. This domination reflected the fact that the premier was usually present in the House for a large proportion of even routine debates; until the mid-1960s the premier also served as his party's House Leader. That responsibility is now shouldered by a Cabinet minister. Other than attending Question Period, premiers spend very little time in the Legislature. In recent years it has become uncommon for premiers to make more than three or four major speeches in the House a year. This sharp reduction in the premier's participation in House business reflects both the exponential growth in the demand on the premier's time, and the lengthening of the legislative session. In Frost's day, the House usually met for six or seven weeks a year, but since the late 1960s the annual session has lasted six or seven months.

While the premier may be rarely present during most of the time the House is sitting, he is clearly the prime focus of the daily, hour-long Question Period. Probably no other question period in a Canadian legislature is so dominated by the party leaders. Table 12.1 presents data on questions asked during the twelve weeks of the 1986 spring sitting. It shows that almost a quarter of all questions were put to the premier, a much higher proportion than that directed to the first ministers studied by Weller.[63] The data also illustrate the extent to which the opposition leaders concentrate on the premier: 45 percent of Conservative Leader Larry Grossman's questions, and 36 percent of NDP Leader Bob Rae's questions were asked of the premier. Even these figures underestimate the importance of exchanges between the leaders, since, under the Standing Orders of the Ontario Legislature, the opposition party leaders not only get to ask the first questions every day, but they are accorded two supplementary questions whereas other members are permitted only one. The strategy of the opposition leaders concentrating on the premier to such an extent, rather than upon

Table 12.1 — Questions in the Spring 1986 Sitting of The Ontario Legislature (Percentages)

	Conservative		NDP		Liberal	Total
	Leader	Backbencher	Leader	Backbencher	(Backbencher)	Percentage
To Premier	45	24	36	13	0	23
To Minister	55	76	64	87	100	77
Number	86	255	83	243	42	709

Source: compiled by author

weaker ministers, owes a good deal to the opposition's perception that the press will not pay attention unless the premier is involved, which in turn reflects the media's recognition that if the opposition has "something good" it will raise it with the premier. This circularity prevails even when, like William Davis, the premier is masterful at withholding a substantive answer through tortuous circumlocution and at sidetracking opposition members' attacks by goading them into the exchange of insults and witticisms.

This concentration on the premier might seem a foolhardy strategy, but it may be one of the few ways in which the opposition leaders can hope to redress the tremendous ascendancy the premier enjoys over them in media coverage. Ontario is unique in that its citizens' attention focusses first on national rather than on provincial politics (which often rank below local politics in terms of popular interest), with the result that opposition party leaders face a constant struggle in simply becoming known to the public. In March of 1985, for example, after three years each as leaders of their parties, David Peterson and NDP Leader Bob Rae were known to only 25 percent and 29 percent of the electorate, respectively.[64]

Lack of responsiveness from the premier to the government caucus has been a perennial complaint in recent Ontario politics. Robarts markedly improved caucus' role in policymaking over what it had been under Frost,[65] but still found his government attacked as, in the words of one disgruntled backbencher, an "un-

approachable, indifferent oligarchy — a clique — that is not listening to its own members in the legislature".[66] Davis' backbenchers repeatedly grumbled in public as well as in private that caucus had become impotent, in large measure because they felt that he paid little attention to caucus collectively or to members individually. His attendance record at caucus was spotty, and when he did come, he often would not stay long. To an extent, this was done purposely, so as not to inhibit caucus discussion; usually Davis went to listen rather than to take part, though if a minister needed or wanted his support for a policy on which he was having trouble, Davis would express his point of view.[67] During his brief time in office, Frank Miller regularly came to caucus meetings both to listen and to discuss, and would summarize the proceedings at the end. Although he would not necessarily have accepted its opinion, Miller did put to caucus the crucial question of whether to call the 1985 election in the spring or the fall, and listened very carefully to the discussion.[68] Peterson has worked harder to cultivate caucus than did Davis or Robarts, but there is little evidence that government backbenchers have any substantially greater influence over policy. If he is in Toronto, Premier Peterson usually attends the weekly party caucus. The Premier's report is a regular feature of the caucus meeting, after which Peterson normally stays to listen and to take part in the discussion, but he does not summarize the meeting as he did while in opposition. In addition, he holds occasional lunches or dinners with small groups of backbenchers and maintains an open-door policy for all Liberal M.P.P.s, some of which do come with their problems and ideas. All premiers spend a good deal of time — more than many M.P.P.s think — meeting informally with their backbenchers and attending to their concerns and discontentments. Peterson's relations with his private members are eased by the unusual composition of his caucus: a sizeable number of the backbenchers were newly elected in 1987 and thus had no experience or expectation of significant access or influence on the leader, while those who form the balance were either elected for the first time in 1985 or are the old guard, content to look after their ridings. It is noteworthy, if hardly surprising, that as Table 12.1 illustrates, Liberal backbenchers do not ask questions of their premier in the House.

CONCLUSION

At the outset of this paper, William Davis was quoted to the effect that the Ontario premiership was more manageable in the simpler days of the 1950s than in the 1970s and 1980s. He was quick to add, though, that this did not imply that Leslie Frost had somehow had an "easier" time of it than he did.[69] Being premier of Ontario has never been easy; Howard Ferguson told (future Premier) Tom Kennedy when he was about to relinquish the premiership in 1930, "it's a slave's life."[70] Evaluating the claim that Ontario premiers are slaves to their positions is beyond the scope of this paper, but some less dramatic conclusions may be advanced.

Recent Ontario premiers' varying involvement in cabinet decision-making provides some perspective on the concept of "strategic intervention" discussed in this volume. Like all leaders, premiers may be arrayed on an interventionist-laissez-faire continuum; that is, some are far more actively involved in routine decisions and administration than others, who prefer to step in only when they are needed.

The development of modern machinery of government has altered the ways in which premiers put into practice their interventionist urges. Specifically, the transition from the "departmentalized" Cabinet to the "institutionalized" Cabinet, to borrow Stefan Dupré's terms,[71] has forced premiers to rely more heavily on strategic intervention.

The key feature of the departmentalized Cabinet, for our purposes, is the high degree of autonomy which individual departments and ministers enjoy from other departments and ministers; except in the person of the premier, little central co-ordination of decision-making occurs, and since the Cabinet as a collective can deal with relatively few matters, this tends to leave ministers quite independent of one another. By contrast, in the institutionalized Cabinet, "various combinations of formal committee structures, established central agencies, and budgeting and management techniques combine to emphasize shared knowledge, collegial decision making, and the formulation of government-wide priorities and objectives."[72]

Both Frost and Robarts had departmentalized Cabinets. Frost was strongly interventionist, whereas Robarts tended to be substantially more laissez-faire, typically letting his ministers have their way unless they ran into trouble. Thus, depending on the premier's style, a departmentalized Cabinet may be dominated by the Premier, who can intervene at will in isolated departments, or it may be comprised of powerful, independent fiefdoms.

The emergence of the institutionalized Cabinet has been in large measure a response to the increasing scope of state activity, yet it implies far more than simply that a first minister will be too busy to do everything himself. In order that ministers take the cabinet committee process, budgetary mechanisms and other components of the system seriously, the premier himself must in significant measure abide by their rules and procedures, though it limit his power. Even with the powerfully enhanced Premier's Office to offset the premier's disadvantage in dealing with central agencies and central agency ministers, the institutionalized Cabinet narrows the range of techniques available to premiers. The premier's intervention at will, with no one to gainsay him, must give way to carefully considered strategic intervention since it is no longer simply a case of overriding one isolated minister; substantial numbers of cabinet ministers may be involved in an issue. Paradoxically, it may also be more difficult for a first minister to remain passive and simply let his ministers go about their business, for "collegial decision-making" is often not all that collegial. Rather, it means that a large number of ministers, with often opposing viewpoints, have a legitimate say in decisions, requiring the premier to interpret or manufacture some sort of a consensus.

The Davis and Peterson premierships reveal quite different froms of strategic intervention. Peterson plays by the traditional rules of the decision-making process, but takes a strong role in setting overall governmental priorities, and on occasion, once the formal process has been completed, forthrightly exercises his prerogative to make the final decision personally. Davis was more circumspect in establishing the direction of his government and in involving himself directly in particular issues. Strategic intervention for Davis often meant approving end runs by ministers or sanctioning other breaches of the formal rules of the process. This more subtle approach can be very effective, for as Peter Aucoin has noted at the national level, "greater flexibility, and thus uncertainty, invariably enhance the power of the prime minister vis-à-vis his cabinet colleagues... [permitting him to avoid] the requirement for initiatives to be put through numerous hoops of collective decision-making."[73]

Throughout this chapter, evidence has been cited demonstrating that every aspect of the Ontario premiership has become more institutionalized over the past few decades. Yet significant ebbs and flows mark the institutionalization process. For example, David Peterson has insisted that the formal channels of the cabinet

committee system be respected, but in other important ways emphasizes people rather than structures — his "fit the job to the person" management philosophy"[74] is surely the antithesis of institutionalization. Moreover, the premiership of Ontario remains substantially less institutionalized than the prime ministership, largely for reasons of scale. This, in turn, is a key reason why in Ontario — though it is less true than in the past — "provincial government is premier's government."

Richard Crossman has written that "as the machinery of government increases in size, the man at the centre of government must also become more powerful."[75] In Ontario, this is only partly true, since only three or four decades ago, the scale of government was still sufficiently small that one person could retain the greater measure of control over the entire Ontario government. More tenable would be the argument that in Ontario, the *individuals* in the centre — the premier's senior officials and personal advisors — have collectively become more powerful. To the extent that government, and the premier's role within government has become more institutionalized; however, those at the centre probably enjoy less power than did their predecessors.

It is evident that even premiers with similar ideological make-up may develop around them substantially different structures and methods of gleaning advice, or of involving their Cabinets in decision-making. The effect this may have on policy is a rather different question, which has not been addressed here as it is really the subject for another full-length article. Both in image and in substance, the premierships of Bill Davis and David Peterson have differed in a number of important particulars. Only time will tell whether, with experience and in a different political environment, Peterson's style of governing will come to resemble the Davis approach more closely. Still, enmeshed in a complex network of cabinet committees, advisory groups, and Premier's Office and Cabinet Office staff, which characterize the institutionalized cabinet, the premierships of Bill Davis and David Peterson unquestionably resemble one another far more than they resemble those of Leslie Frost or of an earlier Ontario.

This paper could not have been written without the information provided in interviews with current and former political advisors and civil servants in the Premier's Office and in Cabinet Office. These respondents, to whom I am most grateful, were promised anonymity, and their comments are therefore not attributed in the footnotes. I am particularly indebted to the Honourable David Peterson, to the Honourable William Davis, and to Mr. Frank Miller for agreeing to be interviewed for this project.

Notes

1. Interview, October 9, 1986.

2. Aucoin, "Organizational Change."

3. Young and Morley, "The Premier and the Cabinet," p. 54.

4. Interview published in *The Catholic Register,* August 16, 1986. The obvious contrast is with Sir Oliver Mowat, who revelled in the nickname "the Christian Statesman."

5. Mowat lived in Toronto for most of his adult life, but his roots were in Kingston and he represented a farm constituency in the Southwest; George Henry's riding is now part of suburban Toronto but in his day it was decidedly rural; George Drew sat for a Toronto seat for several years; Frank Miller lived in Toronto as a child.

6. See Fletcher, "The Prime Minister as Public Persuader."

7. Schindeler, *Responsible Government,* pp. 44-7.

8. McDougall, *John P. Robarts,* p. 77.

9. Ibid., pp. 134-5.

10. Ibid., p. 236.

11. Szablowski, "Policy-Making and Cabinet."

12. Briefly, at the outset of his term, Davis had different people serving as Deputy Minister to the Premier and as Secretary to Cabinet.

13. Management Board of Cabinet, *Expenditure Estimates 1986-87,* Vol. 11 General Government (Part 1), p. G58.

14. Weller, *First Among Equals,* p. 161.

15. Davis interview.

16. The composition and influence of Peterson's inner circle is examined in Collison, "True Grit," pp. 51-5; pp. 84-5.

17. Manthorpe, *Power and the Tories,* p. 226.

18. Peterson interview, November 14, 1986.

19. Segal, "Evolving Cabinet Structure," p. 70; also Manthorpe, *Power and the Tories,* pp. 226-7.

20. Oliver, *Unlikely Tory,* p. 295.

21. D'Aquino, "Prime Minister's Office," p. 76.

22. Davis interview.

23. This paragraph is derived primarily from the Miller interview, October 9, 1986.

24. On the staff changes under Davis and Miller, see Manthorpe, *Power and the Tories,* Chap. 15, and Speirs, *Out of the Blue,* Chap. 3.

25. Schindeler, *Responsible Government,* p. 44.

26. Oliver, *Unlikely Tory,* p. 31, p. 80.

27. Robarts had simply not paid much attention to the so-called "police state bill" until inundated by a torrent of outraged editorialists and Tory backbenchers. See McDougall, *Robarts,* Chap. 9.

28. Davis interview.

29. At least one minister felt undermined by the premier's relations with his deputy. After Government Services Minister Douglas Wiseman complained to Davis that his deputy was disregarding instructions and failing to keep him informed, Wiseman was dropped from the cabinet while the Premier strongly defended the deputy. See Hoy, *Bill Davis,* Chap. 14.

30. Miller interview.

31. Weller, *First Among Equals,* p. 104.

32. Quoted in Alan Christie, "Peterson's Aides: The Weaning is Over," *Toronto Star,* January 11, 1986.

33. Collison, "True Grit" p. 54.

34. On the structure and operation of the cabinet committee system, see Loreto, "The Structure of the Ontario Political System."

35. Segal, "Evolving Ontario Cabinet," p. 73.

36. Ibid., p. 77.

37. Davis has said that with experience, he "developed an instinct" for sending items directly to full Cabinet, or imposing other approaches. (Davis interview).

38. Sterling, "Parliamentary Democracy," pp. 3-4.

39. Davis interview.

40. Hoy, *Bill Davis,* p. 129

41. During his brief premiership, Frank Miller, by expanding its scope and membership, had turned P. and P. into what was effectively an Inner Cabinet.

42. Peterson interview.

43. The Chairman of Cabinet also relieves the premier of a host of routine duties, such as formally signing cabinet papers.

44. Miller interview.

45. Implementation is in train of a recent report recommending a strengthening of the premier's role in a wider range of senior civil service positions and employment issues, chiefly through an advisory council comprised of private sector executives reporting directly to the premier.

46. Office of the Premier, "A Message from Premier David Peterson to OPS Executives," March 5, 1986.

47. Quoted in Collison, "True Grit," p. 84.

48. Not the least of Premier Hepburn's eccentricities was the fact that when he resigned the premiership in 1942, he did not give up the party leadership.

49. Davis interview.

50. On the parties' leadership review mechanisms, see Wearing, "Political Parties: Fish or Fowl?" p. 251.

51. On McKenzie's role, see Manthorpe, The *Power and the Tories,* pp. 45-55.

52. McDougall, *Robarts,* passim.

53. Hoy, *Bill Davis,* Chap. 7.

54. Peterson interview.

55. Weller, *First Among Equals,* p. 99.

56. McDougall, *Robarts,* p. 78.

57. Many key agency positions are awarded to civil servants, or others without party allegiance; see Eichmanis and White, "Government by Other Means," pp. 89-90.

58. Humphries, *Honest Enough to be Bold,* p. 97.

59. Jonathan Manthorpe, "Backroom Breakfast Boys Decide Who Gets the Jobs," *Toronto Star,* November 8, 1977.

60. Hoy, *Bill Davis,* p. 178.

61. See Rosemary Speirs, "Ontario Liberals Discovering Joys of Patronage," *Toronto Star,* July 24, 1986.

62. Ibid.

63. Weller, *First Among Equals,* p. 171.

64. *Toronto Star,* March 29, 1985.

65. McDougall, *Robarts,* pp. 133-4.

66. Quoted ibid., p. 241

67. Davis interview.

68. Miller interview.

69. Davis interview.

70. Quoted in Kennedy, *Tom Kennedy's Story,* p. 28.

71. Dupré, "Reflections on the Workability of Executive Federalism," pp. 3-4.

72. Ibid., p. 4.

73. Aucoin, "Organizational Change," p. 21.

74. Peterson interview.

75. Crossman, *The Myths of Cabinet Government,* p. ix.

CHAPTER 13

The Pattern of Prairie Leadership

Nelson Wiseman

In 1841, Thomas Carlyle articulated a "great man" theory of history in *On Heroes, Hero-Worship, and the Heroic in History.* Carlyle argued that true leaders are geniuses, great individuals who intuitively shape and transform the destinies of their societies. The leader's indomitable will overcomes all obstacles and through his distinctive and brilliant feats and traits history is made. The multitude, in awe or ignorance, follows the leader. Leo Tolstoy, a quarter century later, posited an antithetical concept of history and the role of leaders in *War and Peace.* In his view, history proceeded inexorably, deterministically on its course, and people — both leaders and followers — were merely swept along in the historical unfolding of broader social movements and forces. Leaders, in this perspective, are nothing more than players trapped in a role in a socio-historical script that has been written for them and their times by a larger force. They are simply "in the right place at the right time," and irresistible historical tendencies supersede and dwarf their individual efforts.

In Canada, as elsewhere, historical writing reflects both these diametrically opposite views. Conservative writers have preferred the first; socialist analysts the second. The history of Canada immediately after Confederation, and nineteenth-century party politics and public policy has become, in large part due to the power of skillful conservative writers such as Donald Creighton, the history of John A. Macdonald — his successes and his setbacks, his vision and his foibles. His death spelled the

demise of his party — his successors simply did not have Macdonald's stuff — and the rise of the Liberals is linked to an equally successful, talented and visionary leader, Wilfrid Laurier. Sometimes the "great men" of the day are formal heads of government, as in the cases of Macdonald and Laurier. At other times, they may be renegades or "traitors," as in the case of Louis Riel between the 1860s and 1880s. Or they may be the heads of non-governmental organizations, as in the case of Henry Wise Wood, known the "uncrowned king of Alberta" in the period between the Great War and the Great Depression, by virtue of his presidency of the United Farmers of Alberta, the Canadian Council of Agriculture, and the Alberta Wheat Pool.[1]

One clear example of the alternative to the "great man" tradition of Canadian historical writing is a recent masterfully crafted and award-winning social history, by Gerald Friesen. Entitled *The Canadian Prairies,*[2] it deals with the Métis on 70 of its 524 pages and with Ukrainians and Mennonites on 17 and 10 pages respectively. By contrast, the leader of North America's first socialist government, Tommy Douglas of the Saskatchewan CCF, who was elected and re-elected as premier five times between the 1940s and 1960s, appears only once. Most of the forty Prairie premiers since Manitoba, Saskatchewan, and Alberta entered Confederation are mentioned only in passing in Friesen's study and some, including Hugh John Macdonald (the son of John A., who was premier of Manitoba at the turn of the century) are completely absent. Similarly, a recent study of Canadian public policy overlooks the dimension of leadership and personality and focusses on ideas and competing philosophies of public purpose and public good. Ronald Manzer's *Public Policies and Political Development in Canada* refers to the work and outlooks of a dozen Royal Commissions but rarely to the outlooks of prime ministers and premiers.

The question remains: are leaders unique actors and historic forces in themselves, or just products of their times and of their societies? This may be an unproductive question and the easy answer is in the body of historical and political literature that we have to work with: they are both. They make and define their political times and they are made and defined by them. Leaders are both unique and typical. Canadian premiers must therefore be understood in terms of their own individual personalities, quirks, and behaviour and in terms of the provincial societies and cultures that produced them.

In examining the psychological and sociological traits of forty Prairie premiers, we are hard-pressed to generalize and categorize. With the exception of some trite observations — all of them have been men and Christian — there is no clearly discernible pattern of Prairie leadership, however much the political scientist in us might wish for one. We cannot even assert that all the premiers have been white, for one of them, John Norquay, was an English Métis. Yet neither is the pattern of Prairie leadership completely irregular, however much the historian in us might suggest it to be. Most Prairie premiers, like leaders everywhere, have been articulate, shrewd, reasonable, and perceptive judges of people. Tests for such psychological characteristics are obviously more difficult to conduct and the data are more difficult to evaluate and measure than are concrete facts such as occupation, sex, religion, and political party affiliation. Nevertheless, we must strive to generalize while retaining the power to particularize so that both the macrocosmic and microcosmic character of Prairie society and Prairie leadership may be understood.

The problem in assessing forty Prairie premiers collectively is that their periods of tenure, personal styles, provincial societies and public policy initiatives have been extraordinarily diverse. To focus on those recently in power is to forgo the judgement of posterity and the luxury of 20/20 hindsight. Alternatively, to give each premier equal weight and attention may be democratic and non-discriminatory, but it would misrepresent their individual impact and their collective legacies, creating a misleading perspective. Some stand out, others are forgettable; some shaped or changed the character of their provincial political systems, others did not. Many premiers came and went quickly; others were durable, scored repeated election victories, and left their mark. For example, Manitoba had one premier (D.H. Harrison) whose administration lasted twenty-five days; in Alberta, on the other hand, there was one (E.C. Manning) who governed for over twenty-five years. Analysis of Prairie premierships, moreover, must take into account that the very meaning of governing changed over time: Manitoba's first few premiers did not operate in the context of representative and responsible government, so that the de facto provincial government leader was the federally appointed Lieutenant Governor. In order to squeeze meaning and understanding from a varied cast of characters and a constantly evolving socio-economic environment, it might be instructive to examine three very different premiers whose years in politics overlapped, and whose common story is one of political success and personal triumph. It is impossible to consider the political histories of their individual provinces and the public policies of their governments without acknowledging the formative role of all three of these premiers.

Manitoba's John Bracken, Saskatchewan's Tommy Douglas, and Alberta's William Aberhart were elected or re-elected to office in the mid-1930s — Douglas initially as a federal M.P., the other two as premiers. Bracken became premier in 1922 in the aftermath of an election in which he neither voted nor ran; when he left the premiership in 1943, he was the British Commonwealth's longest serving head of government up to that time. During his two decades in power he headed a government that called itself at first the United Farmers of Manitoba, then alternately the Bracken party or the Progressives, then the Liberal-Progressives, then the Non-Partisan Government (which included the Liberal-Progressives, Conservatives, the CCF, and Social Credit), and finally the Coalition (which contained the above minus the CCF). He left provincial politics to become leader of yet another party, the federal Conservatives, and insisted that they change their name to the Progressive Conservatives. Tommy Douglas served an almost equally long period as Saskatchewan's premier and pioneered some now-common features of the modern welfare state, most notably universal hospital and medical insurance. He led North America's first socialist government. He was the first Canadian premier to pursue systematic economic planning and, as part of the endeavour, used Crown corporations to expand the role of government as employer, entrepreneur, and development agency.[3] In contrast, William Aberhart played the role of evangelical prophet, offering a secular equivalent of biblical truth, and was revered by his followers. Douglas described himself as the servant of a grass-roots socialist party whose policies he was entrusted with implementing and to which he had to answer and submit his leadership for review at annual conventions.[4] Aberhart as party leader had near-dictatorial powers; he personally screened and approved candidates, almost singlehandedly created a winning party from scratch in a matter of five months, and brought the philosophy of Social Credit to national and international prominence. Each of these men — Bracken, Douglas, and Aberhart — represented contrasting features of the political outlooks and backgrounds of Prairie residents. One of the few things they shared was that they came to power as heads of new third parties which symbolized

a rejection of the parties of the East and of the past — the Liberals and Conservatives.

The secondary literature on these three premiers yields conflicting explanations for their success. In accounting for the longevity of Bracken's provincial career, his biographer claimed that "the straitened financial conditions of the thirties underlined that Bracken's low-key, frugal approach to the provinces difficulties was acceptable to most Manitobans."[5] The question that arises in light of similar economic conditions in the other Prairie provinces is, why did this "low-key, frugal approach" not appeal to most residents of Saskatchewan and Alberta, where high-key personalities like Douglas and Aberhart, who both promised less government frugality, came to power? In analyzing Aberhart's Social Credit, John Irving has argued "it was inevitable that a Social Credit rather than a socialist movement would prevail" during the Depression and that "not even Aberhart could have led a socialist movement to victory in 1935... Socialism, as contrasted with Social Credit, had no real roots in the Alberta community."[6] The question is, why was a socialist premier elected in the neighbouring province of Saskatchewan?

DISTINCT POLITICAL CULTURES

The thesis of this paper is that, despite the common agricultural base, the common experience of Depression, and Prairie alienation from Central Canada (or the "East" as it is known in the West), the unique political cultures of the three Prairie provinces were sufficiently diverse to produce quite different premiers and political regimes. Bracken, Douglas, and Aberhart are best seen as mirrors of their distinctive provincial societies. They embodied a diversity of political sentiments and a wide spectrum of policy directions and administrative styles. Their success was based on their ability to understand and express the sentiments of their followers. Through glimpses of their careers, policies, and personalities, I wish to suggest that personality and economic factors are less important than broader cultural, social, and ideological factors in explaining their electoral success and their public policy priorities. The concept underlying this framework of analysis is that Manitoba, Saskatchewan, and Alberta are most influenced by the political cultures of Ontario, Britain, and the American Midwest respectively.[7] Bracken, Douglas, and Aberhart (even though he was not born in the U.S.) were carriers of the ideas and political values of these relatively older societies in the new society of the Canadian Prairies.

That Saskatchewan chose the socialist Douglas and Alberta chose the anti-socialist Aberhart reflected differences in the two provinces' political cultures. In spite of all his charisma and skills of persuasion, Aberhart could not likely have come to power in neighbouring Saskatchewan, nor could he have led a socialist party to victory in Alberta. Similarly, Douglas could never have been successful in Alberta. Aberhart and his Cabinet campaigned actively in the 1938 Saskatchewan election, but only two of the forty-one Social Credit candidates were successful. (In contrast, the fledgling CCF had ten of its thirty-one candidates elected). One thread which runs through the literature on the Prairies ties the political evolution of the provinces to their economic development. It stresses that the Prairies once shared a common and dominant agricultural base and that, in recent decades, the politics of the three provinces have become increasingly diversified and distinct from each other as new staples have emerged. But, if one looks closely at the past, one sees that the politics of the three provinces have always been different from one another, and that economic factors do not appear to explain the differences. The Depression, for example, has been cited to explain the success of Manitoba's Bracken in maintaining power, the success of Alberta's Aberhart in gaining it, and the failure of the Saskatchewan CCF to come by it at all in the 1930s.[8]

An alternative socio-cultural explanation for the differences among Prairie parties, their leaders, policies, and electoral fortunes lies in the ethnically and ideologically heterogenous population of the Prairies, one that grew twentyfold from 100 000 to two million between the 1880s and the 1920s. It was in this formative period of economic and demographic growth that many future premiers, including Bracken, Douglas, and Aberhart settled on the Prairies. We could also include in such a list future prime ministers: Arthur Meighen, R.B. Bennett, and John Diefenbaker. Manitoba premiers are an excellent example of the socio-cultural impact of an older society on a newer society. Initially bilingual and bicultural in practice as well as law, the province had two premiers in the 1870s — one of them a French Canadian — who were born in Quebec. (Before that, a short-lived republican government was led by Louis Riel, a Métis who was an American as well as a Canadian citizen). By the 1890s, however, the province was swamped by Ontario-born immigrants who refashioned it in the image of their native province;[9] so much so that every Manitoba premier in this century — with the sole exception of Ed Schreyer — has been either Ontario-born, or the descendant of Ontarians. In sheer numbers, pioneering Ontarians dominated Legislatures and Cabinets in all three Prairie provinces well into this century.

Although the status of Ontarians as a charter group was never challenged, other settlers, specifically, from Britain, the United States, and Europe, began to make up more and more of the population, and their values and political outlooks contributed to changing the pattern of Prairie politics. British-born settlers, carriers of the class-conscious politics of their homeland, streamed into Prairie cities like Calgary and Winnipeg, where they led unions and not only produced the Winnipeg General Strike, but also came close to producing a parallel strike in Calgary. The British-born had their greatest impact in provincial elections in Saskatchewan, where as many British-born farm operators had settled as in Manitoba and Alberta combined.[10] It is more than coincidence that when the British-born Douglas was leading the Saskatchewan CCF, Saskatchewan's British-born M.J. Coldwell was leading the federal CCF. The influence of British settlers and ideas reinforces the socio-cultural, rather than economic, explanation for differences in Prairie political traditions.

American-born settlers, who stressed liberal individualist and physiocratic values, in contrast to the British labourite group's socialist and collectivist values, had their greatest impact in Alberta, where they made up over one fifth of the population in the second decade of this century. In 1918, eight of the nineteen directors of the UFA were American-born, outnumbering the British-born and the Canadian-born.[11] Their political influence was out of proportion to their actual numbers, because they settled overwhelmingly in the rural areas that held the key to provincial power. Henry Wise Wood, the veteran Missouri populist, could have claimed the Alberta premiership whenever he wanted in the 1920s, but demurred on the grounds that his American background rendered him inappropriate, and because he opposed the entry of organized farmers into politics. He and his UFA followers looked upon the ascendancy of Aberhart and Social Credit with equanimity. It is more than coincidence that in the 1950s, Alberta's Solon Low, the son of Utah immigrants, led the federal Social Credit party. (And when the separatist Western Canada Concept won a seat in the Alberta legislature in the early 1980s, its M.L.A. was a graduate of Utah's Mormon Brigham Young University). The Ontarian, British, and American connections and antecedents in the political histories and cultures of Manitoba, Saskatchewan, and Alberta, respectively, are too numerous to cite exhaustively, and too powerful to ignore.

John Bracken, like his national counterpart, Progressive leader T.A. Crerar, and so many other Manitoba leaders, was born in Ontario and carried with him to the Prairies the Tory-touched liberalism that dominated turn-of-the-century rural Ontario. It was an outlook that stressed individualism and competition but, like the pre-liberal tradition of Britain, also favoured principles of hierarchy, order and privilege through such institutions as the monarchy, a national police force, and expansive government works, as reflected in the early Prairie Crown corporations, such as the telephone systems. Late in life Bracken returned to eastern Ontario to retire not far from his birthplace. Tommy Douglas was born into a British family which, like so many others at the turn of the century, switched its political affiliation from the British Liberal to the British Labour party. Throughout his years in office Douglas looked to Labour party leaders and policies as models to be emulated. His was the socialism of Fabianism, of labourism, of reformism, of gradualism; in brief, it was British socialism. William Aberhart was, like Bracken, a son of Ontario, but his political success was facilitated by the large number of American populists, religious fundamentalists, and monetary reform crusaders who settled in Alberta and became leaders in its farm organizations; in addition to Wood, who was a member of the Disciples of Christ, two examples are J.W. Leedy, the former Populist Governor of Kansas, and George Bevington, the American credit expert who appeared regularly at UFA conventions but was denied a platform by the more conservative UFM.

In Manitoba, Bracken and other Ontarians dominated provincial politics, because the non-Ontarian, class-conscious British workers and poor Eastern European farmers were concentrated in Winnipeg and the marginal rural areas. The former were underrepresented in the Legislature and the latter were content to defer to the leadership of established elites. In Saskatchewan, British immigrants with old-world unionist backgrounds, like L.B. McNamee of the Farmers' Union of Canada, built a viable and successful socialist party because they became leaders in a type of provincial agrarian and cooperative movement which did not develop in

Manitoba and Alberta. In Saskatchewan, where Scandinavian and continental European immigrants counted for more than in any other province, enough of them swung from the Liberals over to the CCF to bring it into power in the 1940s. In Alberta, both the British-born and the continental Europeans, those most likely to support the CCF and the Liberals respectively — were outnumbered and overwhelmed in the rural areas by American farmers who were more sympathetic to the idea of inflating the money supply than to socialist policies as the cure for their economic woes. Social Credit had much in common with American monetary reform schemes like the Townsend Plan which, in 1936, claimed over three million American adherents. Although the Social Credit label originated in Britain, Alberta Social Credit had more material links with the United States. In Britain, Social Credit's appeal was greatest among the Catholic, the urban, and the cosmopolitan.[12] In Alberta, on the other hand, it was viewed most suspicously in Catholic areas and was most popular in rural, Protestant, particularly American fundamentalist, areas.

The foregoing analysis is a bare and simple macrocosmic sketch of the ethno-cultural and ideological bases of Prairie politics when Bracken, Douglas, and Aberhart were in or on the path to power. It does not insist that all the Prairies' Ontario immigrants supported the transplanted parties of the East — the Conservatives and Liberals — or that all British immigrants voted CCF, or that all American immigrants embraced the UFA and Social Credit. It merely contends that the dominant political tendencies among these groups pointed in different directions. But what of Bracken, Douglas, and Aberhart as leaders and personalities in their own right? What does an examination of their behaviour in office yield? In what respects were they similar or dissimilar, and what do such comparisons contribute to the understanding of their policy initiatives and outputs as Prairie leaders?

JOHN BRACKEN

Bracken was cautious, stingy, and administrative in his approach to governing. Low-key, lacking flamboyance and eloquence, if not logic, he did not have a quick mind. In these respects he was very different from both Douglas and Aberhart who, although they preached competing gospels, possessed in common the captivating skills of gifted orators. Nevertheless, Bracken repeatedly won the confidence of Manitoba's electorate and, like Douglas and Aberhart, never lost a provincial election. Bracken replaced Toby Norris, a Liberal reformer, as premier. Norris had introduced compulsory education, established minimum wages for labour, created a Workmen's Compensation Act and a public health nursing system, launched expansive public works and road construction projects, and extended the franchise to women — making Manitoba in this regard a leader in Canada. Both Norris and Crerar were considered by the UFM caucus as their possible leader and premier, but the UFM preferred Bracken. Despite the conventional popular and academic identification of the Progressives with the reform tradition, their inclinations in Manitoba were in many ways conservative. The UFM selected Bracken to lead them precisely because he offered tight-fisted, stable, efficient, honest, and pragmatic government. And Bracken fulfilled their expectations. "Taxes must be kept down to the lowest possible," he declared on the eve of one election. "Social experiments of an unsound or costly nature must be avoided; contracts must not be lightly broken, and the threat of Communistic teaching must be answered."[13]

Bracken was a consummate politician who appeared to be non-political. As a potential premier, he appealed to the farmers in the UFM caucus in part because, like them, he had no parliamentary experience. Few knew each other, none volunteered to lead the government, and none were nominated by their peers. To them, Bracken appeared neutral and competent and, although he had been a Manitoba resident for less than three years, his expertise in the field of scientific agriculture and his principalship of the Manitoba Agricultural College accorded him high status. When interviewed for the job he said "no", but the UFM was taken by his "non-political attitude" and persuaded him to relent. Bracken's style was subdued and his political perspective was, like all political perspectives, ideological. The image that Bracken, his followers, and his biographer presented, however, was that he was non-ideological. His anti-partyism saw government as a simple business operation, a matter of fair-minded administration. His biographer summed him up as

> not by nature a politician. He had no deep
> ideological conviction and no deep respect for
> the narrow exactitudes of party politics. He had
> no compelling vision and no commitment to a
> restructuring or remodelling of society. He saw
> the role of politician as primarily administrative.[14]

Bracken's distaste for partisan politics fit well in a regional political culture that judged parties, especially those with Eastern roots, as corrupt and self-serving. Indeed, he claimed as a major accomplishment the divorce of politics from the business of government.

When in office, Bracken moved quickly to reduce government and the public debt by cutting the size of the civil service and raising taxes. His government's actions meant, among other things, a reduction in provincial allowances to widowed and deserted mothers, and the closing of over one hundred schools for lack of funds in his first year. Only Manitoba decreased provincial government expenditures between 1921 and 1926. Bracken's hold on power benefitted from an improvement in the international economy and a rise in grain prices in the mid-1920s. He astutely maintained and cultivated the support of the UFM by having a large part of his Cabinet attend its annual conventions. Simultaneously, he won the support of Winnipeg's business community. After

the stock market crashed in 1929, further economies were exacted which included a reduction in the monthly allowances for orphans and a marginally lower per capita daily bread allowance for mental-health patients.[15] Bracken preached the virtues of self-denial and administrative husbandry. Although his instincts were decent and certainly devoid of malice, his policies exacerbated more than they alleviated the impact of the Depression. The Conservatives and Liberals were different from Bracken's Progressives only in that they promised even more economy in government and more cutbacks. They were also less receptive than Bracken to public ownership of resources. Like premiers in later years and in other provinces, Bracken was committed to and fought for diversifying his province's economy.

Although he was unimaginative, unadventurous and unspectacular as a premier and party leader, Bracken's style of governing won him the respect of his cabinet colleagues and of a good part, the critical rural sector, of the electorate. He chaired his caucus with a loose rein and rarely participated in House debates, letting others carry the load in legislative sessions that ran for only a few short weeks, unlike the much longer sessions of later years. So long as he secured rural support, his administration was unbeatable, because south Winnipeg, which preferred the Conservatives, and north Winnipeg, which preferred the CCF were dramatically underrepresented in the Legislature: the city had just ten seats in a house of fifty-five between 1920 and 1949. In the 1922 provincial election which brought Bracken to power, Labour's six M.L.A.s captured as many votes as twenty-seven non-Labour M.L.A.s.

TOMMY DOUGLAS

Saskatchewan's Douglas and Alberta's Aberhart, unlike Manitoba's Bracken, were masterful orators and debaters on the hustings and on radio, and both presented closely and carefully structured stories and arguments. Douglas used humour as a way of ingratiating himself with an audience, whereas Aberhart also used imagery and props (such as the "coat of many colours," which he often wore at political rallies and to give speeches), and a hypnotizing voice that modulated through many tones and ranged up and down the octaves.[16] Douglas commanded all the tricks of public speaking: a knowledge of his topic, a tone of sincerity and belief, effective repartee and a ready supply of anecdotes. Unlike Bracken, who was irrelevant in the election that brought him to power, Douglas was his party's "chief campaign weapon" in the CCF's 1944 victory. Like Bracken and Aberhart, Douglas was a religous man, a minister with facility in Hebrew, and the author of a Master's thesis on Christian Sociology. Douglas's reference point was the social gospel; socialism was simply applied Christianity. Like Aberhart, he saw himself as a spokesman for a broadly based social movement, but whereas Aberhart's role models for public speaking were fundamentalist preachers, Douglas's was Nye Bevan, the fiery British Labour minister who had taken on Winston Churchill in debate and eventually fathered his country's socialized health-care system.

Douglas discussed democratic socialism in terms of Christian moral and ethical principles, but it was not a otherworldly, impossibilist socialism. It was, rather, British-style socialism closely modelled on the Labour party pattern. His socialism was reinforced by his studies in theology at Brandon College and sociology at the University of Chicago. The intersection of the social gospel and socialist consciousness in Douglas's vision is demonstrated by his accepting both the post of minister at Weyburn's Baptist Church in 1930 and the presidency of the local Independent Labour Party. His speeches, from the pulpit and from the platform, contained repeated calls for a "new society" where co-operation would replace competition, and concern for public welfare would replace the drive for personal gain. This idealistic vision was expressed in the CCF's motto, "Humanity First," and in Douglas's oft-re-

peated contention as premier that "government is simply the community writ large; it is the instrument by which we do for ourselves co-operatively what we cannot do individually."[17] His attitude as an M.P. to the Depression was in sharp contrast to Bracken's parsimony and Aberhart's Social Credit formula, the A-plus-B theorem. Presaging Keynesian theory, Douglas exhorted the federal government to increase spending on social and economic development programs. Aberhart's Social Credit thinking was similar, although his idea was to increase the direct purchasing power and disposable income of individuals, whereas Douglas wanted to turn the instrumentality of government to satisfying what he perceived as primarily social, rather than individual, needs.

Within a year of attaining power, Douglas's government acted on its promises and on the expectations it had raised. Old-age pensioners were granted free medical, hospital, and dental services and the government assumed all costs for the treatment of cancer, tuberculosis, mental illness, and venereal disease. In the late 1940s, Douglas's government established North America's first universal hospital insurance scheme, the University of Saskatchewan got a medical school, and during 1961-62 a universal medical insurance program was pioneered, the single item of public policy for which Douglas is best remembered, even though by the time it was implemented he was already long-gone to Ottawa, fighting for a national medicare program as the federal NDP leader. Douglas's long-standing commitment to public health care programs may be related to his personal experience as a child when, due to a lack of family funds to treat his bone marrow disease, it appeared his leg would be amputated. By chance, he was selected as a subject for a medical class, operated on, and his leg was saved — a powerful personal incident that planted in his consciousness the idea that medical treatment should be available for all, regardless of ability to pay. Douglas's government initiated many other programs and reforms, including rationalizing and reorganizing the public education system, revamping provincial labour laws, creating a series of Crown corporations, and recasting the civil service so that it was based on merit and imbued with a commitment to planning rather than being a patronage-driven administration, as had been the case under Liberal premiers Jimmy Gardiner and Charles Dunning.[18]

Nevertheless, Douglas's government also exhibited features of retrenchment: in the late 1940s it refused to expand further social services that required increased taxes, employees of the government's Insurance Office went on strike (something civil servants could not have done before the Douglas administration), and old-age pensioners protested the provincial government's proposal to reduce their pensions after the federal government had boosted them.[19] Douglas's socialism with respect to public ownership of natural resources was also muted: he discarded plans to nationalize the oil industry and travelled to Eastern Canada, Britain and New York City in search of private corporations which would invest in mining exploration and development. In its totality, however, the Douglas legacy is one of creative, practical innovation. Douglas showed what a government — a relatively small provincial one with limited resources, at that — could do through the exercise of will and ideological vision.

WILLIAM ABERHART

Whereas Bracken is remembered for his stolidity and longevity and Douglas for his wit and innovation, Alberta's Aberhart is best remembered for his charisma. Like Bracken, he was first perceived as a non-partisan leader and was not a candidate in the 1935 election that brought him the premiership. But he was radically different from Douglas and Bracken in his outlook and style of politicking, administration, and policy-making. Douglas left the established church to participate in more worldly

activities; he wanted to help humanity. Aberhart left the established church because it was too worldly; he wanted to save humanity. Bracken, although deeply religious, did not view religious principles as a guide to political action. Aberhart synthesized economic theory within a theological framework, whereas Douglas synthesized a theological perspective within a political framework. Rather than appeal to reason, Aberhart's success came through an entreaty to emotion and faith. In this he was extraordinarily proficient, gaining a radio audience that ranged from the Okanagan Valley across the Prairies and into the adjacent American states. With a quarter century of preaching experience before he dove into politics, he inspired a fanatical and mysterious zeal in his followers; his folksy performance, including intentional grammatical errors, charmed people and won their confidence. He lifted people's spirits as at a religious revival meeting; many followers labelled him "Our Saviour" and embraced him as a Moses who would lead them out of the bondage of Depression and the grip of evil Eastern financial interests.[20]

Aberhart had boundless energy and a resolute, inflexible will. He was a disciplined and brilliant organizer who emphasized the virtues of hard work and ambition. Unlike Bracken and Douglas however, he was not a team player, and demanded the spotlight. Ideas were black and white; he either accepted or rejected them completely. He could never admit to having made a mistake. As a teacher his notion of education was to make his students memorize and then drill them.

Aberhart's meteoric rise to power was facilitated by the personal misfortunes of his predecessors in office and the conditions of the day. Throughout the 1920s, the American-influenced UFA had clamoured for monetary reform as the answer to economic distress; when Aberhart came along with a simplified version of Social Credit theory, he found a receptive audience. That few of Aberhart's candidates had actually read Major Douglas's Social

Credit writings or that Douglas claimed that Aberhart had a defective grasp of the concept was irrelevant: monetary reform would be instituted by technical experts. "You don't have to understand Social Credit to vote for it," as Réal Caouette was to tell Quebec's voters thirty years later. Aberhart's rise was also aided by the moral debacle within the UFA cabinet: Premier Brownlee had been publicly discredited for "seducing" his young secretary while another cabinet minister had been involved in a divorce featuring salacious speculation. Both resigned, but their cases dragged out over the election period and, compared with them, Aberhart appeared as a figure of shining character and noble principles. The election of Social Credit and the defeat of the UFA was a foregone conclusion: only fourteen people showed up to renominate the new UFA premier, Richard Reid. The refusal of Eastern bank, loan, and mortgage corporations to co-operate with the UFA in adjusting the burden of farm debt also played into Aberhart's analysis of poverty in the midst of plenty and his condemnation of the "Fifty Big Shots" who allegedly ran the country.

In office, Aberhart's major administrative contributions were the reorganization of rural municipal governments and of the provincial education system. Among other things, Aberhart encouraged the formation of co-operatives and credit unions, established minimum wages, guaranteed collective bargaining rights to organized labour, and provided free treatment for cancer, polio, and tuberculosis patients, as Douglas in Saskatchewan was to do later. Similarly, Aberhart introduced legislation guaranteeing farmers security of tenure on their land, thereby protecting them against foreclosures by financial interests.[21] Aberhart's administration was one of activism compared with Bracken's, and it pioneered some programs similar to Douglas's, but he operated differently and was driven by a different vision. Unlike Bracken and Douglas, Aberhart completely dominated his government from the top down and would brook no opposition (al-

though he capitulated to opponents in a short-lived backbenchers' revolt in 1937).

Like Bracken, Aberhart preached the gospel of a reformed capitalism, but presented an alternative solution to the malaise of capitalism. In terms of converting Social Credit from theory to practice, Aberhart's legislation dealing with banking, interest rates, and public debt came to nought: the federal government disallowed eleven Alberta statutes and the Supreme Court declared ten of them ultra vires. In terms of federal-provincial relations, Aberhart rarely rose above fed-bashing, an understandable approach under these circumstances. In contrast to Bracken, who became preoccupied with federal-provincial relations and initiated the idea of a Royal Commission on the subject, Aberhart formed a trio with Mitchell Hepburn of Ontario and T.D. Pattullo of British Columbia which became known as "the three wreckers" and which took every opportunity to oppose the Commission's recommendations on the grounds that they assaulted provincial autonomy. Where Bracken appeared as a strong federalist and centralist in his submission to the Commission, Aberhart refused to appear and addressed his case "to the Sovereign People of Canada and their Governments,"[22] challenging implicitly as many Albertans (but not Manitobans) had done the very legitimacy of the federal government and its parliamentary prerogatives. In central Canada, Bracken became the acknowledged spokesman for the West. Aberhart, in contrast, was a political pariah, attacked in particular by the press both before and after he attempted to restrict press liberty.

FURTHER COMPARISONS

As in the federal arena, parliamentary-cabinet government bestows on the party leader as premier broad authority, including the power to appoint and dismiss cabinet ministers and personnel at the highest echelons of the public service, to make key appointments to boards and commissions, and to control many of government's patronage decisions. In brief, the premier may organize and run his government as he wishes. A revealing difference among Bracken, Douglas, and Aberhart that points to differences in the political cultures of their parties and their provinces is the issue of accountability. Douglas and the CCF, like the British Labour party and other mass social democratic parties, stressed the link between party and government; he defined the party in convention as a "sovereign body" and claimed that his government was responsible to it and was required to take instructions from it. Woodrow Lloyd, Douglas's colleague and successor as premier, had his Cabinet formally agree in 1962 that no person should be appointed to the position of deputy minister, general manager of a Crown corporation, or chairman of a board or commission without consulting the CCF-NDP's provincial executive committee.[23] Aberhart, in contrast, was expected by his followers to lead rather than be led. Although he had endorsed publicly the American idea of "recall," permitting the citizenry to unseat its representative, he dropped his support for the concept when a movement grew to recall him. In Manitoba before, during, and after Bracken's premiership, the relationship of the ruling party and government to each other and the citizenry was rarely discussed. It was as it had been in the older federal parties and in Ontario; although Bracken ran his Cabinet as a team, no one within his party questioned the premier's rights or policy-making powers.

The British-born Douglas was comfortable with the concentration of power in the parliamentary-cabinet form of government; by contrast, UFA-Social Credit leaders like the American-born Wood and Aberhart denounced it. Douglas used the highly centralizing powers of the premier to build a professional civil service with a consciousness of social democratic values. That is why his government became the leader among the provincial governments in federal-provincial fiscal relations in the 1950s and 1960s, and the major provincial beneficiary of new federal conditional grants for the hospitalization and medicare programmes, which it had pioneered. In terms of Manitoba's public administration, Duff Roblin in the 1960s was an imitator of the reforms of Ontario's John Robarts. Although there has been little research in the area, one may hypothesize that Alberta's model of provincial public administration has been more influenced by the American notion of checks and balances than has either Manitoba's or Saskatchewan's.

Collectively, what do these glimpses of Bracken, Douglas, and Aberhart suggest? They were all pragmatists in office, as are leaders everywhere, yet they were strikingly diverse in their party affiliations, their values, and their personal leadership styles. In terms of their public policy output there are similarities as well as divergences. All three, for example, supported the growth of co-operatives, though for different reasons. To Douglas, co-operatives were paving stones on the road to a socialist society. To Bracken and Aberhart, in contrast, co-operatives were merely an efficient and responsive form of capitalism for small entrepreneurs.

PUBLIC POLICY

We may point to specific milestones in provincial public policy and connect them with the premier of the day. Tommy Douglas's health-care policies are a case in point: in a book subtitled *The Seven Decisions that Created the Canadian Health Insurance System,* he is mentioned more than any other political leader, on twice as many pages as Mackenzie King.[24] A quantitative assessment of policy and administrative outputs, however, would suggest that the Prairie provinces have been more, rather than less, similar to each other in their policy behaviour.[25] In this they have much in common with the other English Canadian provinces; less so, of course, with Quebec. This reminds us that while it may be useful and insightful to examine the individual beliefs and values of premiers like Bracken, Douglas and Aberhart, elite preferences and personality types are a flawed guide to predicting policy outcomes. Many of the specific advances claimed by premiers — such as reorganizing municipal governments, providing rural electrification, or treating tuberculosis victims — were the inevitable result of growing administrative and public pressures and advances in technology. Policies may be, and often are, dressed in different ideological clothing, but the outcomes are very similar.

This is not to argue that all policy outcomes are identical. There are nuances that reflect differences: for example, Alberta, like Ontario, continues despite its wealth to levy medicare premiums on its residents, something which NDP governments in Manitoba and Saskatchewan abolished. Similarly, Manitoba and Saskatchewan, under CCF-NDP governments, have created public automobile insurance schemes, whereas Alberta has kept private insurance. That one province (Alberta) levies medicare premiums is not as telling, however, as that all provinces now operate universal, comprehensive, and portable medicare programs. A powerful levelling force in public policy in recent decades has been the federal government: through equalization payments and through transfers such as conditional grants it has coerced, coaxed and bribed the provinces into national programs like medicare despite the recalcitrance of provincial premiers like Manitoba's Walter Weir, Alberta's E.C. Manning, and Ontario's John Robarts in the 1960s. Similarly, Manitoba's Sterling Lyon, despite his longstanding dislike for and denunciation of an entrenched Charter of Rights, was pressured by his peers into accepting it in the context of the broader dynamics of federal-provincial relations at the First Ministers' Constitutional Conference in 1981.

This leads to the subject of federal-provincial relations in terms of parties and their leaders. Much has been made by Canadian political scientists of the alleged "traditional separation

between the federal and provincial wings of the parties, even those sharing the same name."[26] It has been argued that Canada's parties are more confederal than they are integrated; that is, that parties of the same label rely on different sets of voters, financial contributors, organizations, ideologies, and leaders in the two distinct arenas of federal and provincial politics.[27] The experience of Prairie party leadership and the career patterns of premiers, however, belie this alleged inconsistency in the party system. No less than six of Saskatchewan's twelve premiers have served as M.P.s either before or after, or both before and after, their tenure as provincial heads of government (although one of them — Ross Thatcher — sat as an M.P. with the CCF before becoming a virulently anti-socialist Liberal premier.) Today the provincial Saskatchewan Liberal leader is a former Liberal M.P. In Alberta, two of the three early Liberal premiers went on to sit in the federal Cabinet. Similarly, in Manitoba, a number of premiers served as M.P.s and some that did not (e.g. Duff Roblin, Sterling Lyon, and Howard Pawley) did not because they ran but lost. In a number of cases (including those of party leaders Duff Roblin and Gil Molgat of Manitoba and Dave Steuart of Saskatchewan), the prime minister made Senate appointments, further integrating rather than confederalizing Canadian party leadership.

Leadership career linkages between the federal and provincial arenas are all the more noteworthy on the Prairies where the tradition of sectional political protest against the federal government is more deeply ingrained than anywhere else in English Canada. One means employed by prime ministers to mediate such protests has been to seek out Prairie leaders and appoint them to the federal Cabinet. T.A. Crerar and Robert Forke of the Progressives served thus in the 1920s; Stuart Garson went from the premiership of Manitoba into the federal justice portfolio in the 1940s; and Jimmy Gardiner became between the 1930s and 1950s "the prime minister for the prairies."[28]

Aberhart is an example of a party leader with

a career at only the provincial level of politics. Douglas's career is an example of a party leader in the same role at both the provincial and federal levels. Bracken is an example of the same leader of quite different parties in the provincial and federal arenas. Despite his aversion to social experimentation and activist government, Bracken won and retained the respect of leftists in and out of Manitoba until he entered federal politics in the 1940s. He was seen as an effective populist, a defender of the "little man." The local branch of the Independent Labour Party (the CCF's forerunner) in the riding chosen for Bracken in his first election extended him its virtually unanimous support. Similarly, CCF ideologue Frank Scott once described Bracken as the most progressive premier in the country "and one whom the CCF ought to try to win over."[29] The "reactionary" policies of Bracken's government were blamed by CCF members on the right-wing Liberals, and later on the Conservatives and the Social Crediter in his Cabinet.[30] His niggardly ways in the 1920s and 1930s were not as objectionable to socialists as such behaviour was to become in later years and was consistent with the penurious socialist and labour governments of Western Europe, which were tightening rather than expanding government spending.

In the federal scheme of politics, Bracken appeared as a Western reformer, a progressive, and a winner, and the Liberals, Conservatives and the CCF all saw him as a potential convert to their party. Mackenzie King repeatedly pressured Manitoba's Liberals to fuse with Bracken's Progressives and, when the union took place in the early 1930s, it was tied to and facilitated by the transfer of jurisdiction over provincial natural resources from the federal to the provincial government.[31] The federal Conservatives cultivated an image of Bracken as an enlightened man of the soil and of the people when he led them in the 1940s.[32] It was a populist image prefiguring that of John Diefenbaker in the 1950s. Douglas and Aberhart, in contrast, were neither wooed nor seduced by the older federal parties. Rather than being

perceived as progressives or centrists, they were depicted by their opponents in central Canada during their premierships as left-wing and right-wing extremists.

Prairie leadership occurs within a context that is multidimensional; it is both active and reactive to the decisions of others in various centres of power ranging from Parliament Hill in Ottawa, to commodity markets in London, New York and Chicago, to interest groups and voting coalitions closer to home. In an important sense, Prairie premiers have counted more for what they have represented than for what they have done. Some premiers appeared as reformers and won mandates for change (e.g. Aberhart, Douglas, Norris, Duff Roblin and Schreyer); others have represented conservative inclinations (e.g. Thatcher, Manning, Weir and Lyon). All have represented the aspirations of different classes, regions, interests and groups in their provincial societies. Generally, CCF-NDP premiers have been identified with the interests of the less privileged, minorities, and the working class; other premiers have on the whole been identified more with the interests of the established, the propertied, and the entrepreneurial.

The policies and utterances of premiers fulfill a symbolic function: they permit the vote, the people's choice, to be structured around leadership images. One of the most convincing and substantial findings of recent Canadian public opinion surveys is that leadership images have been more important in voters' decisions — whatever the province of residence — than policy issues and local candidates.[33] There is little reason to believe that this was any less crucial a factor in provincial politics in the 1930s and 1940s, when Bracken, Douglas, and Aberhart were premiers, than in the decades before or since. Individual Prairie premiers have set a tone and constituted distinct emblems in political life. They have provided their electorates with concrete, personal expressions of more broadly current ideological outlooks and dispositions.

It would be unreasonable and extreme to

maintain that the development of a public policy is nothing but a function of a premier as a unique individual. At the same time, it is just as unreasonable to deny the role of the political leader in galvanizing people and resources in the forging of policies and initiatives. What has been unique is the particular diversity and context of the Prairie provinces. It is this that has produced the particular leaders, parties, and outlooks that have come to dominate in the three provinces at specific times. To restate the thesis of this article: social context has been primary and personalities have been secondary in explaining the electoral success and policy initiatives of Prairie premiers.

Notes

1. Rolph, *Henry Wise Wood of Alberta,* Chap.8,p.176.

2. Friesen, *The Canadian Prairies: A History.*

3. Cadbury, "Planning in Saskatchewan"; Brownstone, "The Douglas-Lloyd Governments: Innovation and Bureaucratic Response"; MacLean, *Public Enterprise in Saskatchewan.*

4. L.H. Thomas, *The Making of a Socialist: The Recollections of T.C. Douglas,* p.149.

5. Kendle, *John Bracken,* p.248

6. Irving, *The Social Credit Movement in Alberta,* pp.344-6.

7. Wiseman, "The Pattern of Prairie Politics".

8. Lipset, *Agrarian Socialism,* p.205

9. Morton, *Manitoba: A History,* Chap.9.

10. England, *The Colonization of Western Canada,* pp.280-1; *Census of Canada, 1921,* Vol.5, Table 58, p.80.

11. Morton, *The Progressive Party in Canada,* p.39.

12. Finlay, *Social Credit.*

13. *Winnipeg Free Press,* July 4, 1936.

14. Kendle, *John Bracken,* p.248.

15. Peterson, "Manitoba: Ethnic and Class Politics," pp.81-82.

16. Irving, *The Social Credit Movement in Alberta,* p.342.

17. Lovick, *Tommy Douglas Speaks,* p.78.

18. Reid, "The Saskatchewan Liberal Machine Before 1929"; Smith, *Prairie Liberalism: The Liberal Party in Saskatchewan, 1905-1971.*

19. Lipset, *Agrarian Socialism,* pp.334-5.

20. Irving, *The Social Credit Movement in Alberta,* pp.258-9, 342; Schultz, "Portrait of a Premier: William Aberhart".

21. Hooke, "Economic Development and Welfare Policies," pp.162-5.

22. Mallory, *Social Credit and the Federal Power in Canada,* pp.141-2.

23. Eager, *Saskatchewan Government: Politics and Pragmatism,* pp. 171-3.

24. Taylor, *Health Insurance and Canadian Public Policy.*

25. Chandler and Chandler, *Public Policy and Provincial Politics;* Winn and McMenemy, eds., *Political Parties in Canada,* Chap.12.

26. Jenson, "Party Systems," p.118.

27. For this distinction see Smiley, *Canada in Question: Federalism in the Eighties,* Chap.5.

28. Young, "Leadership and Canadian Politics", p.283.

29. F.R. Scott to David Lewis, August 15, 1940, *CCF Records — Public Archives of Canada.*

30. Wiseman, *Social Democracy in Manitoba,* Chap.2.

31. Kendle, *John Bracken,* pp.81-82.

32. *Public Opinion,* November 1, 1943.

33. Clarke et al., *Political Choice in Canada,* p.135.

CHAPTER 14

Governing Amid Division: The Premiership in British Columbia

Neil Swainson

In British Columbia, as elsewhere, the governing process relies on co-operative behaviour, and leadership remains, to paraphrase Chester Barnard, the strategic factor in co-operation.[1] This province, in the Canadian tradition, has relied heavily on its premiers to provide leadership, as exercised not just in their own office, but in association with others also expected to play key roles in the legislative, executive, and administrative branches of government. As Barnard points out, articulating goals, creating ethical codes, managing an economy of incentives to elicit co-operative behaviour, and inspiring, co-ordinating, and in some sense fostering and directing leadership in others, have been and remain continuing concerns for premiers.

Walter Young and Terry Morley argued in 1982-83, with some justification, that "provincial government is premier's government; an oversimplification, perhaps, but one which nevertheless underlines the seminal role of the provincial premiers."[2] In British Columbia, as elsewhere in the Westminster tradition, premiers are outstanding figures in the political executive, and, what is more, exercise power which is primarily conventional. For most of this province's history, the premier was not mentioned at all in the Executive Council section of the provincial Constitution Act.

The office of the premier did not exist when the Crown Colony entered Confederation in 1871, nor at that time did the new province enjoy responsible government. These two deficiencies were remedied before the end of that year, however, although the Lieutenant Governor continued to sit as chairman of the Executive Council until 1875, and to attend it until 1878. From that time the premiership in B.C. evolved much as it did elsewhere in Canada — save for the fact that its occupants were not drawn from the ranks of provincally organized parties (for the simple reason that none existed) until 1903.

In many respects the basic dimensions of the premier's role in all of the provinces have changed little over the last century. This continuity and stability notwithstanding, successive premiers in British Columbia have also had plenty of room in which to manoeuvre. They are not, nor are they expected to be, automatons. Premiers are rather like the batters in a cricket match. They must obey certain rules, but have a good deal of leeway to shape their own innings as they respond to challenges and opportunities presented by their own and their colleagues' strengths and weaknesses, by the Legislature, and the community at large. There is thus a dynamic quality to premiership in action.

The basic intent of this chapter is to identify some of the ways in which both the stability and the flexibility associated with the premier's role in B.C. have been manifested in the postwar administrations of W.A.C. Bennett, David

Barrett, W.R. Bennett, and (thus far only briefly) William Vander Zalm. The chapter pursues this objective by "slicing through" this forty-five-year period from a number of angles, all related to premiers in action. Subsequently, it seeks to stand back from these data, and attempts to account for both stability and flux in the premiership, and to place it in a general Canadian as well as in an even broader setting.

POLITICS IN B.C. SINCE 1940: AN OVERVIEW

British Columbia's premier in 1940 was T.D. "Duff" Pattullo, who had played a major role in reorganizing the provincial Liberal Party after 1929, had led it to electoral victories in 1933 and 1937, and had headed an administration which was one of the most innovative in the province's history.[3] Through 1940 his government and his position within his party appeared to be strong. In 1941, however, Pattullo adopted an openly skeptical stance on the centralizing thrust of the Rowell-Sirois Report, and a very hostile approach to those in B.C. who disagreed with him on this question. His position on the future shape of Canadian federalism, although prescient, in some sense was out of step with the mood of his province at this point in World War II, and appears to have been a major factor in the unfavourable outcome of the October 1941 election, in which the Liberals lost their working majority.[4] When Pattullo subsequently opted for what was in effect minority government, he failed to persuade first some of his leading cabinet colleagues on the issue, and then a convention of his party, which rejected him and replaced him with a new leader, John Hart.

In December, 1941 Hart formed a new coalition administration with the Conservative Party. (The CCF Party declined to join.) This coalition government, which was to win elections in 1945 and 1949, involved a working alliance at the provincial level of two parties which remained organizationally distinct, and, at the federal level, strongly competitive. Hart was the basic architect of the terms of the alliance. He resigned in December, 1947, to be succeeded as Liberal leader and premier by Byron Johnson. Neither man's task was easy, for the Conservatives, with fewer seats than the Liberals, fought hard — though unsuccessfully — to obtain coordinate status in the coalition. The selection of a Cabinet, normally a premier's prerogative, in this context required agreement between two party leaders on the portfolios to be filled from each party. Coalition premiership after 1946 was complicated by the death of the provincial conservative Party leader, R.L. Maitland, and the appointment of the less co-operative Herbert Anscomb as his successor. After Johnson succeeded Hart in December, 1947, the premier's task became still more difficult because of rising factionalism in both coalition parties, increasing opposition to continuing coalition on the part of their federal wings, and the emergence of considerable disagreement among the coalition partners on certain crucial policy issues. Although the Hart-Johnson administrations provided very effective government, and the coalition won a strong majority in the 1949 election, these internal conflicts ultimately led to its dissolution in January 1952. Johnson then became premier with a working majority of a Liberal Party administration, but this new government also generated its own share of publicly aired disagreements — which, combined with those which had surfaced earlier, had an ultimately devastating effect on the appeal of the Liberal and Conservative Parties in B.C.

Such, roughly, was the background to one of the great upsets in B.C.'s political history. In a June 1952 election, the number of Liberal seats was reduced to six, and Conservative seats to four. Johnson and Anscomb were both defeated. The CCF, which led on the first count, lost the election by one seat to a newly emerging political force, the B.C. Social Credit League. While this new party had fought the election nominally with only a campaign leader imported from Alberta, its most prominent and successful candidate had been W.A.C. Bennett, a former Conservative member of the Legislature who had twice unsuccessfully challenged Anscomb for the provincial Conservative leadership. Bennett had left the coalition in 1951, and subsequently joined the Social Credit movement. He was selected by the newly elected Social Credit M.L.A.s as the formal leader of the Social Credit League, and hence as the premier presumptive, in July 1952. Ten colleagues joined his minority government Cabinet, including Robert Bonner and Einar Gunderson, neither of which had been candidates in the June election.

Over the next twenty years, Bennett was to win five more elections with a mix of policies which ranged from conservative to radically innovative. The province prospered; for most of this period its rates of economic and population growth were the highest in the nation. It is important to remember, at the same time, that the Social Credit triumph of 1952 involved a social revolution. This newly powerful and well-organized party for years drew its strength from the ranks of many who previously had been uninvolved politically. Those whom it displaced, including the traditional social elites, were disgruntled, and the province's political dialogue consequently acquired a notable acerbity, much of it directed toward the Premier. In the resulting exchanges he gave every bit as much as he got.

As one electoral success followed another, Bennett faced no significant challenges in his own party. Still, the party and his administration aged with him (he was seventy-two in 1972). Ultimately, he misread the electorate, much as Duff Pattullo and Byron Johnson had done earlier, and in August 1972, he at long last lost an election. Although Bennett retained his own seat, only nine of his colleagues did likewise as the New Democratic Party took thirty-eight seats in a fifty-five-member House.

The party coming to power in B.C. in 1972, which could trace its lineage back to 1932 via the CCF, had served through all but five of the years after 1933 as the province's official opposition. David Barrett, who had assumed the NDP leadership in 1970, had worked hard to revitalize the party, and expand its base into the province's political centre. In 1972 he read the mood of the electorate correctly, as he waged a quiet campaign and made effective use of some inept references from Social Credit Cabinet members concerning the prospect of W.A.C. Bennett's retirement.

Although Barrett's approach to the premiership differed from Bennett's in a number of ways, his government did share one characteristic with its predecessors during its first year and a half in office; namely, a booming economy. During 1972 and 1973 the Gross Domestic Product (GDP) in B.C. rose by at least 18 percent in constant dollar terms, and over 39 percent in current dollars. Inevitably, this economic growth helped strengthen the new government's perception of its fiscal capacity, as it set out to change the face of the province. As the 1970s proceeded, however, the Barrett government encountered two problems. There was a downturn in the resource-industry-led boom in 1975, with the consequence that the GDP in B.C. actually fell that year.[5] At the same time, B.C. was caught up in the worst worldwide inflation of modern times. Eventually, it became clear that fiscal reality would require some checks on the government's spending programme, which had produced its share of difficulties. In addition, much as Barrett apparently had feared when he first became premier, a fusion of anti-NDP forces had begun to occur in the province, and was accelerating. A catalyst in the formation of this coalition, in fact, was the Social Credit Party, now renamed and reinvigorated, and led by W.R. (Bill) Bennett, the previous premier's second son. When Barrett eventually called an election in December 1975, the result was almost a complete reversal of what had emerged in 1972. Social Credit obtained thirty-six seats, the NDP seventeen, the Liberal and Conservatives one each, and David Barrett was defeated in his own riding.

Bill Bennett governed in prosperous times

for the first half of his term as premier. In 1976, the provincial economy again turned around, and the GDP increased (in constant dollars) 7.5 percent. Annual increases in the GDP through 1981 never dropped below 4 percent, again in constant dollar terms. But there was trouble lurking in paradise. During the late 1970s, because of an assumption that this state of affairs would continue indefinitely as well as because of considerable in-migration, the range and cost of public services continued to expand. Simultaneously, B.C.'s key exports faced increasingly intense competition.

The world changed for B.C. and its premier in the latter part of 1981. In 1982 the provincial GDP (in constant dollars) fell 4.8 percent, and in per capita terms hardly changed during the next three years. Indeed, if one corrects for inflation, in real-dollar (i.e. real-wealth) terms, the trouble can be identified earlier, for the provincial government actually began to spend more than it received as income in fiscal year 1980-81.[6] What has to be kept in mind, therefore, is that Bill Bennett straddled two very different eras economically, and had to adapt accordingly.

The Bennett government after 1981 wrestled with the twin problems, as it saw them, of restraining expenditure in the face of ever-expanding health and welfare costs, and of restructuring and restimulating the provincial economy. Five years down the road, with an election fought and won on that issue in 1983, the Premier announced in May 1986 his intention to resign.

William Vander Zalm, a minister in the first two Bill Bennett administrations, who had retired in 1983, easily won the leadership of the Social Credit Party at a July 1986 convention, and formed a new administration (in which he also became the Minister of Finance) in August. Subsequently, he asked for a dissolution, and in the ensuing October election his party won forty-seven seats to the New Democrats' twenty-two. Once again the province had experienced a political revolution.

PREMIERS AND THEIR PARTIES

It is worth recalling at the outset that although W.A.C. Bennett acquired leadership of his party via the (now-obsolete) mechanism of legislative caucus selection, he quickly added to it the influence that is now commonly associated with the convention process of selection. Caucus selection, it should be noted, had been adopted at a Social Credit convention earlier in 1952 partly at his suggestion, and was but one tactical success of a remarkable series which he engineered during 1952-53.[7] Both David Barrett and Bill Bennett assumed party leadership by the convention route, in 1970 and 1973 respectively. In one sense, David Barrett's relationship with his party differed from that of the two Bennetts with theirs. According to the CCF-NDP tradition, his leadership had to be reviewed annually, and he had to meet regularly with his party's provincial council, as well as with its provincial executive. The fact remains, however, that David Barrett's leadership was never seriously challenged over thirteen years. The Social Credit League cum Party never required annual or other leadership reviews.

The relationship of these three men to their parties once they assumed the premiership inevitably varied. Although the early Social Credit movement is difficult to classify, it acquired at the outset many of the characteristics of the cadre party, including a willingness to accept strong direction. W.A.C. Bennett hardly disappointed it in this regard; his son's contribution to the rebuilding and revival of Social Credit after 1973 has its own significance. In a remarkable effort, Bill Bennett grafted onto the earlier populist base new recruits, many drawn from commercial and professional backgrounds. This expanded party gave him strong support during his ten years in office. Interestingly enough, while the older grass-roots component of the party was not so perceptible or powerful after 1975, it had not disappeared, and in fact played a key role at the Vander Zalm convention in 1986. David Barrett started from a different position, as the CCF-NDP tradition involved an ideology of intra-party democracy, ongoing dissent, and considerable reserve with respect to authority. The NDP accepted the need for leadership, but it had to be constrained and decentralized, which fact leaders found it possible to accept, in Walter Young's words, as they could assume a high degree of "consistency in behaviour because of the shared ideology."[8]

All three premiers periodically sought out likely candidates for their parties and recruited members, but, with a few notable exceptions in the W.A.C. Bennett's first premiership, they tried to remain clear of the crossfire so often found in constituency organizations. All insisted on the ultimate freedom of action of the Cabinet. Barrett had the most difficulty on this front, especially in 1974, when his party's provincial newspaper vigorously criticized his administration. With pressure on the editors, he succeeded in changing the paper's direction in 1975.

The experience of these premiers in putting together election platforms varied. The Social Credit League, with only interim leadership, fought and won the 1952 election on a platform drafted and adopted by a party convention in April of that year. The platform of the 1975 "revised version" (of the League) which defeated the Barrett government owed much to the efforts of Dan Campbell and Grace McCarthy, two former cabinet ministers who, with W.A.C. Bennett, had helped revive the party organization after 1972. The NDP campaign of 1972 was waged largely on a platform produced by its leader, with assistance from two strong figures in the party, Robert Williams and Ernie Hall. Subsequently, in the premierships of both Bennetts, the Social Credit Party was to rely very heavily in elections on the manifesto of their leader and premier, as did the NDP in 1975. In the W.A.C. Bennett years and the Barrett premiership of 1972-1974, the premier deliberately distanced himself from the internal organization and politics of his party. Bill Bennett did much the same in his first

premiership, but after nearly losing the 1979 election, turned to an old friend, Hugh Harris, for help. One tactic involved recruiting professional advice in the preparation of election manifestos and campaign strategy. The other involved obtaining professional assistance in reorganizing the Social Credit Party at the provincial and constituency levels. The individuals involved in the first of these tasks, at least after 1981, worked close to or out of the Premier's Office.

After the assumption of power, each premier's familiarity with the details of his party's organization diminished, although this distancing in the case of W.A.C. Bennett seems to have developed very gradually over almost eighteen years. It took only three years in the cases of David Barrett and Bill Bennett. As a result, all three men in the 1970s found themselves heading into elections in which their parties were poorly organized.

Two further observations on the relationship of premiers to their parties are merited. Part of the reason for the victory of Social Credit in 1952 was its organizational superiority over the Liberals and Conservatives. W.A.C. Bennett had played some part, though a limited one, in this development. Subsequently, although he remained aloof from the details of party administration, he encouraged the creation of ongoing provincial and constituency fund-raising mechanisms. Further reference to Bill Bennett's reorganizational efforts in 1974 and 1975 is not needed, other than to point out his battle, with his father's help, against attempts to create a new political umbrella under which the NDP's non-socialist opposition might collect, and his successful maintenance of that role for his party. In any case, he began his premiership possessing a familiarity with his party's organization throughout the province probably unmatched by that of any B.C. premier since Duff Pattullo took office in 1933. After losing contact with much of it by 1979, as we have seen, he sought to reverse the process between 1980 and 1986.

PREMIERS AND CABINETS

The relationships of these premiers with their Cabinets were at least as varied as their relationships with their parties. Cabinets typically were small. W.A.C. Bennett's initially had eleven members, David Barrett's had fourteen and Bill Bennett began with a Cabinet of eighteen. With his near-monopoly of legislative experience and his contributions both to the dismantling of the coalition government, and to the electoral upheaval in 1952, W.A.C. Bennett began his premiership in a powerful position. With his election victory in 1953, it became a dominant one, and one which, if anything, grew over time.

David Barrett's contribution to his party's triumph in 1972 has already been referred to. Still, he commenced his premiership in a different position from Bennett. The fact that he placed in his first Cabinet all of his caucus colleagues with experience in the Legislature had obvious merit, but upset some of those who were left out. A number of his cabinet colleagues matched him, and some exceeded him, in legislative experience. Further, there were continuing strains between Barrett and other candidates of a hard-fought 1968 leadership contest which he had lost.

Bill Bennett faced his own set of initial constraints. These ranged from the disadvantage of his limited experience to his party's new pluralism. His post-1975 caucus contained Social Credit veterans plus new recruits to the party, and at least five former Liberals and Conservatives who had parliamentary or legislative backgrounds. To complicate life for him, this latter group contained much of the most obvious talent from which he had to choose his first Cabinet. However, he consolidated his position with his colleagues more rapidly than many expected.

Apart from the interesting fact that occasionally David Barrett would place a colleague in the chair at cabinet meetings, neither he nor W.A.C. Bennett modified significantly the traditional working of the Cabinet in British Co-lumbia. Agendas and supporting documents were not circulated ahead of time, non-ministerial personnel were seldom invited into meetings — except to report — and minutes were not kept. In Barrett's time, while the deputy provincial secretary and the premier's secretary took the Executive Council Oath, neither regularly attended cabinet meetings, though when Marc Eliesen was appointed a policy advisor to this cabinet in 1974, he did. Treasury Board and an Environment and Land Use Committee were the only significant standing committees in Cabinet. W.A.C. Bennett's Cabinet made limited use, and Barrett's more extensive use, of ad hoc committees. Barrett often relied on these to help fashion a consensus out of the divergent points of view which frequently arose in the debates in his Cabinet. On the other hand, Bill Bennett introduced a set of structured arrangements and working practices which, by 1976, were common in other governmental systems. From the start, relevant documents were circulated prior to meetings. The full Cabinet met less often, inasmuch as a good deal of its deliberating was transferred to standing (and ad hoc) committees — headed, at least in theory, by a Planning and Priorities Committee presided over by the Premier himself. In fact, as time passed he appears to have made decreasing use of this key committee. Indeed, his experience with the extended committee system seems to have matched Ottawa's; some committees (such as the one on Economic Development) worked well; others withered. From 1976, British Columbia's Cabinet had a secretariat of its own — located in the Premier's Office until 1979, in a new Ministry of Intergovernmental Relations from 1979 to 1986, and since the autumn of 1986, back in the Premier's Office. (A secretariat on a very small scale had begun to emerge in 1974-75.)

There were other features of the relationship of these premiers to their Cabinets which merit comment. All three premiers had to restructure their Cabinets to make room for new talent, to more effectively exploit the old, to remake their governments' images, and deal with administrative difficulties. They all met these challenges. W.A.C. Bennett's restructuring was distinguished by a reluctance to appoint newly elected colleagues to his Cabinet. David Barrett's restructuring was notable because some of his ablest colleagues dissented from government policy and so could not be included in the Cabinet. It also involved, late in 1975, giving up the Finance portfolio which he had held since 1972. Bill Bennett's tribulations included at least four outright removals of ministers from the Cabinet for acts of folly, and in 1986 two transfers associated with questionable personal behaviour.

Two premiers had a particularly close cabinet colleague — Robert Bonner in W.A.C. Bennett's case, and Robert Williams in David Barrett's. Bill Bennett does not appear to have retained a special confidant. All three premiers were notably loyal to colleagues, expected loyalty in return, and basically got it. None faced formal challenges to their party leadership during their term of office, although, as we shall see shortly, both W.A.C. Bennett's and David Barrett's Cabinets had confrontations with their caucuses, which produced some changes in policy and practice. The fact that ministers in the Barrett and Bill Bennett Cabinets were allowed to assemble groups of administrative assistants does not appear to have altered the premier-minister relationship. On the other hand, the emergence of analytic assistance for the Cabinet and premier in these last two administrations may well have increased the premier's power. The analytic support in the Barrett years came in part from an interesting innovation (which somehow misfired) — the B.C. Institute for Public Policy Analysis — and in part from the secretariat to the Cabinet's Environment and Land Use Committee, and in part from a small group put together around Marc Eliesen when he became policy advisor to the Cabinet in 1974. In the Bill Bennett years much of the policy analysis for Cabinet came from ministries, but the agency which elicited it, and produced a good deal of its own, was the Treasury Board staff. From 1976 into the early eighties this new group, which in

time came to include over one hundred people, was directly attached to this cabinet committee; subsequently it was moved into the Ministry of Finance.

As both Premiers W.A.C. Bennett and David Barrett were Ministers of Finance, they were in a position to monitor closely their governments' revenue, and to significantly influence government expenditures. Bill Bennett, nominally more removed from the public finance of his administration, in reality was very close to it. He received a detailed monthly review of the state of the government's finances, and worked closely with his two Ministers of Finance — so closely in the case of the first that some deputy ministers felt that Bennett was the de facto minister.

A final word is in order concerning what might be called the generalized premier-cabinet minister relationship during the period under review. Inevitably all three premiers were inclined to give a looser rein to the ministers in whom they had confidence. Overall, Barrett, partly for reasons already suggested, delegated much more to his colleagues than did the other two. All three premiers expected to be consulted on major policy issues. (To facilitate that process — reciprocally by the way — Bill Bennett linked his personal office via a hotline to those of his cabinet colleagues.) All three premiers preferred consultations to be conducted in their offices. Both Bennetts perceived cabinet sessions to be occasions for the transaction of business and the creation of a long-range consensus on policy. While David Barrett's approach to Cabinet was similar, it included as well a readiness to engage in freewheeling debate and, on occasion, a willingness to forgo the premier's veto.

THE PREMIERS AND PUBLIC POLICY

Any review of W.A.C. Bennett's twenty years of premiership will show that while he appreciated policy innovation by his colleagues (as long as he agreed with it), he was the source of many major initiatives. Policies ranging from the imposition of an extra 2 percent on the provincial retail sales tax as an alternative to the collection of hospital insurance premiums, to the progressive extinction of the province's debt, to the introduction of a Homeowner Grant for educational taxation, to the concurrent development of the Peace and Columbia Rivers, to the takeover of the B.C. Electric and Peace River Power Development Companies were essentially his. His sponsorship of a Bank of British Columbia, and his endorsement of both a five-region Canada and of a negative income tax as a means of equalizing to people instead of governments, are other examples of personal initiatives. Not all of his proposals were single-handed, of course — medicare, for example, in the 1960s had broad cabinet support and involvement from the start; similarly, his emphasis on the building of a physical transport infrastructure had long been the goal of several successive provincial governments. Overall, Bennett was convinced that the province would respond favourably to bold, imaginative, large-scale policies, contingent on the understanding that the establishment of an expanded economic base must precede expanded social programmes. Such policies became the hallmarks of his regime.

When David Barrett and his colleagues assumed office they were strongly conscious of the fact that they might not be in power for long; hence they were determined to move quickly on many fronts to implement a variety of programmes which they had endorsed over the years, although these policies had never been formally encapsulated into a planning package. As they assessed their situation in 1972, "caution was the enemy of social democracy."[9] The Premier made no effort to emulate his predecessor as a dominant policy initiator. His task was to co-ordinate the march to the new order: policies as varied as pharmacare, radical improvement of public transit, the preservation of agricultural land, the seeking of

enhanced economic rents in the production of oil, gas, minerals, and forest products, and the introduction of a new Labour Code, state-run automobile insurance — to name just a few — were introduced by his government. Like W.A.C. Bennett, as minister of finance he assumed responsibility for the determination and the allocation of the government's fiscal resources, and here pursued some quite identifiable policies. He essentially endorsed balanced budgets and produced two in 1973 and 1974. These budgets elevated the relative importance of income taxation and health and welfare spending as sources of revenue and objects of expenditure, and slightly downplayed, again in relative terms, sales tax revenue and spending on education. In 1975 he faced a combined slowdown in the resource industry sector, labour strife, and, as noted earlier, a severe bout of inflation, which made balancing the budget very difficult.

In the fall of 1975 Barrett called the Legislature into session to bring to an end four disruptive strikes. Here, in common with both Bennetts, he was prepared to dispense with the ritual dances of the collective bargaining process when convinced that they imposed unacceptable social costs. He endorsed the Anti-Inflation Programme launched by Prime Minister Trudeau early in October 1975, and indeed later that month introduced a ninety-day freeze on basic commodity prices to help start it off.

One feature of Bill Bennett's approach to policy-making was his appreciation of the openness of the province's economy, its vulnerability to trade cycles, and the limited ability of the province to control these two, save by influencing its cost levels. Another was his insistence on giving personal approval to new policies early in the approval cycle; a third feature was his willingness to play a dominant role in winning support for some of these policies. The initial decision to mount Expo '86, the continued commitment to Expo when the opposition of organized labour appeared to have it derailed, and the plan to build the Coquihalla

Highway are cases in point.

Above all, however, his influence seems to have been greatest in structuring his government's response to the recession which began in the last half of 1981. He obviously agreed then to dispense with balanced budgeting, but was convinced as well that this new state of affairs would require not just long-term adjustments in the provincial economy but also adjustments in the agenda of government. The new approach included slower growth in government expenditures, and in those of its related public bodies (such as schools, colleges, universities, hospitals, municipalities) — to be effected in part via salary cuts to civil servants.

After the Bennett government's victory in a May 1983 election, during which the continuation of civil service salary cuts and restraint policies generally became key issues, Bill Bennett also appears to have played a major role in the evolution of a strategy of economic recovery which included the abandonment of rent controls, a significant reduction of the public service, the abandonment of some programmes and agencies, and for a time the assumption of absolute control by the province over school board budgeting, as well as reductions in some categories of public spending, and freezes in others. Mr. Bennett's colleagues candidly assumed their share of the responsibility for the entire restraint package, which, while intensively opposed by labour in the summer and fall of 1983, was largely implemented.

THE PREMIERS AND CANADIAN FEDERALISM

Almost from the moment he became premier, W.A.C. Bennett adopted an aggressive stance vis-à-vis the federal government, echoing then and throughout his years in office Duff Pattullo's claims for better terms for B.C. in Confederation, so clearly articulated in his presentation to the Rowell-Sirois Commission in 1938.[10] Ironically, Bennett's subsequent domestic success hurt him nationally, as B.C. became one of the wealthiest provinces, whose requests for adjustments, subsidies and grants were not difficult to decline. His approach to the federal government was often tinged with a bitterness born of a conviction that provident administration in B.C. was being offset by profligacy elsewhere. His limitations on travel to federal-provincial meetings for public servants and sometimes even for cabinet ministers became legendary, as did his occasional pettiness. These, along with his bitterness, often had the effect of making his perceptions of federal discrimination into self-fulfilling prophecies.

He was never convinced that the fate of the Canadian nation would turn on bilingualism or constitutional reform, although he was a party to the Victoria charter in 1971. Much opposed to latter-day anti-Americanism, he was withal a dedicated Canadian, and disapproved of the provinces assuming powers, such as those concerned with the making of international treaties, which would impair the federal government.

Both David Barrett and Bill Bennett were determined to put behind them W.A.C. Bennett's self-imposed semi-isolation from the national scene. Barrett had no problem with, indeed, supported, the concept of equalization payments as it then existed, and the federal government's commitment to the maintenance of national standards in social policy. Nor was he concerned about jurisdictional niceties; on one occasion he offered to accept federal jurisdiction over all non-renewable natural resources, if the federal government would commit itself to complete public ownership of oil and natural gas production.[12] At the same time some conflicts did arise between Barrett and the federal government, on such matters as the magnitude of the economic rent which the Crown could extract from exploitation of natural resources, and the manner in which such rents should be split between Ottawa and Victoria. Before his defeat in December 1975, Barrett, in fact, had begun to intone a well-known provincial litany concerning inadequate subsidy treatment and unfair freight rates. Barrett also indulged in "America-bashing" on some issues, but his bark on these occasions was worse than his bite.

The major part of Bill Bennett's involvement in federal-provincial exchanges after 1976 concerned the proposed revision and patriation of the Constitution, and culminated, for him, in a highly visible role as the Chairman of the Conference of Provincial Premiers in 1981. Here he found himself initially in a difficult position, as many of the other provincial premiers were lawyers, more familiar than he was with the nuances of the Canadian Constitution. But he learned quickly, and insisted successfully that the province develop a comprehensive set of positions on the broad range of questions raised in the constitutional reform debate between 1978 and 1981. A major feature of the position which he and his administration ultimately advanced was the proposition that the Upper House in Canada's Parliament should be restructured to represent the provincial governments.

PREMIERS AND THE PUBLIC SERVICE

While none of these premiers sought a major and ongoing role in their governments' relationships with the public service, each inevitably had some part to play in them. W.A.C. Bennett essentially supported the merit principle, and most deputy ministers in his day were drawn from the ranks of government employees. He was consulted on, though he basically always had to agree to, all deputy-level appointments. The outstanding feature of his attitude to the public service, however, was his conviction that conceding collective bargaining rights to it would be a mistake. His approach to management-staff relations was essentially paternalistic. In both the 1950s and 1960s as minister of finance he kept a tight rein on civil-service salaries. Had he successfully maintained effective comparability between public service and external working conditions, his

policy might have succeeded, but significant sections of the public service became convinced that they were being unfairly treated. Both David Barrett's personal commitment in 1972 and the New Democrats' campaign promise to introduce collective bargaining in the public service paved the way for such legislation, passed in 1973.

David Barrett shared with his cabinet colleagues a determination to make his government into a model employer, although he was not heavily involved in the major restructuring of the public service and the modification of practice in it introduced after 1973. During these years the service expanded rapidly, and public servants' salaries were significantly increased, especially for those in its lower and middle ranks. Although W.A.C. Bennett had deliberately left in office all of the deputy ministers inherited by his government, Barrett in time demoted nine deputies, and ultimately appointed eighteen new ones, of whom only six were drawn from the public service. The turnover in these ranks when Bill Bennett assumed power was equally dramatic. Such developments led to some uneasiness at the senior management level of the public service in the latter 1970s.

During the first six years of Bill Bennett's decade in office, the major developments in public personnel administration were the designation of a new agency as the government's representative in the collective bargaining process, a further expansion of the public service, considerable reorganization and decentralization of the Public Service Commission, and the introduction of a new classification system for senior management. The direct participation of the premier in these developments is not clear. What is obvious, however, is the relevance to the public service of the restraint programme with which he was so closely connected from 1982 onwards. In time this involved a negotiated one-year salary freeze, a three-and-a-half-year freeze for senior management, and after 1983, the departure from the service of some 10 000 people — out of a total (in 1981) of approximately 45 000. The dismissals went ahead under circumstances which were negotiated with the public sector unions, but not before a host of issues, ranging from the significance of seniority in staff reductions to the possibility of layoffs motivated by partisan considerations, had raised temperatures dramatically across the whole public sector. The crisis of those days passed, in part thanks to Bennett's "grace-under-pressure" style, and external calmness in times of difficulty. Still, the events of 1983 left wounds, as had, after 1980, a few partisan appointments to the public service, and the province's tough bargaining stance with the public service in 1985-86. In summary, since 1952 the relationship between premiers and their governments on the one hand, and the public sector on the other, has involved in varying degrees a dynamic tension.

THE B.C. PREMIERSHIP IN PERSPECTIVE

There are a number of initial observations which can be advanced concerning the evolution of premiership in B.C. since 1952. One is to draw attention to the fact that premiers since that date have all been leaders of third parties, or parties of protest. What this has meant, of course, is that no B.C. premier since 1952 has dealt with a federal administration sharing the same partisan background. It is also important to note that three of these premiers defeated incumbents with whom they differed in party, and from at least some of whose policies they inevitably sought to distance themselves. The record from 1952 to 1986 in B.C. is replete with examples of such behaviour. A good many observers, furthermore, have made much of the manner in which from 1975 onward, Bill Bennett consciously sought to distance himself from his father.[13] The reality, of course, is that whatever the nature of successions, premiers quite reasonably seek to put their own imprint on their leadership. Concurrently, however,

they may, and often do, retain features of their predecessors' behaviour which they deem valuable. One thinks, for example, of David Barrett's retention of the Finance portfolio and the presidency of B.C. Rail — very much in the W.A.C. Bennett tradition. Interestingly enough, Bill Bennett formally eschewed these two roles.

There were similarities and variations in the approaches of the three premiers to the provincial Legislature. All were aware of its ineradicable place in the governing process, and realized that it was a potential minefield. But otherwise their approaches differed. W.A.C. Bennett was a premier very much in the Western Canadian plebiscitary tradition;[14] he believed that an eight- to ten-week legislative session annually was all that the political system needed and that was all that it got. Procedure in the Legislature remained as he found it.

Perhaps understandably, as the Legislature had been the focus of attention for the province's CCF-NDP for thirty-nine years prior to 1972, Barrett assigned to it an enhanced role in the governing process. Under his leadership it met for regular sessions twice a year. During his first calendar year in office it sat for 140 days, and during his term passed more measures than had been enacted in all of the previous decade. Being an M.L.A. was made into a full-time occupation; members were provided with respectable annual incomes, plus, in time, indexed pensions and constituency offices. Caucuses received research assistance, the central building of the parliamentary complex was renovated and reserved for legislative/ministerial use. A whole series of procedural reforms in the Legislature was adopted, which, ironically, had the effect of reducing the power of the premier and the government.[15] Attempts were made to revitalize the committee system, and also to provide a procedural time limit on the annual supply debate. In Bill Bennett's premiership, legislative sessions fell midway in length between those of his two predecessors, and in his last term, in 1985 the Legislature unanimously adopted a further set of procedural reforms.

In still another sense, however, there was a fundamental difference in approach among these three men to the Legislature. W.A.C. Bennett shared with David Barrett a penchant for, as well as considerable, if intimidating, skill in, the cut and thrust of legislative debate. Although in time he became a reasonably effective performer in this environment, Bill Bennett never gave the impression of being comfortable in it.

There were also significant variations in the approach of these premiers to their legislative caucuses. W.A.C. Bennett seldom attended them. David Barrett attended, although he frequently had to leave caucuses which apparently often were the venue for wide-ranging debate. Bill Bennett took them seriously, and insisted that his ministers attend. In all three administrations, of course, caucus served its traditional role as both a safety valve to accommodate the dissenting backbencher, and as an early-warning system. On occasion it was more than this. In 1966 caucus resistance led W.A.C. Bennett to modify a redistribution bill, and in 1968 to remove a minister. According to Kavic and Nixon, the NDP caucus forced David Barrett and a majority of his cabinet colleagues, with great reluctance, to impose rent control in 1974.[16] Recourse to the extensive use of closure to end debate on the Bill Bennett government's restraint legislation in the fall of 1983 appears to have come from pressures within the Social Credit Party caucus and not from the Premier.

Inevitably, the premiership was heavily rooted in the personalities and leadership styles of these very different individuals. All were hard workers, and abler than their opponents initially realized. The two Bennetts differed from David Barrett in demonstrating a willingness to struggle with detail, which was not part of the NDP premier's make-up. All could be tough, even ruthless, political fighters. With some reason, W.A.C. Bennett's style has been described as paternal, and David Barrett's as fraternal.[17] W.A.C. Bennett, in addition, was inclined to hyperbole and the outrageous, as

well — in ways which made his political opponents angry and critical.

All three in private, were pleasant, sensitive and amiable human beings. David Barrett was the most outgoing, the most informal, and most inclined to laugh at himself, although he occasionally dissembled, and had a low boiling point and a propensity to use rough language which damaged his credibility more than he realized. In many respects Bill Bennett was extraordinarily disciplined, a loner who only got to his Okanagan home on weekends, and who regularly carried a full briefcase to his apartment at night. Civil servants and colleagues alike recall the extent to which he mastered cabinet documents, and the embarrassment of ministers who had not done likewise.

All three men had their troubles with the media. For a decade, at least, W.A.C. Bennett skilfully turned media criticism to his advantage, as he insisted that it often spoke for the entrenched interests and privilege which were, he argued, opposed to his government. Most of his contact with print journalists was in formal press conferences, which he dominated. There is some evidence that he was less comfortable with television.[18] Initially, relations between David Barrett and reporters were cordial, and he was notably effective on camera. Over time, however, Barrett became very disturbed at some of the press reporting, and especially at the editorial interpretations of his government's activities. Eventually his criticisms of the *Vancouver Sun* and its owners became as unflattering as any which his predecessor had advanced. When, by 1974, his government realized that its popularity was slipping, it launched a series of in-house publications in an attempt to communicate its own story to the public. Towards the end of his administration he and his colleagues were largely inclined to place blame for their difficulties on the media.

Bill Bennett's relations with the media were determined in part by his reserved manner; reporting was quieter and less intense during his first administration than it had been during

Barrett's. Like Barrett, he had his disagreements with the *Vancouver Sun,* albeit on a subdued scale. However, after the 1979 election and a series of unflattering revelations concerning Social Credit electoral strategy, criticism increased, and remained at a high level until his retirement, although he maintained good relations with most of the press gallery on an individual basis. He found the electronic media difficult to handle, but was determined not to let them get the better of him, and improved his performance before the television camera as he gained experience. His government was noteworthy for the manner in which it sought to professionalize its public relations, adopting a slickness and control in its approach. Where the New Democrats had set up a small Communications Branch in the Provincial Secretary's department in 1975, Bill Bennett's government in time established a large and technically sophisticated Government Information Services Division, headed by a communications advisor who often attended cabinet meetings.

Leadership style can change during a premiership. There is not much evidence that this happened between 1952 and 1972, but there was certainly a centralization of authority in David Barrett's office when he launched his restraint programme in 1975, and in Bill Bennett's office after he nearly lost the 1979 election. When L.J. Wallace, the career non-partisan deputy minister to the Premier, retired for the second time in September 1981, he was succeeded by Patrick Kinsella, who initially sought to pursue both general administrative and partisan advisory functions. This attempt quickly proved to be an embarrassment, and Kinsella was moved sideways to become principal secretary to Bennett. He is widely regarded as a key strategist in the 1983 Social Credit election success — although David Barrett's eleventh-hour commitment to drop the government's programme to cut civil servant's salaries must get some credit for this outcome.[19] When Kinsella formally became a partisan tactical assistant to the premier in 1982 and 1983, his place as

deputy minister to Bennett was assumed by Norman Spector, who became in a sense a chief of staff. The overall effect of these structural changes was to make Bennett, who shared with his father a belief in the wisdom of remaining socially apart from his colleagues, even more remote. Further, cabinet ministers and senior public servants were often unclear after 1982 about the source of inquiries or directives emanating from Spector's office. Complicating life for deputy ministers in this period was the concern that somehow they were being required to demonstrate a loyalty to the Premier's Office impinging on their traditional responsibility to their own ministers. Overall, Bill Bennett's experience with the chief-of-staff arrangement hardly appears to have strengthened the proposition that it can be fitted handily into the working traditions of cabinet government.

Comparing premierships, especially over the span of several decades, is fraught with difficulties. Premiers are never entirely masters of their own fate. Comparison further implies the existence of universal criteria. Is the real key electoral success? Or is it the long-range effectiveness of policy innovation? Should not achievements be assessed in the light of the challenges posed by the general milieu?

There is no need to repeat what has already been said of the premiership of W.A.C. Bennett. The references made in an introductory section to annual increases in economic growth and in the fiscal capacity of government during the 1950s and 1960s were in no sense intended to imply that he had played no part in the prosperity of those years. His mixture of unpredictable energy and caution were part of his skill. A senior public servant with experience through the three administrations we have been examining described these years using the analogy of driving a car, roughly as follows: W.A.C. drove hard, but always with one foot on the brake. For a couple of years David Barrett had both feet on the gas. Bill Bennett started out cautiously, but soon had the car in overdrive. (This is a reference to the 1975-79 government's adoption of some very expensive policies in extended hospital care, dental care and an expansion of pharmacare.) By late 1981, however, he realized that the vehicle was heading straight over a cliff, and put both feet on the brake. In the process, the community got a major dose of whiplash. This characterization has some validity.

The decade of the 1970s was a more difficult one in which to govern than the 1950s or 1960s had been. In many ways, the difficulties have mounted further yet in the 1980s. One has only to recall the turmoil of rising and declining expectations, the breakdown in the social consensus on fundamental values, the decline in civility, the anti-organizations revolution, and the distortions and injustices inherent in the already-mentioned inflation of the 1970s. These were the years when the number and leverage of special interest groups increased, often in the context of a new political culture which was intensely critical of the representative process, enamoured of direct democracy, yet unwilling to accept responsibility or to appreciate the need for authority and leadership in the real world.[20] It is true that being a premier in B.C. has never been easy; in fact during the last sixty years only John Hart and Bill Bennett have escaped the humiliation of electoral rejection.

Since 1975 David Barrett's premiership has been critically reviewed and vigorously defended, not least from within NDP ranks. Some have charged him with letting the agenda get out of hand, with not explaining adequately his government's goals, with not involving the community enough in its decision-making. Inevitably he has had to bear the responsibility for the timing of the 1975 election. Some strategists have argued that it should have been delayed until a redistribution commission had made its report, and a revised electoral law had both limited party expenditures during elections, and publicly subsidized those expenditures. Future historians will have to assess such claims while carefully considering the environment in which

the Barrett government operated, and the long-term impact of its major policies.

The assessment of Bill Bennett's premiership likewise will focus on such features as its reversals of some NDP policies, its innovations in social policy, the building of B.C. Place, Expo '86, Metro Vancouver's Skytrain, new roads and bridges, structural changes in government, moderation of the role of trade unionism, Northeastern B.C. coal development, and, above all, the post-1981 restraint program. The verdict on some of these developments may well be unfavourable. Crucial to an overall assessment, however, will be Bennett's reaction to the fact that the share of his governments' operating expenses represented by natural-resource income fell from 23.3 percent in 1979-80, to 8.6 percent in 1985-86.[21] Bill Bennett concluded that far more than being the result of cyclic change, this decline was structural and likely to persist, and warranted, as noted earlier, a massive reworking of the financing of the entire public sector in B.C. The state of the province's public finances in the last quarter of this century suggests that he was correct, although the jury on this issue may well be out for some time to come.

THE VANDER ZALM PREMIERSHIP

Bill Vander Zalm made history in a number of ways when he became B.C.'s twenty-seventh premier. He was the first in this century to be appointed to the office when not holding a legislative seat; he was also the first premier appointed since 1941 with any cabinet experience at all. His convention victory in July, 1986 was also unique, in that while it was partly the result of a well-organized intra-party campaign, it was primarily a reflection of the fact that, by the time the convention opened, newspaper polls showed him to be, among the twelve candidates, overwhelmingly the people's choice.

In a sense his popularity in mid-1986 was a surprise, for while during his ministerial career he had handled some difficult administrative problems competently, he had occasionally almost asked for trouble and frequently had been disconcertingly frank, in a manner which had created problems both for himself and his colleagues. His frankness, on the other hand, is also apparently one reason for his popularity along with his support of some traditional virtues, his ease with the media, and his open, relaxed style. His appeal may have been helped by the fact that Vander Zalm was not a member of the Bill Bennett Cabinet in the spring of 1986, when it was rocked by no less than four scandals involving ministers, and likewise by the fact that these same ministers, with most of their colleagues, opposed his candidacy. In short, he was viewed at the time as a likely stimulus to cabinet and party renewal.

Renewal and a new look in government were very much his themes from the moment he took office. The October 1986 election, in which his party won a record majority, helped him in this process, for it meant a Legislature with twelve new seats, and the retirement prior to voting of a good many veteran M.L.A.s from both sides of the House. Thirty-nine individuals were elected to the Legislature for the first time. His post-election Cabinet, sworn in on November 6, 1986, contained seven new ministers (five of which were first-term M.L.A.s) out of a total of eighteen members — two fewer than in Bill Bennett's last Cabinet.

As a new premier, he emphasized the commitment to open government by televising the Legislature and reactivating its committees. In this vein, one of his innovations was to begin appearing regularly on radio and T.V. "call-in" shows. Highly reminiscent of former premierships on the other hand were his vigorous endorsement of the case for "better terms" for B.C. and his trips to Ottawa in pursuit of this goal. While he played a major role during his interim administration in settling a long-standing collective bargaining dispute with the

civil service, the outstanding domestic problem in B.C. in the fall of 1986, a forest industry strike, largely played itself out without any effective intervention on his part. He did get involved in a complex set of negotiations at that time concerning the prospect of an American countervailing duty on Canadian softwood lumber exports. In that process, he briefly sparked a considerable controversy when he publicly forecast the emergence of a viable response to this threat. The response duly emerged and in time was adopted, but it involved federal government action and a delicate bargain which, at the time when Vander Zalm made his announcement, Ottawa had not yet agreed to. At this point those Vander Zalm critics who are sure that he will destroy himself believed (or hoped) for a few days that the process had begun, but the excitement passed, and the compromise agreed to may indeed have been the best available.

An innovation in his early premiership was his expressed desire to consult and share confidences with the opposition — a move welcomed by, amongst others, quite a few legislators long disturbed by the antagonism between David Barrett and Bill Bennett which had forestalled such co-operation. The premier gave early indication of an intent to be a policy initiator. In candid expressions of his personal views on such issues as the case against sanctions on South Africa, abortion, and legalized gambling, as well as in some open qualification of policy positions announced by cabinet colleagues, he also gave proof of his intent to remain quite uninhibited.

It is still too soon to label with any precision the mix of continuity and change which ultimately will characterize his premiership. While, in early years at least, it may well be constrained by a severe shortfall in revenue, odds are that it will produce its share of surprises. One surprise already has been the emergence of some echoes of the David Barrett premiership. On present indication, both men share the distinction of having been by far the most newsworthy members of their respective Cabinets, and of possessing a capacity to ensure that life in this province will never be dull.

Notes

1. Barnard, *Functions of the Executive,* p.288.

2. Young and Morley, "The Premier and the Cabinet," p.54.

3. Ormsby, "T. Dufferin Pattullo and the Little New Deal," pp.533-554.

4. See Sutherland, "T.D. Pattullo as a Party Leader," pp.39-41; Alper, "From Rule to Ruin: the Conservative Party of British Columbia, 1928-54," p.159; Abbott, "The Formation of the Liberal-Conservative Coalition in 1941."

5. *B.C. Economic Accounts, 1971-1984.* pp.2-3.

6. Minister of Finance, B.C., "The Economy in a Changing World," March, 1985, p.14.

7. Mitchell, *W.A.C. Bennett and the Rise of British Columbia,* p.150.

8. Young, "Stability and Change," p.17.

9. Young, "Stability and Change," p.38.

10. *British Columbia in the Canadian Confederation,* Parts I, II, VII.

11. Swainson, *Conflict over the Columbia,* p.358.

12. Ruff, "B.C. and Canadian Federalism," p.301.

13. Mitchell, *W.A.C. Bennett and the Rise of British Columbia,* pp.443-446.

14. Smith, "Prairie Revolt, Federalism and the Party System," p.200.

15. Wilson, "The Legislature," p.41.

16. Kavic and Nixon, *The 1200 Days,* p.179.

17. Young and Morley, "The Premier and the Cabinet," p.68.

18. Gamey, "Government-Media Relations: Bennett-Barrett-Bennett," p.4.

19. Garr, *Tough Guy,* pp.83-84.

20. Wildavsky, "The Three Cultures," pp.49-56.

21. Ministry of Finance, B.C., *Financial and Economic Review,* October, 1983, p.115; August, 1986, pp.10-11.

APPENDIX

Canadian Prime Ministers and Premiers, to Date

PRIME MINISTERS

		From	To
1.	Rt. Hon. Sir John A. Macdonald (Conservative)	July 1, 1867	Nov. 5, 1873
2.	Hon. Alexander Mackenzie (Liberal)	Nov. 7, 1873	Oct. 16, 1878
3.	Rt. Hon. Sir John A. Macdonald (Conservative)	Oct. 17, 1878	June 6, 1891
4.	Hon. Sir John J. Abbott (Conservative)	June 16, 1891	Nov. 24, 1892
5.	Rt. Hon. Sir John S.D. Thompson (Conservative)	Dec. 5, 1892	Dec. 12, 1894
6.	Hon. Sir Mackenzie Bowell (Conservative)	Dec. 21, 1894	April 27, 1896
7.	Rt. Hon. Sir Charles Tupper (Conservative)	May 1, 1896	July 8, 1896
8.	Rt. Hon. Sir Wilfrid Laurier (Liberal)	July 11, 1896	Oct. 6, 1911
9.	Rt. Hon. Sir Robert L. Borden (Conservative Administration)	Oct. 10, 1911	Oct. 12, 1917
10.	Rt. Hon. Sir Robert L. Borden (Unionist Administration)	Oct. 12, 1917	July 10, 1920
11.	Rt. Hon. Arthur Meighen (Unionist "National Liberal and Conservative Party")	July 10, 1920	Dec. 29, 1921
12.	Rt. Hon. William Lyon Mackenzie King (Liberal)	Dec. 29, 1921	June 28, 1926
13.	Rt. Hon. Arthur Meighen (Conservative)	June 29, 1926	Sept. 25, 1926
14.	Rt. Hon. William Lyon Mackenzie King (Liberal)	Sept. 25, 1926	Aug. 6, 1930
15.	Rt. Hon. Richard Bedford Bennett (Conservative) (Became Viscount Bennett, 1941)	Aug. 7, 1930	Oct. 23, 1935
16.	Rt. Hon. William Lyon Mackenzie King (Liberal)	Oct. 23, 1935	Nov. 15, 1948
17.	Rt. Hon. Louis Stephen St. Laurent (Liberal)	Nov. 15, 1948	June 21, 1957
18.	Rt. Hon. John G. Diefenbaker (Progressive Conservative)	June 21, 1957	April 22, 1963
19.	Rt. Hon. Lester Bowles Pearson (Liberal)	April 22, 1963	April 20, 1968
20.	Rt. Hon. Pierre Elliott Trudeau (Liberal)	April 20, 1968	June 4, 1979
21.	Rt. Hon. Charles Joseph Clark (Progressive Conservative)	June 4, 1979	Mar. 3, 1980
22.	Rt. Hon. Pierre Elliott Trudeau (Liberal)	Mar. 3, 1980	June 30, 1984
23.	Rt. Hon. John Napier Turner (Liberal)	June 30, 1984	Sept. 17, 1984
24.	Rt. Hon. Martin Brian Mulroney (Progressive Conservative)	Sept. 17, 1984	

(Numbers 2, 4, 6, 20, 21 not members of U.K. Privy Council)

PREMIERS

Alberta

		From	*To*
1.	Hon. Alex. Rutherford (L)	02-09-1905	26-05-1910
2.	Hon. A.L. Sifton (L)	26-05-1910	30-10-1917
3.	Hon. Charles Stewart (L)	30-10-1917	13-08-1921
4.	Hon. Herbert Greenfield (UFA)	13-08-1921	23-11-1925
5.	Hon. John Edward Brownlee (UFA)	-11-1925	10-07-1934
6.	Hon. Richard Gavin Reid (UFA)	10-07-1934	03-09-1935
7.	Hon. William Aberhart (SC)	03-09-1935	23-05-1943
8.	Hon. E.C. Manning (SC)	31-05-1943	12-12-1968
9.	Hon. H.E. Strom (SC)	12-12-1968	10-09-1971
10.	Hon. E. Peter Lougheed (PC)	10-09-1971	01-11-1985
11.	Hon. Donald Getty (PC)	01-11-1985	

Source: For the tables on premiers, the source is *The Canadian Parliamentary Guide,* ed. Pierre G. Normandin, Ottawa, 1987.

British Columbia

		From	To
1.	Hon. J.F. McCreight	-12-1871	23-12-1872
2.	Hon. A. DeCosmos	23-12-1872	11-02-1874
3.	Hon. G.A. Walkem	11-02-1874	27-01-1876
4.	Hon. A.C. Elliott	01-02-1876	25-06-1878
5.	Hon. G.A. Walkem	26-06-1878	12-06-1882
6.	Hon. R. Beaven	13-06-1882	10-01-1883
7.	Hon. W. Smithe	28-01-1883	29-03-1887
8.	Hon. A.E.B. Davie	01-04-1887	-08-1889
9.	Hon. J. Robson	03-08-1889	-06-1892
10.	Hon. T. Davie	02-07-1892	-03-1895
11.	Hon. J.H. Turner	04-03-1895	08-08-1898
12.	Hon. C.A. Semlin	12-08-1898	27-02-1900
13.	Hon. Jos. Martin	28-02-1900	14-06-1900
14.	Hon. J. Dunsmuir	15-06-1900	21-11-1902
15.	Hon. E.G. Prior	21-11-1902	01-06-1903
16.	Hon. R. McBride	01-06-1903	15-12-1915
17.	Hon. Wm. J. Bowser	15-12-1915	23-11-1916
18.	Hon. Harlan C. Brewster	23-11-1916	01-03-1918
19.	Hon. John Olivier	06-03-1918	17-08-1927
20.	Hon. John Duncan MacLean (L.)	20-08-1927	20-08-1928
21.	Hon. Simon Fraser Tolmie (C.)	21-08-1928	15-11-1933
22.	Hon. T.D. Pattullo (L.)	15-11-1933	09-12-1941
23.	Hon. John Hart (Coalition)	10-12-1941	27-12-1947
24.	Hon. Byron Johnson (Coalition)	29-12-1947	01-08-1952
25.	Hon. William Andrew Cecil Bennett (SC)	01-08-1952	30-08-1972
26.	Hon. David Barrett (N.D.P.)	30-08-1972	11-12-1975
27.	Hon. William Richards Bennett (SC)	11-12-1975	06-08-1986
28.	Hon. William N. Vander Zalm (SC)	06-08-1986	

Manitoba

		From	*To*
1.	Hon. A. Boyd	16-09-1870	14-12-1871
2.	Hon. M.A. Girard	14-12-1871	14-03-1872
3.	Hon. H.J.H. Clarke	14-03-1872	08-07-1874
4.	Hon. M.A. Girard	08-07-1874	02-12-1874
5.	Hon. R.A. Davis	03-12-1874	16-10-1878
6.	Hon. John Norquay	16-10-1878	24-12-1887
7.	Hon. D.H. Harrison	26-12-1887	19-01-1888
8.	Hon. T. Greenway	19-01-1888	06-01-1900
9.	Hon. H.J. Macdonald	08-01-1900	29-10-1900
10.	The Hon. Sir R.P. Roblin (C)	29-10-1900	12-05-1915
11.	The Hon. T.C. Norris	12-05-1915	08-12-1922
12.	The Hon. John Bracken (UF)	08-08-1922	08-01-1943
13.	The Hon. S.S. Garson (Coal)	08-01-1943	07-11-1948
14.	The Hon. D.L. Campbell (Coal)	07-11-1948	16-06-1958
15.	The Hon. Dufferin Roblin (PC)	16-06-1958	25-11-1967
16.	The Hon. Walter Weir (PC)	25-11-1967	15-07-1969
17.	The Hon. Edward Schreyer (NDP)	15-07-1969	24-11-1977
18.	The Hon. Sterling R. Lyon (PC)	24-11-1977	17-11-1982
19.	The Hon. Howard Russell Pawley (NDP)	17-11-1982	

New Brunswick

		From	*To*
1.	Hon. A.R. Wetmore (CF)	1867	1870
2.	Hon. G.E. King (C)	1870	1871
3.	Hon. George Hathaway (C)	1871	1872
4.	Hon. G.E. King (C)	1872	1878
5.	Hon. J.J. Fraser (C)	1878	1882
6.	Hon. D.L. Hannington (C)	1882	1883
7.	Hon. A.G. Blair (L)	1883	07-1896
8.	Hon. Jas. Mitchell (L)	07-1896	29-10-1897
9.	Hon. H.R. Emmerson (L)	29-10-1897	31-08-1900
10.	Hon. L.J. Tweedie (L)	31-08-1900	02-03-1907
11.	Hon. Wm. Pugsley (L)	06-03-1907	15-04-1907
12.	Hon. C.W. Robinson (L)	31-05-1907	20-03-1908
13.	Hon. J.D. Hazen (C)	24-03-1908	10-10-1911
14.	Hon. James K. Flemming (C)	16-10-1911	06-12-1914
15.	Hon. George J. Clarke (C)	17-12-1914	01-02-1917
16.	Hon. James A. Murray (C)	01-02-1917	04-04-1917
17.	Hon. Walter E. Foster (L)	04-04-1917	01-02-1923
18.	Hon. Peter J. Veniot (L)	28-02-1923	10-09-1925
19.	Hon. John B.M. Baxter (C)	14-09-1925	18-05-1931
20.	Hon. Chas. D. Richards (C)	19-05-1931	30-05-1933
21.	Hon. L.P.D. Tilley (C)	01-06-1933	14-07-1935
22.	Hon. A. Allison Dysart (L)	16-07-1935	13-03-1940
23.	Hon. J.B. McNair (L)	13-03-1940	08-10-1952
24.	Hon. H.J. Flemming (PC)	08-10-1952	12-07-1960
25.	Hon. Louis J. Robichard (L)	12-07-1960	12-11-1970
26.	Hon. Richard B. Hatfield (PC)	12-11-1970	27-10-1987
27.	Hon. Frank McKenna (L)	27-10-1987	

Newfoundland & Labrador

		From	To
1.	Hon. Joseph R. Smallwood, PC (Lib)	01-04-1949	18-01-1972
2.	Hon. Frank Duff Moores (PC)	18-01-1972	26-03-1979
3.	Hon. A. Brian Peckford (PC)	26-03-1979	

Ontario

		From	To
1.	Hon. J.S. Macdonald (Coal.)	16-07-1867	19-12-1871
2.	Hon. E. Blake (L.)	20-12-1871	25-10-1872
3.	Hon. O. Mowat (L.)	25-10-1872	09-07-1896
4.	Hon. A.S. Hardy (L.)	25-07-1896	17-10-1899
5.	Hon. G.W. Ross (L.)	21-10-1899	07-02-1905
6.	Hon. Sir J.P. Whitney (C.)	08-02-1905	25-09-1914
7.	Hon. Sir William Howard Hearst (C.)	02-10-1914	14-11-1919
8.	Hon. Ernest Charles Drury (U.F.)	14-11-1919	16-07-1923
9.	Hon. G.H. Ferguson (C.)	16-07-1923	15-12-1930
10.	Hon. G.S. Henry (C.)	15-12-1930	10-07-1934
11.	Hon. M.F. Hepburn (L.)	10-07-1934	21-10-1942
12.	Hon. G.D. Conant (L.)	21-10-1942	18-05-1943
13.	Hon. H.C. Nixon (L.)	18-05-1943	17-08-1943
14.	Hon. George A. Drew (P.C.)	17-08-1943	19-10-1948
15.	Hon. T.L. Kennedy (P.C.)	19-10-1948	05-1949
16.	Hon. Leslie Frost (P.C.)	04-05-1949	08-11-1961
17.	Hon. John P. Robarts (P.C.)	08-11-1961	01-03-1971
18.	Hon. Wm. G. Davis (P.C.)	01-03-1971	08-02-1985
19.	Hon. Frank S. Miller (P.C.)	08-02-1985	26-06-1985
20.	Hon. David Peterson (L)	26-06-1985	

Prince Edward Island

		From	*To*
1.	Hon. J.C. Pope (C.)	04-1873	09-1873
2.	Hon. L.C. Owen (C.)	09-1873	08-1876
3.	Hon. L.H. Davies, Q.C.-C.R., (L.)	08-1876	25-04-1879
4.	Hon. W.W. Sullivan, Q.C.-C.R., (C.)	25-04-1879	11-1889
5.	Hon. N. McLeod, Q.C.-C.R., (C.)	11-1889	04-1891
6.	Hon. F. Peters, Q.C.-C.R., (L.)	27-04-1891	10-1897
7.	Hon. A.B. Warburton, Q.C.-C.R., (L.)	10-1897	01-08-1898
8.	Hon. D. Farquharson (L.)	08-1898	27-12-1901
9.	Hon. A. Peters, K.C.-C.R., (L.)	29-12-1901	29-01-1908
10.	Hon. F.L. Haszard, K.C.-C.R., (L.)	01-02-1908	16-05-1911
11.	Hon. H. James Palmer, K.C.-C.R., (L.)	16-05-1911	02-12-1911
12.	Hon. John A. Mathieson, K.C.-C.R., (C.)	02-12-1911	21-06-1917
13.	Hon. Aubin E. Arsenault, K.C.-C.R., (C.)	21-06-1917	09-09-1919
14.	Hon. J.H. Bell, K.C.-C.R., (L.)	09-09-1919	05-09-1923
15.	Hon. James D. Stewart, K.C.-C.R., (C.)	05-09-1923	12-08-1927
16.	Hon. Albert C. Saunders, K.C.-C.R., (L.)	12-08-1927	20-05-1930
17.	Hon. Walter M. Lea (L.)	20-05-1930	29-08-1931
18.	Hon. James D. Stewart, K.C.-C.R., (C.)	29-08-1931	10-10-1933
19.	Hon. William J.P. MacMillan, M.D., C.M., F.A.C.S., (C.)	14-10-1933	15-08-1935
20.	Hon. Walter M. Lea, (L.)	15-08-1935	10-01-1936
21.	Hon. Thane A. Campbell, K.C.-C.R., M.A., (L.)	14-01-1936	11-05-1943
22.	Hon. J. Walter Jones (L.)	11-05-1943	25-05-1953
23.	Hon. Alexander W. Matheson (L.)	25-05-1953	16-09-1959
24.	Hon. Walter R. Shaw (P.C.)	16-09-1959	28-07-1966
25.	Hon. Alexander B. Campbell (L.)	28-07-1966	18-09-1978
26.	Hon. W. Bennett Campbell (L.)	18-09-1978	03-05-1979
27.	Hon. J. Angus MacLean, P.C. (PC)	03-05-1979	17-11-1981
28.	Hon. James M. Lee (PC)	17-11-1981	02-05-1986
29.	Hon. Joseph A. Ghiz (L)	02-05-1986	

Quebec

		From	*To*
1.	Hon. P.J. Chauveau (C.)	15-07-1867	21-02-1873
2.	Hon. G. Ouimet (C.)	26-02-1873	02-09-1874
3.	Hon. C.E.B. de Boucherville (C.)	08-09-1874	07-03-1878
4.	Hon. H.G. Joly (L.) de Lotbinière	08-03-1878	30-10-1879
5.	Hon. J.A. Chapleau (C.)	30-10-1879	05-07-1882
6.	Hon. J.A. Mousseau (C.)	31-07-1882	01-01-1884
7.	Hon. J.J. Ross (C.)	23-01-1884	01-1887
8.	Hon. L.O. Taillon (C.)	25-01-1887	27-01-1887
9.	Hon. H. Mercier (L.)	27-01-1887	16-12-1891
10.	Hon. C.E.B. de Boucherville (C.)	21-12-1891	16-12-1892
11.	Hon. L.O. Taillon (C.)	16-12-1892	01-05-1896
12.	Hon. E.J. Flynn (C.)	12-05-1896	26-05-1897
13.	Hon. F.G. Marchand (L.)	26-05-1897	25-09-1900
14.	Hon. S.N. Parent (L.)	03-10-1900	20-03-1905
15.	Hon. Sir L. Gouin (L.)	23-03-1905	08-07-1920
16.	Hon. Louis Alexandre Taschereau (L.)	08-07-1920	11-06-1936
17.	Hon. Adélard Godbout (L.)	11-06-1936	26-08-1936
18.	Hon. Maurice Duplessis (U.N.)	26-08-1936	08-11-1939
19.	Hon. J.A. Godbout (L.)	09-11-1939	29-08-1944
20.	Hon. Maurice Duplessis (U.N.)	30-08-1944	07-09-1959
21.	Hon. J.P. Sauvé (U.N.)	11-09-1959	02-01-1960
22.	Hon. Antonio Barrette (U.N.)	08-01-1960	15-06-1960
23.	Hon. Jean Lesage (L.)	22-06-1960	05-06-1966
24.	Hon. Daniel Johnson (U.N.)	05-06-1966	26-09-1968
25.	Hon. J. Jacques Bertrand (U.N.)	02-10-1968	29-04-1970
26.	Hon. Robert Bourassa (L.)	29-04-1970	25-11-1976
27.	Hon. René Lévesque (PQ)	25-11-1976	03-10-1985
28.	Hon. Pierre-Marc Johnson (PQ)	03-10-1985	02-11-1985
29.	Hon. Robert Bourassa (L)	02-11-1985	

Saskatchewan

		From	*To*
1.	Hon. Walter Scott (L.)	05-09-1905	19-10-1916
2.	Hon. W.M. Martin (L.)	20-10-1916	05-04-1922
3.	Hon. C.A. Dunning (L.)	05-04-1922	26-02-1926
4.	Hon. James G. Gardiner (L.)	26-02-1926	09-09-1929
5.	Hon. J.T.M. Anderson (C.)	09-09-1929	19-07-1934
6.	Hon. James G. Gardiner (L.)	19-07-1934	01-11-1935
7.	Hon. William J. Paterson (L.)	01-11-1935	10-07-1944
8.	Hon. Thos. C. Douglas (C.C.F.)	10-07-1944	07-11-1961
9.	Hon. W.S. Lloyd (N.D.P.-C.C.F.)	07-11-1961	22-05-1964
10.	Hon. W. Ross Thatcher (L.)	22-05-1964	30-06-1971
11.	Hon. A.E. Blakeney (N.D.P.)	30-06-1971	08-05-1982
12.	Hon. D.G. Devine (PC)	08-05-1982	

Nova Scotia

		From	*To*
1.	Hon. H. Blanchard (C)	04-07-1867	07-11-1867
2.	Hon. Wm. Annand (L)	07-11-1867	11-05-1875
3.	Hon. P.C. Hill (L)	11-05-1875	22-10-1878
4.	Hon. S.H. Holmes (C)	22-10-1878	25-05-1882
5.	Hon. J.S.D. Thompson (C)	25-05-1882	03-08-1882
6.	Hon. W.T. Pipes (L)	03-08-1882	28-07-1884
7.	Hon. W.S. Fielding (L)	28-07-1884	20-07-1896
8.	Hon. Geo. H. Murray (L)	20-07-1896	24-01-1923
9.	Hon. Ernest Howard Armstrong (L)	24-01-1923	16-07-1925
10.	Hon. Edgar N. Rhodes (C)	16-07-1925	11-08-1930
11.	Col. The Hon. Gordon S. Harrington (C)	11-08-1930	05-09-1933
12.	Hon. Angus L. Macdonald (L)	05-09-1933	10-07-1940
13.	Hon. A.S. MacMillan (L)	10-07-1940	08-09-1945
14.	Hon. A.L. Macdonald (L)	08-09-1945	13-04-1954
15.	Hon. Harold Connolly (L)	13-04-1954	30-09-1954
16.	Hon. Henry D. Hicks (L)	30-09-1954	20-11-1956
17.	Hon. Robert L. Stanfield (PC)	20-11-1956	26-09-1967
18.	Hon. George I. Smith (PC)	26-09-1967	27-10-1970
19.	Hon. Gerald A. Regan (L)	27-10-1970	05-10-1978
20.	Hon. John M. Buchanan (PC)	05-10-1978	

Sources Cited

Abbott, G.M. "The Formation of the Liberal-Conservative Coalition in 1941." Master's thesis, University of Victoria, 1978.

Adorno, Theodor W., et al. *The Authoritarian Personality.* New York: Harper and Row, 1950.

Alexander, David G. *Atlantic Canada and Confederation: Essays in Canadian Political Economy.* Toronto: University of Toronto Press, 1983.

Alford, R.R., and R. Friedland. *Powers of Theory: Capitalism, the State and Democracy.* Cambridge: Cambridge University Press, 1985.

Alper, Donald K. "From Rule to Ruin: the Conservative Party of British Columbia, 1928-1954." Ph.D. dissertation, University of British Columbia, 1976.

Armstrong, Christopher. "Ceremonial Parties: Federal-Provincial Meetings Before the Second World War." In *National Politics and Community in Canada,* edited by R. Kenneth Carty and W. Peter Ward. Vancouver: University of British Columbia, 1986.

———. *The Politics of Federalism: Ontario's Relations with the Federal Government, 1867-1942.* Toronto: University of Toronto Press, 1981.

Assimopoulos, N., et al. *La transformation du pouvoir au Québec.* Montréal: Editions Albert Saint-Martin, 1980.

Atkinson, Max. *Our Masters' Voices.* London: Methuen, 1984.

Atwood, Margaret. *Survival.* Toronto: Anansi, 1972.

Aucoin, Peter. "Organizational Change in the Machinery of Canadian Government: From Rational Management to Brokerage Politics." *Canadian Journal of Political Science* 19 (March 1986): 3-28.

Aucoin, Peter, and Herman Bakvis. "Regional Responsiveness and Government Organization: The Case of Regional Economic Development in Canada." In *Regional Responsiveness and the National Administrative State,* edited by Peter Aucoin, 51-118. Toronto: University of Toronto Press for the Royal Commission of the Economic Union and Development Prospects for Canada, 1985.

Aucoin, Peter, and Richard D. French. *Knowledge, Power and Public Policy.* Ottawa: Science Council of Canada, 1974.

Baccigalupo, A. *Les grands rouages de la machine administrative québécoise.* Montréal: Editions d'Arc, 1978.

Banting, Keith. *The Welfare State and Canadian Federalism.* Montreal and Kingston: McGill-Queen's University Press, 1982.

Barber, James David. *The Presidential Character: Predicting Performance in the White House.* Englewood Cliffs, N.J.: Prentice-Hall, 1972.

Barnard, C.I. *The Functions of the Executive.* Cambridge: Harvard University Press, 1962.

Bashevkin, Sylvia. *Toeing the Line: Women and Party Politics in English Canada.* Toronto: University of Toronto Press, 1985.

Beck, J.M. and D.J. Dooley. "Party Images in Canada." In *Party Politics in Canada,* edited by Hugh A. Thorburn. Toronto: Prentice-Hall, 1963.

Beck, Murray. "An Atlantic Region Political Culture: A Chimera." Paper presented at the Western Canadian/Atlantic Canada Studies Conferences, Calgary, February 1978, and Fredericton N.B., April 1978.

———. "Elections." In *The Provincial Political Systems,* edited by David J. Bellamy, Jon H. Pammett, and Donald C. Rowat. Toronto: Methuen, 1976.

Behiels, M.D. *Prelude to Quebec's Quiet Revolution.* Montreal and Kingston: McGill-Queen's University Press, 1985.

Bélanger, A.-J. *L'apolitisme des idéologies québécoises.* Québec. Les Presses de l'Université Laval, 1974.

Bellamy, David J. "The Atlantic Provinces." In *The Provincial Political Systems,* edited By David J. Bellamy, Jon H. Pammett, and Donald C. Rowat. Toronto: Methuen, 1976.

Bendix, R. *Kings or People: Power and the Mandate to Rule.* Berkeley and Los Angeles: University of California Press, 1978.

Benjamin, J. *Comment on fabrique un premier ministre de la machine administrative québécoise.* Montréal: Editions d'Arc, 1978.

Bergeron, G. *Notre miroir à deux faces.* Montréal: Editions Québec-Amérique, 1985.

Bernard, J.P. *Les rébellions de 1837-1838.* Montréal: Boréal Express, 1983.

Bernier, G. "Le Parti Patriote, 1827-1838." In *Personnel et partis politiques au Québec,* edited by V. Lemieux, 207-229. Montréal: Boréal Express, 1982.

Binington, H. "Review Article: The Fiery Chariot: British Prime Ministers and the Search for Love." *British Journal of Political Science* 4, no. 3 (1974): 345-369.

Black, C. *Duplessis.* Toronto: McClelland and Stewart, 1976.

Black, E.R. "The Progressive Conservative Party in British Columbia: Some Aspects of Organization." Master's thesis, University of British Columbia, 1960.

Blondel, J. *World Leaders: Heads of Government in the Post-war Period.* Beverly Hills: Sage Publications, 1980.

Boily, R. "Les hommes politiques du Québec, 1867-1967." *Revue d'histoire de l'Amérique française* 21, no. 3a (1967): 626.

Boismenu, G. *Le Duplessime: Une biographie politique de Maurice Duplessis.* Montréal: Les Presses de l'Université de Montreal, 1981.

Borden, Henry, ed. *Letters to Limbo.* Toronto: University of Toronto Press, 1971.

Bothwell, Robert. "'The Canadian connection': Canada and Europe." In *Foremost Nation: Canadian Foreign Policy and a Changing World,* edited by Norman Hiller and Garth Stevenson. Toronto: McClelland and Stewart, 1977.

Bothwell, Robert, and W. Kilbourn. C.D. Howe: A Biography. Toronto: McClelland and Stewart, 1979.

Boudreau, Joseph A. *Alberta, Aberhart and Social Credit.* Toronto: Holt, Rinehart and Winston, 1975.

Bourassa, G. "Les élites politiques de Montréal: de l'aristocratie á la bureaucratie." In *Personnel et partis politiques au Québec,* edited by V. Lemieux, 255-276. Montreal: Boréal Express, 1982.

Bourassa, R. *Le défi technologique.* Montréal: Québec-Amérique, 1985.

———. *L'énergie du Nord.* Montréal: Editions Québec-Amérique, 1985.

Brand, Cynthia W. "Recruitment of deputy and associate deputy ministers in the NDP Government in British Columbia." Master's thesis, Queen's University, 1975.

Brecher, Michael. *The Foreign Policy System of Israel: Setting, Images and Process.* London: Oxford University Press, 1972.

British Columbia, Minister of Finance. "The Economy in a Changing World." Victoria: March 1985.

Brodie, Fawn. *Thomas Jefferson: An Intimate History.* New York: W.W. Norton, 1974.

Bromke, Adam, and Kim Richard Nossal. "Trudeau rides the 'third rail'." *International Perspectives* (May/June 1984).

Brown, Patrick, Robert Chodos, and Rae Murphy. *Winners, Losers: The 1976 Tory Leadership Convention.* Toronto: James Lorimer, 1976.

Brown, Robert Craig. *Robert Laird Borden: A Biography.* 2 vols. Toronto: Macmillan, 1975, 1980.

———. *Canada's National Policy, 1883-1900.* Princeton: Princeton University Press, 1964.

Browne, G.P., ed. *Documents on the Confederation of British North America.* Toronto: McClelland and Stewart, 1969.

Brownstone, M. "The Douglas-Lloyd Governments: Innovation and Bureaucratic Adaptation." In *Essays on the Left: Essays in Honour of T.C. Douglas,* edited by Laurier LaPierre, et al. Toronto: McClelland and Stewart, 1971.

Brunet, Michel. "Trois dominantes de la pensée canadienne-française: l'agriculturisme, l'antiétatisme et le messianisme." In *La présence anglaise et les Canadiens,* edited by M. Brunet, 113-166. Montréal: Beauchemin, 1964.

Bunce, Valerie. *Do New Leaders Make a Difference? Executive Succession and Public Policy Under Capitalism and Socialism.* Princeton: Princeton University Press, 1981.

Bureau, L. *Entre l'Eden et l'utopie.* Montréal: Editions Quebec-Amerique, 1984.

Burns, James MacGregor. *Leadership.* New York: Harper and Row, 1978.

Cadbury, George. "Planning in Saskatchewan." In *Essays on the Left: Essays in Honour of T.C. Douglas,* edited by Laurier LaPierre et al. Toronto: McClelland and Stewart, 1971.

Caldwell, G., and E. Waddell. *Les Anglophones du Québec: De majoritaires a minoritaires.* Montreal: Institut québécois de recherche sur la culture, 1982.

Cameron, David R. "The Expansion of the Public Economy: A Comparative Analysis." *American Political Science Review* 72 (December 1978): 1243-1261.

Campbell, Colin. *Governments Under Stress: Political Executives and Key Bureaucrats in Washington, London and Ottawa.* Toronto: University of Toronto Press, 1983.

Campbell, R.M. *Grand Illusions: The Politics of the Keynesian Experience in Canada 1945-1975.* Peterborough, Ont.: Broadview Press, 1987.

———. "The Diefenbaker Years Revisited: The Demise of the Keynesian Experience in Canada." *Journal of Canadian Studies* 18, no. 2 (Summer 1983): 106-131.

Careless, J.M.S., and R. Craig Brown, eds. *The Canadians, 1867-1961.* Toronto: Macmillan, 1967.

Carlyle, Thomas. *On Heroes, Hero-Worship, and the Heroic in History.* Edited by John Chester Adams. New York: Houghton Mifflin, 1907.

Castles, Francis G. "How Does Politics Matter?: Structure or Agency in the Determination of Public Policy Outcomes." *European Journal of Political Research* 9 (June 1981): 119-132.

Chandler, Marsha A., and William M. Chandler. *Public Policy and Provincial Politics.* Toronto: McGraw-Hill Ryerson, 1979.

Charbonneau, P. *Le projet québécois d'Honoré Mercier.* Saint-Jean-sur-Richelieu, Qué.: Editions Mille Roches, 1980.

Charron, C. *Désobéir.* Montréal: VLB Editeur, 1983.

Cheffins, R.I., and P.A. Johnson. *The Revised Canadian Constitution.* Toronto: McGraw-Hill Ryerson, 1986.

Chrétien, Jean. *Straight From The Heart.* Toronto: Key Porter Books, 1985.

Christian, William, and Colin Campbell. *Political Parties and and Ideologies in Canada.* 2nd ed. Toronto: McGraw-Hill Ryerson, 1983.

Christie, Alan. "Peterson's Aides: The Weaning is Over." *Toronto Star* 11 January 1986.

Clark, Kenneth B. "The pathos of power: A psychological perspective." *American Psychologist* 26 (1971).

Clark, Ian D. "Recent Changes in the Cabinet Decision-Making System in Ottawa." *Canadian Public Administration* 28 (1985): 185-201.

Clarke, Harold D., et al. *Political Choice in Canada.* Toronto: McGraw-Hill Ryerson, 1980.

Clarkson, Stephen. *Canada and the Reagan Challenge.* Toronto: Canadian Institute for Economic Policy, 1982.

Clift, D., and S.M. Arnopoulos. *Le fait anglais au Québec.* Montréal: Libre expression, 1979.

Clouscard, M. *Le capitalisme de la seduction.* Paris: Editions sociales, 1981.

Cocking, Clive. *Following the Leaders: A Media Watcher's Diary of Campaign '79.* Toronto: Doubleday Canada, 1980.

Cohen, Andrew. "Fish Dispute Turns Focus on Province's Discontent." *Financial Post* (Toronto), 16 February 1987.

Coleman, W.D. *The Independence Movement in Quebec, 1945-1980.* Toronto: University of Toronto Press, 1984.

Collison, Robert. "True Grit." *Toronto,* a magazine supplement to the *The Globe and Mail* (Toronto), September 1986.

Comber, Mary Anne, and Robert Mayne. *The Newsmongers: How the Media Distort the Political News.* Toronto: McClelland and Stewart, 1986.

Cook, Ramsay. *Provincial Autonomy, Minority Rights and the Compact Theory, 1867-1921.* Studies of the Royal Commission on Bilingualism and Biculturalism, No. 4. Ottawa: Queen's Printer, 1969.

Copps, Sheila. *Nobody's Baby.* Toronto: Deneau, 1986.

Courtney, John. "Prime Ministerial Character: An Examination of Mackenzie King's political leadership." *Canadian Journal of Political Science* 9, no. 1 (March 1976): 77-100.

———. *The Selection of National Party Leaders in Canada.* Toronto: Macmillan, 1973.

———, ed. *The Canadian House of Commons.* Calgary: The University of Calgary Press, 1985.

Creighton, Donald. *Towards the Discovery of Canada.* Toronto: Macmillan, 1972.

———. *John A. Macdonald: The Old Chieftain.* Toronto: Macmillan, 1955.

———. *John A. Macdonald: The Young Politician.* Toronto: Macmillan, 1952.

Cronin, Thomas. *The State of the Presidency.* Boston: Little, Brown and Company, 1980.

Crossman, Richard H.S. *The Myths of Cabinet Government.* Cambridge: Harvard University Press, 1972.

Dafoe, John. *Laurier: A Study in Canadian Politics.* Toronto: Thomas Allen, 1922.

Daignault, R. *Lesage.* Montréal: Libre Expression, 1981.

D'Aquino, Thomas. "The Prime Minister's Office: Catalyst or Cabal?" *Canadian Public Administration* 17 (Spring 1974).

Davey, Keith. *The Rainmaker: A Passion For Politics.* Toronto: Stoddart, 1986.

David, H. "La grève et le Bon Dieu." *Sociologie et société* 7, no. 1 (1975): 249-275.

Debord, G. *Society of the Spectacle.* Detroit: Black and Red, 1970.

Dechêne, L. *Habitants et marchands de Montréal au XVIIe siècle.* Paris: Plon, 1974.

Dery, David. *Problem Definition in Policy Analysis.* Lawrence, Kan.: University Press of Kansas, 1984.

Desbarats, P. *René: A Canadian in Search of a Country.* Toronto: McClelland and Stewart, 1976.

Descrochers, F. *Les remaniements ministériels au Québec.* Master's thesis, Department of Political Science, McGill University, 1987.

de Tocqueville, Alexis. *Democracy in America.* Vol. I, edited by Phillips Bradley. New York: Random House, 1945.

Dewitt, David B., and John J. Kirton. *Canada as a Principal Power.* Toronto: John Wiley, 1983.

Diamond, S. "Le Canada français au XVIIIe siècle: une société préfabriquée." *Annales* 16, no. 2 (1961): 317-353.

Dion, Leon. "The Concept of Political Leadership: An Analysis." *Canadian Journal of Political Science* 1, no. 1 (1968): 1-17.

Dobell, Peter C. *Canada and World Affairs, 1971-73.* Canada and World Affairs Series, Vol. 17. Toronto: Canadian Insitute of International Affairs, 1985.

Doern, G. Bruce. "The Politics of Canadian Economic Policy: An Overview." In *The Politics of Economic Policy,* edited by G. Bruce Doern, 1-109. Toronto: University of Toronto Press, 1985.

———. "The Policy-Making Philosophy of Prime Minister Trudeau and his Advisers." In *Apex of Power.* 2nd ed., edited by Thomas A. Hockin, 189-196. Scarborough, Ont.: Prentice-Hall, 1977.

———. "Recent Changes in the Philosophy of Policy Making in Canada." *Canadian Journal of Political Science* 4 (1971): 243-63.

———. "The Development of Policy Organizations in the Executive Arena." In *The Structures of Policy-Making in Canada,* edited by G. Bruce Doern and Peter Aucoin, 39-78. Toronto: Macmillan, 1971.

Doern, G. Bruce, and Peter Aucoin, eds. *Public Policy in Canada.* Toronto: Macmillan, 1979.

Doern, G. Bruce, and R.W. Phidd. *Canadian Public Policy: Ideas, Structures and Process.* Toronto: Methuen, 1983.

Dror, Yehezkel. "On Improving the Performance of Rulers." Paper presented at the annual meeting of the American Political Science Association, Chicago, 1983.

———. *Design for Policy Sciences.* New York: Elsevier, 1971.

Drouilly, P. *Le paradoxe canadien.* Montréal: Editions Parti Pris, 1979.

Dufresne, J., and J. Jacques, eds. *Crise et Leadership.* Montréal: Boréal Express, 1983.

Dunsire, Andrew. *The Execution Process.* Vol. 2. *Control In a Bureaucracy.* London: Martin Robertson, 1978.

Dupré, J. Stefan. "Reflections on the Workability of Executive Federalism." In *Intergovernmental Relations,* edited by Richard Simeon. Toronto: University of Toronto Press, 1985.

Dyck, Rand. *Provincial Politics in Canada.* Scarborough, Ont.: Prentice-Hall, 1986.

Dye, Thomas R. *Politics, Economic and the Public: Policy Outcomes in the American States.* Chicago: Rand-McNally, 1966.

Eager, Evelyn. *Saskatchewan Government: Politics and Pragmatism.* Saskatoon: Western Producer Prairie Books, 1980.

Eayrs, James. *In Defence of Canada.* 5 vols. Toronto: University of Toronto Press, 1964-1984.

———. "The Foreign Policy of Canada." In *Foreign Policies in a World of Change,* edited by Joseph E. Black and Kenneth W. Thompson. New York: Harper and Row, 1963.

———. *The Art of the Possible: Government and Foreign Policy in Canada.* Toronto: University of Toronto Press, 1961.

Edelman, Murray J. *The Symbolic Uses of Politics.* Urbana, Ill.: University of Illinois Press, 1964.

Edinger, Louis J. *Political Leadership in Industrial Societies.* Huntington, N.Y.: Robert E. Krieger, 1976.

———. "Editor's Introduction" In *Political Leadership in Industrialized Societies: Studies in Comparative Analysis,* edited by Louis J. Edinger, 1-25. Huntington, N.Y.: Robert E. Krieger, 1976.

———. "The Comparative Analysis of Political Leadership." *Comparative Politics* 7, no. 2 (1975): 253-369.

Eichmanis, J., and G. White. "Government by Other Means: Agencies, Boards and Commissions." In *The Government and Politics of Ontario.* 3rd ed., edited by Donald C. MacDonald. Toronto: Nelson, 1985.

Eisenstadt, S.N., and S. Rokkan, eds. *Building States and Nations.* Beverly Hills: Sage Publications, 1973.

England, Robert. *The Colonization of Western Canada.* London: P.S. King and Son, 1936.

English, J. "The French Lieutenant in Ottawa." In *National Politics and Community in Canada,* edited by R.K. Carty and W.P. Ward, 184-200. Vancouver: University of British Columbia Press, 1986.

Epstein, Edward Jay. *News From Nowhere.* New York: Vintage Books, 1973.

Erikson, Erik. *Gandhi's Truth: On the Origins of Militant Nonviolence.* New York: W.W. Norton, 1969.

———. *Young Man Luther: A Study in Psychoanalysis and History.* New York: W.W. Norton, 1958.

Esberey, Joy. "Prime ministerial character: An alternative view." *Canadian Journal of Political Science* 9, no. 1 (March 1976): 101-106.

Evans, Peter B., Dietrich Rueschemeyer, and Theda Skocpol, eds. *Bringing the State Back In.* Cambridge: Cambridge University Press, 1985.

Farrell, R. Barry. *The Making of Canadian Foreign Policy.* Scarborough, Ont.: Prentice-Hall, 1969.

Fecteau, J.-M. "Prolegomènes a une étude historique des rapports entre l'Etat et le droit dans la société québécoise, de la fin du XVIIIe siècle à la crise de 1929." *Sociologie et société* 18, no. 1 (1986): 129-138.

Finlay, John L. *Social Credit.* Montreal: McGill-Queen's University Press, 1972.

Fletcher, Frederick J. "The Contest for Media Attention: The 1979 and 1980 Federal Election Campaigns." In *Politics and the Media.* Toronto: Readers' Digest Foundation of Canada and Erindale College, University of Toronto, 1981.

———. "The Prime Minister as Public Persuader." In *Apex of Power.* 2nd ed., edited by Thomas A. Hockin. Scarborough, Ont.: Prentice-Hall, 1977.

Foucault, Michel. *Power/Knowledge: Selected Interviews and Other Writings, 1972-1977.* Edited by Colin Gordon. New York: Pantheon Books, 1980.

Fox, Paul. "Psychology, Politics, and Hegetology." *Canadian Journal of Political Science* 13, no. 4 (December 1980): 675-690.

———. "The Representative Nature of the Canadian Cabinet." In *Politics: Canada.* 3rd ed., edited by Paul Fox. Toronto: McGraw-Hill, 1970.

Fraser, Graham. "Learning How to Live With Gang of 10." *The Globe and Mail* (Toronto), 10 February 1987.

———. *P.Q.: René Lévesque and the Parti Quebecois in Power.* Toronto: Macmillan, 1984.

Frégault, G. "Politique et politiciens." In *Le XVIIIe siècle canadien,* 159-241. Montréal: Fides, 1968.

French, Orland. "Media Like a Tool That's Used." *Globe and Mail* 24 November 1986

French, Richard D. *How Ottawa Decides: Planning and Industrial Policy-Making, 1968-1984.* 2nd ed. Toronto: James Lorimer, 1984.

———. *How Ottawa Decides: Planning and Industrial Policy-Making 1968-1980.* Toronto: James Lorimer, 1980.

———. "The Privy Council Office: Support for Cabinet Decision-Making." In *The Canadian Political Process.* 2nd ed., edited by R. Schultz, et al. Toronto: Holt, Rinehart and Winston, 1979.

Freud, Sigmund, and William C. Bullitt. *Thomas Woodrow Wilson: A Psychological Study.* Boston: Houghton Mifflin, 1966.

Friesen, Gerald. *The Canadian Prairies: A History.* Toronto: University of Toronto Press, 1984.

Frizzell, Alan, and Anthony Westell. *The Canadian General Election of 1984.* Ottawa: Carleton University Press, 1985.

Fromm, Erich. *Escape From Freedom.* New York: Farrar and Rinehart, 1941.

Gamey, Carol. "Government-Media Relations: Bennett-Barrett-Bennett." B.C. Project Working Paper, University of Victoria, November 1980.

Garr, Allen. *Tough Guy: Bill Bennett and the Taking of British Columbia.* Toronto: Key Porter Books, 1985.

George, Alexander, and Juliette George. *Woodrow Wilson and Colonel House: A Personality Study.* New York: Dover, 1956.

Gibbins, Roger. *Conflict and Unity: An Introduction to Canadian Political Life.* Toronto: Methuen, 1985.

Gillies, J. *Facing Reality: Consultation, Consensus and Making Economic Policy.* Montreal: Institute for Research on Public Policy, 1986.

Globe and Mail (Toronto), 2 January 1980.

Goar, Carol. "Is Mulroney Era of 'National Reconciliation' Over?" *Toronto Star,* 10 February 1987.

Godin, P. *Daniel Johnson.* 2 vols. Montréal: Editions de l'Homme, 1980.

Gossage, Patrick. *Close To The Charisma: My Years Between the Press and Pierre Elliott Trudeau.* Toronto: McClelland and Stewart, 1986.

Gow, J. *Histoire de l'administration publique québécoise, 1867-1970.* Montréal: Les Presses de l'Université de Montréal, 1986.

Graham, Roger. "Charisma and Canadian Politics." In *Character and Circumstance: Essays in Honour of Donald Grant Creighton,* edited by John S. Moir. Toronto: Macmillan, 1970.

Graham, Ron. *One-Eyed Kings: Promise and Illusion in Canadian Politics.* Toronto: Collins, 1986.

Granatstein, J.L. *Canada's War: The Politics of the Mackenzie King Government, 1939-1945.* Toronto: Oxford University Press, 1978.

Gray, Charlotte. "The PM's office and the media square off." *Globe and Mail* (Toronto), 28 November 1986.

Greenstein, Fred. "The Impact of Personality on Politics: An Attempt to Clear Away Underbrush." *American Political Science Review* 81, no. 3 (September 1967): 633-34.

Gros d'Aillon, P. *Daniel Johnson: L'égalité avant l'indépendance.* Montréal: Stanke, 1979.

Groupe de recherche sociale. *Les préférences politiques des électeurs québécois en 1962.* Montréal: 1962.

―――. *Les électeurs québécois: Attitudes et opinions a la veille de l'élection de 1960.* Montreal: 1960.

Gwyn, Richard. *The Northern Magus: Pierre Trudeau and the Canadians.* Toronto: McClelland & Stewart, 1980.

―――. *Smallwood: The Unlikely Revolutionary* Toronto: McClelland and Stewart, 1968.

―――. *The Shape of Scandal: A Study of Government in Crisis.* Toronto: Clarke Irwin, 1965.

Gwyn, Richard, and Sandra Gwyn. "The politics of peace." *Saturday Night* (May 1984).

Hamelin, J. *Economie et société en Nouvelle-France.* Québec: Presses de l'Université Laval, 1960.

Hamelin, J., and L. Beaudoin. "Les Cabinets provinciaux, 1867-1967." In *Personnel et partis politiques au Québec,* edited by V. Lemieux, 119-140. Montréal: Boréal Express, 1982.

Hamelin, J., and Nicole Gagnon. *Histoire du catholicisme québécois* Montreal: Boréal Express, 1984-1987.

Hamelin, J. and Y. Roby. *Histoire Économique du Québec, 1851-1896* Montréal: Fides, 1971.

Hamelin, M. *Les premières années du parlementarisme québécois, 1867-1878.* Québec: Presses de l'Université Laval, 1974.

Hamilton, G.G., and N.W. Briggart. *Governor Reagan, Governor Brown: A Sociology of Executive Power.* New York: Columbia University Press, 1984.

Hardy, A. *Patronage et patroneux.* Montreal: Editions de l'Homme, 1979.

Hartsock, Nancy. *Money, Sex and Power: Toward a Feminist Historical Materialism.* New York: Longman, 1983.

Hartz, L. *The Founding of New Societies.* New York: Harcourt Brace, and World, 1984.

Heclo, Hugh. *A Government of Strangers.* Washington: Brookings Institute, 1977.

Heintzman, R. "The Political Culture of Quebec, 1840-1960." *Canadian Journal of Political Science* 16, no. 1 (1983): 3-60.

Herzik, E.B. "The President, Governors and Mayors: A Framework for Comparative Analysis." *Presidential Studies Quarterly* 15, no. 2 (1985): 353-371.

Hockin, Thomas A., ed. *Apex of Power: The Prime Minister and Political Leadership in Canada.* 2nd ed. Scarborough, Ont.: Prentice-Hall, 1977.

Hockin, Thomas A. "The Prime Minister and Political Leadership: An Introduction to Some restraints and Imperatives." In *Apex of Power: The Prime Minister and Political Leadership in Canada.* 2nd ed., edited by Thomas A. Hockin, 2-21. Scarborough, Ont: Prentice-Hall, 1977.

Hoffman, Stanley. "Heroic Leadership: The Case of Modern France." In *Political Leadership in Industrialized Societies: Studies in Comparative Analysis,* edited by Louis J. Edinger, 108-154. Huntington, N.Y.: Robert E. Krieger, 1976.

Hogg, Peter W. *Constitution Law of Canada.* Toronto: Carswell, 1977.

Hollander, Edwin P. *Leadership Dynamics: A Practical Guide to Effective Relationships.* New York: Free Press, 1978.

Holmes, John W. *Life With Uncle: The Canadian-American Relationship.* Toronto: University of Toronto Press, 1981.

Holsti, Ole. "Foreign Policy Formulation Viewed Cognitively." In *Structure of Decision: The Cognitive Maps of Political Elites,* edited by Robert Axelrod. Princeton: Princeton University Press, 1976.

———. "The 'Operational Code' Approach to the Study of Political Leaders: John Foster Dulles' Philosophical and Instrumental Beliefs." *Canadian Journal of Political Science* 3 (March 1976): 123-57.

Hook, Sidney. *The Hero in History: A Study in Limitation and Possibility.* Boston: Beacon Press, 1943.

Hooke, A.J. "Economic Development and Welfare Policies." In *William Aberhart and Social Credit in Alberta,* edited by Lewis H. Thomas. Toronto: Copp Clark, 1977.

Hoy, Claire. *Bill Davis: A Biography.* Toronto: Methuen, 1985.

Humphries, Charles W. *'Honest Enough to be Bold': The Life and Times of Sir James Pliny Whitney.* Toronto: University of Toronto Press, 1985.

Huntington, Samuel. *American Politics: The Promise of Disharmony.* Boston: The Belknap Press of Harvard University, 1981.

Hurmuses, Paul. *Power without glory.* Vancouver: Balsam Press, 1976.

Ichikawa, Akira. "The 'helpful fixer': Canada's persistent international image." *Behind the Headlines* 37 (March 1979).

"Interview with the Right Honourable John G. Diefenbaker." In *Apex of Power: The Prime Minister and Political Leadership in Canada,* edited by Thomas A. Hockin. Scarborough, Ont.: Prentice-Hall, 1971.

"Interview with the Right Honourable Lester B. Pearson." In *Apex of Power: The Prime Minister and Political Leadership in Canada,* edited by Thomas A. Hockin. Scarborough, Ont.: Prentice-Hall, 1971.

Iremonger, L. *The Fiery Chariot: A Study of British Prime Ministers and the Search for Love.* London: Secker and Warburg, 1970.

Irving, John A. *The Social Credit Movement in Alberta.* Toronto: University of Toronto Press, 1959.

Jackman, S.W. *Portraits of the Premiers: An Informal History of British Columbia.* Sidney, B.C.: Gray's Publishing, 1969.

Jackson, Karen. "Ideology of the NDP in British Columbia." B.C. Project Working Paper, University of Victoria, August 1980.

Jackson, Robert, Doreen Jackson, and Nicholas Baxter-Moore. *Politics in Canada: Culture, Institution, Behaviour and Public Policy.* Scarborough, Ont.: Prentice-Hall, 1986.

James, William. *The Will to Believe and Other Essays in Popular Philosophy.* New York: Dover, 1956.

Janus, Irving. *Groupthink.* Boston: Houghton Mifflin, 1982.

Jenkin, Michael. *The Challenge of Diversity: Industrial Policy in the Canadian Federation.* Science Council of Canada, Background Study No. 50. Ottawa: Minister of Supply and Services, 1985.

Jennings, E.E. *Anatomy of Leadership: Princes, Heroes and Supermen.* New York: McGraw-Hill, 1960.

Jenson, Jane. "Party Systems." In *The Provincial Political Systems,* edited by David J. Bellamy, Jon H. Pammett, and Donald C. Rowat, 118-131. Toronto: Methuen, 1976.

Jervis, Robert. *Perception and Misperception in International Politics.* Princeton: Princeton University Press, 1976.

Johnson, D. *Egalité ou indépendance.* Montreal: Editions de l'Homme, 1965.

Johnston, Donald. *Up The Hill.* Montreal and Toronto: Optimum Publishing International, 1986.

Jones, L.R. "Financial restraint, management and budget control in Canadian Provincial governments." *Canadian Public Administration* 29, no. 2 (Summer 1986): 259-281.

Karlen, Arno. *Napoleon's Glands and Other Ventures in Biohistory.* New York: Warner Books, 1984.

Kavic, Lorne J., and Garry B. Nixon. *The 1200 Days: A Shattered Dream.* Coquitlam, B.C.: Kaen Publishers, 1978.

Kearns, Doris. *Lyndon Johnson and the American Dream.* New York: Harper, 1976.

Keene, Roger, and D.C. Humphreys. *Conversations with W.A.C. Bennett.* Toronto: Methuen, 1980.

Kellerman, Barbara. "Leadership as a Political Act." In *Leadership: Multidisciplinary Perspectives,* edited by Barbara Kellerman. Englewood Cliffs, N.J.: Prentice-Hall, 1984.

———. *The Political Presidency.* New York: Oxford University Press, 1984.

Kendle, John. *John Bracken: A Political Biography.* Toronto: University of Toronto Press, 1979

Kennedy, T.L., with Ralph Hyman. *Tom Kennedy's Story.* Toronto: Globe and Mail, 1960.

Kernaghan, Kenneth, and David Siegel. *Public Administration in Canada: A Text.* Toronto: Methuen, 1987.

Key, V.O. Jr. *American State Politics: An Introduction.* New York: Alfred A. Knopf, 1956.

King, Anthony. "Ideas, Institutions, and the Policies of Governments: A Comparative Analysis." *British Journal of Political Science* 3 (1973): 291-313, 409-23.

———, ed. *The British Prime Minister.* 2nd ed. Durham, N.C.: Duke University Press, 1985.

Kirton, John. "The Foreign Policy Decision Process." In *Canada Among Nations — 1985: The Conservative Agenda,* edited by Maureen Appel Molot and Brian W. Tomlin. Toronto: James Lorimer, 1986.

———. "Managing Canadian Foreign Policy." In *Canada Among Nations — 1984: A Time of Transition,* edited by Maureen Appel Molot and Brian W. Tomlin. Toronto: James Lorimer, 1985.

Klapp, O.E. *Heroes, Villains and Fools.* Englewood Cliffs, N.J.: Prentice-Hall, 1962.

Lachance, A. *Crimes et criminels en Nouvelle-France.* Montreal: Boreal Express, 1984.

Laforest, G. "Le sculpteur collectif et l'Etat pastoral." *Recherches sociographiques* 27, no. 1, (1986): 133-151.

Lamontagne, Maurice. *Business Cycles in Canada.* Toronto: James Lorimer, 1984.

Lanctôt, G. *L'administration de la Nouvelle-France, 1627-1760.* Québec: Les Presses de l'Université Laval, 1970.

Langer, Walter C. *The Mind of Adolf Hitler: The Secret Wartime Report.* New York: Basic Books, 1972.

Lasswell, Harold. *Psychopathology and Politics.* Chicago: University of Chicago Press, 1930.

Latouche, Daniel. "The Organizational Culture of Government Myths: Myths, Symbols and Rituals in a Québécois Setting." *International Social Science Journal* 35, no. 2 (1983): 257-278.

Laundy, Philip. "Legislatures." In *The Provincial Political Systems,* edited by David J. Bellamy, Jon H. Pammett, and Donald C. Rowat. Toronto: Methuen, 1976.

Leduc, Lawrence, and Richard Price. "Great Debates: The Televised Leadership Debates of 1979." *Canadian Journal of Political Science* 18 (March 1985): 135-153.

Léger, M. *Ce n'était qu'un début.* Montréal: Editions Québec-Amérique, 1986.

Lemco, Jonathan. "Canada and Central America: a review of current issues." *Behind the Headlines* 43 (May 1986).

Lemieux, V., and R. Hudon. *Patronage et politique au Québec, 1944-1972.* Montréal: Boréal Express, 1975.

Lerner, Daniel, and Harold D. Lasswell, eds. *The Policy Sciences.* Stanford, Calif.: Stanford University Press, 1951.

Lesage, Jean. *Jean Lesage s'engage.* Montreal: Editions politiques du Québec, 1959.

Lévesque, René. *Memoirs.* Toronto: McClelland and Stewart, 1985.

———. *An Option for Quebec.* Toronto: McClelland and Stewart, 1968.

Lichter, Robert, Stanley Rothman, and Linda Lichter. *The Media Elite.* Bethesda, Md.: Adler and Adler, 1986.

Lindblom, Charles E. *Politics and Markets.* New York: Basic Books, 1977.

Lindblom, Charles E., and David K. Cohen. *Usable Knowledge: Social Science and Social Problem Solving.* New Haven, Conn.: Yale University Press, 1979.

Linton, R. *The Study of Man.* New York: Appleton, 1936.

Lipset, Seymour Martin. "Historical Traditions and National Characteristics: A Comparative Analysis of Canada and the United States." *Canadian Journal of Sociology* 1, no. 2 (1986): 113-155.

———. *Revolution and Counter-Revolution.* 2nd ed. Garden City, N.Y.: Anchor Books, 1970.

———. *Agrarian Socialism: The Co-operative Commonwealth Federation in Saskatchewan.* Garden City, N.Y.: Doubleday, 1968.

Loreto, Richard. "The Structure of the Ontario Political System." In *The Government and Politics of Ontario.* 3rd ed., edited by Donald C. MacDonald. Toronto: Nelson, 1985.

Lovick, L.D. *Tommy Douglas Speaks.* Lantzville, B.C.: Oolichan Books, 1979.

Lowi, Theodore J. *The Personal President: Power Invested, Promise Unfulfilled.* Ithaca, N.Y.: Cornell University Press, 1985.

Lyon, Peyton V. "The Trudeau Doctrine." *International Journal* 26 (Winter 1970-71).

MacDonald, Flora. "Minister, Civil Servants, and Parliamentary Democracy." *Dalhousie Review* (Summer 1980).

MacDonald, L.I. *From Bourassa to Bourassa.* Montreal: Harvest House, 1984.

MacKinnon, Frank. "Prince Edward Island: Big Engine, Little Body." In *Canadian Provincial Politics: The Party Systems of the Ten Provinces,* edited by Martin Robin. Scarborough, Ont.: Prentice-Hall, 1972.

MacLean, Gordon W. *Public Enterprise in Saskatchewan.* Regina: Crown Investments Corporation of Saskatchewan, 1981.

Mallory, J.R. *Social Credit and the Federal Power in Canada.* Toronto: University of Toronto Press, 1954.

Manthorpe, Jonathan. *The Power and the Tories: Ontario Politics 1943 to the Present.* Toronto: Macmillan, 1974.

———. "Backroom Breakfast Boys Decide Who Gets the Jobs." *Toronto Star.* November 8, 1977.

Manzer, Ronald. *Public Policies and Political Development in Canada.* Toronto: University of Toronto Press, 1985.

Martin, Chester. *Dominion Lands' Policy.* Toronto: Macmillan, 1938.

Martin, Patrick, Allan Gregg, and George Perlin. *Contenders: The Tory Quest for Power.* Scarborough, Ont.: Prentice-Hall, 1983.

Marx, Karl. *The Eighteenth Brumaire of Louis Bonaparte.* New York: International Publishers, 1963. (Originally published 1852.)

Matheson, William. "The Cabinet and the Canadian Bureaucracy." In *Public Administration in Canada,* 5th ed., edited by Kenneth Kernaghan. Toronto: Methuen, 1985.

———. *The Prime Minister and the Cabinet.* Toronto: Methuen, 1976.

May, Judith V., and Aaron B. Wildavsky, eds. *The Policy Cycle.* Beverly Hills: Sage Publications, 1978.

Mazlish, Bruce. *The Revolutionary Ascetic.* New York: Basic Books, 1974.

———. *In Search of Nixon: A Psychohistorical Inquiry.* New York: Basic Books, 1972.

McCall-Newman, Christina. *Grits: An Intimate Portrait of the Liberal Party.* Toronto: Macmillan, 1982.

McClelland, David. *Power: The Inner Experience.* New York: Irvington, 1975.

———. *The Achieving Society.* New York: Free Press, 1961.

McDaniel, R. Brian. "Some aspects of provincial deviance within Canada's federal political party system." Bachelor's essay, University of British Columbia, 1970.

McDougall, A.K. *John P. Robarts: His Life and Government.* Toronto: University of Toronto Press, 1986.

McGeer, Patrick L. *Politics in Paridise.* Toronto: Peter Martin Associates, 1972.

McGregor, Douglas. *The Human Side of Enterprise.* New York: McGraw-Hill, 1960.

McGregor, Gaile. *The Wacousta Syndrome.* Toronto: University of Toronto Press, 1985.

McMenemy, John, John Redekop, and Conrad Winn. "Party Structures and Decision-Making." In *Political Parties in Canada,* edited by Conrad Winn and John McMenemy, 167-190. Toronto: McGraw-Hill Ryerson, 1976.

McRoberts, K. "Unilateralism, Bilateralism, and Multilateralism: Approaches to Canadian Federalism." In *Intergovernmental Relations,* edited by R. Simeon. Toronto: University of Toronto Press, 1985.

Meisel, John. "The Boob-Tube Election: Three Aspects of the 1984 Landslide." In *The Canadian House of Commons,* edited by John Courtney. Calgary: The University of Calgary Press, 1985.

Meyer, P. *Québec.* Paris: Editions du Seuil, 1980.

Michels, Robert. *Political Parties: A Sociological Study of the Oligarchical Tendencies of Modern Democracy.* New York: Collier, 1962.

Millan, Betty. *Monstrous Regiment: Women Rulers in Men's Worlds.* Windsor Forest, Berks.: Kensal Press, 1982.

Milne, David. *Tug of War: Ottawa and the Provinces Under Trudeau and Mulroney.* Toronto: James Lorimer, 1986.

Miner, J.B. "The Uncertain Future of the Leadership Concept: Revisions and Clarifications." *Journal of Applied Behavioral Research* 18, no. 3 (1982): 293-307.

Mitchell, David J. *W.A.C. Bennett and the Rise of British Columbia.* Vancouver: Douglas & McIntyre, 1983.

Monière, D. *Le développement des idéologies au Québec.* Éditions Montréal: Québec-Amérique, 1977.

Moore, Thomas, "Personality Tests are Back." *Fortune,* 30 March 1987, 74-82.

Morton, Desmond. "Television: Does the Image Reflect Reality?" In *Politics and the Media.* Toronto: Readers' Digest Foundation of Canada and Erindale College, University of Toronto, 1981.

Morton, W.L. *Manitoba: A History.* Toronto: University of Toronto Press, 1967.

———. *The Progressive Party in Canada.* 1950. Reprint. Toronto: University of Toronto Press, 1967.

———. *The Progresive Party in Canada.* Toronto: University of Toronto Press, 1950.

Mulroney, Brian. *Where I Stand.* Toronto: McClelland and Stewart, 1983.

Murray, Charles. *Losing Ground: American Social Policy, 1950-1980.* New York: Basic Books, 1984.

Murray, D., and V. Murray. *De Bourassa à Lévesque.* Montréal: Les Quinze, 1978.

Neatby, H. Blair, and R. MacGregor Dawson. *William Lyon Mackenzie King.* 3 vols. Toronto: University of Toronto Press, 1958, 1963, 1973, 1976.

Neustadt, Richard. *Presidential Power: The Politics of Leadership from FDR to Carter.* 2nd ed. Toronto and New York: John Wiley and Sons, 1980.

Newman, Peter C. *The Distemper of Our Times: Canadian Politics in Transition: 1963-1968.* Toronto: McClelland and Stewart, 1968.

———. *Renegade in Power: The Diefenbaker Years.* Toronto: McClelland and Stewart, 1973.

Nish, C., ed. *Quebec in the Duplessis Era, 1935-1959: Dictatorship or Democracy?* Toronto: Copp Clark, 1970.

Noel, S.J.R. "Leadership and Clientelism." In *The Provincial Politicial Systems,* edited by David J. Bellamy, Jon H. Pammett, and Donald C. Rowat. Toronto: Methuen, 1976.

———. *Politics in Newfoundland.* Toronto: University of Toronto Press, 1971.

Nossal, Kim Richard. *The Politics of Canadian Foreign Policy.* Scarborough, Ont.: Prentice-Hall, 1985.

———. "Personal diplomacy and national behaviour: Trudeau's North-South initiatives and Canadian development assistance policy." *Dalhousie Review* 62 (Summer 1982).

Oliver, Peter. *Unlikely Tory: The Life and Politics of Allan Grossman.* Toronto: Lester and Orpen Dennys, 1985.

O'Neill, P., and J. Benjamin. *Les mandarins du pouvoir.* Montréal: Editions Québec-Amérique, 1978.

Ormsby, Margaret A. "T. Dufferin Pattullo and the Little New Deal." In *British Columbia: Historical Readings,* edited by W.P. Ward and R.A.J. McDonald. Vancouver: Douglas & McIntyre, 1981.

Osbaldeston, Gordon. "The Public Servant and Politics." *Policy Options* 8, no. 1 (January 1987).

O'Sullivan, Sean. *Both my Houses* Toronto: Key Porter Books, 1986.

Ouellet, F. *Papineau: Textes choisis.* Québec: Les Presses de l'Université Laval, 1958.

Owram, Douglas. *The Government Generation: Canadian Intellectuals and the State 1900-1945.* Toronto: University of Toronto Press, 1986.

Paige, Glenn D. *The Scientific Study of Political Leadership.* New York: Free Press, 1977.

Pal, Leslie A. *Public Policy Analysis: An Introduction.* Toronto: Methuen, 1987.

————. *State, Class and Bureaucracy: Canadian Unemployment Insurance and Public Policy.* Montreal and Kingston: McGill-Queen's University Press, 1988.

Paquet, G., and J.-P. Wallot. "Sur quelques discontinuités dans l'expérience socio-économique du Québec: une hypothèse." *Revue d'histoire de l'Amérique française* 35, no. 4 (1982): 483-522.

Patton, Michael Q. *Utilization-Focused Evaluation.* Beverly Hills: Sage Publications, 1978.

Payette, Lise. *Le pouvoir? Connais-pas!* Montréal: Éditions Québec-Amérique, 1982.

Pearson, Michael, Gregor Mackinnon, and Christopher Sapardanis. "'The world is entitled to ask questions': The Trudeau peace initiative reconsidered." *International Journal* 41 (Winter 1985/86).

Persky, S. *Son of Socred.* Vancouver: New Star Books, 1979.

Peterson, Thomas. "Manitoba: Ethnic and Class Politics." In *Canadian Provincial Politics: The Party Systems of the Ten Provinces.* 2nd ed., edited by Martin Robin. Scarborough, Ont.: Prentice-Hall, 1978.

Phidd, R.W., and G. Bruce Doern. *The Politics and Management of Canadian Economic Policy.* Toronto: Macmillan, 1978.

Pollard, Bruce. *Managing the Interface: Intergovernmental Affairs Agencies.* Kingston: Institute of Intergovernmental Relations, Queen's University, 1986.

Pontaut, A. *René Lévesque, ou l'idéalisme pratique.* Montréal: Leméac, 1983.

Pressman, Jeffrey L., and Aaron Wildavsky. *Implementation.* 3rd ed. Berkeley and Los Angeles: University of California Press, 1984.

Prince, Michael J. "The Mulroney Agenda." In *How Ottawa Spends 1986-87: Tracking the Tories,* edited by Michael J. Prince. Toronto: Methuen, 1986.

Prince, Michael J., and John Chenier. "The Rise and Fall of Policy Planning and Research Units: An Organizational Perspective." *Canadian Public Administration* 23 (Winter 1980): 519-541.

Prindle, D.A. "Toward a Comparative Science of the Presidency." Paper presented at the Annual Meeting of the American Political Science Association, 1983.

Pross, A. Paul. *Group Politics and Public Policy.* Toronto: Oxford University Press, 1986.

Provencher, J. *René Lévesque: Portrait of a Quebecker.* Toronto: Gage, 1975.

Province of Canada, *Parliamentary Debates on the Subject of the Confederation of the British North American Provinces.* Quebec: 1865.

Public Opinion. Brampton, Ont.: Progressive Conservative Party, 1 November 1943.

Punnett, R.M. *The Prime Minister in Canadian Government and Politics.* Toronto: Macmillan, 1977.

Quinn, H.F. *The Union Nationale.* 2nd ed. Toronto: University of Toronto Press, 1979.

Radwanski, George. *Trudeau.* Toronto: Macmillan, 1978.

Redekop, Clarence G. "Trudeau at Singapore: the Commonwealth and arms sales to South Africa." In *An Acceptance of Paradox: Essays on Canadian Diplomacy in Honour of John W. Holmes,* edited by Kim Richard Nossal. Toronto: Canadian Institute of International Affairs, 1982.

Regina Morning Leader, 13 September 1917.

Reid, Escott M. "The Saskatchewan Liberal Machine Before 1929." *Canadian Journal of Economics and Political Science* 2 (1936): 27-40.

Renshon, Stanley. "Assessing Political Leaders: The Criterion of 'Mental Health.'" In *Leadership: Multidisciplinary Perspectives,* edited by Barbara Kellerman, 231-262. Englewood Cliffs, N.J.: Prentice-Hall, 1984.

Rioux, M. *Les Québécois.* Paris: Éditions du Seuil, 1974.

Roberts, L. *Le Chef.* Montreal: Editions du Jour, 1972.

Robins, Robert S. "Paranoia and Charisma." Unpublished paper.

Rockman, B.A. "Presidential and Executive Studies: The One, the Few, and the Many." Paper presented at the annual meeting of the American Political Science Association, Chicago, 1983.

Rolph, William Kirby. *Henry Wise Wood of Alberta.* Toronto: University of Toronto Press, 1950.

Rose, Richard. "British Government: The Job at the Top." In *Presidents and Prime Ministers,* edited by Richard Rose and Ezra N. Suleiman, 1-49. Washington: American Enterprise Institute for Public Policy Research, 1980.

————. "Government Against Sub-governments: A European Perspective on Washington." In *Presidents and Prime Ministers,* edited by Richard Rose and Ezra N. Suleiman, 284-347. Washington: American Enterprise Institute for Public Policy Research, 1980.

Rose, Richard, and Ezra N. Suleiman, eds. *Presidents and Prime Ministers.* Washington: American Enterprise Institute for Public Policy Research, 1980.

Ross, Douglas A. *In the Interests of Peace: Canada and Vietnam, 1954-1973.* Toronto: University of Toronto Press, 1984.

Rotschild, J. *Ethnopolitics: A Conceptual Approach.* New York: Columbia University Press, 1981.

Royal Commission on the Economic Union and Development Prospects for Canada. *Report.* 3 vols. Ottawa: Minister of Supply and Services, 1985.

Roy, J.-J. *La marche des Québécois: Le temps des ruptures 1945-1960.* Montréal: Leméac, 1976.

Ruff, N.J. "British Columbia and Canadian Federalism." In *The Reins of Power: Governing British Columbia,* edited by J.T. Morley, et al., 271-305. Vancouver: Douglas & McIntyre, 1983.

Rumilly, R. *Maurice Duplessis et son temps.* Montréal: Fides, 1973.

Russell, Bertrand. *Power: A New Social Analysis.* New York: W.W. Norton, 1938.

Rustow, D.A., ed. *Philosophers and Kings: Studies in Leadership.* New York: George Braziller, 1970.

Saint-Aubin, B. *Duplessis et son époque.* Montréal: La Presse, 1979.

Savoie, Donald J.. *Regional Economic Development: Canada's Search for Solutions.* Toronto: University of Toronto Press, 1986.

Schindeler, F.F. *Responsible Government in Ontario.* Toronto: University of Toronto Press, 1969.

Schmidt, Manfred G. "The Welfare State and the Economy in Periods of Economic Cristis: A Comparative Study of Twenty-three OECD Nations." *European Journal of Political Research* 11 (1983): 1-26.

Schultz, Harold J. "Portrait of a Premier: William Aberhart." *Canadian Historical Review* 45 (1964): 201-26.

Schultz, Richard J. *Federalism, Bureaucracy and Public Policy: The Politics of Highway Transport Regulation.* Montreal and Kingston: McGill-Queen's University Press, 1980.

Schumpeter, Joseph. *Capitalism, Socialism and Democracy.* New York: Harper and Row, 1962.

Schwartzenberg, R.-G.. *L'Etat spectacle.* Paris: Flammarion, 1977.

Scott, F.R., and A.J.M. Smith, eds. *The Blasted Pine.* Toronto: Macmillan, 1957.

Segal, Hugh. "The Evolving Ontario Cabinet: Shaping The Structure to Suit the Times." In *The Government and Politics of Ontario.* 3rd ed., edited by Donald C. MacDonald. Toronto: Nelson, 1985.

Seidman, Harold. *Politics, Position and Power.* 3rd ed. New York: Oxford University Press, 1980.

Sherman, Paddy. *Bennett.* Toronto: McClelland and Stewart, 1966.

Silver, A.I. *The French-Canadian Idea of Confederation, 1864-1900.* Toronto: University of Toronto Press, 1982.

Simeon, James C. "Prime Minister Brian Mulroney and Cabinet Decision-Making: Political Leadership in Canada in the Post-Trudeau Era." Paper presented at the annual meeting of the Canadian Political Science Association, Montreal, 31 May 1985.

Simeon, Richard. *Federal-Provincial Diplomacy: The Making of Recent Policy in Canada.* Toronto: University of Toronto Press, 1973.

Simonton, Dean Keith. *Genius, Creativity and Leadership: Historiometric Inquiries.* Cambridge: Harvard University Press, 1984.

Simpson, Jeffrey. *Discipline of Power: The Conservative Interlude and the Liberal Revolution.* Toronto: Collins, 1986.

———. "The Missing System." *Globe and Mail* (Toronto), 3 July 1985.

———. "Problems in the PMO." *Globe and Mail* (Toronto), 3 July 1985.

Skelton, O.D. *The Life and Letters of Sir Wilfred Laurier.* 2 vols. Garden City, N.Y.: 1922.

Smiley, Donald V. *The Federal Condition in Canada.* Toronto: McGraw-Hill Ryerson, 1987.

———. *Canada in Question: Federalism in the Eighties.* 3rd ed. Toronto: McGraw-Hill Ryerson, 1980.

———, ed. *The Rowell-Sirois Report.* Book I, abridged. Toronto: Macmillan, 1978.

Smircich, L., and G. Morgan. "Leadership: The Management of Meaning." *Journal of Applied Behavioral Research* 18, no. 3 (1982): 257-273.

Smith, A.D. *The Ethnic Revival in the Modern World.* New York: Cambridge University Press, 1981.

Smith, David E. "Party Government, Representation and National Integration in Canada." In *Party Government and Regional Representation in Canada,* edited by Peter Aucoin, 1-68. Toronto: University of Toronto Press for the Royal Commission on the Economic Union and Development Prospects for Canada, 1985.

Smith, David E. *Prairie Liberalism: The Liberal Party in Saskatchewan, 1905-71.* Toronto: University of Toronto Press, 1976.

———. "The Prairie Provinces." In *The Provincial Political Systems,* edited by David J. Bellamy, Jon H. Pammett, and Donald C. Rowat. Toronto: Methuen, 1976.

Smith, Denis. "President and Parliament: The Transformation of Parliamentary Government in Canada." In *Apex of Power: The Prime Minister and Political Leadership in Canada,* edited by Thomas A. Hockin. Scarborough, Ont.: Prentice-Hall, 1971.

———. *Gentle Patriot.* Edmonton: Hurtig, 1973.

———. "Prairie Revolt, Federalism and the Party System." In *Party Politics in Canada,* edited by Hugh Thorburn. Scarborough, Ont.: Prentice-Hall, 1967.

Sparrow, James H. "Royal Commissions: A Study of Five Provinces." In *Provincial Policy-Making: Comparative Essays,* edited by Donald C. Rowat. Ottawa: Carleton University, 1981.

Speirs, Rosemary. "Ontario Liberals Discovering Joys of Patronage." *Toronto Star* 24 July 1986.

Speirs, Rosemary. *Out of the Blue.* Toronto: Macmillan, 1986.

Stacey, C.P. *Canada and the Age of Conflict.* Vol. 2, *1921-1948 — The Mackenzie King Era.* Toronto: University of Toronto Press, 1981.

Stairs, Denis. "The Political culture of Canadian foreign policy." *Canadian Journal of Political Science* 15 (December 1982).

Stanbury, W.T. "The Mother's Milk of Politics: Political Contributions to Federal Political Parties in Canada, 1974-1984." *Canadian Journal of Political Science* 19 (December 1986): 795-821.

Statistics Canada. *Labour Force Annual Averages, 1975-1983.* February 1984.

Sterling, Norman W. "Parliamentary Democracy: Who Rules — Cabinet or Parliament?" Notes for an address to the Churchill Society, Toronto, April 3, 1986.

Stevens, Geoffrey. "Prospects and Proposals." In *Politics and the Media.* Toronto: Readers' Digest Foundation of Canada and Erindale College, University of Toronto, 1981.

———. *Stanfield.* Toronto: McClelland and Stewart, 1973.

Stevens, Paul. "Wilfrid Laurier: Politician." In *Les Idées politiques des Premiers Ministres Canadiens,* edited by Marcel Hamelin. Ottawa: University of Ottawa Press, 1969.

Stevenson, Garth. "Federalism and Intergovernmental Relations." In *Canadian Politics in the 1980s,* edited by Michael Whittington and Glen Williams. Toronto: Methuen, 1984.

———. *Unfulfilled Union: Canadian Federalism and National Unity.* Toronto: Gage, 1982.

Stoessinger, John. *Crusaders and Pragmatists: Movers of Modern American Foreign Policy.* New York: W.W. Norton, 1979.

Sullivan, Martin. *Mandate '68.* Toronto: Doubleday, 1968.

Sutherland, J. Neil. "T.D. Pattullo as a Party Leader." Master's thesis, University of British Columbia, 1960.

Swainson, Neil A. *Conflict over the Columbia.* Montreal and Kingston: McGill-Queen's University Press, 1979.

———. *Symbolic Leaders: Public Dramas and Public Men.* New York: Minerva Press, 1964.

Szablowski, George. "Policy-Making and Cabinet: Recent Organizational Engineering at Queen's Park." In *Government and Politics of Ontario,* edited by Donald C. MacDonald. Toronto: Macmillan, 1975.

Taras, David. "Brian Mulroney's Foreign Policy: Something for Everyone." *Round Table* 293 (1985): 35-46.

Taylor, Charles. *Snow Job: Canada, the United States and Vietnam, 1954-1973.* Toronto: Anansi, 1974.

———. "Political Leadership and Polarization in Canadian Politics." In *Apex of Power: The Prime Minister and Political Leadership in Canada,* edited by Thomas A. Hockin. Scarborough, Ont.: Prentice-Hall, 1971.

Taylor, Malcolm G. *Health Insurance and Canadian Public Policy.* Montreal and Kingston: McGill-Queen's University Press, 1978.

Thomas, L.G. *The Liberal Party in Alberta: A History of Politics in the Province of Alberta, 1905-1921.* Toronto: University of Toronto Press, 1959.

Thomas, Lewis H. *The Making of a Socialist: The Recollections of T.C. Douglas.* Edmonton: University of Alberta Press, 1982.

Thomson, Dale C. *Jean Lesage and the Quiet Revolution.* Toronto: Macmillan, 1984.

Thordarson, Bruce. "Posture and policy: Leadership in Canada's external affairs." *International Journal* 31 (Autumn 1976).

———. *Trudeau and Foreign Policy: A Study in Decision-Making.* Toronto: Oxford University Press, 1972.

Tilly, Charles, ed. *The Formation of National States in Western Europe.* Princeton: Princeton University Press, 1975.

Touraine, A. *Sociologie de l'action.* Paris: Éditions du Seuil, 1965.

Tousignant, P. "Problématique pour une nouvelle approche de la Constitution de 1791." *Revue d'histoire de l'Amérique française* 27, no. 2 (1973): 181-234.

Tremblay, L.-M. *Le syndicalisme québécois.* Montréal: Les Presses de l'Université de Montréal, 1972.

Tremblay, R. *Le Québec en crise.* Montréal: Editions Select, 1981.

Troyer, Warner. *200 Days: Joe Clark in Power.* Toronto: Personal Library, 1980.

Trudeau, Pierre Elliott. "Some Obstacles to Democracy." In *Federalism and the French-Canadians,* by Pierre Elliott Trudeau, 103-123. Toronto: Macmillan, 1968.

———. *Federalism and the French-Canadians.* Toronto: Macmillan, 1968.

Tucker, Michael. "Canadian security policy." in Maureen Appel Molot and Brian W. Tolin, eds. *Canada Among Nations — 1985.: The Conservative Agenda.* Toronto: James Lorimer, 1986.

———. "Trudeau and the politics of peace." *International Perspectives* (May/June 1984).

———. *Canadian Foreign Policy: Contemporary Issues and Themes.* Toronto: McGraw-Hill Ryerson, 1980.

Tucker, Robert C. *Politics as Leadership.* Columbia, Mo., and London: University of Missouri Press, 1981.

Tufte, Edward. *The Political Control of the Economy.* Princeton: Princeton University Press, 1978.

Turnbull, A. Douglas. "Reminiscences of a Coalition M.L.A." Manuscript, November 1984.

Vachon, A. *L'administration de la Nouvelle-France, 1627-1760.* Québec: Presses de l'Université Laval, 1970.

Van Loon, Richard. "Planning in the Eighties." In *How Ottawa Decides: Planning and Industrial Policy Making 1968-1984,* edited by Richard French. Toronto: James Lorimer, 1984.

———. "The Policy and Expenditure Management System in the Federal Government: The First Three Years." *Canadian Public Administration* 26 (1983): 285.

Van Loon, Richard, and Michael S. Whittington. *The Canadian Political System: Environment, Structure, and Process.* 3rd ed. Toronto: McGraw-Hill Ryerson, 1981.

Vigod, B.L. *Quebec before Duplessis: The Political Career of L.-A. Taschereau.* Montreal and Kingston: McGill-Queen's University Press, 1986.

von Riekhoff, Harald. "The impact of Prime Minister Trudeau on foreign policy." *International Journal* 33 (Spring 1978).

von Riekhoff, Harald, and John Sigler. "The Trudeau peace initiative: the politics of reversing the arms race." In *Canada Among Nations — 1984: A Time of*

Transition, edited by Brian W. Tomlin and Maureen Appel Molot. Toronto: James Lorimer, 1985.

Waite, P.B. "The Political Ideas of John A. Macdonald." In *Les Idées politiques des Premiers Ministres canadiens,* edited by Marcel Hamelin. Ottawa: University of Ottawa Press, 1969.

Wallace, Donald. "Provincial Central Agencies for Intergovernmental Relations." Ph. D. diss. University of Toronto, 1985.

Walker, Russell R. *Politicians of a Pioneering Province.* Vancouver: Mitchell Press, 1969.

Ward, Judith B. "Federal-provincial relations within the Liberal Party of British Columbia." Master's thesis, University of British Columbia, 1966.

Weber, Max. "Politics as a Vocation." In *From Max Weber: Essays in Sociology,* edited by H.H. Gerth and C. Wright Mills, 77-128. New York: Oxford University Press, 1958.

Wearing, Joseph. "Political Parties: Fish or Fowl." In *The Government and Politics of Ontario.* 3rd ed., edited by Donald C. MacDonald. Toronto: Nelson, 1985.

Weller, Patrick. *First Among Equals: Prime Ministers in Westminster Systems.* London: George Allen and Unwin, 1985.

West, Laurie. "The Man In The Middle: The Role Of The Prime Minister's Press Secretary." Research Project, Carleton University School of Journalism, 1986.

Whitaker, Reginald. *The Government Party: Organizing and Financing the Liberal Party of Canada, 1930-58.* Toronto: University of Toronto Press, 1977.

Wildavsky, Aaron. *The Nursing Father: Moses as a Political Leader.* Tuscaloosa, Ala.: University of Alabama Press, 1984.

———. "The Three Cultures: Explaining Anomalies in the American Welfare State." *Public Interest* 69 (Fall 1982): 45-58.

Willhoite, Fred H., Jr. "Primates and Political Authority." *American Political Science Review* 70, no. 4 (December 1986): 1110-1127.

Wilson, R.J. "The Legislature." In *The Reins of Power,* edited by J.T. Morley, et al., 11-14. Vancouver: Douglas & McIntyre, 1983.

Winn, Conrad. "Elections." In *Political Parties in Canada,* edited by Conrad Winn and John McMenemy, 114-128. Toronto: McGraw-Hill Ryerson, 1976.

Winn, Conrad, and John McMenemy. *Political Parties in Canada.* Toronto: McGraw-Hill Ryerson, 1976.

Winnipeg Free Press, 4 July 1936.

Wiseman, Nelson. *Social Democracy in Manitoba.* Winnipeg: University of Manitoba Press, 1983.

———. "The Pattern of Prairie Politics." *Queen's Quarterly* 88 (Summer 1981): 298-315.

Wolfenstein, E. Victor. *The Revolutionary Personality.* Princeton: Princeton University Press, 1971.

Young, B.J. *Promoteurs and Politicians: The North Shore Railways in the History of Quebec, 1854-1885.* Toronto: University of Toronto Press, 1978.

Young, Walter D. "Leadership in Canadian Politics." In *Approaches to Canadian Politics,* edited by John H. Redekop, 267-291. Scarborough, Ont.: Prentice-Hall, 1983.

———. "Stability and Change: Politics in British Columbia in the 1970s." N.p., n.d. Mimeo.

Young, Walter D., and J.T. Morley. "The Premier and the Cabinet." In *The Reins of Power,* edited by J.T. Morley, et al., 45-82. Vancouver: Douglas & McIntyre, 1983.

Young, Walter D. "Leadership and Canadian Politics." In *Approaches to Canadian Politics,* edited by John H. Redekop, 267-291. Scarborough, Ont.: Prentice-Hall, 1983.

Zaleznik, Abraham. "Charismatic and Consensus Leaders: A Psychological Comparison." In *Contemporary Issues in Leadership,* edited by William Rosebach and Robert Taylor. Boulder, Colo.: Westview Press, 1984.

Zeldin, T.T. *The Political System of Napoleon III.* New York: W.W. Norton, 1958.

Zolf, Larry. *Dance of the Dialectic.* Toronto: James Lewis & Samuel, 1973.

INDEX